'A timely update of the very influential handbook on educational theatre... I commend the authors for their painstaking research, the quality of their scholarship and outreach, and for the groundbreaking and timely contribution of *Theatre for Change*' – Philip Taylor, Associate Professor of Educational Theatre, New York University, USA

'As one who teaches undergraduate and graduate students in the fields of drama and theatre education, theatre for young audiences, and applied theatre, I would draw on this book in each of those courses as a means of helping students understand the connections among these disciplines. The work simultaneously provides an eagle's eye overview and a thoughtful, close analysis of specific praxis.' – Robert Colby, Associate Professor and Graduate Programme Director, Emerson College, USA

Building on Robert J. Landy's seminal text, *Handbook of Educational Drama and Theatre*, Landy and Montgomery revisit this richly diverse and ever-changing field, identifying some of the best international practices in Applied Drama and Theatre. Through interviews with leading practitioners and educators such as Dorothy Heathcote, Jan Cohen Cruz, James Thompson and Johnny Saldaña, the authors lucidly present the key concepts, theories and reflective praxis of Applied Drama and Theatre.

As they discuss the changes brought about by practitioners in venues such as schools, community centres, village squares and prisons, Landy and Montgomery explore the field's ability to make meaning of a vast range of personal and social issues through the application of drama and theatre.

ROBERT J. LANDY is Professor of Educational Theatre and Applied Psychology and Director of the Drama Therapy Program at New York University. His publications include *The Couch and the Stage: Integrating Words and Action in Psychotherapy* (2008), *Essays in Drama Therapy: Unfinished Business* (2001), *Drama Therapy: Concepts, Theories and Practices* (1994) and *Persona And Performance (1993)*. He is also a playwright and composer.

DAVID T. MONTGOMERY is a clinical assistant professor for the Program in Educational Theatre at New York University. He is a specialist in drama education, theatre for young audiences, student teaching and integrated arts.

# Theatre for Change

## Education, Social Action and Therapy

Robert J. Landy
and
David T. Montgomery

First published 2012 by
PALGRAVE MACMILLAN

Palgrave Macmillan in the UK is an imprint of Macmillan Publishers Limited,
registered in England, company number 785998, of Houndmills, Basingstoke,
Hampshire RG21 6XS.

Palgrave Macmillan in the US is a division of St Martin's Press LLC,
175 Fifth Avenue, New York, NY 10010.

Palgrave Macmillan is the global academic imprint of the above companies
and has companies and representatives throughout the world.

Palgrave® and Macmillan® are registered trademarks in the United States,
the United Kingdom, Europe and other countries.

ISBN 978–0–230–24365–1   hardback
ISBN 978–0–230–24366–8   paperback

This book is printed on paper suitable for recycling and made from fully
managed and sustained forest sources. Logging, pulping and manufacturing
processes are expected to conform to the environmental regulations of the
country of origin.

A catalogue record for this book is available from the British Library.

A catalog record for this book is available from the Library of Congress.

10  9  8  7  6  5  4  3  2  1
21 20 19 18 17 16 15 14 13 12

Printed and bound in Great Britain by
CPI Antony Rowe, Chippenham and Eastbourne

*In memory of Dorothy Heathcote and Nancy Swortzell,
who were always mindful that change comes from a deep
immersion in the art forms of drama and theatre where
the mind and heart are eternally alive.*

# Table of Contents

# List of Illustration and Photographs

## Illustration

## Photographs

# Foreword

Theatre, in all of its manifestations, is essentially concerned with change. The title of this book clearly reflects the potential of drama and theatre to transform the lives of individuals and communities around the world. As well as accounts of national and international practice, detailed case studies of individual practitioners and companies give glimpses of the depths of transformative thinking and feeling that may be generated by agents of change functioning in educational, cultural and therapeutic settings. Many practitioners aim to achieve positive adaptations in outlook or understanding among their clients, and the range and ambition of their work is inspiring. But any promise of individual or social change immediately raises difficult questions. Who or what needs to be changed, why and by whom, and what kinds of changes are likely to take place?

The efforts of these impressive individuals will be most effective when their work obeys the essential rules of theatre. It's worth remembering that the most powerful kinds of theatre and drama defy appropriation. They should never be reduced to convenient ways of transmitting information or transparent methods of achieving some kind of moral, social or political health. This book demonstrates that, like the greatest practitioners in theatre, experienced and exceptional facilitators are likely to work indirectly, raising problems and generating questions so that moral, social and political values are highlighted and challenged. Human conduct, situations, issues and relationships – 'tangled lives' as Dewey calls them – become both visible and palpable. Once visible they demand reflection, interpretation and in some cases, action.

But art, and perhaps most of all the drama, is essentially anarchic and volatile. In the unpredictable medium of theatre it is not always possible to anticipate the directions in which any desired changes may occur.

As the German dramatist Peter Weiss puts it:

> Everything that we see and hear
> Can add to or increase us in some way,
> And so it might be with this play.
> Some seeds have drifted from our stage. A few
> May even have entered and taken root in you.
> But what these seeds are – even though

> In your darkest places they feed and grow,
> Whatever these seeds are – you will never know.[1]

There is no doubt that involvement in drama and theatre will 'increase' us, even if any of the 'seeds' that take root may remain unknown and unavailable to ordinary discourse. Many of the case studies included in this book demonstrate this 'increase'. It is always engagement in the dramatic encounter, whether as participant or spectator, that will be truly transformational. This will not arise just because of any intention on the part of the facilitator to induce change in the participants. The greater the struggle to discover emerging meanings, the greater will be the commitment to the encounter. Shallow texts, banal themes, an explicit 'message' and the absence of any irony or ambiguity will all limit the effects of the work. Emerging speculation, interpretation and reflection will demand sensitive and informed responses. The engagement becomes transformational because of the insight, the delight, the enlargement of identity, the alternative perspectives that are offered and the developing sense of artistry that arises from that engagement.

Harley Granville Barker (1877–1946), playwright, director, critic, scholar and all-round man of the theatre, insists that the dramatic form, if used honestly and artistically, can be the vehicle for a very vital sort of truth. In 'Exemplary Theatre' (1922) he introduces a Minister of Education who argues against allowing professors of theatre to spread abroad 'a respect for complicated lingo, because 'they'll go on complicating it indefinitely for their own greater credit'.[2] The result, he believes, will be to muddle up teachers' minds. Even in 1982, when the predecessor to this book, Robert Landy's *Handbook of Educational Drama and Theatre*, was published the field suffered from a proliferation of designations as practitioners and theorists attempted to identify and define their practice.[3] Three decades later some labels and titles have fallen out of favor, but instead of a consolidation and simplification of the field, further terms have been added to the already extensive catalogue. This book lists an astonishing number of locations, applications and objectives of possible practice in education, health and social welfare.

In the decades since 1982 the struggle for practitioners in drama and theatre remains the same. The challenge is to find an effective balance between form and content, skill and spontaneity, process and product, acceptance and exclusion. As in all other aspects of human endeavor, fashions have come and gone. Dramatic play, small group improvisation, games, exercises, conventions, structures, all had their moments of success in the hands of outstanding practitioners and most of the approaches surveyed in 1982 continue to be popular, although they may have acquired different names.

In this book Robert Landy and David Montgomery show us a remarkable range of philosophies, theories and practice in a variety of contexts, and demonstrate that gifted and ethical practitioners can bring about beneficial changes in the lives of others. But the greatest challenge remains. How do we identify, train and support the kinds of teachers, directors, facilitators and therapists who will be capable of constructively employing the many-faceted art that is theatre? This book reveals the huge potential of drama and theatre in the hands of such agents of change and their impressive capacity to achieve positive transformations in the lives of individuals, groups and communities.

Cecily O'Neill

# Acknowledgements

We begin with our immense gratitude to our dear colleague, friend, mentor and question poser, Philip Taylor, who organized the mix of Educational Theatre and Drama Therapy students to study with Boal in Rio in 2008, where we met and planned this book. Philip also introduced us to Kate Haines of Palgrave Macmillan, who brought this work to fruition.

Our deep appreciations to Teresa Fisher, our research assistant, for her keen intelligence, grace and good cheer. Her contributions to this book are monumental.

We thank the NYU Research Challenge Fund for providing a generous grant to complete our research. We are grateful for the abiding support and friendship of the intrepid chair of Steinhardt's Department of Music and Performing Arts Professions, Larry Ferrara.

We acknowledge the kindness and precision of the editors at Palgrave Macmillan in realizing this project, most notably Jenni Burnell and Felicity Noble.

We and our publishers wish to thank the following for permission to reproduce copyright material:

Broadway Bound Children's Theatre, Jim D'Asaro, Executive Director, for *God Lives in Glass*, photo by Nigel Cooper (2010)

Alex Sarian, Aminisha Ferdinand, Edmund Chow, James Webb, Emily Bolton Ditkovski, and Gretchen Peters for Theatre of the Oppressed at CTO-Rio, photo by Alex Sarian (2007)

Zerka T. Moreno for photo of J. L. and Zerka Moreno (1971)

Hsiao-hua Chang for two photographs: Mask Drama with the Elderly at the County Senior Citizen Home for Compassion, Tapei, photo by Hsieh, Tsai-miao; and Mask Drama with the Disabled at Pai Ai-hsin Home for Persons with Disabilities, Taipei, photo by Lin, Yi-shiuan (2010)

Geo Britto at CTO-Rio for photo of Augusto Boal and his jokers, Olivar Bendelak, Helen Sarapeck, Augusto Boal, Claudete Felix, Barbara Santos, and Geo Britto (n.d)

Sai Ye for photo of Robert Landy leading Drama Therapy group in China, photo by Sai Ye (2010)

Adam Kalesperis and Joe Quintero for photo of B.R.I.D.G.E Project (2008)

Peggy Stern, producer, for photos of *Standing Tall* (2004)

Chianan Yen, Jessica Schechter, and Derek Nason for photo of *Kindertransport*, photo by Chianan Yen, Courtesy NYU Steinhardt (2008)

David Saar of Childsplay for photo from his play, *The Yellow Boat*, photo by Hal Martin Fogel (1993)

Richard Termine for photo of the Les Freres Corbusier production of *Hell/House*, directed by Alex Timbers, photo by Richard Termine (2006)

Every effort has been made to trace rights holders, but if any have been inadvertently overlooked the publishers would be pleased to make the necessary arrangements at the first opportunity.

David acknowledges the following:

Robert Landy, for your generosity, providing cogent and useful criticisms, along with moral support, and for the opportunity to collaborate and learn from you.

All of my curious students, especially Nofisat Sonekan and Annie Crowley, who posed and explored critical questions.

Colleagues Amy Cordileone, Joe Salvatore and Nan Smithner for their ongoing support, and my mother and father for their encouragement.

My family – wife Annie, daughter Mary Leigh and sons Danny and James. They motivate me daily to do my best. Special thanks to Annie, a constant inspiration, for her sacrifices and love.

Robert acknowledges the following:

David Montgomery, for your dedication, openness and superb grasp of the field. Without you, this wouldn't have happened.

Lowell Swortzell, who brought me to the field in 1979, and nurtured my creativity and scholarship.

My colleagues in Drama Therapy: Maria Hodermarska, Lucy McLellan, Nina Garcia, Sara McMullian, Cecilia Dintino, Anna-Marie Weber, whom I respect and admire.

To my students, Jason Frydman, for transcribing many of the interviews, and Lizzie McAdams, for critiquing early chapters.

To my dear children, Georgie and Mackey, who are in my heart.

Above all, we are grateful to our extraordinary students and colleagues who toil daily on the front lines to work toward change. Your collective passions inspire us to give all that we have.

# List of Interviewees

| | |
|---|---|
| Ela Weissberger | Holocaust survivor and original cast member of Brundibar, in Terezin |
| Johnny Saldaña | Professor, Arizona State University |
| Philip Taylor | Associate Professor of Educational Theatre, NYU |
| David Booth | Professor Emeritus, University of Toronto |
| Cecily O'Neill | Scholar, artist and practitioner of Educational Theatre |
| Gavin Bolton | Scholar, artist and practitioner of Educational Theatre |
| Kristy Messer | Drama Specialist, Inner-City Arts |
| Adam Kalesperis | Co-founder, B.R.I.D.G.E Theatre Project |
| Joe Quintero | Co-founder, B.R.I.D.G.E Theatre Project |
| Emelie Fitzgibbon | Artistic Director/CEO, Graffiti Theatre Company |
| Nan Smithner | Clinical Assistant Professor of Educational Theatre, NYU |
| Chrissie Poulter | Head of Media, Film and Culture Department, Leeds Trinity University College |
| Lisa Citron | Founder and Executive Director, (Out)Laws and Justice |
| Linda Cook | Drama therapist and drama educator, New Orleans, Louisiana |
| Judge Helen Berrigan | Judge, US District Court, Eastern District of Louisiana |
| Soohyun Ma | Drama therapist and drama educator, Seoul, Korea |
| Akeyo Onoe | Drama therapist and drama educator, Professor, Ritsumeiken University, Japan |
| Jun Watanabe | Drama educator and Professor, Nihon University, Japan |
| William Sun | Professor and Vice-President, Shanghai Theatre Academy, China |

| | |
|---|---|
| Dorothy Heathcote | MBE, innovator of Drama in Education |
| Jay Pecora | Assistant Professor, Theatre and Dance, Potsdam, The State University of New York |
| Jennifer Holmes | Adjunct Faculty, Manhattanville College and Founder and Director of Global Empowerment Theatre (GET) |
| Chris Vine | Academic Director, Master of Arts in Applied Theatre, The City University of New York |
| James Mirrione | Playwright and Professor, United Arab Emirates University |
| Peter Harris | Lecturer and Practitioner, Tel Aviv University |
| Michael Rohd | Artistic Director, Sojourn Theatre; Visiting Chair in Theatre, Northwestern University |
| Jan Cohen-Cruz | Professor, Syracuse University; Director, Imagining America |
| Hazel Barnes | Senior Research Associate, Drama and Performance Studies, University of KwaZulu-Natal, Pietermaritzburg Campus |
| Teresa Fisher | Adjunct Lecturer at Bronx Community College, Coordinator of the NYC Arts in Education Roundtable, and Producer/Administrator of New Plays for Young Audiences |
| James Thompson | Professor of Applied and Social Theatre at the University of Manchester |
| Nisha Sajnani | Director of the Drama Therapy, Community Health, and Prevention program at the Post Traumatic Stress Center in New Haven, CT, and is on faculty at the Institutes for the Arts in Psychotherapy (NYC) and at New York University. |
| Nancy Swortzell | Founder and Artistic Director Emeritus, New Plays for Young Audiences |
| Edie Demas | TYA and Arts Education Specialist |
| Carol Korty | Playwright for children and young adults |
| José Cruz González | Professor of Playwriting and Directing, California State University, Los Angeles |
| Tony Graham | Visiting Artist in Educational Theatre, NYU and noted director of plays for young audiences |

| | |
|---|---|
| Natalie Burgess | Educator/Puppeteer/Musician, Brooklyn Children's Museum |
| Sally Fairman | Executive Director, The Unusual Suspects Theatre Company |
| Jonathan Shmidt | Assistant Director of Education, The New Victory Theater; Co-Director, Trusty Sidekick Theatre Company |
| Renée Emunah | Director of the Drama Therapy program at California Institute of Integral Studies |
| Zeina Daccache | Executive Director, Drama Therapist, Catharsis – Lebanese Center for Drama Therapy |
| Zerka T. Moreno | TEP, along with her late husband, J. L. Moreno, developed the theory and practice of psychodrama |
| Armand Volkas | Clinical Director of the Living Arts Counseling Center |
| Jonathan Fox | Founder/Emeritus, Playback Centre |
| Tom Magill | Voluntary Artistic Director of ESC: Understanding through Film |
| Christopher Odhiambo Joseph | Associate Professor of Literature and Intervention Drama, Department of Literature, Theatre and Film Studies, Moi University |
| Hsiao-Hua Chang | Professor of Drama, National Taiwan University of Arts |

# Introduction: The Praxis of Theatre for Change

Drama and theatre are aesthetic forms of performance with historical roots in ritual and religion. Both trace their etymology to ancient Greek, which speaks to drama as an action taken, and theatre as a place for observing an action. Both are intimately linked in their confluence of acting and witnessing. As drama is conventionally performed in a theatre, each theatrical space presages an action compelling enough to be seen.

We begin this book with the assumption that drama and theatre truly matter and not only to actors and audiences. They matter to teachers and students, social activists and spiritual celebrants, therapists and clients, those who apply aspects of performance toward understanding and changing their life circumstances. As such, performance elucidates pedagogical structures in classrooms, social, political and religious structures in communities and psychological structures in the heart and mind. When applied to learning, social action and therapy, performance becomes a means for changing understanding, power dynamics, consciousness and behaviour.

This performative model of action and observation also encompasses a critical element when the actors and observers reflect upon their experience. Furthermore, such reflection can lead to transformational action in the world on the part of the actor and the observer.

This is a book about drama and theatre praxis in the service of personal and collective change. We view praxis as a practice informed by theory (and vice-versa), or, more specifically, a model of action–observation–reflection–re-action, where re-action points to change. With etymological roots in Greek, praxis, which means action, is deeply grounded in drama through Aristotle's conception of tragedy as *mimesis praxeos*, an imitation of an action.[1] The concept of praxis, with applications to philosophy, politics, aesthetics, religion and more recently, pedagogy, will frame our discussion of drama and theatre for change. We will also adhere to Paul Taylor's understanding of praxis as a creative process, steeped in dialogue, an idea consistent with the educational philosophy of Paolo Freire who writes: 'Liberation is a praxis: the action and reflection of men and women upon their world in order to transform it.'[2]

Throughout this book, we will work toward describing and analyzing the praxis of drama and theatre as it is applied to the education, social action and therapy of individuals and groups. By social action, we mean efforts within a community to enhance a social justice agenda. In addition, we will make some remarks about religious expression through drama and theatre, again situating our discussion within the framework of praxis.

This book builds upon a previous text, *Handbook of Educational Drama and Theatre*, written by Robert Landy and published in 1982.[3] That volume was based upon a 48-part television series 'Drama in Education,' which Landy created and hosted on WCBS-TV in 1980.[4] In the series many of the leading figures in the field were interviewed, including Gavin Bolton, Brian Way, Geraldine Brain Siks, Richard Courtney, Nellie McCaslin, Nancy and Lowell Swortzell. In his book, Landy incorporated many of the ideas of these and other leading figures in an attempt to define and survey the field of Educational Drama and Theatre as it existed in the US and the UK in the early 1980s.

In the current volume, Landy and his colleague David Montgomery, re-examine the field 30 years later. This time the authors cast a wider net, looking at the field more globally for signs of development. In this new endeavor, they not only identify many of the best practices, associated with specific practitioners and performance groups, but also critically examine these practices through the lens of praxis. As in the previous volume, the authors interview practitioners and theorists worldwide and incorporate their points of view. They also interview some of the original figures in the 1982 volume and ask them to discuss the changes they see over a 30-year span.

One constant from 1982 to 2012 is the lack of a coherent and integrated understanding of the discipline. In fact, few then or now would even agree on an optimal title. In 1982 Landy proposed the title 'Educational Drama and Theatre' as an umbrella for the field as a whole, integrating many of the discrepant parts including: Creative Drama, Drama in Education, Developmental Drama, Theatre in Education, Children's Theatre, Drama Therapy and Psychodrama.

What was clear in the early 1980s, and remains so 30 years later, is that these forms of drama and theatre exist in many environments, including schools, community centers, hospitals and auditoriums. Given the technology in common usage since the end of the 20th century, drama and theatre are also practiced globally in the virtual spaces of the World Wide Web. In one example, 'World of Warcraft', an internet game played by millions, players take on fictional roles, called avatars, and enact transformational journeys within the frame of cyberspace.[5]

Although much of the terminology is similar today, a conceptual shift has occurred over the last 30 years, based in the development of theory, practice and research, as well as political and psychological concerns. This is especially clear in the domains of social action and therapy. Action has become a mainstay of several forms of psychotherapy,[6] and Drama Therapy has matured and expanded internationally as a praxis. In education and social action, the field of Applied Theatre has burgeoned, consistent with the need of adherents to address issues of social justice through performance.

Many in Applied Theatre, influenced by the political and philosophical implications of globalization, post-colonialism and postmodernism, embrace a position of critical consciousness, also known as conscientization or *conscientização*, a term coined by Brazilian educator Paolo Freire, whose theory springs from work with oppressed people in Brazil in the 1970s.[7] Conscientization in practice urges people to raise essential questions about their circumstances and to expose the mechanisms of oppression. Freire's work provided the philosophical basis for that of theatre artist, Augusto Boal, who has influenced generations of practitioners of Applied Theatre and related forms.

Applied Theatre, discussed in Chapter 4, is based not only in the ideas of Freire and Boal, but also the critical theory of Giroux, Kincheloe and McLaren, among others.[8] Critical theorists offer an intellectual perspective that challenges assumptions about privilege, culture, gender, race and class. These perspectives inform our understanding of Theatre for Change.

In this book, we present a holistic view of a field still very much in development. Many will argue that a single umbrella is too inclusive and that fields like Applied Theatre and Drama Therapy are and ought to be separate. However, going against the stream that foregrounds specializations, we take the point of view that the several forms of drama and theatre that apply to education, social action and therapy are more similar in praxis than not and can be viewed as one discipline. As such, we open an expansive umbrella and let go of the previous, more limited name, Educational Drama and Theatre.

Our vision is of a discipline that holds together forms of drama and theatre which exist to facilitate change. Our focus is upon three parts of the whole: Drama and Theatre in Education, Applied Theatre and Drama Therapy. Because these fields are in themselves so burdened with terminology, we attempt to clarify each major field and sub-field. In addition, we look briefly at related applications of drama and theatre to the spiritual domain as religion deeply impacts people's lives in the 21st century.

We are well aware of the problems associated with an umbrella for the three applied fields of drama and theatre. There are certainly key differences as pointed out by many writers in Applied Theatre and Drama in Education who make it abundantly clear that they are not therapists equipped to swerve into the dangerous traffic of the inner lives of their constituents. They are correct in asserting that the training and contract between therapist and client in Drama Therapy is different from that between facilitator and participant in Educational Drama or Applied Theatre. And yet, theatre artists have been grappling with the problem of aesthetic distance for at least a century, debating whether or not to delve too deeply into an actor's psyche and whether or not to preserve the sanctity of the fourth wall to protect the spectator from psychological harm, or, in some cases, physical engagement with the actors.

Given the political and psychological agendas of contemporary drama/ theatre practitioners, these issues are very much alive as all use methods of performance to nudge and sometimes startle viewers out of their comfort zones into new dimensions of seeing, thinking and acting. The problem of containing and generating too much or too little emotion continues to challenge most all in the drama/theatre profession.

As an umbrella term, we propose Theatre for Change, a phrase which speaks to the purpose of the several dramatic forms applied to educa- tion, social action and therapy. We acknowledge that some may question whether theatre and its applied forms really do foment change and if so, how can the change be measured.[9] And yet, through our research within the three domains, we have discovered that change is a shared principle that guides and motivates so many practitioners and researchers.

We conceptualize change in a way consistent with Freire's notion of critical consciousness. Change concerns two basic processes: awareness and action. In Theatre for Change, the actor and viewer are provided the opportunity through an engagement with the aesthetic object of perform- ance to develop their critical consciousness and to rehearse options toward action. We also recognize that change is not necessarily indicated in all circumstances. For some, taking personal action in a repressive political arena can lead to further repression and harm.[10]

What are some of the unique qualities of Theatre for Change? For one, Theatre for Change is an applied form. It can be applied to many locales that require change. In this book, we look at three: educational settings, community settings, with a strong orientation toward social justice issues, and therapeutic settings.

Further, practitioners apply aesthetic performance for specific reasons, in our three cases, pedagogical, political and therapeutic. Consistent with many others in the field, we believe that changes in cognition, conscious- ness and behaviour can occur optimally through an aesthetic process of drama/theatre. We also believe that these aims are not mutually exclusive and that practitioners in all three domains work at least implicitly toward changes in cognition, consciousness and behaviour.

Finally, Theatre for Change brings to the forefront issues of values and ethics, consistent with the theory that underlies much of the debate. Critical theory has become prominent in the fields of Applied Theatre and Educational Theatre, as scholars and practitioners debate the efficacy of post-colonial praxis and globalization, for example.[11] Some in the field take on a particular ideological point of view, consistent with their political and/or spiritual orientation. As you will see throughout this book, we do not embrace a particular ideology, but rather take an eclectic stand, valuing dialogue and multiple points of view. As such, we look at both the critical theory-based ideas of Nicholson and Thompson in Applied Theatre, and the more conservative ideas of faith-based forms of theatre, which attempt to change audiences into true believers.

In Drama Therapy, ethical issues of informed consent and confidentiality provide guidelines for practitioners who are trained to value the human rights and dignity of all clients and research subjects.[12] Similar issues are inherent in practice and research throughout all the fields to be discussed.

Theatre for Change, then, is an applied art form, with specific objectives, ethics and values. It is eclectic in its attention to pedagogical, social/political and psychological change. In 1982, many conceived of its precursor, Educational Drama and Theatre, as atheoretical. Today, we find specific theory informing the practice and, in fact, a shift from scholarship on practice to that of praxis.

In 1982, Educational Drama and Theatre was centered in children and young people. In the three fields of Theatre for Change we find performances by and for people of all ages and conditions within diverse venues. In 1982, there was much debate as to whether the field was primarily about process, the non-scripted, improvisational, child-centered work, or product, the more formal presentation of plays to audiences. Today, that separation is not as clear-cut as many scripted performances are based in a lengthy process of devising and reflecting which incorporates both process and product. Further, non-scripted, improvisational experience in the classroom and community often leads to some form of formal performance or sharing with an audience of peers. Throughout the book, we will address the question of change over the 30-year span, 1982–2012.

Given the range and scope of the field at this juncture, it is difficult in many ways to distinguish it from the more generic forms of drama and theatre. These terms are, in themselves, complex and dynamic, existing on a continuum from the drama of everyday life through theatrical performances of plays to audiences.

Does the use of the term Theatre for Change alter the traditional aesthetic and entertainment intentions of theatre? Although this book may not fully answer the question, we will provide examples in the following chapters that address it. Let us offer some preliminary thoughts. Theatre for Change, although retaining clear aesthetic and entertainment values, seeks to inform and transform its participants and viewers in a more conscious way than conventional drama and theatre. Its pedagogical, political and therapeutic aims are often eschewed by theatre artists. For many in Theatre for Change, entertainment is just the tip of the iceberg. For the most committed, this is a process that truly matters, that goes deep into the fabric of social and psychological life, attempting to realize Bertolt Brecht's call to action: 'Change the world: it needs it.'[13]

In the following pages we present Theatre for Change as a hybrid discipline. It is drama/theatre *and* education, social action, therapy. It veers within poetics, politics and therapeutics, with side excursions to religion. It is quite eclectic theoretically, informed by humanism, Marxist-based critical theory, and a mix of psychological and sociological theories. In practice, it is also eclectic, mixing forms of non-scripted improvisation and scripted performance.

Although much research in the field has been limited to descriptions of practice and theory, Theatre for Change entered the 21st century with an attention to praxis and a commitment to methodologies of critical analysis and performance ethnography as well as evidence-based research.

As a discipline that has developed more in its separations than in its integrations, we seek to envision the whole, with each part retaining its own identity yet sharing a common praxis, determined as much by its action as its reflective observation, and a common goal, that of change.

We begin Part I of the book with a discussion of Drama and Theatre in Education. This part includes chapters on Drama and Theatre in the Elementary School, Drama and Theatre in the Secondary School, and Drama and Theatre for, by and with Young People. Many subsets of Educational Drama and Theatre will be carefully described and contextualized. Through presenting case vignettes, we will highlight drama and theatre praxis in US, UK and other international classrooms.

Part I will include interviews with several generations of leaders in the field. We examine changes in practice and theory since 1982 and present contemporary examples of exemplary praxis.

In Part II, we move from the school into the community at large and focus upon Drama and Theatre in Social Action. In Chapter 4 we examine Applied Theatre and several of its forms including Theatre for Development, Theatre of Faith and Prison Theatre.

In Part III, we turn to Drama and Theatre in Therapy. We explore the praxis of Drama Therapy and related fields in Chapter 5, discussing their growth and development over a 30-year span.

Having surveyed a broad terrain, we then revisit some of our key questions about the nature of Theatre for Change. Taking an arts-based approach, we create an imaginary dialogue among the many voices of scholars, teachers, therapists, activists and artists represented in this book. Through the discussion we seek responses to our central questions: What is the scope and breadth of Theatre for Change? Is this a useful name for the field? Can it hold all of its discrepant pieces under one umbrella and inspire productive dialogue? How has the field changed over a 30-year span? And given that the world needs change, what parts do drama and theatre play in effecting that change?

Beyond the body of the text, we present a glossary of terms used throughout the book.

## Journeys to places where theatre really matters

We got to know each other while eating *empadinhas* and *açaí* in small outdoor cafes in Lapa, an old neighborhood in Rio de Janeiro where the Center for the Theatre of the Oppressed (CTO) is located.[14] We came to Rio in 2008 with our students – half in Educational Theatre, half in Drama Therapy – to study Rainbow of Desire with Augusto Boal and his jokers. We were excited to work with Boal and to explore a confluence of our two fields. The results were mixed, as we will discuss later in Chapter 5, but the food was tasty, as was the conversation which led to the research and writing of this book.

While in Rio we spoke often about the connection between Educational Theatre and Drama Therapy. And we spoke every day about Boal's influence upon both fields. This was especially poignant as Boal focused upon Rainbow of Desire, his approach to exploring personal oppression, born in the days when he was in exile in France and realized that more Parisians were oppressed by inner demons of fear and self-doubt than by exploitative landowners and repressive military regimes.

In working with Boal, the group created some very intense dramas concerning relationships between daughters and fathers, friends and lovers, leading to powerful emotional expression. True to his approach, Boal steadfastly worked to explore each personal story through the sculpting and performance of several alternative scenarios. Boal was clear with us that his work was not about resolution, but about empowering the protagonist to understand her oppressive dilemma from several points of view and become aware of her options. Some noted that because such raw emotion was expressed, there needed to be time for closure and questioned Boal about the safety of his work. His response was direct: 'This work is theatre and not therapy. Theatre is not safe.'

Boal's statement resonated with us since and adds another layer to explore in this book. We recalled extreme examples in performance history of ritual human sacrifice in Mayan and Aztec cultures, and the slaughter of slaves and gladiators in the ancient Roman amphitheatres for the entertainment of mass audiences. Landy recalled working as an actor in New York City's experimental theatre in the 1960s in productions that removed the aesthetic distance of the fourth wall, conflating reality and illusion as actors and viewers became confused in their non-theatrical performance of private acts.

And yet, in our excursions to CTO sites in Rio for the incarcerated and mentally ill, we were protected by the aesthetic distance of the theatre. We wrestled with Boal's dictum and realized that in order for us to do our work ethically in education, social action and therapy, theatre had to be safe.

And yet again, Boal challenged us then and now to re-think this premise. When engaged in drama and theatre, does too much safety lead to complacency and inaction? When we, as citizens, let our actors do the work we need to do, then are we forever condemned to the couch and the iPhone, unwilling to question the circumstances that lead to a perpetuation of inertia and injustice? On the other hand, does too much exposure to the drama of cruelty and oppression shut us down, numbing us to the realities of cruelty, and in some cases, re-traumatize rather than empower us to reflect and to act? When we delve too deeply into the heart of darkness, condemned to tell the same stories and repeat disturbing actions over and again, how do we find a way out?

Shortly after working with Boal in Rio, Landy joined a Psychodrama group in Poland to explore ways that the Holocaust plays out in contemporary family life.[15] The group convened in the concentration camps of Auschwitz and Birkenau and consisted of those whose relatives perpetrated the Holocaust and those who were victimized by the Holocaust. In Psychodrama sessions and dramatic rituals in the camps, group members discovered that intergenerational trauma plays out on both sides and that dramatic action is one way to break its insidious cycle.

Landy thought often of Boal's statement that theatre is not safe, especially when enacting his own pain and observing the equally painful enactments of the others. By crossing the line and going too far in confronting the past psychodramatically, many in the group were able to acknowledge the moral complexity of the issues and take steps toward change. The therapeutic drama, performed on a stage that was once a killing field, did matter for all participants.

After Auschwitz, Landy journeyed to the Czech Republic and on to Terezin (Theresienstadt), a particularly cynical concentration camp that Hitler designed not only as a ghetto and way-station for those to be transported to their deaths at Auschwitz, but also as a stage set, forcing its inhabitants to act as if they were well-treated, and to participate in a propaganda film in order to convince the Red Cross and the allies how well he treated the Jews of East Europe. Landy knew that many prominent artists had been incarcerated at Terezin, and he knew of the publication *I Never Saw Another Butterfly*, containing poems and drawings by several of the incarcerated children expressing a desire to return home.[16] Of the 15,000 children that passed through Terezin, fewer than 100 survived.

Landy also knew that the children's opera *Brundibár* was performed at Terezin.[17] Upon visiting the camp, he learned that *Brundibár* was performed more than 50 times, once to an audience that included Adolf Eichmann and Heinrich Himmler, and that following these performances, many of the child actors were transported to Auschwitz to their immediate deaths.

Landy also learned that Kurt Gerron, a prominent German Jewish actor and director, was incarcerated at Terezin, where he performed and directed dozens of cabarets and plays. Gerron, coincidentally, played the Streetsinger and the Police Chief of London in the original 1928 production of Brecht and Weill's *The Threepenny Opera*, an ironic musical about oppression and crime. Knowing full well the impact of Brecht's epic theatre, Gerron used his talents as an actor and director in the direst of circumstances to stay alive and to help others do the same. Ironically, in the 1928 production of *The Threepenny Opera*, he performed a song called 'What Keeps Mankind Alive', which ends with the line: 'Mankind is kept alive by bestial acts.'[18]

Gerron eagerly volunteered to direct Hitler's propaganda film, hoping it would buy him time to survive the transports. As soon as the film was completed, Gerron was transported to Auschwitz where he was gassed. Learning this at Terezin, Landy again recalled Boal's admonition: 'Theatre is not safe.'

Despite the thousands of ways that theatre was powerless in the face of a relentless killing machine, it did have a salubrious effect in the camps. *Brundibár* tells the story of poor children who need money to buy milk for their sick mother. They go to the village and raise money, only to be cheated by the evil hurdy-gurdy man, Brundibár. With the help of the neighborhood animals, the children overcome the tyrant and win the day. For the children of Terezin living daily in highly stressful conditions, *Brundibár* provided a moment of hope. The children were victorious in every performance, singing the lines: 'If we all pull together, we'll win the children's dispute with the ugly dictator, giving the world a good example.'[19] Their zeal gave others hope, like the writer Josef Bor, a witness to the performances, who reflected:

> The children are singing about milk, knowing only too well that it is about life they are thinking of. We don't want a greedy hurdy-gurdy man, the children told us. He knows only his old worn-out melody about oppression and war. We want to live free and in peace. ... And it was that revolutionary spirit that nurtured the imagination of the children in Terezin – and ours, spectators, too.[20]

A few from the casts of *Brundibár* survived and found their way out of the Holocaust to build full lives. Landy interviewed one, Ela Weissberger, who played the role of the cat in all 55 productions at Terezin. Landy wanted to know how the experience of performance helped her and other children survive. Weissberger said that it was the Nazis' intention to ban any formal education for the Jewish children. And yet the children needed activities. Visual art activities, as well as singing and acting, kept the children occupied and excited. 'Theatre was our nourishment. It took us out of our fear,' she said.[21] For Weissberger and the other children, Brundibár represented Hitler and in their theatricalized defeat of the tyrant, they hoped that soon they would return home, victorious.

In an American production of *Brundibar* in 2005, translated and adapted by Tony Kushner and designed by Maurice Sendak, the original ending is modified. Rather than sending the tyrant fully packing, Kushner writes a final stanza suggesting that evil is alive and well in the world and will return:

> Nothing ever works out neatly,
> Bullies don't give up completely.
> One departs, the next appears,
> And we shall meet again my dears![22]

For Weissberger, this was an unacceptable ending as the purpose of the original was to give everyone hope, without ambiguity, of an imminent victory. Weissberger best expresses that sense of hope in describing her interaction with her beloved art teacher, Feidl Dicker-Brandeis, a gifted Viennese artist and teacher, who inspired the children to create art envisioning a better, safer world:

> She would tell us that everything we found – a little piece of paper – you can create something really special. She would take us to the window and say: 'Kids, look out. The fortress is surrounded by mountains and the sun. It's a beautiful day. Behind those mountains is hope for you to survive.' Today, whenever I wake up and see a beautiful day, there is always hope.[23]

Although it will remain unknown why some survived this and other atrocities and others perished, it seems clear that for Ela Weissberger and other children who entered into the alternative reality of art and theatre in Terezin, there was always hope. For them, theatre was safe.

Kushner is certainly correct in his theatrical allegory that bullies will return. But Weissberger is also correct – children in hopeless situations need to believe in a hope beyond sorrow. Krasa and Hoffmeister, the composer and librettist of *Brundibár*, gave the children of Terezin a moral and revolutionary education, a theatre for change that really mattered.

As Kushner well knew, Hitler was hardly the last of the great tyrants to perpetrate genocide. In the 30 years from 1982–2012, the world has witnessed the rise and fall of apartheid in South Africa, genocide in Bosnia, Rwanda, Sudan, Sri Lanka and in the Democratic Republic of Congo. The terrorist attacks on the United States on September 11, 2001, have effectively killed the fantasy that the US is safe. Hot wars continue to rage in many corners of the earth. What can drama and theatre do?

Boal tells the story in *Rainbow of Desire* of his early attempt in the 1960s to spread revolution through theatre in a small Brazilian peasant community where no one had ever seen a play.[24] Boal's company performed an *agit-prop* play intended to rouse the peasants to action, capped by a chorus: 'Let us spill our blood.' In response, one man named Virgilio was so ready for action that he invited Boal and his actors to take up weapons and fight the local landlord. Aware that he had gone too far in blurring the lines between theatre and reality, Boal shamefully declared that although his intentions were real, his guns were mere stage props and he and his colleagues were only actors.

Reflecting on that story, Boal tells us that he changed his aesthetic and philosophical approach, going on to develop his signature Theatre of the Oppressed, which offers no solutions, but instead awareness and options. As such, it is a safer theatre than the previous one.

In the chapters to follow, we explore many attempts to create applied forms of drama and theatre that really matter in the lives of children and adults living in times of peace and war. In laying out the praxis of these forms, we look toward understanding a wide range of approaches that taken together can provide a way to see many of the possibilities of changing the world through the art of performance.

As we proceeded with our research, we met many people doing the work of applied forms of drama and theatre outside the mainstream. They had no knowledge of the field as such and no awareness of the distinctions between various forms of applied drama and theatre. Some, like Helen Berrigan, a federal judge in New Orleans, who worked with at-risk adolescents through the format of a dramatized mock trail, did the work because it coincided with her sense of social justice. Others, like Johannes Galli, a German clown and entrepreneur, were also motivated by a desire to help oppressed children. But in his case, there was also an economic incentive, which he acquired from working in the corporate world with business people who reported experiencing a boost in creativity after engaging in Galli's dramatic exercises.

This book is primarily for students and for a professional audience aware of the bounty of life as an actor/teacher, community activist or drama therapist. But it is also for the clowns, the entrepreneurs, the amateurs, the mavericks and the idealists who intuit that drama and theatre can change lives. And this book is for those who simply want to explore their own unsafe journeys safely and maybe even help others in need to do the same.

Although our desires to create a book representative of the multiplicities of culture, ethnicity, gender and sexual orientation were grand, our perspectives were necessarily limited by the realities of being two white, North American, heterosexual men, teaching groups of predominantly female students. As we learned from Boal, it is ever useful to look beyond the personal into the world of possibilities and alternatives. And so, given our limitations, that is what we do in the following pages. Our face-to-face conversations with Boal in the summer of 2008 were incomplete. Several months after we returned home, Boal passed away. In part, this book is a continuation of unfinished dialogues with Boal and Brecht and J. L. Moreno and many other guides who still feel very much alive.

# PART I    DRAMA AND THEATRE IN EDUCATION

In this section we examine various forms of Educational Drama and Theatre in schools and performance spaces. Special attention is paid to our model of praxis as action–observation–reflection–re-action. We explore praxis through case vignettes and interviews, through observations and reflections, to offer a broad view of theory and practice, past and present.

## Educational drama and theatre in school settings

In so many ways, theatre aims for change. The spectrum of change runs from a shift in mood that a good comedy engenders in audience members, to a shift in thinking inspired by a provocative drama. In applied theatre settings, a primary goal is to develop participants' critical thinking skills which inevitably leads to change in understanding. This focus is aligned with the school's goal to create change through education. Consequently, the opportunity exists for Educational Theatre to make a key contribution to the school curricula. How this relationship between schools and theatre has fared over the years is one area we explore.

One of Aristotle's most significant contributions to theatre was a theory based on exploration and contemplation of theatre practice. If theory is a form of knowledge, and practice is the application of that knowledge, then artist educators engaging with acts that shape knowledge can be seen as theorists. Do drama teachers think of themselves as theorists as they practice their art? Are they even aware of the theories driving their teaching? We argue that often drama teachers are unacquainted with the theory informing their practice.

This section illustrates that despite the unfamiliarity some have with terminology and theory, their work is Educational Theatre praxis and should be recognized as such. By placing noteworthy drama practice alongside an investigation of Educational Theatre history and theory, readers can situate their practice within the field and build their own philosophies of the practice.

Consider these first three vignettes of drama praxis in school settings:

### ❖ Case vignette one: Drama in the elementary school setting

At primary grade three levels in an all-boys school in Hong Kong, students were shown how to engage with drama and role work for the first time. In a lesson called 'The Disappearance of Rice', boys were put into role as researchers in the future who traveled back in time to investigate why farmers no longer grow rice, considering the hardships that farmers faced under a variety of circumstances.[1] The impact of the drama helped promote a multi-dimensional perception of events for students, particularly regarding the real-life demonstrations held against the World Trade Organization (WTO) in Hong Kong in 2005.[2] One student reported, 'If I had not taken part in this drama, I would never have understood why Korean farmers have to go on protest.'[3] Another boy added, 'If I had not taken part in this unit, I would have thought that the police were absolutely right [in dispersing the demonstrators]. Now I still think the police were right, but I think the WTO had some wrong-doings.'[4]

### ❖ Case vignette two: Playwriting in the middle school

Raul has enjoyed working on a playwriting unit for almost three years at his middle school in Nebraska. As part of a recurring unit that began in sixth grade and continued through seventh and eighth grade, he enjoyed taking part in improvisations that helped with character development. He also liked creative reading and writing exercises. Now, during his eighth grade year, he is putting the final touches on writing a script that is rooted in his own experience. He cannot wait to hear his play read aloud in a staged reading by semi-professional adult actors, many of whom are parents of students that attend Raul's school.

### ❖ Case vignette three: Devising theatre in the high school

Drama students at the Wilton High School in Connecticut worked on devising a piece of theatre as a class project. After getting approval from the school administration and with the guidance of their drama teacher, Bonnie Dickinson, students worked on creating *Voices in Conflict*, a play based on interviews, letters and essays written by Iraqi civilians and American soldiers serving in Iraq. When individual members of the Wilton community heard about this project and complained to the school's principal, he decided it was too controversial and cancelled all performances, much to the dismay of the students. These students, however, learned that sometimes confronting controversy has its rewards.[5] After their story appeared in *The New York Times*, the students received thousands of letters of support and were subsequently provided numerous opportunities to perform the play in professional theatre settings. *Voices in Conflict* is now a published play and an organization with an impressive website. The students were awarded a 'Courage in Theater' award for their 'non-performance' from Music Theatre International, a New York agency that licenses many high school productions.[6] 'I'll probably look back on this in 20, 30 years and say, "I can't believe I did this,"' expressed sixteen-year-old cast member Dagan Rossini after a performance at the Vineyard Theatre.[7] 'It was a huge, overwhelming experience,' said Rossini adding, 'It's changed me.'[8]

In surveying the field, we find an enormous variety of drama praxis that extends far beyond the three examples presented here. To illustrate the myriad of questions that arise from such drama work, Cecily O'Neill writes: 'Drama offers almost too rich an array of topics and potential lines of inquiry, ... with a maze of pathways and blind alleys leading off in all directions.'[9] Indeed, it was challenging to decide what to include in this text. In the end, we chose examples of best practices from four sources: published literature, interviews with experts, direct observation and personal experience.

While a tremendous amount of research went into completing this book, our core findings emerged from our personal experiences in and reflections on the field. Likewise, as a narrative device, the interviews and vignettes highlight the personal experiences of others, helping the reader build bridges to ideas. We have seen how many learners understand theory more clearly when they are able to explore cases and hear the voices of practitioners in the context of interviews. In sifting through our interviews and collected data, we sought to discover and reveal several core principles and questions within each section of the book. Sometimes this necessitated more in-depth contextualization and, at other times, a more limited focus upon the work itself.

All the narrative devices, whether long or short, are intended to convey themes and questions dynamically and to allow for the authors' reflections to emerge. Likewise, much of what is presented intentionally leaves an open space for readers to render their own reflections and interpretations. Driving our choices of vignettes, interviews and descriptions was clear evidence of praxis that raised compelling issues and spoke to the theme of theatre for change.

Given that educational objectives determine how various theatre projects are designed, it is necessary to identify those objectives. Returning to the opening vignettes, we find the objective of case vignette one was to encourage the boys from Hong Kong to develop a multi-dimensional perception of historical events through drama. Undoubtedly, drama and theatre help develop multiple perspectives when students caught up in a particular moment can build well-informed interpretations. As Cecily O'Neill writes, 'If students are unable to imagine things differently and consider the world from unfamiliar perspectives, they will be unable to bring about any change in their circumstances. The arts and drama in particular have always provoked these shifts of perspective.'[10]

Case vignette two is about a student playwright's quest to develop a dramatically engaging play through a sequential playwriting program. Working within a theatre-making paradigm, Raul is provided the opportunity to convey personal experiences through playwriting, a significant objective in Educational Theatre. In addition to drama-based pedagogical practice to create change, in the following pages we also find more traditional theatre-making examples maintaining the objective of change.

In many school theatre programs the objective is purely to stage a musical or a play. The reasons for this can vary. In addition to providing opportunities for students to hone their acting and technical theatre skills, play productions give family and friends the chance to see students in a different light. For many theatre teachers, the discipline learned through rehearsing and performing is likely to induce feelings of pride and accomplishment. However, a question to consider when engaging in such an undertaking is: What constitutes a developmentally, conceptually, culturally and politically appropriate play or musical to produce with young people?

Case vignette three is also about theatre production, but with students as creators of the performance piece. The objective was for students to become researchers, authors, producers and actors of a piece written in a documentary style similar to Moisés Kaufman's *The Laramie Project*.[11] As creators, students needed to maintain a critical stance. The principal of the school, fearing potential backlash from the community, cancelled the performance. From this setback, however, students gained insight into what it means to be silenced. The students' critical stance and curiosity, perceived as dangerous by some, led to suppression. In response students became eager advocates for themselves and the play. They learned how committing to dialogue and art, despite obstacles, can create change.

Thus we see that the learning objectives provide different ways to approach and implement drama and theatre work. In all three vignettes participants express themselves through the aesthetic of theatre. In educational institutions it can be difficult to cultivate artistic expression when governmental policies dictate teaching and learning objectives. Likewise, it becomes stressful for teachers when emphasis is placed on teaching to the state standardized tests. Adding to the teachers' pressure is the sobering reality that too many young people drop out of school, and marginalized communities are not getting the education they need to compete with their more privileged counterparts.

Another compelling reality is that some students who excel in school get accustomed to daily non-critical learning routines and are startlingly resistant to exploration. Too many teachers note how their high-achieving students just want to know what is needed to get an 'A' grade. Students are frustrated by open-ended questions and, at first, balk at the complex puzzlements that arise from exploring multiple perspectives. In this, drama work can meet the needs of all levels of learners. Drama can help underachieving students internalize and understand affective skills, for example empathy, which are related to cognitive skills such as making inferences, and are required on standardized tests. For students who test well, drama provides opportunities to learn other valuable skills, including appreciation of nuance and dramatic irony, qualities which are critical to many life and learning situations.

Three decades ago Landy described an issue that still holds true today. He wrote: 'One of the key issues in the field of educational drama and theatre involves the relationship between the nonperformance, informal process of drama and the more performance-oriented product of formal theatre.'[12] In educational settings we find that some schools and teachers privilege performance, others focus on the process of theatre and many more are in the middle, making decisions based on desired educational outcomes. Regardless of where a teacher is positioned on this spectrum, a constant of best practice is in facilitating students to engage in critical analysis of their work. Likewise, the posing of questions in various educational settings establishes dramatic contexts and deepens the students' capacity to reflect on the experience.[13] Further, in using open and compelling questioning teachers can lead students toward an understanding of the aesthetic and philosophical dimensions of drama.

In his biography of renowned drama teacher Dorothy Heathcote, Gavin Bolton described how some of Heathcote's pupils in Newcastle took away a shallow understanding of her pedagogy and consequently applied her techniques in superficial ways. Bolton wrote: 'Teachers on her short courses who picked up the surface features of her methods faced disastrous consequences when they failed to grasp the underlying philosophical and artistic values.'[14] This type of shallow understanding can be avoided when time is taken to absorb theory and reflect on practice. As Sharon Grady writes, 'by engaging in practice and research from informed positions, that is, through careful examinations of our own and others' paradigmatic assumptions, we can actively choose challenging theoretical and methodological tools that allow us to focus and attend to the complexities of the practice of theory in practice.'[15]

As we will see, practitioners who look beneath the surface to consider the complex ways in which teachers create and participants engage in drama experience are able to infuse their work with purposefulness and meaning on a consistent basis.

## Educational drama and theatre outside schools

This section also examines the art form of theatre-making and performance with, by and for youth that transpires outside the school setting. Though there are examples of drama and theatre in schools provided in Chapter 3, the work originates outside the school setting, from an outreach or theatre education program, for example.

At the onset it might appear that a chapter on Theatre by, for and with Young People is far afield from the book's focus on change and the intersections of drama in education, social action and therapy. However, an examination of theatre-making practices with young people is included because of its explicit link to pedagogy. In essence, all of the theatre work highlighted in Chapter 3 is an extension of the classroom.

Here the reader will find the praxis of theatre positioned within three forms. The first is Theatre for Young Audiences, or TYA. The aim of TYA is to perform a staged play for an audience of young people. The second form is Theatre in Education (TIE). TIE aims to offer issue-based theatre experiences for young people where they are both the audience and participants. The third form is Youth Theatre. Working toward theatre performance, Youth Theatre aims toward providing young people the opportunities to participate as actors, directors, playwrights and designers.

Conspicuously absent from this chapter is a discussion of Puppet Theatre and Puppetry in Education. Puppetry maintains a well-deserved audience, and Puppetry in Education has enjoyed much success and acceptance. In educational contexts puppetry is applied to the curriculum, to music, daily routine and social growth. There are many varieties of puppets utilized in TYA including marionettes, shadow puppets and *Bunraku* puppets developed in Japan over a thousand years ago. However given its broad scope and multiple applications, we decided to eliminate a discussion of puppetry.[16]

The following case vignettes are exemplary of theatre projects in TYA, TIE and Youth Theatre.

### ❖ Case vignette four: Theatre for young audiences

Imaginate, an Edinburgh-based development agency in Scotland, focuses on promoting and developing performing arts for children. Since 1999 the government has helped fund pilot projects, and showcases have been staged annually by Imaginate at various venues across Scotland. Emerging from one pilot and launched in 2006, the Starcatchers Project was the first of its kind in Scotland for the creation of theatre work for babies and young children, zero to three years old, and their parents or care-givers.[17]

Starcatchers' one-man show, called *My House*, explored textures and sounds for children between the ages of 18 months and three years. It traveled to New York where it ran at the New Victory Theater, New York City's first and only full-time performing arts theatre for young people. *My House* played in a studio space that only admitted 25 audience members. It featured artist Andy Manley as a resident of a multi-layered painted box house who engaged in a quirky relationship with a watermelon that wanted to move in.

### ❖ Case vignette five: Theatre in education

In England, Big Brum Theatre in Education has been working in Birmingham and the West Midlands since 1982. Working with ages three to 17, the company tours TIE programs throughout the region to schools and colleges.[18] Like others, a distinctive feature of Big Brum's TIE is both participation and reflection. Before, during or after a performance, Big Brum sometimes has children take on roles to solve problems. For example, in a play exploring the death of village people as a result of contaminated water, 'The children are in role as investigators for the UN whose task is to produce a report which will bring those responsible for contaminating the water to account and set up a more accountable and efficient means of water purification.'[19]

### ❖ Case vignette six: Youth theatre festival and competition

In October 2010 the fourth annual Dubai Festival for Youth Theatre showcased the theatre skills of young people across the UAE. The event was organized by the Dubai Culture and Arts Authority, the Emirate's dedicated authority for culture, heritage and the arts. UAE-based youth theatre groups performed eight plays that were evaluated by a jury. The event was in Arabic and comprised of Emiratis, as well as participants from other Arabic-speaking countries. Plays were selected by an internal committee in Dubai that made sure that the quality of plays maintained high standards and that any political and/or controversial references were screened out.[20] Salem Belyouha, projects and events manager in the Dubai Culture and Arts Authority, noted, 'Some of the plays talk about personal relationships; others present the bigger picture of how the Arab youth perceive significant global events.'[21]

Case vignette four illustrates a relatively new genre of TYA called Theatre for the Very Young (TVY). A subset of TYA, TVY is also sometimes called Theatre for Toddlers, Babies or Infants. As we will see, bringing young audience members into the world of the play through direct contact is important in such work. As children get older and go to school, TYA makes connections with schools. TYA productions invite classrooms to shows and almost always supplement the production with teacher resource guides. Pre- and post-show drama workshops dealing with the production are often implemented in school classrooms as well. These workshops are designed to make students curious about a play before seeing it, and to help them further process a performance afterwards.

Likewise, processing a play before or after performance is built into TIE as plays travel to schools to help students further explore the theatre experience. As in TYA, actors in TIE are usually adults who perform plays for young people. Unlike TYA, TIE plays are primarily created to address a specific issue – a social problem like drug use, for example. Similarly, in case vignette five we find the Big Brum Theatre investigating the issue of contaminated water and pollution. Usually performed in an educational setting, as opposed to a TYA theatre, TIE workshops are always facilitated with young people before and/or after the play. While workshops around TYA plays are designed to help young people understand a play, TIE workshop are first and foremost about unpacking the specific issue at hand. These issue-based drama workshops are facilitated by the actors, often called actor-teachers. Undoubtedly, TIE workshops are of equal importance to the performance. For Big Brum, like most TIE companies, reflection and participation are key components.

Chapter 3 also explores how ideologies can challenge notions of Theatre by, for and with Young People, thus shaping its praxis in various contexts throughout the world. Consistent with our notion of Theatre for Change, we discuss ways in which theatre has been used to help young people critically reflect upon society, making reference to such examples as the Federal Theatre Project, Holocaust Theatre for Young Audiences and Theatre of Faith.

Youth Theatre is an umbrella term describing any program that develops young people as theatre artists. Here the role of the teacher is to direct, guide and mentor young people in theatre-making. At times this culminates in a theatre production that is acted, and sometimes written, by youth theatre participants.

Case vignette six provides an example of Youth Theatre festivals in Dubai. Festivals like this one can be exciting for young people to learn theatre and social skills. But there are also concerns when they promote competition and create strict rules that stifle creativity. In Chapter 2 we consider the pros and cons of competition in similar high school festivals. Nevertheless, festivals like this can broaden the critical perspective of young people, exposing them to values and ideas outside their own communities.

The complexities of drama, theatre and education are evident when looking at the various titles given to such work – Creative Drama, Process Drama, Story Drama, Curriculum Drama, Drama in Education, Theatre in Education, Theatre for Young Audiences, to name a few. As if the titles alone are not perplexing, the multiple meanings given to these various forms of drama and theatre in schools make both teachers and students weary. 'Can't we just delve into the work without rigidly defining it?' they might ask. However, we welcome the range of terms for what they teach us about the intersections of drama, theatre and education in the classroom, while remaining aware of the ways in which terminology can initially distract drama practitioners. We choose to identify the variety of terms to better understand the depth and breadth of dramatic activities used by drama practitioners.

We conclude this section with a portion of an interview with Johnny Saldaña, professor of theatre at Arizona State University (ASU), whose work became well known since the publication of the 1982 *Handbook* and whose career covers a broad spectrum of Curriculum Drama, arts-based research, Theatre for Social Change and Ethnodrama.

MONTGOMERY: Do you still offer a course at ASU called Creative Drama?

SALDAÑA: No. We used to have a course called Creative Drama, but Lin Wright changed it to Improvisation with Youth in 1990.

MONTGOMERY: Why?

SALDAÑA:   Roger Bedard, who currently heads the Theatre for Youth MFA and PhD programs at ASU, had just come on board. Lin Wright felt that Creative Drama was outdated and she wanted to call it improvisational process. She eventually settled on Improv with Youth. Children's Theatre was also the outdated term. Roger wanted to call it Theatre for Young Audiences. Theatre for Youth was Coleman Jennings' term.

LANDY:   So a lot of the name changes were based on individuals' preferences?

SALDAÑA:   Yes. The entire faculty brings their signature to the places they work. But for years I taught my students the definition from the Children's Theatre Association of America, which was that 'Creative Drama is an improvisational, non-exhibitional process form of drama where participants are guided by a leader to imagine, enact and reflect upon human experience.' That's the official definition burned in my memory. Now I simply call it drama. Sometimes when I teach Improv with Youth it's primarily with non-education majors, and in that case it's about creating the artist within you. Last year, with this focus of using drama as a teaching modality, we learned how to teach English and social studies and math through these forms. There's some school that says: We don't follow trends, we set them.[22] I loved that. That's when I realized my own autonomy. But I also acknowledge this wonderful hybridity and variations within the field.[23]

In researching this field, we discovered that it is reflective practitioners rather than special commissions who decide terminology. While these terms have at times obfuscated the field, we embrace them for the debate they spark. Rather than narrowing the field, the definitions help broaden our understanding and deepen our practice. So, too, do they collectively help us embrace Saldaña's theme of hybridity, which becomes a central feature of this book, traversing the landscape of drama and theatre in education, social action and therapy.

# 1      Educational Drama in the Elementary School

## Introduction

From a young age, children play to explore their hopes and fears through creative expression. The idea that natural play is educationally important was amplified by John Dewey who placed art in the realm of experience.[1] He believed it was important to integrate the mind with physical activity in learning. If games, pleasures and instincts are developed, the senses are cultivated, so that by the age of twelve, play and work become synonymous. Dewey influenced multitudes of drama educators who share the belief that education should focus primarily on children's interests and needs, and that purposeful play helps children express their interests and needs.

Viola Spolin, as others, emphasized play in her work but also viewed drama as developing relaxation, trust, concentration, imagination and awareness of one's self and social world. With these skills, the child is better able to work collaboratively with others in the classroom. For Spolin, drama work began with exercises in physical and creative movement to ground young people in their bodies and connect movement to thought and action. From there, Spolin moved participants into pantomime, sense awareness, voice and characterization.[2]

Creative Drama, Developmental Drama, Child Drama and Story Drama are process-oriented approaches that are particularly relevant to elementary-age participants who are generally more interested in playing for play's sake than in performing to an audience.

## Creative Drama

Drama in Education practitioners frequently proclaim the benefits of creating drama without the intention of performing for an audience. The philosophy dates back to Winifred Ward in the early 1930s. Ward pioneered the practice and coined the term 'Creative Drama'. She mentored the early generations of American drama practitioners including Geraldine Brain

Siks and Nellie McCaslin. Ward outlined her work in *Creative Dramatics* and her second book, *Playmaking with Children*.[3] Ward also helped found the Children's Theatre Association of America, the first professional organization for children's theatre practitioners.[4]

Creative Drama emerged from Ward's work in a public school in Evanston, Illinois, and the School of Speech at Northwestern University where she was Assistant Professor of Dramatic Production. Recognizing that educators of her day saw drama as 'a frill, grudgingly allowed to deck holiday attire, but of no possible use for everyday wear,' she worked to make drama a more acceptable and integral form of teaching and learning.[5]

Sadly, while there have been positive changes in theatre education with the advent of theatre teaching certification in US states such as New York, this view of drama as a frill in the classroom still persists in educational institutions throughout the world. Too many schools have no drama or theatre programs. Some have no arts programming at all. Likewise, some schools that have a theatre program do not value it as much as the school sports teams or test preparation programs.

The ideas of Harriet Finlay-Johnson and Caldwell Cook deeply impacted the development of Creative Drama. Finlay-Johnson, a head teacher in an elementary school in England during the early 1900s, believed drama led to better retention of material and aroused a new desire for knowledge among students.[6] This belief persisted in the classroom of Caldwell Cook, also from England, who authored the influential book, *The Play Way*. For Cook, children would 'learn to require less from the teacher and therefore enjoy the sense of pride in being able to work on their own.'[7] Cook advocated making learning fun, providing children a balance of work and play to develop into well-rounded adults. Through his methods of 'active play' he inspired students who were 'not only able to learn but anxious to continue their work.'[8]

Nellie McCaslin, whose work spanned more than 50 years, was highly influenced by Ward. McCaslin's book, *Creative Drama in the Classroom and Beyond*, remains a valuable resource for introducing a variety of drama approaches, including mime, puppetry, improvisation, and drama in special education.[9] Due to her publications and numerous international presentations, McCaslin influenced generations of practitioners in the US, Asia, the Middle East and Europe.

According to McCaslin, Creative Drama 'refers to informal drama that is created by participants,' for the purpose of acting out a story, or to 'explore, develop, and express ideas and feelings through dramatic enactment'.[10] The replaying of scenes occurs to deepen understanding and strengthen the skills of the performers rather than to perfect a product.

Geraldine Brain Siks, who worked for 30 years at the University of Washington, was another pioneer in the development of Creative Drama.[11] In dramatizing a story already told by a storyteller, students pick characters to play. She described her creative process with young people as follows:

> They'd talk a little bit about the characters, and then they'd start to play it. Sometimes the children were very embarrassed and shy, and they didn't know what to do. Now that I look at it from a concept point of view, I say the child creates a character from two particular aspects: physical aspects and dominant personality traits. So now we're reducing it down to what I call fundamental concepts of the art form – helping the child really learn to create form, to give form to his inner thoughts and feelings, the things he perceives.[12]

Winifred Ward also worked with concepts of the art form by concentrating on skills relevant to performing plays.[13] In the creation and acting of plays, she adhered to the literary model of the Western well-made play with its use of causally-related plot structure and climax. Therefore it is not surprising that Ward cautioned teachers, 'A story which takes place on the back of a camel, or jumps from one spot to another in many short episodes is seldom a wise choice.'[14] Whereas such storytelling could occur in the spontaneous play of children, teachers needed to develop a cohesive, linear plot in their dramatic practice. Ward also asserted:

> Poetic justice almost invariably characterizes the outcomes of stories for little children. It does not give them an entirely realistic view of life as it is. But it is life as it should be, and while their standards are forming, it would be utterly confusing to them to hear stories in which evil triumphs over good.[15]

Ela Weissberger, the Holocaust survivor who played the Cat in *Brundibár* in Theresienstadt, as discussed in the introduction to this book, would certainly agree. Nevertheless, while potentially useful for some teachers, this advice places limitations on the imagination of the group. It could shut down possibilities for critical analysis on the part of children. Though indicative of the times in which Ward worked, such a conservative perspective potentially stifles the natural play process.

In considering contemporary praxis in the field, it is useful to note how some of Ward's practices have fallen out of favor. For instance, Ward offered her thoughts on casting as follows: 'We find it is better to choose our casts by letting the children volunteer for parts, because in that way they have a choice as to what they will play.'[16] Today, while many teachers call on student volunteers in drama work, others feel this approach silences the students who do not wish to volunteer but who still want to be involved in the performative drama experience.

Ward also wrote: 'It is a good rule of the game to stay in character once they have assumed it.'[17] As we see later in this chapter, Process Drama methods encourage students to play multiple roles, engage in improvisations as a whole group simultaneously and come in and out of role for reflection. Thus, although Ward set many parameters for the work, her ideas are challenged in Process Drama and current praxis.

While Creative Drama as a movement has impacted the field, it has been on the decline as a term since Dorothy Heathcote began lecturing in the US in the 1970s. Heathcote called her work in the UK Drama in Education (DIE) – which implied that drama was used as a means of teaching other subject areas. The term Drama in Education was appropriated by practitioners in the US and is often the umbrella used to describe not only curriculum content, but any dramatic process that engages students in meaning-making.

The term Curriculum Drama is a more specific term used to identify Educational Drama that services the teaching of curricula content. Other terms used synonymously with Creative Drama and DIE are Improvisation with Youth or simply Drama Education.

While Creative Drama developed in the US, DIE developed in the UK. Process Drama, a methodology to be discussed, is a popular form of DIE. As both Creative Drama and DIE evolved and crossed paths, so did Creative Drama and Process Drama, as exemplified by McCaslin, who further described Creative Drama as 'an umbrella term that covers playmaking, process drama, and improvisation.'[18]

'I would have to say that Nellie McCaslin is wrong on that if she thinks that Process Drama comes out of Creative Drama,' said Philip Taylor in an interview for this text.[19] Undoubtedly, there are many similarities in these two approaches, particularly the de-emphasis of future performance. However, we are again reminded of the definition dilemma – can Process Drama fit within Creative Drama if Creative Drama has been replaced by DIE, the field from which Process Drama was born? As we saw from Johnny Saldaña's opening interview, terms change over time and place of origin.

## Child Drama

Preceding Creative Drama, DIE and Process Drama was the term Child Drama, coined by Peter Slade. A key figure in drama education, Slade also emphasized the need for teachers to nurture children's play, creativity, self-expression and personal growth. As a theorist, he developed an understanding of Child Drama that, like Jean Piaget's stages of cognitive development, provided a model for praxis in the field. His influential book, *Child Drama*, first published in 1954, promoted drama for personal development. 'Many people ask what are the aims of Child Drama,' wrote Slade, 'probably the shortest answer is: a happy and balanced individual.'[20]

Slade believed that happy and balanced children developed through sincerity and absorption in the work, concepts that played a part in Stanislavski's earlier system of actor training.[21] According to Slade, sincerity and absorption are cultivated when teachers create supportive environments.[22]

Slade, like Ward, his contemporary, was interested in drama as it related to imaginative play, but he advocated more directly for the element of play emanating from the child: 'When you see attempts at Play which you may feel are more obviously linked with Drama, take care not to rush any notion or conception of adult drama,' he wrote.[23] By adult drama, he was referring to audience-centered performance in which improvisation is shaped into a coherent story with a beginning, middle and end. Slade remained child-centered, always supporting the values of spontaneous play.

Slade's Child Drama was developmental in nature. With an emphasis on physical action and dance, the drama teacher was encouraged to guide students through the lessons. The teacher narrated stories for children to enact. In practice, Slade asked young people to imagine being within certain situations related to a story and to individually move and react accordingly.[24] Slade often accompanied the narrative with recorded music and guided students into groups to collaboratively enact the stories.

Gavin Bolton, who recognized the positive impact of Slade's praxis, criticized his narrative/instructional methodology for being too future-oriented and 'anticipatory of the *next* action of the story rather than exploratory of the present moment.'[25] Toward the end of his prominent career, Slade's work shifted from the specifics of drama to a more general view of human nature and play. As we shall see later, Slade's influence spread into the field of Drama Therapy.

## Developmental Drama

Brian Way echoed Slade's division between Educational Drama and Educational Theatre in his influential text, *Development through Drama*. Expanding on Slade's ideas, Way was interested in drama 'to develop people, not drama.'[26] Way was also not concerned with the performance of young people and worked toward developing the whole child through a series of specific life skill exercises in focus, concentration, relaxation, imagination and sensitivity.[27] He warned, 'By pursuing professional theatre conventions – some dating back more than three hundred years – the point may be missed altogether, the activity reduced to one of interest only to a few, achievable by fewer still, and all quite outside any fundamental aspect of general education.'[28]

Way often had students work individually, then in dyads, then small groups, and finally, in whole group improvisations. Although participants engaged individually for a period of time, Way emphasized the importance of developing group ensemble. He believed his model echoed various developmental stages in the lives of children, beginning with solo play alongside others, and gradually moving into collaborative play.[29] As his work progressed, Way, like Slade, adopted a 'narrative/instructional methodology' at times, but also added the 'exercise' dimension of the activity with music played to serve as unifying element to the physical activities.[30]

Way believed teachers should structure drama experiences where a student is seen 'exploring, discovering and mastering his own resources, and attaining a sensitive, confident relationship with his environment.'[31] He outlined the role of the teacher towards achieving these goals, emphasizing that the teacher avoid 'imposing (through demonstration or explanation) particular ways of doing things.'[32] This is a constructivist idea of teacher as facilitator, not expert. He suggested, 'in the early stages the teacher may suggest "what" but not "how," and in the later stages the teacher constantly helps each young person to develop and enrich his actual approach and achievement through his own effort and consideration, not through any short cut based on consideration of the end product.'[33]

It is clear that Way calls for expression and interpretation to emanate from the participants. However, his methods also require the teacher to be the expert on enhancing the creative spirit of the student. According to Bolton, Way 'seems to eschew Slade's occasional use of story-building from the children's suggestions, preferring to use a sequence of his own (often less whimsical and more imitative of "real life").'[34] In other words, in Way's practice, many narrative ideas originate from the teacher who leads the students through realistic scenarios. Bolton further criticized the non-dramatic, individualized emphasis of Way's exercises for taking the risk out of classroom drama.[35]

Participatory Theatre was another significant technique originated by Way. This method permitted the child audience to become active participants in a play performance in schools. Staying away from the traditional proscenium stage, performances occurred in all-purpose rooms in schools, with children seated on three sides.[36] Within the play structures, spaces were provided for audience involvement as actors questioned, requested help or convinced students to come into the playing space with fellow actors.[37] As McCaslin noted, Way offered an approach to children's theatre that combined 'the formal with the informal in its attempt to establish a closer relationship between actor and audience.'[38] With Participatory Theatre we find strong connections to Theatre in Education, discussed in Chapter 3, and Forum Theatre, discussed in Chapter 4.

## David Booth and Story Drama

Story Drama involves using a pre-existing narrative to create drama with participants. We have seen that for Ward, drama was often a re-enactment of a story with a beginning, middle and end. Since her time, practitioners increasingly approach story in non-linear ways. This development, influenced by post-modernism, has occurred over the past 30 years as drama educators increasingly changed their practice based on self-critiques and critiques of their predecessors.

David Booth speaks of drama as '[a]n exploration of topics and issues that can surprise and shock the participants into deeper awareness at every level.'[39] He works with students to explore these topics within an ensemble.

Booth began teaching drama to grade seven and eight students in 1962. Soon Booth met Brian Way, who changed his understanding of teaching drama 'by involving everyone inside the activity.'[40] Booth later became a professor of Drama at the University of Toronto and brought many experts to his program, including Dorothy Heathcote and Gavin Bolton. 'This caused me to study in England for two years with Dorothy and Gavin, where I met many significant drama educators including Jonothan Neelands, Tony Goode and Cecily O'Neill.'[41]

Booth's influential text, *Story Drama*, describes a multitude of strategies for moving students inside the stories they experience together. He shows how teachers can help students build stories through pair work, small group work or large gatherings.[42] 'Events such as meetings, assemblies, inquiries and protests allow the whole class to participate in this way, contributing in and out of role,' thus building the drama cooperatively into a playmaking event.[43]

As we will see, this sort of interaction with story shares many similarities to Process Drama, discussed in the next section. Both forms utilize conventions that enable participants to interact in an imaginary world where they generate ideas for dramatic action.

This interface of student and story is similar to Louise Rosenblatt's focus on the uniqueness of a particular, momentary transaction between reader and text which has become known as 'transactional theory'. Rosenblatt, best known for her text, *Literature as Exploration*, argued that the meaning of any text comes not in the work itself, but in the readers' interaction with it.[44] Therefore, teachers of literature play a pivotal role in shaping how students perform in response to a text. Rosenblatt's transactional theory also emphasized the interaction between emotion and reason to help students make meaning of text, a synergy well exemplified in drama. 'Reason should arise in a matrix of feeling,' said Rosenblatt who quoted Dewey to emphasize the value teachers must place on feeling: 'More "passions," not fewer, is the answer over reason.'[45] This does not mean that teachers open up the floodgates in their classrooms, but rather utilize drama for a deeper, more nuanced exploration of literature, recognizing that students' emotional reactions inform their understanding. Most importantly, the act of reflecting and questioning is clearly illustrated in the transaction between reader and text.[46]

How do teachers decide which strategies to utilize? Booth points out: 'The needs of the students determine my approach to working in drama. ... If they are in a performance class, I try to understand their reference points, but my teaching style and dynamic always remains the same – to deepen participants' roles through guided group improvisation.'[47] For Booth, a primary teaching goal is to 'teach and reach all students, regardless of natural talent or particular dispositions to this art form and to adapt to their needs.'[48]

At the University of Toronto, Booth continues to demonstrate his praxis each week with a group of elementary students who work alongside his graduate students. After 45 years in Educational Theatre, Booth sees positive changes in the field:

> In Ontario, drama is now mandated in every classroom in elementary school, and is an option in every secondary school. As well, Master's and Doctoral degrees are now offered in each province. The level of in-service instruction in many places is very high.[49]

While it is certainly a positive sign that drama is required in Ontario elementary classrooms, as we see in Chapter 2, Ontario is an exception when it comes to mandating drama and theatre in schools.

## Process Drama

As in Story Drama, many drama experts neither begin drama with exercises nor move progressively to play production. Rather, they work with an eclectic, less linear form that combines many elements, techniques and aims of the drama experience. This way of working is referred to as Process Drama, a term that first appeared in print in 1991 in an article by Brad Haseman published in *The Drama Magazine*. John O'Toole also used the term extensively at the time.[50] Cecily O'Neill explains:

> In what is one of the first uses of this term in print, Brad Haseman notes that those working in process drama have created, appropriated, and reshaped a range of dramatic forms that establish its unique character. For Haseman, these forms include role taking and role building, the 'key strategy' of teacher in role, the means of being inside and outside the action, and distance and reflection.[51]

Process Drama is a set of drama skills and a methodology used to explore themes, issues and curriculum content. When Process Drama conventions are integrated for meaning-making, it often results in a 'structured improvisational activity in which teachers and students jointly contract to an imaginary world.'[52] It is structured so that participants take on multiple roles, not just one character throughout the drama experience. It is framed this way to allow participants to consider multiple perspectives. At the same time, Process Drama is a methodology that empowers students to take ownership in the meaning they make of any given topic. As the drama is developed, it takes on a reflective component that impacts the unfolding action, moving it more clearly into our conception of praxis.

While Process Drama is almost entirely improvised, it usually starts with a pretext. The pretext, a term used by O'Neill, refers to the inspiration for the drama that allows teachers to consider how they will establish location, roles, circumstances, atmosphere and the initial action.[53] The pretext can be a word, an object, a play script, a letter or any other form that frames the Process Drama and suggests the roles and responsibilities for participants in the drama's development.[54]

Process Drama also involves 'careful sequencing and layering of dramatic units or episodes, often in non-linear ways.'[55] This concentrated series of episodes bring about the tension of the drama that both teachers and students collectively attempt to resolve.

Process Drama experts share a constructivist view of education and maintain that knowledge is acquired through engagement with content instead of imitation or repetition. The role of the teacher is to structure, stimulate, challenge and develop the students' contributions.

Process Drama grew out the DIE movement that Dorothy Heathcote pioneered when she developed the conceptual groundwork for drama as an effective learning medium.[56] She emphasized that teachers need to develop an awareness of pedagogical objectives and take structural responsibility in creating lessons. Heathcote was highly detailed and methodical in her approach toward planning a drama experience. Interestingly, despite the value she put on spontaneity and flexibility, her teaching drew criticism from those who argue that her methods confine children's creativity within a severe structure.[57]

David Hornbrook was most critical of the DIE movement.[58] As a researcher, noted author on theatre education and arts inspector for the London Borough of Camden, Hornbrook advocated an approach that focuses on theatre aesthetics rather than the imprecise humanistic goals of process:

Through the mid 1960s and early 1970s book after book professed to demonstrate how Drama in Education developed 'self-confidence', or encouraged 'personal awareness and an awareness of others' or taught students how to co-operate in groups, or fostered qualities of 'tolerance and understanding', or helped children become more 'self-disciplined.' Just about the only thing it made no claims to do ... was to equip young people with an understanding of actors, theatres and plays.[59]

Hornbrook called on educators to make use of the wealth of plays available. Although he claimed to bridge the gap between drama and theatre, his strategy at times was to attack the DIE movement. In reflecting on past DIE teachers, he wrote:

the important issue for drama teachers was not drama at all, but rather how they should deal with questions like: 'Why can't I get the job I choose? Why is my Dad never going to work again? Why do we let blacks in when there aren't enough jobs for whites? Why do we spend money on bombs rather than jobs?'

... Important questions. And there is little doubt that by asking students to put themselves 'into other people's shoes' in this way, skillful and sensitive teachers may well be able to draw from students' insights into questions of social and individual morality. Yet, uncouple role-play from the distinctive questions, procedures, knowledge and traditions of the theatre arts and all that is left is a bag of pedagogical tricks likely to be of interest less to radical politicians than to personal and social education teachers, management trainers and therapists.[60]

Philip Taylor, program director of Educational Theatre at NYU, recalls the impact of Hornbrook's ideas and critical writings:

> In the early 1990s, I was reading a lot of journals. And in those journals there were a couple of articles by David Hornbrook. And he was taking a very hostile stand against Process Drama. And he got a lot of celebrity through two articles in *Youth Theatre Quarterly* where he was alienating practitioners. And I was kind of livid with Hornbrook's writing because he made Dorothy Heathcote and Gavin Bolton look foolish. I remember when Hornbrook was invited to speak at a graduate student study abroad course in the UK where I was a participant. At one point Hornbrook held up this magazine from *London Drama* and said, 'Look at the title of this!' The title was 'Teaching Shakespeare through Drama.' '"Teaching Shakespeare through Drama?" What does that mean? Shakespeare *is* drama.' And that was the first time I realized that, 'Oh, there's controversy brewing in the field.'

> I attended a huge conference in England called *The Fight for Drama, The Fight for Education*. Talk about the red flag being raised at that conference! England had just brought in The Education Act where they were introducing standards and outcomes. The Progressive Era, which is how I was trained, was dying! But I was brought up on process and trained in...Viola Spolin and Brian Way, which I sort of enjoyed but found myself a little self-conscious doing. I kind of felt it wasn't right for me. But the discovery of the Heathcote school was right for me. So I went off to this conference, and that's when I really hooked into the British drama education movement in a powerful way. And I became one of the clan and started to write about how Hornbrook doesn't have the solutions for us. And this business about how drama teachers are not interested in theatrical products is wrong, but I couldn't really get the language right.[61]

This passage helps contextualize the initial rise and resistance to DIE. While Taylor felt he couldn't get the language right at first, he eventually did, and authored several significant drama education texts advocating DIE, including *Structure and Spontaneity: The Process Drama of Cecily O'Neill*.[62]

Cecily O'Neill is a prolific educator and researcher, as well as playwright and director. Her books have influenced scores of current leaders in the field like Taylor.[63] In an interview for this book, O'Neill reflected on the state of Process Drama work in British classrooms today:

> There's very little Process Drama work happening in the UK. Today there's almost no exploration in the drama work at all. It's 'go into groups and make up a little play' – which is what we tried to get away from with Bolton and Heathcote. I think that as people get into the higher levels of schooling they do some very, very interesting theatre work. But too often with Process Drama, the teacher is merely a stage manager and a time keeper and disher out of the task. Because the drama training isn't there![64]

Some will disagree with O'Neill's assessment here, which is based on observations made through her ongoing facilitation of workshops in schools. Though it's important not to generalize O'Neill's claim, Montgomery's experiences observing London drama classrooms over seven years confirms her view to a degree. Some teachers admitted to him of not knowing enough about Process Drama to implement it, or revealed that they avoided engaging with Process Drama because it was too time-consuming to fit into their curriculum. In a number of instances Montgomery observed work that was termed Process Drama by teachers, but the philosophical underpinning of student ownership was absent. Many activities typically utilized in Process Drama, like Teacher-in-Role, discussed in the next section, were implemented by teachers. However, students' ideas were not driving the lessons, nor informing the shape of the topics explored. Rather, students interpreted teacher-directed tasks, and the outcomes of the lesson guided the work.

Jonothan Neelands, known for his work in Process Drama, is an expert trainer of drama teachers. For Neelands, Drama in Education embodies two forms – the representational and the presentational, the latter of which is frequently referred to as the 'conventions' approach.[65] The representational mode describes any performance 'that seeks to create a "virtual" or parallel reality, which co-exists with but does not inter-penetrate the audience's reality.'[66] Examples of the representational mode in theatre include realistic plays where actors strive to inhabit the world of the play presented on stage. The presentational mode is closely associated with the Brechtian style of theatre in that actors acknowledge the audience and the dramatic world which 'is not experienced as "reality" but shown to be a version or interpretation of actuality.'[67]

Serving both the representational and presentational forms, Neelands describes dramatic activities as conventions. Heathcote first introduced the notion of conventions in her article 'Signs and Portents'.[68] While Neelands does not cite Heathcote's conventions, he advocates using them as building blocks to structure drama work. As such, conventions introduce students to an increasingly wide and complex choice of 'means' for depicting the world, which are helpful for teachers to have at their disposal when creating a Process Drama lesson.[69] A valuable resource outlining these drama conventions is Neelands and Tony Goode's book, *Structuring Drama Work*, which details how the conventions can be used to achieve certain objectives in a Process Drama lesson.[70]

While there is substantial literature deconstructing Process Drama, it is difficult to understand the work without experiencing it first-hand as a participant or observer.[71] Even if one disagrees with the premise that Process Drama is waning in the UK, it is undoubtedly the case that Process Drama is less known and practiced in the US. When we introduce Process Drama to NYU students, some express they are hearing about it for the first time. Others are resistant to the method, saying it is too complicated, or pointing to the curriculum as the culprit for not permitting content flexibility.

While Process Drama is well suited to adolescent participants and practiced in secondary schools, it is included in this chapter for its effectiveness in preparing younger students to experience drama and theatre work. When Process Drama is introduced at the elementary level, students learn the art of drama and theatre, analyze ideas emerging from the work, raise questions and reflect on the action of the drama. Critical thinking is an outcome of Process Drama that young students can build upon as they face more complex developmental tasks, both on cognitive and affective levels. As elementary students are less removed from natural play, they are often more willing to dive fully into the process.

## Teacher-in-Role

One of the key strategies used in Process Drama is Teacher-in-Role, where the teacher takes on a fictional role within the imaginary world of the drama. It provides facilitators with the opportunity to interact with students from inside the drama. In such situations, students can communicate freely with high and low status characters played by the teacher. This kind of role-play gives students the opportunity to develop a sense of their own power as they are drawn into forms of dialogue not possible in the everyday teacher–student relationship. It raises the stakes of the learning experience because students and teachers alike are required to think on their feet and address issues in the moment. We will later see in Chapter 5 how this form is used within the Drama Therapy approach of Developmental Transformations.

Teacher-in-Role in many ways crystalizes an essential goal of Process Drama – helping students make meaning of ideas within a dramatic context. Interestingly, some teachers in training perceive that Teacher-in-Role, because of its pretend nature, is more suited to elementary students. However, if undertaken with commitment and sincerity by the facilitator, Teacher-in-Role can make a tremendous impact on participants of any age.

In her book, *Role Reconsidered*, Judith Ackroyd writes: 'I suggest that teachers should understand that they can draw upon the work of actors to find what is appropriate in their drama and in their contexts.'[72] Ackroyd offers a compelling analysis of Teacher-in-Role which has implications for the training of dynamic drama teachers. However, in some situations, as in arts partnerships where classroom teachers are asked to develop pedagogical drama strategies following a residency, some are confused by the word 'role'. As Prendiville and Toye point out: 'The word "role" can be used in a theatrical context to describe a written part in a scripted play, but it is used in Drama in Education to describe taking on a particular attitude or viewpoint, in an unscripted, improvised context.'[73] Not understanding this, many untrained teachers will connect being in role to acting in a play, which scares them. Optimal process-based training in Teacher-in-Role should dispel this fear.

In a qualitative research study, Montgomery examined the experience of three English Language Arts (ELA) school teachers who partnered with drama specialists in order to learn and teach drama lessons on their own.[74] Two of the three participants were teachers who used drama to help their sixth grade students study the novel, *The Last Book in the Universe* by Rodman Philbrick.[75] The following vignette explores one of the teacher participant's experiences.

### ❖ Case vignette: An ELA teacher's experience using Teacher-in-Role

When one of the sixth grade teachers, Tina, a pseudonym, first heard about Teacher-in-Role, she expressed concern that if she went into role, 'the students wouldn't buy it.'[76] However, after she observed Teacher-in-Role and tried it out in the classroom, Tina revealed:

> One of the most powerful lessons happened when I took on a role. And I think it worked because the students were so shocked. It was a side of

me that they had never seen before. And the students really got into it and they will remember that.[77]

While Tina identified success, she also revealed in an earlier part of the interview that she distanced herself from the experience by letting students know beforehand that she was going to try out new activities that had already been initiated by the teaching artist. 'It was a kind of disclaimer in case things didn't work out well,' said Tina.[78] In framing the drama, Tina felt safest being detached from the theatre aesthetic. However, she became more involved once she entered into role. This initial distancing allowed Tina to practice the new technique more comfortably and move into it at her own pace.

Before trying Teacher-in-Role, the two ELA teachers feared that students would be overly confused and ask them why they were teaching class in a 'different' way. By the end of the residency, however, the primary benefit of the work was learning to work in role, because it allowed students to see new and diverse sides of the teachers' personalities.

Tina particularly liked playing the role of Billy Bangor, a high status villain from Rodman Philbrick's novel, as it compelled students to play lower status characters. Tina noted that the role-playing gave her the opportunity to raise her voice and act antagonistically towards the students under the guise of a role. While she made sure to articulate that she would never act this way with the students in reality, she also expressed delight in threatening the students in a dramatic and playful manner.

Throughout the residency, Tina experimented with a variety of roles of both low and high status. However, although she had success with a lower status role, her enthusiasm for playing the villain role was greater. Why was that the case? Did she like the theatricality of 'acting' the higher status role? Did it allow her to guiltlessly act out feelings of aggression towards the kids?

Although we can only speculate on the answers, generally speaking, a higher status role will keep the teacher more in control, while a lower status role will provide students the opportunity to enact superior intelligence. It is in the choosing of role that Cecily O'Neill offers a downside of Teacher-in-Role:

Mistaking the nature of their function, some leaders and teachers may decide to take on a role in the drama process in order to acquire control over it. Typically, the roles chosen under these circumstances may appear to possess the greatest authority – kings or queens, prison governors, ships' captains, the leader of the explorers, and so on. Drama teachers sometimes fall into this error and attempt to subvert the drama to their own ends.[79]

O'Neill has always advocated role work that permits ideas to flow from students.[80] Yet, teachers sometimes fear they will lose control of a class if they sanction this type of student–teacher dynamic through playing the lower status. However, when the teacher really listens and builds upon ideas that students bring to the improvisational exchange, students become more engaged with the work.

Freire said that teachers who are influenced by authoritarian attitudes can suffocate the curiosity of the learner as well as their own curiosity.[81] And yet, authoritative teaching is still pervasive in the classroom. Playing and enjoying the authoritative role in a class drama does not necessarily mean that Tina is an authoritative teacher. It does, however, mean that she is willing to risk change, and thus set a positive precedent for her students.

Shifting from an analysis of Teacher-in-Role but staying within the framework of Process Drama, we present a vignette written by Kristy Messer. This example of Process Drama was used to explore media representations with elementary students.

Messer is a teacher at Inner-City Arts, a non-profit arts education center in Los Angeles, California. In attempts to bring media education into the elementary classroom, she utilized a Process Drama framework that allowed students to create their own television show. Far removed from authoritative teaching, her reflection in the following vignette shows how role-playing led to a complex exploration of representations in popular media. Perhaps most interesting is how creating a television show, an inherently theatrical task, was played out within the Process Drama framework. The framework also resonates with Heathcote's notion of Mantle of the Expert, which we discuss in Chapter 2.

### ❖  Case vignette: Media education and drama: Transforming representations

While working with students through the years, I noticed how often popular media came up in their daily conversations. In my research to find out the ways in which media may influence students, I discovered an entire field focused on teaching media education through production methods. From producing their own media, students become more aware of the processes involved in creating it. Instead of focusing on fixed negative messages about the evils of television, production work encourages students to use their imaginations in order to create original content. Through these activities, students begin to interrogate current media systems and understand how media work in their lives. This realization holds the possibility for students to bring social change by creating alternative ideas for media or making changes in current popular media. The course, taught to a class of second graders, was called 'Exploring Television through Drama'. As a reflective practitioner, I analyzed my own creation and execution of this original curriculum. I observed and reflected upon my teaching and interaction with students. I documented the transformation of the curriculum in my field notes, beginning with my initial thoughts, describing what actually happened in the classroom, and noted where the curriculum might go in coming weeks. The documented changes, mistakes, and triumphs made in and outside of the classroom led to more complex theories about the possibilities of interactions between drama and media education in the elementary classroom.

In this Process Drama, students played the roles of writers, producers and directors in the television field with the overall task of creating a new show. By the end of the curriculum, my aim was for the students to have explored the following aspects of media education: agency (Who is involved in the creation of the show?), category (What characteristics make each genre of television its own category?), language (What are the typical codes and conventions of this genre?), audience (What kind of audience are the students trying to reach?), and representation (How are characters on the show represented, and what types of characters are found in different genres?). It was not my intention to answer every question or explore each aspect equally. In the end, the most interesting discoveries were the ways in which drama allowed for manipulating and shifting ideas about stereotypical representations in media.

As part of creating the show, the students and teacher in role as television experts wrote and acted out characters in a pilot comedy sitcom. In this drama world, students spent class time debating and refining the actual language used in the script. Classmates shouted out suggestions, and the actors/students onstage tried several different lines before deciding on one. The students' own experiences with television helped supply some of the traditional dialogue, like a police officer shouting 'Hands in the air!' when making the arrest. However, through creating characters and making choices in their expert roles about identity, students were able to play with various representations on television.

The biggest space for transformation was in allowing the students to change roles each day, so the cast was constantly in flux. Male and female students played multiple roles and everyone portrayed their characters in very different ways. Patricia, for example, played the role of the cop as a not-so-intelligent character. The role was originally created as a 'straight' and serious police officer, but Patricia's representation was all for laughs. Why was her portrayal amusing? What elements of her performance were stereotypical, if any? Do we have a responsibility as producers of television to not perpetuate stereotypes, or to make the sitcom as funny as possible? Patricia's choices were discussed and analyzed amongst the students within the world of the Process Drama.

The students crossed traditional gender and age lines through their improvised portrayals. Mixing their own character portrayals with their role as television sitcom makers made room for complex perspectives and discussion to transpire. As I reflected on the work, I recognized that student ownership and flexibility in the Process Drama framework were the keys to interrogating representations, and that it was the students' enjoyment in creating and acting out the sitcom that resulted in the most powerful moments of discovery.

For a form that is intended to be about process, there is a lot of attention paid to performance in Messer's Process Drama, including how Patricia altered her acting to get laughs. This was appropriate given that the Process Drama was about enactment and understanding how decisions of representations are made in television. In Chapter 3 we provide a case demonstrating how Process Drama is used in the rehearsal process for a Theatre for Young Audiences (TYA) play, which reminds us that Process Drama, though not intended to satisfy an external audience, is nevertheless rooted in theatre.

In his article, 'It's All Theatre', Bolton re-directs the discourse to theatre.[82] He writes, 'In the past we would do anything to avoid calling it theatre, qualifying the term "drama" into "child" drama or "process" drama or replacing the name of specific classroom practice with non-drama expressions such as "movement" or "speech-training"'.[83] Like Saldaña in the opening interview, Bolton outlines reasons for terms changing over time. What makes them all theatre, Bolton maintains, is the presence of an audience: 'And this is where we have to accept the idea of "self-spectatorship"'.[84]

If we accept the notion that participants are their own audience, every activity is theatre, according to Bolton. Yet there are still a multitude of definitions practitioners identify with and work from. Tackling head on the question of what should be done with all these definitions, Bolton writes that 'to recommend an immediate change of usage would be absurd, for there are too many branches of education that still rely on alternative expressions to make it clear to others that what they are doing is something other than or bigger than putting on plays.'[85]

Along with his prolific writing, Bolton's teaching has had a tremendous impact on Educational Theatre. 'Many of these [Bolton's] graduates, among them Cecily O'Neill, John O'Toole, David Booth and David Davis, cultivated what they knew of Gavin's work and adopted it to their own styles of working, but consistently acknowledged the seed which had been planted by Gavin,' wrote Jardin.[86]

In Bolton's writing we find clear expressions of praxis. Not only does he ask questions of others, but he questions his own practice and biases over time. Bolton discussed his views of the field, past, present and future, in an interview with us, which we refer to throughout the book. We note here, however, that when asked about the future of the field, Bolton replied: 'World-wide the main development will be in different forms of Applied Theatre, offering learning experience for a group with personal or social problems.'[87]

It is noteworthy that Bolton embraces Applied Theatre, a term used to describe drama and theatre in social action. Chapter 4 is devoted to Applied Theatre, but the practice of helping young people address social issues through drama has often been a prevalent objective of drama work in schools.

We have seen how Drama in Education strategies can be used to explore social issues, but theatre-making can also be effective for exploring social issues with students.

The B.R.I.D.G.E Theatre Project provides a global example of work in elementary schools that is applied from an outside organization to address social issues. As such, it could be considered an Applied Theatre project. We include B.R.I.D.G.E here because of its focus on elementary students in school settings and its philosophy that theatre-making transcends cultural boundaries in exploring social issues.

B.R.I.D.G.E Theatre Project offers playwriting and acting programs to communities worldwide, providing opportunities for cultural exchange and artistic communion. Their name, in fact, is their mission: B.R.I.D.G.E – Building Relationships and Inspiring Dialogue through Global Exchange.[88]

Focusing on Western theatre playmaking, the methodology of B.R.I.D.G.E is entirely different from that of Drama in Education. For B.R.I.D.G.E, the collaborative nature of theatre work inherently leads to understanding, dialogue and conflict resolution. For example, participants learn about the acting 'objective' of a scene, a term associated with Stanislavski, to illustrate how someone can use various tactics to get what they want from another person.

Participants also learn about ensemble, improvisation, character creation, conflict and dialogue. This active work fuels the children's writing. Later in the process, youth exchange and rehearse plays written by B.R.I.D.G.E participants from other countries. Simultaneously, one of their new plays is selected to be performed at a B.R.I.D.G.E program in another country, promoting cross-cultural exchange.[89]

During summer 2008, Joe Quintero, an actor and teacher, collaborated with his colleague, Adam Kalesperis, to facilitate a series of theatre workshops in Los Angeles. A year later, Quintero invited Kalesperis to accompany him on his trip to South America to help facilitate theatre workshops with elementary school students. Very quickly, the two launched B.R.I.D.G.E Theatre Project.[90] The following vignette, written by Kalesperis, describes this experience:

### ❖ Case vignette: Exploring social issues in the elementary school: The B.R.I.D.G.E Theatre Project

After stopping in Guayaquil, Ecuador's largest city, to meet with a journalist about our project, we arrived in Milagro where we held introductory theatre workshops at two schools. The children were very poor. The classrooms themselves were small shacks, yet all the students proudly wore a clean school uniform. Such was the importance, and privilege, they placed on education.

We worked with the fifth graders, teaching them the basics of improvisation and character development. The entire school gathered

Photograph 1.1   B.R.I.D.G.E Project, photo courtesy of Adam Kalesperis and Joe Quintero

around the courtyard to observe. Two brave souls volunteered to improvise a scene together, as we asked the kids watching how they could use different tactics to achieve their objectives and overcome their characters' conflict.

After our introductory workshop, the students showed us a native folkloric dance performance. We celebrated further by sampling authentic Ecuadorian cuisine as the kids excitedly raided their backpacks to share their drawings and favorite toys with us. By morning's end, we bid a heartfelt goodbye as the students gathered by the front gate of the school and waved farewell to send us off.

Our next destination in Milagro was a special education school. Rather than doing improvisation exercises or scene-work here, Joe and I focused more on theatre games that would help the children work together, explore different characters, and just have a good time. During one particular exercise, we asked for a student volunteer to lead the group in a round of 'Che Che Coole'. The game consists of chanting nonsensical phrases with movement, which are repeated by the group. Our first volunteer eagerly approached us, but as we tried to teach him the phrases, we found out he was deaf. We called for another volunteer to help him out, but the next student who came up couldn't speak. We then asked once more for another volunteer, and low and behold, the third child couldn't speak or hear. Despite these challenges, the three students stood with us as we led the group in this exercise.

After our time in Ecuador's coastal region, Joe and I flew to the city of Cuenca in the mountainous sierra, nestled in the Andes. There we visited Centro Educativo Crecer, another elementary school, and worked with the third and fourth graders on their first day of school, as their families watched and reacted in the audience. Again, we were outside in the school's courtyard where we engaged the kids in ensemble-building games and a character profile exercise. The students created a half-human, half-wolf character named Hombre-Lobo (Man-Wolf). To get a feel for their character, all the third and fourth graders crawled around the courtyard growling and pawing the air. The children vigorously engaged in the character walk, and the parents in the audience joyfully reacted to what they were witnessing.

When Joe and I returned to the States, we took some time to reflect on the wealth of experiences our inaugural trip to Ecuador provided us. A first viewing of the video footage from workshops gave us the opportunity to re-live our wonderful moments with the students. We then needed to put clips together outlining our mission and philosophy for B.R.I.D.G.E Theatre Project, a task that helped us clarify our objectives and long-term goals. This required recursive viewing of the video, which in turn helped us to step away and more deeply analyze our practice. This was immensely valuable for us. We quickly became aware that the outreach potential for B.R.I.D.G.E was far greater than we initially considered. Different communities – varying not only in culture, but also in socioeconomic background and physical or mental capabilities – have the chance to create their own stories and at the same time share the stories of people from another country, to whom they may have otherwise never been exposed. Imagine the understanding that can come of such an exchange. Imagine the dialogue that can occur between different cultures as a result.

Although still new at the time of writing this book, the state of B.R.I.D.G.E as an organization is on an upward trajectory as it begins to make an impact in Nepal, South Africa, France, Norway and Germany. From its birth consisting of two teachers sharing ideas, to its launch in Ecuador, to its ongoing development, B.R.I.D.G.E exemplifies not only a powerful praxis, but also a collaborative spirit as two artist-educators with passion and a mission work toward enhancing the lives of children.

While their main goal is to promote peace, the facilitators do not come into the elementary classroom and say, 'We're here to explore your situation of poverty or oppression.' Rather, they believe that the shared experiences of the theatre-making process will in itself lead to transformation, and help participants move toward change.

## Drama for Conflict Resolution

Drama for Conflict Resolution, like B.R.I.D.G.E's work, can be valuable in the elementary classroom, as well as upper grades, during a time of social confusion or crisis, one that cannot be scheduled within the timetable of the school day. It can be applied to various situations, such as a rash of bullying or sexting, a school shooting or similar crisis in the community. Undoubtedly, all teachers have to deal with emotionally charged issues at some point in their teaching. If any of these issues are so pronounced as to impede the educational process, they must be dealt with in some fashion. Sometimes they are addressed by bringing in social workers, counselors or motivational speakers. Most classroom teachers feel unprepared, and principals often believe it is inappropriate for the school to deal with volatile social and emotional matters.

Drama is one way of examining such issues. In the elementary school, role-playing experiences can be basic; for example, in exploring feelings of disappointment toward teachers, students may be asked to assume a teacher's role and answer questions put to them by other students. Or, a disappointed student may be asked to switch roles with another in the role of teacher, so that the situation is explored dramatically. Following the demonstration, students can be asked to reflect upon the drama and discuss their insights.

The challenge of applying such drama lies, of course, in teachers who are not trained in role-playing and who are generally uncomfortable and unprepared to deal with emotion in the classroom. Such teachers should not experiment with these uses of drama. But for teachers who have learned the techniques of role-playing and have explored their own fears of leading such dramas, the charged situation can be defused and attention can be freed for other curricular matters.

Not all teacher training in conflict resolution is optimal. Several years ago while in graduate school, Teresa Fisher, a drama and health specialist, participated in a workshop with other graduate students. In that the lesson was intended for elementary children, the facilitator asked the graduate students to take on the role of young people so they could understand the drama from the inside out. At the end of the workshop, there was an opportunity to reflect on the experience as participants and as practitioners. The workshop led Fisher to question issues of safety and containment in conflict resolution training, as Fisher's following vignette demonstrates:

## ❖ Case vignette: Reflections on a workshop on bullying

The theme of the workshop was bullying. The drama teacher solicited volunteers to play the role of the victim and the victim's friend. The rest of us took on the role of bullies. In the drama, the victim and his friend played catch near an electrical power unit. When the bullies came, the ball was tossed into the electrical unit area. The lead bully, played by the facilitator, forced the victim to retrieve the ball. In so doing, the victim was electrocuted and died. A frozen image of this death pose was created, with the volunteer student still in role as the victim.

In a later portion of the workshop, the facilitator took on the role of the victim before the electrocution incident. We participants sat in a circle offering advice to the victim. The victim shot down our ideas. I was left with a sense of hopelessness, especially knowing how the victim's story would end. I also got confused during the reflection activities. I wasn't sure when I was a graduate student reflecting on the work and when I was in role. Furthering my confusion, I wasn't always certain when the facilitator was in role and when he was facilitating.

While still in this state of hopelessness and confusion, our facilitator brought the Process Drama to an end. As we were almost out of time, we had only a brief period of reflection. In responding to a question about how this workshop was received by young people, the facilitator made a joking comment that he did not know the effects of the drama as he never checked back with groups after the lesson. A few days later, I remarked to one of the other course instructors that I wondered if the drama had ended so abruptly because of the time factor. She assured me that she had seen the workshop facilitated before and it ended the same way when there was more time.

This answer prompted me to ask other students their reactions to the work. The workshop seemed to bring out mixed feelings in students. Some students loved the workshop and thought the facilitator was brilliant. Other students were concerned that he did not protect them from emotional reactions. For me, the activity felt unfinished. While I recognize that Process Drama is not meant to solve all problems for/with students, but to open up discussions and minds, I still felt that there were many feelings left unresolved from the session. When one is a teacher coming in for a one-off lesson, as was the case in this instance, I wonder how the facilitator would make sure that post-activity processing happened for participants?

In contrast to this approach to Process Drama, Dorothy Heathcote taught that students can learn metaphorically, with distance from the actual event.[91] As O'Neill noted, 'While encouraging identification, it [Process Drama] promotes distance and reflection – key concepts in the arts and in learning. The arts represent a different way of knowing and responding to the world.'[92]

By taking on a role, participants in Process Drama are provided a safety net. In the bullying workshop, while we participants were in role, we were not metaphorically addressing the issue of bullying, but were facing it head on. As graduate students, we had the benefit of being distant from childhood, whereas elementary children or even adolescents participating in this workshop would be essentially playing themselves. The drama in the workshop was not set in another time or in a significantly different location in which to encourage distance. Thus, the level of distance from the role could very easily be next to nothing.

As a former mental health counselor, I am especially attuned to the emotional reactions from charged Process Drama work. I feel it is important to prepare participants for emotionally charged drama work as well as provide them with the support to deal with strong emotions and the option to step out of the drama if they do not feel ready to open up those emotional channels.[93] Without pre-establishing healthy responses to feelings which may arise during the drama, students may act out violently or turn to other unhealthy coping strategies. As Heathcote said, 'one student's therapeutic indulgence may overstep the threshold of another's vulnerability.'[94] Heathcote also noted that drama should be structured so as to stay away from therapeutic/emotional issues/reactions. In connecting her observations to this particular workshop, I did not feel safe in the bullying workshop nor did I feel that we accomplished anything beyond feeling hopeless about the situation for the school children portrayed in the Process Drama.

Drama works best with elementary students when it provides safety through aesthetic processes of metaphor and distance, which the teacher in Fisher's narrative did not incorporate. Structuring drama with these factors in mind is not easy. Thus, the work frequently is not led by classroom teachers but by trained actor/teachers from organizations specializing in problem solving. Some, however, are not effective and teach by negative example or simply look for a quick fix of complex issues. Emelie Fitzgibbon, Artistic Director of the Graffiti Theatre in Cork Ireland, addresses the latter:

> There's a fashion, I think at the moment, which is that drama can solve everything. And we're inundated with requests like – 'can you do a workshop on bullying? Can you do a workshop on self-esteem? Can you do a workshop on human development and *can you do it tomorrow?*' And so you wonder whether it can be effective. We've been put in a position here where we won't take on a workshop unless we believe in it and have time to develop it. But there is also a sense that people are just grabbing other people to do drama workshops in a way which is ill prepared.[95]

The 'quick fix' is unlikely to build a thoughtful, well-scaffolded classroom drama lesson. That requires the proper time and knowledge of the students, utilizing their ideas and facilitating reflective activities. It is helpful to note that reflection can occur during as well as following an experience, which Schön terms 'reflection-in-action'.[96] Heathcote consistently endorsed the notion of refection-in-action in the structuring of dramatic activities, where reflection is interspersed throughout the drama lesson.

Many organizations, such as the Creative Arts Team, to be discussed in Chapter 4, work through metaphor to help participants better understand the motivations and consequences of bullying or other behaviors. While drama often generates more questions than answers to societal problems, these questions can lead toward understanding and ultimately change when explored through an optimal balance of action and observation, of feeling and thoughtful reflection.

Thus far, we have looked at several forms including Creative Drama, Story Drama, Process Drama and theatre-based approaches in elementary school settings. We examined theories and methods of drama and looked at Drama for Conflict Resolution with its inherent requirement of safety. We have noted that much of the most exciting and innovative work in Educational Drama occurs at the elementary school level when young learners are still very much open to the values inherent in role-playing, movement and story work. The elementary drama teacher has the advantage of drawing upon the child's natural predisposition to play, for drama is not a new skill to be taught, but a natural process to hone and refine. Unfortunately, as children grow older this process often becomes blocked as the instinct to play is buried under the weight of academics and socially acceptable behavior.

As expressed by Ken Robinson: 'The dominant forms of education actively stifle the conditions that are essential to creative development.'[97] Educational Drama and Theatre counteracts the deleterious effects of these dominant forms of education by bringing students together in imaginary circumstances where they are encouraged to freely participate, to raise questions and to engage in reflective action based upon the search for answers.

As we shall see in the next chapter, the aims, techniques and values that are valid in the elementary classroom are applicable across the educational spectrum.

# 2 Educational Drama and Theatre in the Middle and Secondary School

## Introduction

In secondary education, drama continues to be used to make meaning of ideas and to teach curriculum subjects. Instances of exemplary Curriculum Drama praxis are presented in this chapter. However, as has been the case for decades, secondary dramatic education predominantly focuses on theatre-making. Schools that offer drama/theatre studies tend to stress performance, production techniques and dramatic literature courses. In the US one needs only look at the national standards for the arts to see the value placed on theatre product.

Developed by the Consortium of National Arts Education Associations, the National Standards for Arts Education outlines basic arts learning outcomes integral to the comprehensive K–12 education of every American student.[1] The eight standards include:

1. Script writing through improvising, writing and refining scripts based on personal experience and heritage, imagination, literature and history
2. Acting by developing, communicating and sustaining characters in improvisations and informal or formal productions
3. Designing and producing by conceptualizing and realizing artistic interpretations for informal or formal productions
4. Directing by interpreting dramatic texts and organizing and conducting rehearsals for informal or formal productions
5. Researching by evaluating and synthesizing cultural and historical information to support artistic choices
6. Comparing and integrating art forms by analyzing traditional theatre, dance, music, visual arts and new art forms
7. Analyzing, critiquing and constructing meanings from informal and formal theatre, film, television and electronic media productions
8. Understanding context by analyzing the role of theatre, film, television and electronic media in the past and the present.

All of these standards revolve around formal theatre production. There is no mention of using drama and theatre informally as a learning medium. Furthermore, theatre appears to weaken altogether with the recent US emphasis on the Common Core State Standards Initiative. Adopted by a majority of US states in summer 2010,[2] the Common Core are standards focusing on what students should learn in math and English.[3] Math and English are at the center of the curriculum, and while there is certainly a place for theatre and other subjects to be taught within the Common Core, the standards offer a constricting view of education when the arts and other subjects are not identified for the unique ways they contribute to student learning and development.

Looking outside the US, the Government of Alberta, Canada, refers to 'Programs of Study' to identify standardized curriculum and learning expectations. In middle school, students study movement, speech, improvisation/acting, theatre studies and technical theatre. In high school, units of playwriting and directing are added.

In Ontario the curriculum is similar, but at the elementary level it is stressed that students should not be given 'instruction in formal drama or theatre techniques,' a point of view consistent with that of Winifred Ward, Peter Slade and many others.[4] While formal theatre is reserved for upper grade levels, there remains a strong recognition of integrated drama at all levels.

The UK employs the Key Stages of the national curriculum which outline the educational knowledge expected of UK students at different ages, with outcome expectations very similar to the standards of the US. As in the US, criticism has been aimed at schools for concentrating too much on preparing students for national tests in English, math and science. A 2003 study found that 'Teachers often narrow down the teaching of the core subjects by not drawing on the wealth of other subjects, including arts subjects.'[5]

A number of countries, including Brazil, Chile and South Africa, do not identify arts standards at all. In Australia the National Minimum Standards do not include arts standards, but the Australian Curriculum Assessment and Reporting Authority (ACARA) is responsible for the development of Australian curriculum from K–12, working collaboratively with schools, government and community groups. This curriculum, at the time of writing, is still in development. The first phase of the Australian curriculum for English, math, science and history is well under way, but the second phase for languages, geography and the arts is barely beginning.[6]

The conception of arts curricula varies greatly among European countries. In roughly half of the countries with standards, each arts subject is considered separately in the curriculum, while in the other half, the arts are conceived as an integrated area of study. The breadth of the arts curricula also varies, although in virtually all countries, curricula include music and visual arts.[7] The same cannot be said for dance and drama. In Lithuania, despite an increase in time devoted to the arts since 1992, the National Council for Curriculum and Assessment revealed that theatre is given considerably less weight and commitment from their schools.[8]

Critical appreciation, or aesthetic judgment, is one of the most recognized standards in Europe. This aim is concerned with raising students' awareness of significant features of a performance and developing students' capacity for critical judgment in evaluating artistic work.

Despite this focus, the 2009 study, 'Arts and Cultural Education at Schools in Europe', found significant cross-curricular links between the arts and other areas of the curriculum in the Czech Republic, Greece, Latvia, Luxembourg, Hungary, Finland and Sweden.[9] In these countries, using drama to make meaning of curriculum content is specifically outlined, which is not the case in the US. Nevertheless, later in this chapter we outline examples of Curriculum Drama in the US from practitioners who understand the value of incorporating drama to teach a variety of subjects.

Further findings of the 2009 study revealed that 'Half of the countries include drama as a compulsory subject forming part of the arts curriculum, or as part of other compulsory subject areas.'[10] Drama is an entirely optional subject in seven countries. In Austria, drama is either an optional subject with assessment, or a voluntary course without assessment.[11]

While various European countries speak to the importance of arts integration across the curriculum, it can be said that in most countries that have standards, a primary weight in the upper grades is given to learning the skills inherent in theatre-making.

## Theatre performance skills

Formal performing arts schools dedicated to providing comprehensive theatre training for teenagers exist around the world. The National Taiwan Junior College of Performing Arts (NTJCPA) is the first vocational school of its kind in Taiwan to offer ten years of continual education in the performing arts. NTJCPA students begin their studies in the fifth year of elementary school, at ten years of age, and continue through high school. Students at the elementary and junior high levels are fully sponsored by the government, while students at the high school and junior college levels are given financial support.[12]

39

In Russia, Oleg Tabakov, a renowned actor and director of the Moscow Theatre, founded a high school with a curriculum that combines theatre with academic subjects. Tabakov's school provides a free four year education, and after four years, the school's graduates can apply directly for further study at the Moscow Art Theatre School, where they receive higher education in theatre.[13]

Other samplings of international performing arts schools include the Australian International Performing Arts High School in Sydney; the Victoria School of the Arts in Edmonton, Alberta and the National School of the Arts, a full-time high school in Braamfontein, South Africa.

While there is certainly not a plethora of specialized performing arts schools internationally, their reputations strengthen the emphasis upon formal performance in schools. Fiorello H. LaGuardia High School of Performing Arts, otherwise known as the 'Fame' school featured in the 1980 movie of the same title, is arguably the most famous of the specialized arts schools in the US. New York City Mayor LaGuardia founded the school in 1936. In 1948 the School of Performing Arts was created to provide training in dance, music and drama. The two schools merged in 1961, and LaGuardia became the first school in the US to provide a free, publicly funded program for arts students. The school's mission is 'to provide a balanced opportunity for students to pursue both rigorous conservatory style training and a challenging academic program.'[14] This model has been replicated in many cities throughout the US.

Most states in the US have such schools. In Colorado, the Denver School of the Arts is the only comprehensive secondary arts magnet in the Rocky Mountain region, and in Nevada, students from all over the Las Vegas area wake up well before dawn to ride the bus to be at the Las Vegas Academy by 7:00 a.m. to begin their training. In almost all cases, students are required to audition to get into the schools.

In such schools there is a wide variety of praxis. However, because of a lack of research, it is not clear what kinds of performance models are applied at the high school level. At the college and university level, it is easier to evaluate the range of acting programs, as many are based on performance models, that is, Stanislavski, Suzuki, Lecoq or a combination of all. In their original form, these models of training were intended for adult actors. One is left to wonder how they translate to adolescents.

❖ **Case vignette: Valuing tears**

The following fictionalized excerpt, based on a combination of stories relayed to Montgomery by student teachers, highlights a recurring theme in theatre-based schools. In the passage, we get a critical glimpse of teaching methodology as the student teacher reflects on the value of tears:

> I have recently been struggling with my feelings toward some of the training techniques used with the high school actors that I see every day. The problem I have is that the work appears to be heading in a direction wherein raw, guttural acting could progress into the realm of what may become emotionally dangerous.
>
> I began to deeply consider what was going on when a student, Olivia, worked herself up into hysterical tears at the first line of her scene. The running technique in this class for focusing the students is a type of 'emotional preparation' that involves sitting by one's self, focusing inward and prepping for the demands of the scene. This is usually done with the help of iPod playlists chosen to provoke certain responses from the listeners.
>
> As the scene began, Olivia and her scene partner choked out two or three lines amidst streaming tears before their teacher offered his congratulations. While I certainly admired the student's skill in achieving that level of vulnerability and honesty in front of classmates, I had some concerns.
>
> The praise coming from the teacher wasn't so much in reference to the richness of her line coloring, pauses, gestures or relationship with her scene partner. Rather, the fact that she managed to well up real tears was commended. A teachable moment for the rest of the class could have occurred if the girls' actual *acting choices* were complimented.
>
> Olivia was fervently applauded for her obvious willingness to 'go there' more than anyone else that day. This irritated me as my thoughts instantly went to all of the other students who were told that they weren't putting themselves on the line as courageously as Olivia, just because they weren't bawling onstage. Most significantly, I had questions as to whether these emotional reactions were being brought about for the actors in the most effective ways.
>
> Of course, the ability to convey powerful emotion when necessary as an actor is a valuable skill. However, these things must be done mindfully and safely, which in my opinion can only come from careful preparation from a dramaturgical standpoint.

The student teacher's reflection on observed practice leads him to believe that in his school there was not enough emphasis placed on text, dramaturgy and the reasons *why* students engage with the work. While he realizes that actors must often develop their own techniques for bringing out necessary levels of emotion, once again, as we saw with Fisher's bullying vignette in Chapter 1, a question of safety emerges. This student teacher makes the argument that for adolescent students, overwhelming praise and pressure should not be placed on an actor's ability to crank out real tears from personal places. He believes it is unsafe.

Through observation and critical written reflections, the student teacher developed a teaching philosophy that calls for students to learn to make tangible acting choices based on evidence in the text that inspires physical and emotional responses, so as to keep the world of the play as real as possible.

## Significant theatre education organizations, journals and competitions

When the 1982 *Handbook* was published, there was little evidence in the field of a scholarly tradition. Nor was there a plethora of PhD graduates leading programs across the world. Today we find both happening. These developments mirror the rise of significant educational theatre organizations that attract practitioners and scholars to conferences.

We note, too, a shift into Applied Theatre, discussed in Chapter 4, as we track organizations over the years. For example, in 1992 the International Drama/Theatre in Education Association (IDEA) brought together diverse countries and movements in educational theatre.[15] From this emerged *The Applied Theatre Researcher/IDEA Journal*, a worldwide e-journal for theatre and drama in non-traditional contexts.[16]

Another noteworthy journal that played an important role in the development of educational theatre praxis is *Research in Drama Education* (*RiDE*), which later became *Research in Drama Education: The Journal of Applied Theatre and Performance*.[17] For some, this new title suggested a split between Drama Education and Applied Theatre. For others, it signified the joining of Applied Theatre to Drama Education. We accept the latter, noting that *RiDE* has become a well-established journal aimed at those interested in 'applying performance practices to cultural engagement, educational innovation and social change.'[18]

We also acknowledge the importance of the International Drama in Educational Research Institute (IDIERI). The aim of the first IDIERI conference in 1995 'was to critique the different modalities of research design, to draw connections between them, and to probe how knowledge can be advanced by their application.'[19] The term 'institute' was chosen specifically because an 'institute connotes a body that produces and promotes educational advancement, a place where ideas can be investigated and new visions proposed.'[20]

The American Alliance for Theatre and Education (AATE) is the largest networking organization for theatre artists and educators in the US.[21] AATE consistently holds annual conferences, and from the organization has emerged two publications. *Incite/Insight* is a non-peer-reviewed digital magazine that is 'intended to ignite conversations between emerging and established theatre artists and educators and build connections that strengthen the field.'[22] The scholarly journal of AATE, *Youth Theatre Journal*, is a juried publication dedicated to advancing the study and practice of theatre and drama with, for and by people of all ages.[23]

In addition to these organizations and scholarly journals, we find professional organizations that specifically foster secondary school theatre. One is the Educational Theatre Association (EdTA) with more than 4,600 members. The EdTA and its International Thespian Society (ITS) branch have been in operation since 1929.[24] The ITS is an honorary organization for middle and high school theatre students located at more than 3,600 affiliated secondary schools across the US, Canada and elsewhere.[25] Their mission is to honor student excellence in theatre arts.

Thespian Festivals are held annually at the district, state and national levels. The season culminates with the International Thespian Festival held at the University of Nebraska–Lincoln each June, where theatre troupes qualifying at the district and state levels are showcased. More than 50 productions are presented by participating schools, in front of adjudicators and large audiences.

At the 2008 festival productions with remarkably talented young people were showcased. The plays were primarily commercial theatre offerings, but many encompassed imaginative staging and top notch performances. Offerings included the musicals *Rent* and *Sweeney Todd*, and the dramas *Proof* and *Noises Off*.

A production of *Hairspray* staged solely for the festival featured students who were selected in regional auditions throughout the country. Marc Shaiman and Scott Wittman, composers of the score for *Hairspray*, addressed the audience. According to Charles Isherwood, critic for *The New York Times*, 'Mr. Wittman, himself a former Thespian, was wiping away copious tears at its conclusion.'[26]

Charles Isherwood did not go unnoticed by the high school students at the festival, for most of them were well aware of the role critics play in the success or failure of a Broadway production. In a subsequent article, Isherwood described the impact of watching Athol Fugard's *Master*

*Harold and the Boys*, performed by the Westminster School in Atlanta, Georgia:

> I practically crawled from the Lied Center after the 10 a.m. staging ended, so moved was I by the performances of James Franch, Omar Ingram and Hampton Fluker in Mr. Fugard's drama about the complex relationship between a white South African adolescent and the black workers in his parents' cafe. It took me a full hour to recover.[27]

On a similar scale, for many years in Texas, the University Interscholastic League (UIL) has run massive theatre competitions. The UIL's One-Act Play Contest, founded in 1927, is the largest high school play production contest in the world. According to Luis Muñoz, the state contest director, over 23,000 Texas high school students in more than 12,000 plays participate in the contests.[28] On their website, Muñoz explains the rules of the competition:

> The plays have a time limit of forty minutes and students have seven minutes to set up and strike the set. Since the contest is primarily about acting and directing, there are numerous rules that restrict the amount of scenery [...] Students are recognized at each level of competition with acting awards. A maximum of eight students are named to the all star cast and to the honorable mention cast. A best actor and actress is [*sic*] named at each level.[29]

For some teachers, the notion of drama competitions is problematic in educational settings as the added weight of competing detracts from more natural and creative school-based work. Indeed, the rules of the competition do not promote student spontaneity. Further, directors are charged to make sure that the chosen play 'does not offend the moral standards of the community' and to 'eliminate profane references to a deity and obscene language or scenes from the approved production.'[30]

Such restrictions fly in the face of our model of praxis promoting critical exploration and freedom of expression. Nevertheless, the spirit of these competitions is highly energetic; much like it would be for the school football team. Perhaps most importantly, the UIL competition is a motivating reason why Texas continues to increase the number of schools offering theatre arts as an academic subject. But does quantity equal value? Undoubtedly it helps, but the value Texas places on winning performance competitions threatens the elements of exploration and dialogue within the work.

The English-Speaking Union of the United States (ESU) was founded in 1920, two years after the establishment of its counterpart in the British Commonwealth. It was conceived as a nonpolitical association dedicated to furthering friendship and understanding among English-speaking peoples around the world.[31] One of its curriculum-based programs, the ESU's National Shakespeare Competition, is designed to help high school students develop their language skills and dramatic talents through acting a monologue and/or sonnet. Day-long competitions between contestants from local high schools transpire in communities across the nation, and the local semi-finalists go to New York City for ESU's National Shakespeare Competition. The national winner receives a month-long summer acting scholarship at the British American Drama Academy.[32]

Although ESU focuses on Shakespeare monologues and sonnets, in many schools teachers are charged with mounting an entire Shakespeare play. How can this be achieved effectively when decoding Shakespeare's language can be a challenge in itself for many students?

Nancy Smithner, a professor in the Program in Educational Theatre at NYU, believes it is important to encourage young people to make a strong connection between the body, the emotions and the intellect when working on a Shakespeare play. Hers is a search for quality in the work. Despite the US mania for competitions, we often find smaller, individual programs like the following example from NYU, more concerned with quality exploration whilst working toward performance.

In the Looking for Shakespeare program at NYU, secondary school students work with a director and graduate students to shape an original production of Shakespeare.[33] Ensemble members work intensively for four weeks with the creative team to discover how a Shakespearean play resonates for them, within their own personal experiences. Using these connections as a source and inspiration, young actors rehearse and perform their own vision of the play. In the following vignette, Smithner discusses her approach to directing Shakespeare plays with the young people.

### ❖ Case vignette: Looking for Shakespeare

I explored ways to lead middle and high school students forward in the rehearsal process of a Shakespeare play using physical play, improvisation and collaboration to create deeply meaningful characters. It is necessary to carefully scaffold this process, in the form of a progression of warm-ups, improvisational structures and teaching of aesthetic skills. Initially, it is important to warm up the whole body so that students will not injure themselves in the flush of full-bodied improvisation. To accomplish two goals at once, I always combine vocal warm-ups with physical ones, which has the added benefit of introducing playfulness and release. Part of my warm-up includes a series of stretches in which the participants hold each other's wrists and lean back, stretching and releasing the back muscles. Through the element of physical contact, trust and human exchange are introduced, creating a different level of communication.

Students are then invited to work with a series of sound and movement improvisations, wherein the essence of play fosters spontaneity and humor, building a framework to further engender trust. I then work extensively with Viewpoints, a technique defined and implemented by experimental dance and theatre artist Mary Overlie, and then expanded upon by director Anne Bogart. In this practice, the students work with improvisational and abstract movement to create shapes, investigate different rhythms and explore space with the entire body.

Once students become comfortable moving as an ensemble, specific themes of the play are explored through movement, such as vengeance, greed or ambition (*Macbeth*). Words are then added slowly, and the students are encouraged to discover a deeply intuitive side, in their exploration of human nature. They are then ready to embody the worlds of the play. For example in *Macbeth*, the entire ensemble moves as if they are in the realm of the royals, and then repeat the process in the world of the supernatural. In *A Midsummer Night's Dream*, the physical environments of the forest, the town and the castle are embodied. In *Love's Labour's Lost*, the differentiation in the status of the characters is explored, and then related to the universal archetypes of Commedia dell'arte, taking on the exaggerated physicalities of the Harlequino, Capitano, Columbina and Dottore.

Other exercises focus on exploring the complexities of the text, such as working with tableaux to physicalize the imagery within Shakespeare's poetry, and to learn more about the progression of the story. Also, to investigate the rhythm of the verse, pairs speak dialogue while manipulating various props, such as a tug of war with a rope or having a mock sword fight with sticks, and move from one prop station to another. Students are thus able to offer their own interpretations of the themes, characters, subtext and action of the play.

As the ensemble works together, they become aware of the importance of collaboration, in an atmosphere in which all members are viewed as equal and active participants. The teacher/director draws ideas from the individuals in the group through frequent reflection, infusing the personal and cultural experiences of each member into the process. I operate under the premise that if a teacher engages her students with a physical approach, not only will their creative work be greatly enhanced, but they will also learn to listen to and trust each other, which will then be readily apparent in their performances on stage. Young people should be encouraged to enter into a perpetual state of discovery, in order to find their own performance styles and identities. It is my firm opinion that if teachers offer a full training of physical theatre in rehearsal, a creative and inspiring production will ensue, adding the visceral interpretations of the young members of the ensemble to the mix.

While play productions remain popular in secondary school settings, it is difficult to generalize as to their pedagogical practices. The school play has a prescribed structure: auditions, casting with its inherent caste system, rehearsals, performance, ensemble interaction, striking the set, cast party and award ceremony.

At NYU, in asking adult graduate and undergraduate students to reflect on their experiences with play production, we have heard countless stories of teachers who directed plays authoritatively using ridicule, threat and favoritism in pursuit of a 'professional' theatrical product. On the other hand, we have also heard stories of nurturing teachers devoted to building supportive environments in realizing such goals as listening, speaking, collaborating, empathizing and interpreting texts.

To avoid the pitfalls of a product orientation, the director should allow the element of spontaneous play to be firmly rooted in the rehearsal and performance experience, as Smithner described in her vignette. It is important to find a balance between the spontaneous play aspects and more controlled performance aspects of the rehearsal. In order to cultivate students' improvisational skill, teachers often turn to games and exercises.

## Improvisation exercises and theatre games in middle and high schools

Theatre games are frequently utilized in the elementary classroom, yet they also remain popular throughout secondary school where they become more sophisticated both physically and cognitively. Boal's seminal text *Games for Actors and Non-Actors* provides numerous examples of games plus rationales for using the games to develop the adult actor's physical and mental awareness.[34]

Viola Spolin, who pioneered improvisational theatre games, began her career in the 1930s in Chicago settlement houses, then became drama supervisor for the Works Progress Administration's recreational project, using drama exercises to cross the cultural barriers of participants.[35] Her classic book, *Improvisation for the Theater*, outlined a sequence of dramatic exercises to help students develop spontaneity for acting on stage.[36]

While Spolin had an eye toward performance, she appeared more interested in the kind of drama that occurs spontaneously when groups of people work together toward a common goal:

> Through spontaneity we are re-formed into ourselves. It creates an explosion that for the moment frees us from handed-down frames of reference, memory choked with old facts and information and undigested theories and techniques of other people's findings. Spontaneity is the moment of personal freedom when we are faced with a reality and see it, explore it and act accordingly. In this reality the bits and pieces of ourselves function as an organic whole.[37]

Spolin's texts have remained quite popular in the classroom for decades, which is ironic given that, according to Hoetker, 'Spolin [...] had little interest in the application of her games to teaching in formal classroom settings.'[38]

Like Spolin, Keith Johnstone from the UK influenced generations in the use of improvisation. His book *Impro: Improvisation and the Theatre* outlines the use of improvisational exercises in relation to comedy.[39] As Irving Wardle explains in the Introduction, 'Johnstone's analysis is not concerned with results, but with showing you how to do it; and his work ranks as a pioneer contribution to the exceedingly sparse literature of comic theory from which comic practitioners really have something to learn.'[40]

Given the emphasis on theatre skills in many high school drama programs, these texts have become essential reading for drama teachers. With the growing influence of Boal, Spolin and Johnstone, game-playing has become a valid form of theatre education.

Chrissie Poulter, a director, devisor and drama teacher based in Ireland and the UK, stresses the need for constant reflection on action when leading games and dramatic activities. Her influential book, *Playing the Game*, offers a multitude of activities in which to build ensemble with students.[41] Her work spotlights the application of theatre arts to non-theatre contexts as her book categorizes and breaks down activities into variations of high and low focus work.

When leading any activity, Poulter checks in with the individuals in the group, asking questions that compel all members to take note of their feelings. In observing her work with drama school teachers and Applied Theatre practitioners at Trinity College in Dublin, we noted Poulter's praxis. Even the simple rituals of forming a circle during introductions led

Poulter to ask questions such as: 'How many of you felt a sense of panic when I asked you to introduce yourself?', 'What is it about a circle that can make some people in a group feel uncomfortable?', and 'What was it for you?'

In raising these questions, Poulter pointed out that every decision facilitators make has an impact on the group, and that constant reflection on action and dialogue builds trust and ensemble.

In an interview with Poulter, she advocated for the reflective component as well as guardianship of the work:

I'm looking at guardianship in group work. What I want to do is see if I can inscribe in my writings some of the things that I can unpack in workshops. So that when someone looks at my book they aren't just getting a lot of recipes without also pausing for thought about what the implications of using the exercises might be. In the first edition of the book, I'd say, 'well this game might be a good preparation for that.' But then I started thinking, 'Oh, this needs language skills! Let's do some speaking and listening work before we launch into the games and activities.' And so now my work is focused on what is guardianship of group work in terms of analysis and reflection – both in terms of the work and in terms of who's in the group.

I'm also looking at the work of others on a spectrum from teacher training to actor training. Dorothy Heathcote talks about the social behavior of the group. She talks about reading the group and that one must decide what strategy to use because of where the group is at. However, when you read the manuals of Augusto Boal, even though he's full of anecdotes, and he will at some point say, 'use this exercise because it's impossible and it makes everybody laugh and they stop feeling so nervous at the beginning,' he doesn't do something similar for all the other exercises. So unless you've read it chronologically and imbibed all of the advice, you can't dip in and mix. He doesn't say what he does, how he reads a group, and who *he is* in the workshop. I'm wondering – can we as drama practitioners take more responsibility for consciously inscribing what we understand of our role as facilitator, without it saying this is the only way of doing it? Can we enable someone else to take the work, make it their own, and be a good guardian? Can the players take on the ethics of guardianship in terms of how they look after themselves, and how they look after the people with whom they are working? Can they spot the danger signs that this is going a bit too far, or that this person obviously isn't following what's going on? Do leaders understand about scaffolding?[42]

Poulter's deconstruction of games and her view of the responsibility of the facilitator and players reveal the complexity of theatre games. Drama teachers often say that they play games to build ensemble. However, playing games does not in itself ensure an effective ensemble. A game is successful in ensemble-building when there is continual reflection by the participants and teachers who raise such questions as: Why did we play this game? What did we observe? How did we feel? What did we learn? What will we do with our learning? What is the connection between our game and the curriculum?

Once again we stress the importance of praxis for drama teachers, who can only adapt this approach if they acknowledge their role as learners. We have discovered the most effective drama teachers are those who remain curious and willing to let go for a while of their privileged status as experts. Aronowitz, in his introduction to Freire's *Pedagogy of Freedom*, noted the distinction between teacher as expert and learner.[43] As two learners occupy somewhat different spaces in an ongoing dialogue, 'both participants bring knowledge to the relationship, and one of the objects of the pedagogic process is to explore what each knows and what they can teach each other.'[44]

This notion also applies to successful arts partnerships. Remaining open to learning from other teachers in professional relationships is of the utmost importance when various school and arts organizations collaborate to bring drama and theatre into the classroom. In the next section we discuss arts partnerships that exist to teach curriculum content.

## Arts partnerships

Arts partnerships refer to the connections that are made between K–12 schools and outside arts organizations. These organizations include cultural institutions, community arts education providers, social and human service agencies, public agencies and foundations, and colleges and universities. Arts partnerships are formed in an effort to integrate the arts into the curriculum by pairing Teaching Artists with classroom teachers. Teaching Artist (TA) refers to an artist who earns income providing educational services through a cultural partner to schools and other settings. The time a TA works in a school is called a residency.

In New York City, high school graduation rates and access to effective arts education programs are closely linked, according to a study by The Center for Arts Education (CAE).[45] CAE's report outlines recommendations for the Department of Education to close this education gap, which include finding and sustaining arts partnerships. Although this study was specific to New York City, one wonders if similar results would be found in other regions.

Ostrower analyzed arts partnerships in the US to reveal how partnering has 'become increasingly fashionable among grantmakers'.[46] Her study surveyed 1192 grantmakers and found that 69 percent actively encouraged collaboration among grantees, and 42 percent sometimes required partnering as a condition for funding.[47]

In Australia arts partnerships thrive as they are used to strengthen community identity and local cultural traditions. Being home to one of the world's oldest indigenous cultures and enriched by a diverse citizenry, arts partnerships are encouraged so that schools can celebrate their 'wealth of cultural diversity and strengthen traditions of cultural knowledge and expression in ways relevant to the 21st century'.[48]

For many partnerships the goal is for TAs to help teach curriculum content through the art form, which makes many principals happy because it bolsters the core courses of math, science and English. Sometimes there is an expectation that TAs will help classroom teachers learn to implement drama so they can eventually facilitate it on their own. However despite the support arts partnerships provide for classroom teachers, many articulate their hesitation.

The following vignette is taken from a study examining the experience of three middle school classroom teachers involved in an arts partnership.[49] The goal was to pair classroom teachers and TAs who collaboratively created curriculum and delivered drama infused lessons that explored English Language Arts (ELA) content. The intention here was for the classroom teachers to teach the lesson on their own after the drama residency ended.

For this partnership a unit around the novel *The Last Book in the Universe* was implemented.[50] This unit is also referenced in our section on Teacher-in-Role in Chapter 1. Process Drama techniques were used to make deeper meaning of the book, including the use of tableaux, Teacher-in-Role, whole-group improvisations, role-playing in pairs and other dramatic activities that allowed students to physicalize their interpretations of the text.

### ❖ Case vignette: Bonnie's drama residency

As a first-year seventh grade teacher, Bonnie found the activities in the drama residency valuable: 'The lessons are so different from what I'm used to doing. They're more abstract, creative, open-ended, and interpretive.'[51] At the same time Bonnie found the work overwhelming, particularly when students were asked to physically explore ideas, themes and characters from the book through their bodies. She was concerned about managing students after they became enthused by the drama work:

> When there's controlled chaos in my room, it's different from the way I usually run my class. But you know, whenever I take the mentality of just loosening it up, I calm down. When they seem out of control, there's a little voice in my mind and I keep telling myself, 'Calm down, they're okay. They're still focused. They can come back. ... They're not going to jump out the window.'[52]

Note Bonnie's analysis in this passage. She recognized that her uneasiness with controlled chaos is an issue partly based in her personality. However pages of interview transcripts and log entries revealed Bonnie's increasing ownership of the drama work. Nevertheless after the collaboration ended, Bonnie began to investigate how to get one of the TAs to lead the final lesson, a lesson intended for her to facilitate alone:

> It's just that I'm feeling so overwhelmed with all the assignments, the test-prep, and this scene-writing project that I just don't know if I can do it. I'm still not entirely comfortable with the drama stuff. It's not that I don't think it's fabulous and meaningful; I just can't do it now. It's nothing to do with the drama work – it's just curriculum stuff.[53]

Looking only at the above passage, one might assume Bonnie did not take ownership of the partnership since she felt she could not teach the final lesson. However during interviews she spoke of caring about the drama work and felt it was vital for the students and for her development as an educator. As a first year teacher preparing students to take standardized tests and trying to keep up with the prescribed curriculum, she started to look about for additional help. This situation reveals that in spite of research indicating the value of the arts in learning, many teachers succumb to the pressure of getting high scores on the next round of standardized tests.

Another roadblock for arts partnerships comes from teacher misconceptions about educational partnerships. These misconceptions speak to an interesting binary in the arts where the artist is put on a pedestal but the art form is treated as mere fluff, a distraction. For some there is an inherent fear and mistrust when it comes to arts in the classroom. However these misconceptions can change once teachers are given the opportunity and time to work with a professional development program that is neither rushed nor superficial in its approach to collaboration.

# Curriculum Drama

In the preceding vignette an arts partnership was formed in an effort to give classroom teachers opportunities to learn and take ownership of drama-based teaching strategies. Shifting to the students, we note how ownership was key to the work of Harriet Finlay-Johnson as she integrated drama across the curriculum as a way 'to increase children's respect for science and humanities as well as the arts'.[54] She believed a set curriculum should not be forced upon the children, but rather they should 'find it and remould it, making it their own'.[55] Although she taught in an elementary school in the early 20th century, Finlay-Johnson's goal for student ownership of drama remains significant to our discussion of contemporary praxis in secondary schools.

Another important advocate for the use of drama as meaning-making across academic subjects was Richard Courtney who was interviewed in the 1982 book. He conceived of the field of Educational Drama as truly multidisciplinary and wrote theoretically about drama across the curriculum.[56] Courtney favored an approach that accounted for each student as unique; encouraged sound learning experiences in thinking, feeling and experiencing; recognized the application of play to the continued growth of adolescents; and provided for a 'genuine encounter between teacher and student'.[57] With these principles in mind, Courtney used role-playing, improvisation, play-making, dance and speech in combination with more theatrical aspects of performance in his curriculum.

Drama integration is exemplified here through Curriculum Drama vignettes. We look at Curriculum Drama from the perspective of those who teach drama or theatre in school settings full time, as well as TAs involved in art partnership residencies.

### ❖ Case vignette: Drama in the English Language Arts classroom

The following lesson occurred in a seventh grade ELA classroom in a public school in Jersey City, New Jersey. The class was working with the Educational Arts Team on exploring the novel *Johnny Tremain* by Esther Forbes.[58] Since 1974 the Educational Arts Team, under the leadership of Carmine Tabone, has conducted countless educational workshops for children, families and teachers. As an observer Montgomery sat in on the following lesson.

As students settled in the TA held up the book *Johnny Tremain* and said: 'Follow me as I read this... Who can remember where we left off?' One student raised his hand and offered, 'We were staging a family portrait of the characters from *Johnny Tremain*.' 'Right,' affirmed the TA who asked: 'Who were some of the characters?' Students responded with names like Johnny,

Mrs. Lapham, Madge and Dusty – all characters from the book. The TA continued:

'The last portrait was created with your understandings from the beginning of the book, but now that we're further along in the story, let's see how things change. Before we do that, however, I'm going to read a few pages. As I read, I want you to think about the relationship of the characters to one another, even if some characters are not in the scene.'

The TA read a passage while the students followed along. Afterwards the TA asked, 'Based on what I read, do you think the family portrait picture has changed?' A handful of students called out 'Yes.' The TA continued: 'Good, now let's get a few students to come up and create the picture of where we left off in the last class.' Eight volunteers struck poses for a family portrait. The TA proceeded: 'Now I'm going to tap you on the shoulder and you are going to tell us your name and what you think of Johnny Tremain at this point in the story.' When tapped, student responses included: 'Johnny's a worthless piece of garbage.' 'I thought he was a hot-shot apprentice, but he burnt his hand and now he's useless.' 'He's as useless as a horse with broken knees.'

The character of Dove, who caused the protagonist Johnny to permanently damage his hand, was revealed in the portrait. The TA encouraged students to ask Dove questions. One student asked: 'Why did you do this to Johnny?' The student-in-role as Dove replied, 'Because at the time I thought he deserved it.' A second student asked: 'Do you regret doing this to Johnny?' Dove responded: 'Yes, I do regret it.' A third student cried out: 'He did it on purpose because he was jealous of Johnny.' A fourth student reasoned: 'It was Johnny's fault too because he was cocky all the time, but ultimately Dove must take responsibility for setting Johnny up.'

The TA transitioned into a 'Role on the Wall' activity and posed the question: 'What did you think about Johnny in the past, and what do you think about him now?' The Role on the Wall activity used an outline of a body drawn on the white board. A line was drawn down the middle of the body with the label 'Past' written at the top left of the body, and 'Now' at the top right of the body. Students were instructed to write their thoughts on either side expressing Johnny's view himself now and in the past. Outside the body students were to write what other people in the story think of him now and in the past. Students made their way to the white board and wrote eagerly:

Outside past – *talented, valuable, cocky, self-assured*
Outside now – *untalented, worthless, useless, saddened*
Inside past – *proud, the best, talented, skilled, smart*
Inside now – *remorseful, disheartened, sad, depressed, unsure*

'What are the differences between how he sees himself and how others see him? Is it balanced?' the TA asked. Among others, a student responded:

'People used to put up with his attitude but now that he has nothing to offer, they don't tolerate him anymore.'

The TA asked: 'Does anyone know a person like this in their own lives?' Many students vocalized 'Yes.' Transitioning into a new activity, the TA asked the students to write a letter to Johnny Tremain. Simultaneously, the TA put himself in role as Johnny Tremain. This activity is known as 'Hot-Seating' as he allowed the students to question him in role. The following is part of the ensuing dialogue:

STUDENT 1:   Are you as strong as you were before the accident?
TA:          What do you mean by strong?
STUDENT 1:   Mentally.
TA:          Mentally I'm weak right now. I want to find work but I feel
             so overwhelmed.
STUDENT 2:   If the accident never happened, would you feel this way?
TA:          You can't go backwards.
STUDENT 3:   Why do you keep running away from your problems?
TA:          Did you ever have anything bad happen to you, and did
             you overcome it quickly?
STUDENT 4:   Do you think you have the same courage you had before?
TA:          I sure hope so. What do you think?

More often than not the TA responded by posing more questions rather than answering questions directly, compelling students to consider their own answers. When the TA de-roled he encouraged students to write letters to Johnny Tremain, considering their letters as a first draft. Students were soon paired up and assigned to read their letters to one another. Afterwards four volunteers read their letter to an empty chair representing Johnny placed in front of the classroom. The first student offered Johnny advice. The second analyzed Johnny's emotions. Two other students revealed their empathy for Johnny, though one expressed frustration as well when she read: 'So what if your hand is bent! It shows you've dealt with pain in your life, and that perhaps you can help me with my pain.'

The TA offered: 'I have an observation to make. At the beginning of the class I didn't think that Johnny was very likeable, but now there are more dimensions to him. He's more complex. Also, I love how you're relating his situation to your own life!'

The TA then established dyads and instructed: 'Tell your partner what you think is going to happen in the story, and then, together, shape your bodies into a sculpture of what you think is going to happen.' Afterwards students shared and reflected upon the images.

From Montgomery's point of view the lesson successfully enhanced literacy as the students: (a) created a tableau to express character relationships; (b) engaged with a role-on-the-wall activity to unpack the protagonist's feelings; (c) wrote a letter to Johnny Tremain that expressed their reactions to the character; (d) collaborated to create images depicting how the story might unfold; and (e) posed pivotal questions for characters in the story.

After the lesson ended three students informally expressed to Montgomery how much they enjoyed the activities and the entire drama residency. Students were consistent in noting that one reason they liked it was because the lessons permitted them to engage with reading through physical action.

The lesson observed was alive with students' desire to commit to the activities. When students were paired up to sculpt their ideas about what was going to happen next, there was a palpable feeling of anticipation and excitement in the room. Every activity in the lesson had a purpose directly related to literacy, and writing was encouraged throughout the entire lesson. Consequently the writing activities were engaging for students. Classroom management was not an issue, and a genuine curiosity arose from the class when they listened to the letters written and shared by their peers.

From ELA we move toward a vignette demonstrating how drama was used to teach science. In this example getting students to physically explore ideas using their bodies transpires again, this time to help them understand properties of light and sound.

### ❖ Case vignette: Drama in the science classroom

Montgomery and two student teachers collaborated with a classroom teacher to teach the properties of light and sound to middle school students. Using superheroes as a framing device, Montgomery wanted students to engage in an activity where they had to use their light or sound powers to battle someone else who possessed a power connected to light or sound. The teaching team decided that some of the students would be in role as super-villains with others as superheroes.

Following a brief preparatory warm-up, students were assigned to work in pairs with the properties of either sound or light. Science cards were distributed to the class. On the front of each card was a description of a superhero/villain's power and on the back the property of sound or light was identified with a scientific explanation. All the villains and heroes had the same goal: to defeat their arch enemy.

After receiving their cards, students read them aloud to the group. One concept of sound, for example, was called 'Timbre Superhero'. On the card was written:

The sound quality of a sound source is called timbre. Why do different sound sources have a unique timbre? Sounds are produced by a source when it vibrates at a certain frequency. Each frequency produces a sound with a specific pitch. The blending of the pitches gives the sound its timbre, which explains why you can tell the difference between the sound of a trumpet and the sound of a flute even when they are both playing the same note.

Written on the front of the card was: 'Your timbre superhero can identify every sound source it hears and change the sound. So, for example, your hero can change the sound of a human scream into the sound of a violin.'

Based on these properties of light and sound, and their given super powers, students created a name for their character and their character's alter ego, a secret identity character. Each student shared their character's name with their partner. The students then created a pose for their character and their character's alter ego. Students practiced transitioning from one pose to the other, saying their superhero/villain's name and their alter ego's name out loud. Students shared these two poses with their partner, and volunteers shared their poses with the rest of the class.

Afterwards, the question was posed, 'How do your superheroes or super-villains use their powers?' After soliciting answers which referred to the scientific properties, the class was asked to create movements that revealed their characters' powers. Students took five minutes to practice this sequence of gestures in slow motion while the soundtrack to the film *Superman* played in the background. One at a time, volunteers shared their movement with the rest of the class.

The question was posed, 'Which super-villain has the best chance of defeating this superhero?' Students were encouraged to give scientific reasons for their responses. It was at this point that the specific scientific properties were discussed in more depth.

Following the discussion, new student dyads were established, pairing up one sound or light superhero with one super-villain. The pairs choreographed two action sequences in slow motion with dialogue – one in which the super-villain won and the other in which the superhero won the battle. The lesson ended with a reflective discussion by all involved in order to evaluate how the dramatic process related to an understanding of the actual properties of sound and light. In most cases, students felt they better understood the science properties through physical exploration.

## Drama in the social studies classroom

Teaching science through drama is challenging when stories are not a mainstay of the curriculum. The social studies curriculum, on the other hand, is well suited to drama exploration because students are required to learn stories from the past. However, stories are not the only reason why social studies and drama work well together. The multidisciplinary nature of the field draws upon many areas of a school's curricula.

According to the National Council on Social Studies (NCSS) in the US, social studies are concerned with knowledge of and involvement in such civic issues as health care, crime and foreign policy. The NCSS specifies the multidisciplinary nature of the field drawing upon history and geography, the social sciences, law, philosophy and religion.[59]

This understanding implies a myriad of approaches to teaching a social studies curriculum. And yet, in the US, in order for students to pass state-wide tests, social studies teachers are encouraged to concentrate on the teaching of accurate historical information, omitting the multidisciplinary education described above. Consequently many teachers allow the social studies text to dictate their curriculum and practice.

The textbook industry is a big business, and many schools choose to adopt best-selling titles. Unfortunately, in most of the popular social studies textbooks, the point of view expressed is profoundly limited. Issues of race, class and gender are often downplayed or ignored in the quest to present a positive image of American society. 'What is most important in a textbook is not what is in there and how they treat what is in there,' said noted historian Howard Zinn, 'but … what is omitted.'[60]

In 2010 conservatives in Texas approved radical changes to the state educational social studies curriculum. Those opposed to the changes argued that far-right ideas were injected into the curriculum. Since Texas is one of the largest textbook purchasers in the country, it was feared that the updated 'white-washed' standards could end up indoctrinating students across the country with conservative values. Some of the proposed changes include minimizing the political impact of minority leaders like César Chávez and Supreme Court Justice Thurgood Marshall, eliminating a discussion of the separation of church and state, and erasing liberal US Senator Ted Kennedy from the texts. According to *The New York Times*, 'Liberals – on the Texas board and beyond – detected an attempt to force-feed children conservative dogma, whether it is the putative religiosity of the nation's founders, the historic contribution of the Moral Majority and Rush Limbaugh, or the elevation of John Wayne into the pantheon of patriotic heroes.'[61]

Controversies such as this can be explored through drama in the classroom. In the case of the history textbook, questions about the choice of historical narratives can be explored. A class can even take on the roles of historians and create their own social studies textbook. What do the students think is important to include? Within such a frame students can explore the nuances of political decision-making and educational policy.

### ❖ Case vignette: (Out)laws and Justice

An example of a program that compels students to critically examine history through Process Drama is (Out)Laws & Justice (OLJ), based in Los Angeles and New York City.[62]

Lisa Citron, the director of OLJ, described their praxis to us in an interview. she noted that in the early days of OLJ students were asked to do performance-based work immediately, but that this approach 'was subverting the work' as it shifted the focus away from the students and the issues.[63] Shortly thereafter OLJ began incorporating Process Drama in professional development workshops. However, while teachers were positive about the work, Citron did not see a transition of learning Process Drama to teaching Process Drama in the classroom. 'Teachers were unaccustomed to the ways that Process Drama depends upon both guiding and following students' ideas,' said Citron.[64]

A turning point, however, came after OLJ conducted Process Drama training with the teachers and students together. 'When the teachers saw how alive the students were as they inched into the drama world of belief, and when they saw students responding in focused ways that they had never experienced before in their classrooms, that was the conversion point,' recalled Citron.[65]

As a praxis OLJ helps students explore significant questions that get to the heart of historical events. These events still have strong resonance today. One assumption of the OLJ curriculum is that the myths and realities surrounding the conquest of Western America continue to shape the life and politics of this nation. Citron described the first teacher training workshop with the classroom teachers, TAs and students:

Students were introduced to the life of Jesse James by entering into a make believe museum. This museum was set up on card tables on the stage of the school auditorium, and the adults in the room, who were classroom teachers and TAs, took on the role of docents. The museum's mission was to glorify Jesse James, who was lauded as a hero, a kind of Robin Hood who robbed from the rich and gave to the poor. Students were encouraged to examine artifacts and documents, and ask questions of the docents.

The class was then divided into smaller groups who looked at various large posters displaying archival photographs of people of that time. A photograph of Jesse James' family home and farm was included. The groups went through what we call 'I see, I think, I wonder,' where the students scrutinize the poster, think about what they are looking at, then write their questions, or their wonderings, on post-it notes, placing them alongside the photographs.

Shortly thereafter, a curtain was drawn to reveal the docents arranged in frozen images, representing the people in the photographs. The students were told that one of the really fun things they can do in drama is to travel backwards in time. Students were then encouraged to gently touch the people in the frozen tableaux to 'wake them up.' We explained that if students asked the characters questions based on their wonderings, the characters would share aspects of their story. Once the adult characters told the students their story, they went back to being frozen images of the past.

From this activity, the students heard stories of Jesse James as a young child and the perspectives of the slaves who were owned by James' family. They heard from neighbors who saw the violence and murders that Jesse James committed. They also heard stories from James' neighbors who admired him. Students then reported out to the class what they had learned.

The groups were then assigned to devise a reenactment of a particular aspect of Jesse James' life. So, for example, one scene involved Jesse James as a child, a second scene dealt with a bank robbery, and a third scene depicted the assassination of Jesse James. The students performed these reenactments for the rest of the class. This was followed by reflection.

The culmination of these steps concluded in a complex interpretation that Jesse James was not the hero they met at the beginning of the lesson. Students believed he was a criminal who had committed heinous acts. But what was satisfying to me was not just that they reversed their view of Jesse James, but their reversed perspective was nuanced. They had compassion for him. They had empathy for a boy their age who was beaten by his father, lost his biological father at an early age, witnessed violence done to his stepfather, and survived a near hanging from a tree. They had empathy for why he made the decisions he made, which was to become a violent criminal.

The students incrementally gathered information and learned what conflicts drove Jesse James. These conflicts represented a larger picture of the conflicts of the Civil War. By studying the life of Jesse James, students were ready and eager to further study and comprehend the conflicts that caused the Civil War and defeated Reconstruction.[66]

This lesson examined the particular stories of a historical figure to arrive at a more general understanding of issues surrounding the Civil War. Students examined the values that drove these events and considered what justice means for themselves. 'And when students were able to bridge the past to their present, that made the past meaningful to them,' said Citron.[67]

The OLJ curriculum is framed in such a way that compels students to critically reflect on the Wild West Frontier in the US, and, in fact, begin to question what actually constitutes the American frontier, as opposed to finding right or wrong answers about events of the time period.

## ❖ Case vignette: The mock trial

This next case of drama in a social studies class is an example of collaboration between a school system and a legal system in New Orleans, Louisiana. In some ways it echoes Boal's notion of Legislative Theatre, where Theatre of the Oppressed methodology is used to effect legislation within a community.[68] And yet this example is unique in that it is not focused upon changing laws, but upon changing attitudes and competencies among a group of secondary students all but excluded from the public school system.

As context the Mock Trial experience was developed at the New Orleans Alternative High School (AHS), a public-funded school for adolescents, most from a background of poverty, all expelled from regular school and labeled at risk for committing crime. The idea was born in a collaboration between Linda Cook, drama teacher/drama therapist and former Drama Coordinator for the New Orleans public school district; Helen Ginger Berrigan, Chief Judge of the US District Court, Eastern Division; and Keith Bartlett, teacher at AHS.

For six weeks in 2003, 31 AHS students participated in the Mock Trial project. A core group of 16 students took on the roles of prosecutors, defense lawyers and witnesses. They were given a legal scenario and descriptions of the characters involved in the trial. The scenario was about a group of young people in a bar who got into an altercation that turned violent, leading to a charge of assault and battery. The students developed both the scenario and the characters through discussion and improvisation, finding their own voices and nuances.

The students developed and rehearsed their roles as part of the Language Arts, Civics, and American History classes which Cook team-taught. In Bartlett's Civics class attorneys coached the students in courtroom procedure, strategies and law. The students learned the formal steps of a trial, which they implemented in the Federal Courtroom of Judge Berrigan. The mock trial was convened by a student in role of the judge. The remaining students participated as court staff and jury members, each bringing a citizen's role to the proceedings.

According to Cook the experience promoted core academic and communication skills, as well as addressed the social/emotional needs of the students. Cook, citing Ruby Payne, speaks to a number of deficits endemic to children of poverty, many of which were ameliorated during this project: lack of a systematic method of exploration; limited vocabulary; lack of impulse control; lack of precision in data gathering and difficulty asking questions.[69] In working through a model of praxis, Cook based this experience on current research on children of poverty as well as current theories of role and distance in Drama Therapy.[70]

Reflecting upon the process Federal Judge Berrigan noted how the experience changed the lives of the students:

> The Mock Trial was invaluable in changing how these kids felt about themselves and the criminal justice system. Many came from dysfunctional families with little encouragement and support. Most already had negative encounters with the criminal justice system. They had been stopped by police, belittled, shaken down, perhaps arrested and even convicted of juvenile offenses. Their view of the criminal justice system was that it was there to harass and intimidate them. The Mock Trial, which focused on a criminal case about adolescents, allowed them to actually participate in the criminal justice system in a very positive and empowering way. They took command of the courtroom and unfolded their case with minimal flaws. Some of the students actually did a better job than the real lawyers that regularly appear. They were well organized in their presentations, asked relevant questions, and clearly cared about their side of the case. I remember one female student, who was to play the key role, froze when she came into the courtroom, claiming she was too scared to get on the stand. Her teachers encouraged her and she relented. When she took the stand, the fear evaporated and she completely adopted the role, including an insolent sassiness. When the student on cross-examination tried to challenge her, she responded

with a shot back at the interrogator that ended the cross examination right there. When she stepped down, her pride was palpable.

All of the students, I think, had a similar feeling of empowerment as a result of the experience. They came to also understand how an important part of the criminal justice system actually works. In the preparation for the trial, they learned about analyzing witness statements, preparing questions for witnesses, creating a theme for the opening and closing arguments, and how to organize their presentation to be persuasive. They learned at least one aspect of the criminal justice system by participating in it from the inside, rather than being buffeted by it from outside. They also saw how they could in fact play these roles in real life.[71]

In an interview with Judge Berrigan, Landy asked, 'How can theatre impact and advance a social justice agenda?' She answered:

Theatre exposes audiences to realities of life that they would not otherwise likely see. It is relatively easy to marginalize classes of people that are comparatively powerless and 'not like us' – convicts, the mentally ill, the homeless. A play that presents such people as real people allows for empathy to develop between the characters and the audience, so the audience can no longer simply discount them as hopelessly different and irrelevant. The book and film *To Kill a Mockingbird* was pivotal for many people (including myself) in becoming lawyers and even committing to the South to do social justice work.[72]

Through this one example of drama in an alternative high school we clearly see a merging of our several concerns of education, social action and therapy within a praxis that is theoretically based, reflective and geared toward real-life consequences.

A final example of a drama-based social studies lesson is presented within the following discussion of a key method in Educational Drama praxis, Mantle of the Expert.

## Dorothy Heathcote and Mantle of the Expert

Mantle of the Expert, developed by Heathcote, is a drama approach that addresses student needs and in many ways compels them to create their own culture. It is another significant way to approach curriculum by facilitating students to take ownership of the research, writing and role-playing of the drama.

The Mantle of the Expert methodology comprehensively puts the responsibility for learning into the students' hands. In essence students take on actual occupational roles and use their own skills and knowledge to solve problems related to the demands of both the role and the curriculum. In role as workers where groups of people make products or decisions, the students become the experts.

In his illuminating biography of Heathcote, Bolton explained how during the mid-1970s, after her disillusionment with the education system in the UK which she felt set too many young people up for failure, Heathcote began to shift her emphasis from general drama work to Mantle of the Expert:

> The most significant change in Dorothy's approach came when she pondered on whether fiction could be generated not by stepping into someone else's shoes, not by attending to a still picture, not by awakening an adult in role, but by the setting. Supposing this classroom takes on a role. Supposing it were to become a laboratory, or a factory or an advice bureau or travel agency or any place that implies: 'people in here are committed to carrying out tasks'. Such fictional labeling of the setting dictates the function of those in it, teacher and pupils alike: 'we are the people who work in this laboratory, factory etc.' And Dorothy has thus found a fictional setting that, at least partially, matches her vision of education, that automatically redirects pupils along channels of purposefulness, responsibility and industry. What these pupils do in their classroom will not be just getting ready for one day; they will be working now, honoring the contract to whatever clients the fictional setting generates. And they are barely in role; it is the setting that carries the role and defines how they are to function.[73]

Additionally, in Mantle of the Expert, Heathcote pointed out that,

> Any one thing you want to teach must become meshed within a broad curriculum, [...] so (that) the five or six sessions in role as experts will not be confined to bullying (although this of course will turn out to be a critical learning area); the five or six sessions will cover many selected aspects of the curriculum: science, math language, art, etcetera.[74]

### ❖ Case vignette: The ring

Heathcote's teaching was showcased during a week she spent at NYU in the summer of 2006, where she demonstrated a variety of Teacher-in-Role scenarios and revealed aspects of Mantle of the Expert. Heathcote facilitated drama work in the morning with eighth grade students, observed by NYU graduate students, and in the afternoon she reflected upon her process.

In morning sessions Heathcote put student participants into role as documentary filmmakers. In groups it was their job to decide on the theme and process of making their film. Heathcote wisely used this structure so that as filmmakers they could work with the adult observers in the room. The adults were interviewed, played roles in devised documentary scenes and helped whenever they were called upon by the adolescents.

Heathcote modeled Teacher-in-Role because it is integral to Mantle of the Expert work. As we saw in Chapter 1, Teacher-in-Role allows teachers to guide the work from within the drama. In this case, however, it was also used to help students understand power dynamics that exist in their daily lives. Using a variety of status roles, students were asked to consider status for their documentary films.

In one instance Heathcote took on a mid-status role as a colleague, asking students to discuss the implications of office plans they created for their production companies. This type of role was useful for generating discussion and questions from students as they built belief in the drama and moved forward in the work.

She also demonstrated a lower status role, asking a female student questions about a ring she was wearing, wondering where she (Heathcote) might find a similar ring for herself. Afterwards Heathcote provided an example of Teacher-in-Role using higher status as she interacted with the same ring-wearing student. She did so to illustrate how seemingly more subtle forms of power should be noticed in the students' documentary films. The following is an excerpt of her exchange with the student.

HEATHCOTE: So, I am a police officer at this moment. Right? I have called this lady in. She's now sitting in my office. This time I have power. So I can ask very direct questions. And I can, if I choose, make her feel very uncomfortable, because that may be what this film is about – how police can interrogate and make people afraid. [...] But she's got some power too. (Dorothy turns to face the student, signifying the role work is beginning).

HEATHCOTE: We've asked you to come in because it's come to our notice that you were in a certain store yesterday that sells jewelry.

STUDENT: (Pause) Okay. I like jewelry.

| | |
|---|---|
| HEATHCOTE: | It's quite obvious you do. (Pause. Pointedly.) We are interested in a ring. |
| STUDENT: | I buy plenty of rings at the jewelry store. |
| HEATHCOTE: | You *buy* plenty of rings! |
| STUDENT: | I *buy* plenty of rings. |
| HEATHCOTE: | In that store. |
| STUDENT: | In that store. |
| HEATHCOTE: | The store manager tells us that you have many times come in and examined rings, (pause) but you hardly ever bought. |
| STUDENT: | Is anything wrong with that? I have a low paying job. Is it wrong to just stare at some rings that I wish I could pay for? Is anything wrong with window shopping? |
| HEATHCOTE: | (Calmly but deliberately) You are not being accused of anything. I merely told you what the manager has reported. How would you describe the ring you're wearing? |
| STUDENT: | (Looks down at her ring, smiles, put her hand over her heart). It's beautiful. |
| HEATHCOTE: | And... |
| STUDENT: | (Takes a moment to look at it again) Silver. |
| HEATHCOTE: | (Leaning back in her chair towards another student near her, saying to him as an aside) Take a note, will you? The witness described it as beautiful and made of silver. (Back to student being interrogated) What is the hallmark inside it that says that it is solid silver? (The student takes off her ring and examines it). |
| STUDENT: | It says 'Silver Company'. |
| HEATHCOTE: | Had you seen the hallmark before? |
| STUDENT: | The company? |
| HEATHCOTE: | No. That it is solid silver. It has been tested as such. |
| STUDENT: | Well yes, it has the mark right here! (She attempts to show Dorothy the hallmark on the ring.) |
| HEATHCOTE: | I see this. Now, if I may hold it (leaning back in her chair again directing the following statement to both the interrogated student and all the students in the room). There are witnesses. I shall not hurt your ring. (A pointed look at interrogated student) *Your* ring! (To all the students) She's a tough witness, isn't she? (Heathcote examines the ring.). How much did you pay for it? |
| STUDENT: | I didn't pay for it. |
| HEATHCOTE: | (displaying a look of surprise) You didn't pay for it? |

| STUDENT: | (Snatching the ring) I received it as a gift! |
|---|---|
| HEATHCOTE: | (To student near her) Make a note … the student snatched the ring (laughter erupts from the students as Dorothy comes out of role). |
| HEATHCOTE: | We're seriously looking, though, that if we are making a film, some people are in the power of the situation and some people are not. You know this happens all the time. Officials who have the right to ask for things, or all the power that you go through if you come from Britain into an American airport! This is all power. Now … as we're going to make our films, we've got to be looking at the different kinds of power we can operate because we are making this film! |

Heathcote was not interested in the quality of acting or the theatrical skills demonstrated by the student with whom she played the scene. In preparing the students to take on roles as documentary film-makers, she explicitly encouraged young people to consider the implications of power in society.

The good teacher, said Freire, 'is the one who manages to draw the student into the intimacy of his or her thought process while speaking,' a philosophy Heathcote embraced throughout the week.[75] When guiding sessions, she consistently drew students into her thought process, moving in and out of various status roles and making decisions along the way about optimal activities to serve the students and provoke their thinking.

James Pecora, director of Educational Theatre at the State University of New York at Potsdam, used Mantle of the Expert extensively as a high school social studies teacher in New York City. In the following vignette Pecora describes an early attempt at implementing Mantle of the Expert with his students at a high school for young people who failed in previous schools, much like the New Orleans Alternate High School mentioned earlier. Pecora's example reminds us how important reflection is to becoming a better teacher.

❖ **Case vignette – What happened at My Lai?**

After my first couple of years teaching social studies, I stumbled upon Philip Taylor's book *Redcoats and Patriots*. His account of teaching social studies in NYC, where he challenged the traditional textbook driven curriculum, changed my understanding of how drama could be used with my students. He illustrated how students could become participants in history rather than mere observers of it.

Where I taught, the school's mission was to help students overcome their negative feelings about school, incurred from their experiences at prior high schools, and to become active participants in their own learning. Because our students had generally come to us from schools where they were not given individual and sympathetic attention, my school's philosophy was to allow teachers to take ownership of their curriculum. Thus my classroom became a place to use the new forms I was learning about in graduate school: Process Drama, Theatre of the Oppressed and Creative Drama, to name a few. When I reflect on that time, over ten years ago now, one lesson I taught proved very instrumental in my development as a theatre educator. Part of an eight week course on the Vietnam War, this lesson was about the American massacre of Vietnamese citizens in the village of My Lai.

What follows is an example of my practice in the hope that it illustrates obstacles educators face when they use Process Drama and Heathcote's Mantle of the Expert, and how important reflection is to becoming a better teacher. Through reflection, I recognized problems with my lesson, determined how to change the lesson for the better, and [this] re-enforced in me the knowledge that 'clever' teaching is not always good teaching.

The title of the lesson was 'What Happened at My Lai', and essential questions I identified included: What happened and how do we know what happened at My Lai? How did Americans learn about what happened at My Lai and what were their reactions? Did the American reaction have any political effects?

From this lesson I hoped the drama work would help students to describe their own feelings about the massacre and to discover and write about conclusions they drew from the historical event as it related to global human rights and American political and military policy.

We began class by discussing the Joint Chiefs of Staff. I pointed out that the presence of civilian advisors to the President, which were to be used in this drama, was not usual to meetings of the Joint Chiefs. I also explained that while the documents we were using were real, the meeting we were running probably did not happen. I then told students that when I entered the room, they were to salute me and listen to my instructions.

I left the room and re-entered as the Chairman of the Joint Chiefs of Staff. The Process Drama began with the students saluting me. I saluted back and I told everyone to be seated. I provided the following instructions: 'Welcome to this special meeting of the Joint Chiefs of Staff. Each of you is here because you are the best in your field.'

Since we were engaging with a Mantle of the Expert approach to the drama investigation, students were put in role as highly placed individuals in the government. I gestured to each table and said: We have representatives from the Air Force, the Army, the Navy, the Marines and a special group of visitors, civilian advisors to the President. On the table in front of you is a folder with top-secret documents in it. These documents may not leave the room. With your colleagues at your table you will need to read all of the documents in the folder. There is a lot of reading there, and some documents you may all want to read, but each of you do not need to read everything. Instead, divide the reading up amongst your group and summarize what you have read to one another. Pick someone to report out to the larger committee. As a group, consider the information and decide: (a) who, if anyone, is responsible for criminal behavior in this incident and (b) if you decide someone or ones have behaved illegally, what should they be charged with? The results of our deliberations will go to the President for his consideration.

'It happened at a small village called My Lai,' I said. I continued to explain that the My Lai Massacre was a mass murder conducted by a unit of the US Army during the Vietnam War where unarmed civilians in South Vietnam, the majority of whom were women, children and babies, were not only killed, but many victims were also tortured and sexually abused.

Because the task concerned the outcome of the massacre, I did not explain the historical results: 26 US soldiers were initially charged with criminal offenses for their actions, but only William Calley, the Army officer, was found guilty of ordering the My Lai Massacre on 16 March 1968. He went on to serve a reduced sentence. When the incident became public knowledge in 1969, it prompted widespread outrage around the world.

As students worked in their groups, I moved around the room to provide help and further information where it was needed, all the while continuing to play the role I had established in the drama. This supported the Mantle of Expert roles that the students played. As they needed more information, like the legal definition of manslaughter, homicide and murder, for example, I allowed them access to the Internet. A few students in one group had learned about the United Nations declaration of human rights from another class they had, and printed out a copy to support their findings.

Each group reported out their answers to questions posed in the folders, writing each report on the board. When everyone was finished, we considered what was written on the board to see if we could come to consensus on what to recommend to the President.

Some powerful work came out of this 90-minute lesson. I learned conclusively that Mantle of the Expert can excite students about a research project unlike any other teaching tool I have seen. I also learned that what *seems* like a compelling and meaningful end to a story can have detrimental effects when not fully considering all the possible ways it could be interpreted. This lesson was eagerly taken up by my students, who had been using drama throughout the semester and vocally supported the use of it. They took quite seriously their charge and roles as advisor to the President of the United States. They genuinely wanted to provide the best advice possible.

However my students were deeply disturbed to hear about the events of the My Lai massacre. Many of these young people had countless reasons to mistrust government, and indeed all authority, for in addition to having all been unsuccessful in other high schools, many had negative experiences at the hands of police officers, teachers and guidance counselors. Nearly all were African America or Latino/a and over two-thirds were eligible for free lunch. This context, when combined with my curriculum, resulted in a group of young people who found the actions of the American government during the Vietnam War disturbing and possibly criminal.

Because of the sympathies I describe above, when it came time to decide who, if anyone, was guilty of crimes and if so, what crimes, the students were extremely critical of American soldiers. They charged dozens of individuals with a great number of crimes, and even considered genocide charges against the United States.

Thus when I revealed what the actual results were in criminal court, there was deep despair. Students were angry at the country for not punishing soldiers they saw as out of control. They left class that day depressed, expressing dismay that such behavior could go unpunished. I had not anticipated the reaction, although had I considered it more deeply I should have been able to predict it. Had I predicted it, though, what would I have done? Is there a way to teach very much the same lesson, but not end with such a nasty surprise? My students' despair and anger struck me deeply and I felt bad about how I ended our work that day. As I reflected and discussed my thoughts with my colleagues I came to a few conclusions.

The lesson could have just as easily been conducted in a very similar fashion to the one above, with a simple change of focus. Instead of being advisors to the President at the time of My Lai, they could have been advising a future president about whether to apologize for the actions of the military on that day. The teacher in role could be the same, as could the Mantle of the Expert, but the students would *start* with the knowledge of the outcome rather than be surprised by it.

My choice to contrast the student's findings with the actual results also surprised me in retrospect. At the time I was planning it seemed like a strong way to bring home the message that those who killed the Vietnamese villagers received very little punishment. But it failed in one major respect; the lesson did not consider how environment, history and context would intersect and how that encounter might trouble the students.

Pecora's vignette speaks to the necessity for thoughtful contemplation of participants' needs when structuring drama work and for reflective dialogue following the work, so that the situation can be further contextualized politically and psychologically. Despite the students' despair at the end, the Mantle of the Expert method was quite effective. However, we can see that often a powerful method developed by a master teacher requires considerable supervision and reflection when implemented by a novice. Optimal supervision should not only be about technical and pedagogical matters, but also ethical, political and psychological ones.

While the two examples here took place in the US, Heathcote's praxis was far reaching. She influenced practitioners from around the globe. On Landy's travels to China and Japan he heard many people he interviewed mention Heathcote's name, even though they did not study with her directly.[76]

In the next section we focus on Taiwan, Korea, Japan and China to see how theories and practices discussed thus far have impacted praxis in these Asian countries.

## Educational drama and theatre in Taiwan

Despite traditions of authoritative teaching and rote learning in Asia, there have been substantial developments in DIE within several Asian cultures over the past 30 years. Many of the experts who practice in Chinese and Korean cultures have been trained in the US.

For example Hsiao-hua Chang, professor of Applied Drama and Theatre at National Taiwan University of the Arts, studied Educational Theatre at NYU in the 1980s. He trained with Nellie McCaslin and Robert Landy, both of whom he considers primary academic mentors. Chang's work in Taiwan is of particular importance as he was the architect of a public school curriculum for drama and theatre that was implemented by the Educational Administration in Taiwan in 2004.[77] This means that all elementary and middle school students are required to study drama as part of their standard curriculum.

For Chang DIE is both a way of learning about drama and theatre, and a method for learning other subject areas, such as history and literature.

Chang has created an eclectic model that informs his practice. It is based upon the praxis of seven British and Canadian experts, including Gavin Bolton's learning through drama, Carole Tarlington and Patrick Verriour's role drama, Cecily O'Neill's Process Drama, John Somers' compound stimulus, Dorothy Heathcote's Mantle of the Expert and David Booth's Story Drama.[78] His work is also informed by Landy's Role Theory.[79]

In practice Chang applies one or several of these approaches, depending upon the specific goals of the population served. In addition he has adapted many of these Western approaches to suit the culturally specific needs of his Taiwanese students.

Chang works within both educational and community organizations, with public school students and special needs students. Further, he works with groups of disabled children as well as frail elderly, with whom he applies Landy's projective work with masks. Chang's influence in Taiwan has extended to China where he consults with experts in theatre on how to develop educational applications. In the following vignette we find an example of a successful Taiwanese drama educator who was strongly influenced by Chang.

### ❖ Case vignette: Teaching English as a second language through drama

Like Chang, Professor Yung Ching Chen was mentored by several Westerners. One was John Somers, who guided her doctoral studies at the University of Exeter in the UK. The other was Robert Landy, who mentored her studies in Drama Therapy in Taiwan. In this vignette Chen played the dual role of teacher and researcher, gathering data on the experience of teaching English as a second language through drama to 40 eleven-year-old children in a public school in Kaohsiung, Taiwan.

Chen's research interest was to see if a DIE approach could enhance the children's learning of English. She supplemented the traditional Taiwanese approaches to learning English with more interactive choral readings from textbooks. In addition she applied the following DIE activities: voice training, movement, tableaux and role-play. In implementing these activities she aimed toward developing vocabulary comprehension and pronunciation, listening skills, creativity, imagination and the ability to write dialogue in English. She also added her own exercise of having the children develop and sing a theme song in English.

Finally she used a rehearsal process that led to the performance of an original play in English. As part of her qualitative methodology Chen encouraged students to reflect upon the process throughout by articulating their observations orally and in journals. She transcribed her own daily observations and also interviewed the children and their teachers following the performance.

In her results Chen found that DIE activities and performance enhanced her students' learning of English. In analyzing student's journals, for example, she found that more than 70 percent of the students experienced enjoyment and improvement of their English skills. Several mentioned that the drama and performance experience changed their attitudes toward English language learning. For a smaller percentage of students (3.85 percent), the experience was less positive due to difficulty memorizing lines and experiencing stage fright. Thus the negative comments were primarily from the performance aspect of the process.

In conclusion Chen noted that the optimal method for teaching English as a second language to children is through a combination of traditional methods and dramatic ones. Of the dramatic ones, she listed three types: drama games, drama tasks and drama projects. Although noting that the performance aspect of drama projects can lead to pressures to produce a superior product, she also felt that such an activity enhances the objectives of motivating learning and developing listening, speaking and writing skills.[80]

This vignette, though based upon a small sample, offers some qualitative evidence for the effectiveness of drama in the ESL classroom. In many ESL classrooms we find drama providing a multi-sensory approach to language acquisition by involving second language learners physically, emotionally and cognitively in the language learning process.

Like many of their Taiwanese colleagues in Educational Drama, Hsiao-hua Chang and Yung Ching Chen have studied in the US and UK, where they were mentored by Westerners. They, like others, continue to discover ways to integrate their learning with the cultural realities of their country. Whether developing an entire Taiwanese drama curriculum or a single English language protocol, they struggle to find the right cultural blend of East and West.


## Educational drama and theatre in Korea, Japan and China

In Korea the developing field of Educational Drama and Theatre is led by practitioners trained in the West. You-Jin Hong studied Educational Theatre at NYU with Nellie McCaslin, Nancy and Lowell Swortzell and Robert Landy. She earned her doctorate in 1992 and is a professor of performing arts at Dongduk University in Seoul. In 2007 Hong established a concentration in Drama Therapy within the Department of Performing Arts. Further, Yun-Tae Kim, another graduate of NYU's Educational Theatre Program, has invited a number of Western scholars and practitioners in the field to train and educate Korean students.

Soohyun Ma, a drama therapist and doctoral student in Educational Theatre from NYU reports that since the late 1980s there has been a shift from a purely academic curriculum to one more open to the humanities and arts.[81] This development has led to the appearance of drama and theatre classes in Korean higher education.

Drama Therapy classes are a newer addition, and have become popular since Landy presented a workshop in Seoul on 'Storytelling and Role-Playing in Drama Therapy' in 2003. Around that same time You-Jin Hong introduced Drama Therapy by discussing it on mainstream broadcasting networks MBC, KBS and SBS. Ms Hong also established the Korean Institute for Drama Therapy (KIDT) in 2009 as a professional organization, one that offers registry to trainees. Since then KIDT has been subsidized by the Korean government to conduct work with several targeted populations – the elderly, disabled, immigrants and single mothers.

Many of the theoretical ideas and approaches to Drama Therapy are Western-based. However Hong and her colleagues are working toward developing culturally specific practices. Hong's doctoral research concerned an analysis of the performance of Korean shamans.[82] She sees the value in linking traditional performance-based healing traditions to Western models of dramatic healing. Soohyun Ma, her former student, is following a similar path, integrating her Western education with praxis steeped in Korean cultural traditions.

Since 1998 undergraduate courses in Educational Theatre have been offered to drama majors in over 160 Korean universities. In 2003 official certification from the Korean government was given to the top 10 percent of students in drama programs, preparing them to teach drama and theatre in schools. At the graduate level only Korea National University of the Arts offers a Master's program in Educational Theatre. It is within the Department of Theatre for Children and Adolescents.

Since 2000 Educational Drama and Theatre scholars have worked to develop an interdisciplinary framework responsive to Korean culture. The Ministry of Education has encouraged public schools and arts schools to include theatre classes in their curriculum and organize drama clubs as a part of extracurricular activities. As a consequence university graduates of drama programs are able to work as theatre teachers in public and private schools.

In 2005 the Korean Arts and Culture Education Service was founded by the government to support arts and culture education for children in the public schools and for groups in the community such as multi-ethnic families, prisoners and elderly welfare recipients. It has a variety of programs to train teachers in Educational Theatre as well as other arts and has trained more than 5000 arts teachers. In addition it sponsors professional conferences. In 2010 the organization teamed up with UNESCO to host the second World Conference on Arts Education in Seoul.

Japan, like Korea, is in a relatively early developmental stage in Educational Drama and Theatre. Akeyo Onoe, who studied Educational Theatre and Drama Therapy at Kansas State University, tells us that interest in the field is growing even though drama is not a required subject in the Japanese compulsory educational curriculum.[83] Onoe, who is presently director of the Japanese Drama Therapy Education and Research Center and professor of human services at Ritsumeikan University in Kyoto, notes an expansion of research and practice in Educational Theatre and an application of the work within secondary and university classrooms.

She cites the work of several Japanese educators: Professor Fumiko Takeda of Ritsumeikan University who uses an improvisational drama method in a class of environmental studies, and Professor Kumagai Yaushiro of Nihon University College of Art, Tokyo. Yaushiro developed various Applied Theatre projects since the mid-1990s in theatres, museums and village streets, working with the disabled and elderly, immigrants and school truants. He initiated the first Applied Theatre minor in Japan, at Nihon University.

Jun Watanabe, also of Nihon University, originally a social studies teacher, played a key role in the development of Educational Drama and Theatre in Japan. In an interview with Watanabe he told us that there is a long history of drama in education in Japanese schools through the performance of school festivals.[84] In these festivals students are given prescribed dialogue and movement and enact cultural celebrations and well-known folk tales. School plays, focusing upon classical Japanese and Western dramas have also been a staple of extra-curricular activity in schools.

For Watanabe these forms were too static. In searching for a more dynamic way to use drama and theatre, he transformed the structure of debates, popular in the 1990s in Japanese secondary schools, into active forms of role-playing and role-reversal, urging his students to take on multiple perspectives. Watanabe conceives of his drama work as praxis, and developed a three-tier theoretical model integrating aspects of discussion and debate with those of Drama-in-Education and theatre performance.

Watanabe was influenced by several Western experts, including Viola Spolin, Dorothy Heathcote and Jonathan Neelands, with whom he published the book *Using Drama as a Medium of Instruction*.[85] In his work Watanabe makes use of 16 dramatic activities, including role-play, tableau and Teacher-in-Role, some of which are firmly based in Japanese cultural traditions.

Of the several Asian countries surveyed, China is the latest to develop Educational Drama and Theatre. With a moderation of controls by the Communist party since the publication of the 1982 *Handbook* affecting not only economic policies, but also cultural and intellectual ones, a number of options have opened in the arts as applied to education and therapy.

The pageantry of festivals mentioned above by Watanabe is also a highlight of Chinese cultural life and many school and community-based performances concern the celebration of Chinese culture and politics. During the years of the Cultural Revolution, the government oversaw all public performances. Under the supervision of Jiang Qing, Mao's wife, eight revolutionary operas were developed and performed, all intended to promote the ideology of Communist China. Within this political system, proclaimed Mao, 'art must serve the interests of the workers, peasants, and soldiers and must conform to proletarian ideology'.[86]

One of the exciting newer cultural developments in China is the use of the classical Chinese opera form to tell new stories, some taken from the canon of Western dramatic literature. William Huizhu Sun, professor of theatre at the Shanghai Theatre Academy, is at the forefront of this development. Sun, who studied theatre at NYU with experimental theatre artist and performance theorist Richard Schechner, is interested in developing Educational Drama within Chinese public schools. In addition he has expressed an interest in incorporating culturally relevant forms of Drama Therapy within Chinese institutions. Sun invited Hsiao-hua Chang to China to speak about his Taiwanese model of Educational Theatre and Robert Landy to speak about his model of Drama Therapy and its application to Chinese culture. Although his academic training is in part Western, Sun is always mindful of developing creative forms fully applicable to Chinese culture. The following is an excerpt from an interview with Sun:

SUN:    There is a long tradition in Chinese education, especially in arts education, of starting with imitation of typical types, or models. This is also a model in the West in music education. You would not ask future musicians to play whatever they feel like playing. You give them a set of eight tunes that have been tested for generations. This is actually the training method of Chinese opera.

The philosophical basis of this approach is not individualism, but collectivism, or a type theory we can say is a variation of Landy's role theory. Even though art requires individual creativity, you have to tell students what the general form is like. Even for Creative Drama.

My plan is to start with a general requirement that every school has to fulfill. Children will do a physical exercise every day that is based on the six decades long practice of broadcast exercise. This is a robotic torso and limb movement that is gender neutral and cultural neutral. My almost utopian proposal is to re-choreograph this broadcast exercise with Chinese opera choreographers and kung fu masters. In fact there are schools that have begun doing this kind of Chinese opera-flavored physical exercise. If this is implemented nationally, then we could say every Chinese student is doing something related to theatre, even though there is no character or plot yet.

Then, I hope some of the kids may want a more advanced level, and we could organize a drama/theatre class to teach them more advanced Chinese opera movement patterns with plots and characters. This is what I call theatre études, exemplary short plays with basic character types and movement patterns. The plays are there to help them take the first step. Based on the theatre études, students will create their own plays. I am planning on working with my students to create a series of short plays around the theme of Confucius and his disciples, using three set role types derived from Chinese opera. And I will ask Chinese choreographers to make it distinctively entertaining and fun.

LANDY: Do all high school students know these role types?

SUN: Not necessarily, but once these plays are presented to them, it will be easy for students to know.

LANDY: What are the role types?

SUN: One is a painted face, a warrior type. Another is a clown. The third is a woman impersonating a man because in Confucius' time, a woman could not travel with a man.

I am also working on professional Chinese opera productions based on Western classics like *Miss Julie*, *Hedda Gabler*, *Oedipus*, plays that I love, to help revitalize and promote Chinese opera to Chinese children. One reason why so many schoolchildren know so little about Chinese opera is because they think: 'They don't speak to me at all.' Even the Chinese version of Romeo and Juliet is set in an ancient time 'and that has nothing to do with my life.' On the other hand Western plays, even when they were written 500 years ago, can still speak to us.

But Chinese theatre also has its advantage, which is mostly in its stylized form. So we can take the best from Chinese theatre and Western theatre. That's why I call my idea the Chinese brand of Creative Drama. We will never forget Chinese opera. I also believe, philosophically, to start with types would be much easier to implement. I don't want children to stick with the types all of their lives like some of the Chinese Opera actors. I want them to start with the types. Once they have mastered the types, they don't have to be limited by them. Then they can create their own stories with new forms.[87]

There are many other experiments in Educational Drama and Theatre throughout Asia: in Singapore, India, Pakistan, Malaysia, the Philippines, among other countries, all of which have their own unique performance traditions. And especially in the developing countries, there are many examples of Applied Theatre, some of which are discussed in Chapter 4. All practitioners grapple with their culture and with their training, sometimes at odds, in searching for an approach that best suits the needs of their students and citizens. For example in the following vignette we see practitioners grappling with Heathcote's training.

In 2007 Heathcote returned to NYU once more for a week of workshops. Most of the NYU graduate students in attendance were focused on issues of classroom management. They were concerned that drama could potentially reinforce unruly behavior from students, and they wondered how challenging behavior could be dealt with positively in drama work.

### ❖ Case vignette – Blowing up the drama

During Heathcote's demonstration with another group of seventh and eighth grade students from Brooklyn, New York, a pivotal moment came at the end of the week. It involved one male student and his two friends. Their interaction became the hot topic for discussion amongst observing graduate students. Some were highly critical of how Heathcote dealt with the boys' behavior. Others marveled at how well she contained the student disturbance in role, without stopping the drama, and how everyone was able to reflect upon the choices that were made. This example transcended the mere explication of a single technique, such as Mantle of the Expert, but was instead about the more basic meaning of the educational drama process.

Reflecting upon the experience Jennifer Holmes, a doctoral student in Educational Theatre, wrote the following:

The young students volunteered to be observed by graduate students during a drama workshop about creating a community for recent immigrants. In role, students interviewed other students for jobs and helped recent immigrants establish homes and community centers for their families. It was all interesting and I learned a lot throughout the week, but what transpired at the end of the workshop changed the way I view classroom management in Educational Drama.

The students had busied themselves with the tasks Heathcote assigned, including filling out applications for job interviews and designing homes for newly arrived immigrants and their families. They were very engaged in the process and allowed themselves to 'play' along with her. Heathcote maintained the serious nature of the tasks on the first day during the 'application process' when three boys all put down 'silly' answers on their forms, such as references to mob connections and burying dead bodies. Despite these answers, Heathcote gave value to everything they said and allowed it to be real in the context of what was needed.

These boys laughed and talked amongst themselves continually during the five days of workshops. I did not get the impression that this bothered Heathcote in the least, despite the fact that the same three boys distracted each other by chatting and giggling. After a while Dorothy split the boys up, but in the final stages of the last workshop the three boys were allowed to work together one last time.

The final activity improvised a welcoming ceremony for the immigrants. It was a deeply reflective activity that allowed the young people and adults together to consider all the work that had transpired and consider all the discoveries that had been made throughout the week. Most participants, including me, had been deeply invested in the experience and felt the final ceremony was a touching experience.

However the very last moment found all the participants being led into another part of the theatre by one of the three boys. There was a sense of anticipation for what the boys were going to do. Then, slowly and quite deliberately, one boy, the leader, raised his hand and said, 'Boom! I set off a bomb. You're all dead!'

My heart dropped, and so did most everyone else's. If I were his teacher, I would have been devastated. I would have focused on the fact that he wasn't committed to the experience all week and that this boy had not properly learned the sense of humanity that theatre teaches.

Immediately following the moment the bomb was set off, this single act, for many, almost negated the entire experience.

With great authority, though without raising her voice, Heathcote said, 'You had some beautiful moments, but that was self-sabotage.' Heathcote then stated, 'There is nothing we do in this room that isn't happening somewhere in the world.' The other students, the young man's classmates, looked upset. Heathcote shared that she had recently read about a family who had been blown up in Iraq, and wondered aloud about the lack of humanity those soldiers must have had. She turned to the three boys and quietly but pointedly said, 'And we have three of them here.' The boy with the 'bomb' put his head in his hands.

It took me a little while to come to, and so many people in the room were focused on the student's insensitive deed at first, but I found Heathcote's response to be an incredibly useful way to deal with what happened. Heathcote had included the dramatic act as part of the lesson. I don't think this young man will ever forget that moment. Neither will I. She continued to endow what happened in that room with importance and meaning. She never gave in to any silliness by stifling student choices; she just made students responsible for them. This moment made me realize how everything that transpires in drama can be a 'teaching moment'. You give the students power, but you never take away the power of having them face the real consequences of their choices.

In the two summers that Heathcote came to NYU, she demonstrated how teachers need to be flexible and adjust their curriculum towards the needs of the students. She also stressed how important it is to make drama a special time, and take students 'out of the casual'. Further, we learn by example that drama is both about spontaneous action and its consequences, and that optimal dramatic learning occurs when an individual is able to take responsibility for creating an action that can have serious consequences, and when a group is able to make sense of that action.

Heathcote's ideas emerged from praxis, from trying out theories in practice, reflecting on her practice and making adjustments moving forward. In an interview for this book Heathcote expressed it this way: 'Praxis is doing to understand. All the tasks, any part I play in keeping the tasks going or initiating them, is active – it's about doing so that the students understand the doing of it. And I learn what I realize I didn't know when I started.'[88]

# 3    Theatre for, by and with Young People

## Introduction

This chapter examines theatre practice with young people as audience members and theatre makers, considering examples both in and out of schools. Unlike school-based work described in the first two chapters, here the discussion includes organizations that bring their programs and performances into schools. We also describe work happening separately from schools at theatres or local community centers. We look to history and compare it to current developments in the field, and share perspectives from interviews with leading artists and practitioners.

Whether transpiring in or out of schools, educational objectives remain at the core of all the performance work presented here. With this in mind we look to practitioners, playwrights, artists and organizations devoted to Theatre for Young Audiences, Theatre in Education and Youth Theatre to help us reflect on the varied praxis. We begin with Theatre for Young Audiences.

## Theatre for young audiences

Theatre for Young Audiences (TYA) can be traced back to the politically-based theatre of Bertolt Brecht, an artist who challenged the audience to critically examine social issues. Brecht's *Lehrstücke* or 'learning plays' were performed in schools and intended to raise awareness on the part of the children. Brecht, in fact, actively solicited children's criticism, sometimes revising texts as a result.[1]

Though not generally as provocative as Brecht's Epic Theatre, several TYA plays adhere to similar goals – to educate young people, to stimulate critical reflection and to inspire them to take action in the world.

There are many theatres around the globe that devote a part or all of their season to presenting plays written with the young audience in mind. Most often, TYA plays are produced using adult, professional actors. Some

TYA plays deal with contemporary and explosive issues, some are purely for entertainment, and others consist of modern adaptations of literary classics. Since the 1982 *Handbook* was published, many TYA professionals feel that the term, Children's Theatre, does not aptly describe the range of plays produced and the audiences served.

During those same three decades TYA has addressed the needs of our youngest audiences through the development of Theatre for the Very Young (TVY). TVY was created so that young children could have a direct theatrical experience. As noted by researcher Tony Mack, in TVY child participation is necessary 'to overcome age and developmental barriers in order for art to make contact with the consciousness of the very young audience members.'[2]

This high level of engagement is seen 'in a number of recent German productions which welcome children onto the stage to play with the set and props' writes Mack.[3] For example, Theater von Anfang an (Theatre Right from the Very Beginning) produced *Light and Shadow*, a play about a tree that needed to grow. The production used many objects to capture the young child's attention and encouraged children to directly participate. One young audience member held the branch of a tree, while another used an overhead projector to cast the shadow of it on to a wall. The child holding the branch experimented with moving it closer to the light source, which made the shadow of the tree grow.[4] Through this activity, the young audience members played a part in creating the world of the play.

In another example of TVY, Suzanne Osten, the influential artistic director of Unga Klara in Stockhom, Sweden, created a memorable TVY piece with Ann-Sofie Bárány, a psychoanalyst and playwright.[5] In 2008 Osten and Bárány's experimental *Babydrama* won the prize as the best performance at the BITEF Festival, an acclaimed international theatre festival in Belgrade, Serbia.[6]

Although an increasingly popular form, TVY is not without skeptics. Some question why it is important to bring such young children to a show that they won't remember. From our point of view, children create a muscle memory from the experience. Their involvement initiates them into the world of theatre as observers and creative participants. TVY also provides a different experience from TV or film, and while very young children may not be able to watch television for very long, they can participate in a 45-minute interactive theatre experience.

Though they found success presenting it, Linda Hartzell, artistic director of the Seattle Children's Theatre admits: 'We were embarrassed to do toddler theater for a long time'.[7] In assessing TVY in the US, Kim Peter Kovac, director of youth and family programs at Washington, DC's Kennedy Center, said 'We all know how to do theatre for the fourth- to eighth-grade range. The question is, How do we get the really young ones? Can we create a dramaturgy for babies? Right now there are a lot of people who know very little; the form is wrestling its way into coherence. The Europeans have such a head start on us.'[8]

Jumping ahead in age, theatre for adolescents, also known as Theatre for Youth, is more prevalent in 2012 than it was 30 years ago. This rise corresponds to the increasing popularity of young adult novels. Noted theorist and practitioner Roger Bedard describes how theatre companies in the US have also focused more on adolescent audiences by creating unique performance experiences. He points to the Coterie Theatre in Kansas City and the Children's Theatre of Minneapolis as examples:

> The Coterie children's theatre offers teen programming at a local coffee house, geographically distinct from its children's theatre playing space, under the auspices of its 'Coterie at Night program (Breakfast Club).' Night time performances are also rarely associated with the children's theatre. The Children's Theatre Company of Minneapolis has created a programming unit, called ctc4teens, and they produce teen theatre in the Cargill Theatre, which was built as a second performing space in the children's theatre facility but was dedicated primarily for teen programming.[9]

By recognizing that adolescents have different desires and needs than their younger counterparts, creators of Theatre for Youth engage teenagers in productions that speak to their own experiences.

Whether the focus is on babies, children or teens, TYA playwrights and organizations believe that young people should have the same quality theatrical entertainment as adults. It is within this philosophical position that Moses Goldberg, an international expert in TYA, developed an age-appropriate plan for a child's exposure to theatre.[10] Goldberg wrote theatre pieces for specific audiences in order to nurture their development as playgoers and to increase their knowledge of various theatrical forms and styles.[11] He believed playwrights could write for children without writing down to them, a charge often leveled against TYA playwrights. Goldberg has also been critical of Children's Theatre practitioners who sacrifice sincerity to marketability.

Influential playwright Aurand Harris wrote a wide range of original plays for young audiences that significantly impacted the TYA canon. Like Goldberg, he believed in substance over marketability. 'Instead of using familiar stories the child may already have known, he selected that which is new and unusual for a children's theatre audience,' wrote Jennings.[12]

Harris also explored a range of different theatrical styles. As a teacher of elementary students, Harris often allowed his pupils to guide his plays' development. In one anthology of Harris' works, *Short Plays of Theatre Classics*, he included 12 historical comedies adapted for his elementary school students to perform.[13]

McCaslin wrote that Harris was an important playwright because he insisted that the materials he used have 'substance and value', and he was critical of work that was 'condescending', 'cute' or 'camp'.[14] His play *The Arkansaw Bear* was one of the first children's plays to deal with the issue of death and dying.[15]

And yet we share in the criticism that Harris' plays are often too safe and conservative in content, raising few questions and avoiding any truly critical point of view. An example is one of his oft-produced plays, *Rags to Riches*, based upon Horatio Alger novels.[16] In the play Harris recapitulates the theme of the American dream popularized by Alger in the early 20th century – with hard work and pluck and a large dose of luck, a street urchin can strike it rich in the land of unlimited opportunity.

In the mid-1970s Landy directed a production of *Rags to Riches* in the style of Brechtian Epic Theatre, posing questions about the social and political implications of the Alger/Harris vision. Following the production Landy and a colleague, Portuguese developmental psychologist Luis Joyce-Moniz, interviewed a number of children from the audience to determine their levels of identification with the characters and comprehension of the scenes of varying complexity. They discovered that there was a developmental sequence of identification and comprehension consistent with Piaget's epigenetic theory of cognitive development.[17] This meant that older children from seven to eleven were able to understand aspects of the play such as irony and political commentary on a more sophisticated level than younger ones whose identification and understanding were based upon such external factors as color and costume, broad movement and humorous dialogue.

Landy followed up this directing experience by adapting another Alger novel, *Phil, the Fiddler*, into the musical play *The Padrone*, written within the style of epic theatre and intended to raise a number of questions about the American dream among audiences of young people.[18]

Raising questions and trusting that children can comprehend complex material, playwright Suzan Zeder emphasizes the emotional truth of stories and characters. *Wiley and the Hairy Man* is arguably her most popular play, based upon a southern folktale.[19] Two other plays, *Step on a Crack* and *Doors*, explore issues of divorce through a mix of realism and fantasy.[20]

In 1985 Zeder wrote *Mother Hicks*, a play about three outsiders told in dialogue, poetry and sign language set in the small town of Ware in southern Illinois, during the Great Depression.[21] In 1995, Zeder wrote a prequel to *Mother Hicks* with her play about Tuc, the play's deaf character, called *The Taste of Sunrise*.[22] Then in 2010, at the New Visions/New Voices play development series at the Kennedy Center, described below, Zeder returned to Ware for her third play *The Edge of Peace*.[23] This time the play was set in 1945 at the very end of World War II during a period of upheaval in traditional family life. Zeder's scripts have been appreciated on many levels by both children and adults, for depicting child characters as clever, complex and full of feeling.

David Saar also reveals great depth of emotion in *The Yellow Boat*, developed with Zeder's dramaturgical assistance. *The Yellow Boat* is a meditation on the life of Saar's son Benjamin, a hemophiliac who died of AIDS in 1987 at the age of eight.[24] This was the first play for young audiences to take on the subject of AIDS. It revealed not only Benjamin's struggle with the virus, but also with a hostile and ignorant community. It also revealed the healing power of art to express feeling and make meaning out of that which seems so hopeless.[25] Co-commissioned by Childsplay and the Metro Theater Company of St Louis, *The Yellow Boat* made a tremendous impact on the field when it premiered in 1993.

**Photograph 3.1** *The Yellow Boat*, **Childsplay, April 1993, premiere (Tempe Performing Arts Center), photo by Hal Martin Fogel, courtesy of David Saar**

Despite the emotional impact of Harris, Zeder, Saar and many international TYA playwrights, some perceive TYA as a less respected art form than mainstream theatre. Additionally TYA actors are often paid less than their mainstream counterparts. For some performing in TYA is a stepping stone to bigger and better adult theatre roles. On the other hand many companies and artists put extensive thought and care into creating work that is relevant, aesthetically pleasing, thought-provoking, funny and moving, the same qualities that all theatre strives to achieve.

The Dutch have long rallied around cultivating meaningful theatre for youth, as Manon Van De Water, a TYA scholar, explains:

> Dutch TYA really took off in the 1970s, as an aftermath of the turbulent 1960s, to create an emancipatory theatre, meant to empower its youth and offer them acting perspective. The emancipatory TYA was part of a wider, Western movement that included the Unga Klara in Sweden and the Grips Theatre in Berlin. Many of these early theatre makers still work successfully today, and one of the hallmarks of their work is that the artists seem to practice their theories [...] Although not explicitly analyzed in scholarly terms, much of Dutch TYA is socially engaged and clearly rooted in the specific conditions of Dutch society, in content and aesthetic vision.[26]

The culturally based vision of individual artists plays a large role in generating theory. As such, examining their work within a cultural context can benefit TYA praxis. As Van De Water notes, 'Looking at TYA as cultural production, producing meanings in specific contexts, for specific audiences, through specific performances, can illuminate our practice and shed light on some of the problems that hamper the field and contribute to a marginalized status.'[27]

## TYA Organizations

In further considering the development of TYA, it is useful to identify the mission and progress of organizations devoted to the work. Established in 1958 the Children's Theatre Foundation of America (CTFA) still retains Children's Theatre in its title. Its mission is to advance the artistic and professional interests of theatre for the young by 'funding proposals from American theatres, artists, scholars, and special projects of national import to the field'.[28]

Not to be confused with CTFA, the Children's Theatre Association of America (CTAA) raised the standards of theatre for young people.[29] In 1932 as part of the Association of Junior Leagues of America, a children's theatre committee (CTC) was formed, chaired by Winifred Ward. The committee went through various name changes, settled on CTAA, and in the 1970s and 80s held national and regional meetings with children's theatre-makers across the US.[30] Today CTAA's functions are filled by the American Alliance for Theatre and Education (AATE).

The most prominent international organization is called ASSITEJ, an acronym for the Association International du Théâtre pour l'Enfance et la Jeunesse, or the International Association of Theatre for Children and Young People.[31] With chapters around the world ASSITEJ links thousands of theatres, organizations and individuals through national centers on six continents in more than 70 countries.

The history of ASSITEJ is told in a series of books by Nat Eek, Ann Shaw and Katherine Krzys who meticulously document the steps that were taken towards organizing AASITEJ with dedicated artists worldwide.[32] In 1965, 187 representatives from 26 countries met in Paris to 'encourage the development of fine theatre for children and young people with particular emphasis given to the art of theatre and its presentation by adult professional actors'.[33]

Today the research network of ASSITEJ International continues to grow. This can be seen on the Internet with the emergence of Facebook pages from the countries involved in ASSITEJ. Also connected is the International Theatre for Young Audiences Research Network (ITYARN) and the International Performing Arts for Youth (IPAY) organization.[34]

## Three experts reflect on TYA in 2011

Longtime colleagues and friends Emelie Fitzgibbon, the founder and artistic director of Graffiti Theatre Company in Cork, Ireland; Cecily O'Neill, the international authority on Process Drama and TYA; and Nancy Swortzell, co-founder of the Program in Educational Theatre at NYU, discussed the state of TYA in a joint interview:[35]

MONTGOMERY: In Landy's 1982 *Handbook*, he refers to the CTAA definition of theatre with young people as 'the performance of a largely predetermined theatrical art work by living actors in the presence of young people, either children (young persons' typically of elementary school age, five through 12) or youth (young persons typically of junior high school age, 13 through 15).' Is there a better way to define TYA today?

FITZGIBBON:     The definition – I was puzzled by it. ... It somehow doesn't capture the spirit of TYA and the aesthetic comparatives of TYA. It seems to be very ... prescriptive. And I think that TYA and its overall definition have loosened up in the past 30 years. There isn't the gap that there used to be between theatre for children, TIE and Theatre for Youth.

SWORTZELL:      The historical definition was originally devised during the reign of Winifred Ward and the CTC. The feeling of the committee was that it was to be a written text, which obviously ruled out improvisational drama. ... The 'living actors' was to delimit it so that the art of puppetry was excluded, and the art of musical theatre was excluded. This was to be theatrical activity where fully mounted productions ... for a child audience were included. But Children's Theatre somehow terminated the activity at the age of 12. No one who was 13 through 20 needed these activities anymore. But I think that we have seen a tremendous shift in that Children's Theatre is no longer Children's Theatre. It is young people's theatre but sub-divided into the early years, the middle years, and then ... the open years. And the open years can be anywhere from 13 to the early 20s. So it has become much more sophisticated and devoted to plays which develop significant contemporary issues for children. Also arising now is something that I question but that Emelie Fitzgibbon endorses, which is Infant Drama. There are many subdivisions to what Youth Theatre is today. Do you agree with me Cecily?

O'NEILL:        Yes. Absolutely! I think so many things have changed and I think the thing to remember is that things have changed in the adult world of theatre as well to encompass cutting edge shows, physical theatre and performances without words. I mean if you take a show like *Shockheaded Peter* which the Improbable Theatre in England did, which was very strange and ...

FITZGIBBON:     from the German book?

O'NEILL:        Yes. Did you see it Nancy?

SWORTZELL:      Yes. I've seen it twice.

O'NEILL:        And it was a great success. It was full every night. And teenagers saw it. I don't know if it was marketed to younger children but they would probably have been scared.

FITZGIBBON:     Terrified!

O'NEILL:      Yes, terrified. But I think practitioners in TYA, if they have any artistic pretentions, would be using those materials. These types of wordless pieces we've seen would have been unusual 30 years ago. They would've been seen as mime or something else. And we also see the kind of things that are more like art installations than a dramatic encounter happening more frequently.

SWORTZELL:      I think you would have to say that many more forms are included now. It was a gradual evolution. Theatre centers in England began exploring more topics and then some of the resident children's theatre and authors turned to forms and ideas which normally were not considered appropriate for youth. And certainly there was a questioning of what was the educational component. Did every play have to have an educational focus? And I think that children's aesthetic sense has grown as well...

O'NEILL:      ...to be much more sophisticated. You know with television or interactive games or the speed of modern films, for example. I think they have a much wider range of references and styles.

FITZGIBBON:      Yes. And their response times on things have changed.

SWORTZELL:      The real boost to young people's theatre came through the LORT [League of Resident Theatres] professional theatres in communities because they didn't have any money. And they discovered that they could get grants from the Department of Health, Education and Welfare to have a theatre outreach team. And so in the US, theatres like the McCarter in New Jersey and the Cleveland Playhouse applied for grants. I'm very interested in trends of new work for multiple-aged audiences. And there are three centers in the US to help give playwrights the experience and support they need in writing their texts –the Bonderman event in Indianapolis; the Kennedy Center's New Visions/New Voices; and the wee little Provincetown Project [New Plays for Young Audiences].

The play development projects that Swortzell refers to here, including New Plays for Young Audiences (NPYA) where she served as artistic director with Montgomery, are significant to the process of creating exciting and innovative TYA plays in the US, although international playwrights are also represented in these programs. In the next section we describe these play development programs further.

## New play development in TYA

NPYA at the Provincetown Playhouse was established in 1997 by Lowell and Nancy Swortzell, co-founders of the Program in Educational Theatre at NYU. Lowell Swortzell, the artistic director of the series, was a prolific writer and scholar who passionately dedicated his life to theatre for young people. The field lost a profound voice and advocate of TYA when he passed away in 2004. In 2005 Nancy assumed the artistic directorship of NYPA, and she and Montgomery co-directed it from 2008 to 2011. The field suffered another profound loss during the editing of this book when Nancy passed away in July 2011.

The Swortzells recognized a need to encourage the development of plays for young audiences and worked with many of the finest TYA playwrights in this pursuit. They saw the value of these plays not just for entertainment, but for creating opportunities for young people to learn about themselves and their world. The Swortzells created a supportive atmosphere for playwrights to take risks as their writing is put on its feet, evaluated, reworked and read aloud by a cast of actors in front of an eager audience of youth and their families.

On a larger scale, as part of the Kennedy Center in Washington, DC, New Visions/New Voices is a week-long festival for playwrights and theatres to stimulate and support the creation of new plays and musicals for young audiences. It culminates in a weekend festival of rehearsed readings and discussions with professionals in the field. Since it began in 1991 the festival has helped develop 73 new theatre pieces from 47 US and five international theatre companies.[36]

The 'Bonderman', another biennial play development program, was first conceived by Dorothy Webb in 1983 when she became aware that there were few opportunities for playwrights to come together and explore issues surrounding the creation of high quality dramatic literature for young audiences.[37] Webb, then a professor of theatre at Indiana University/Purdue University at Indianapolis (IUPUI), conceived of a place where playwrights writing for young audiences could share their plays, their ideas and the everyday problems existing in the field.[38]

In 1997, Webb added a classroom link for the finalist playwrights. Playwrights were assigned an age-appropriate school group that provided feedback about the play at different points during the week of the residency.[39] Webb recognized that youth involvement was a key to the future success of these plays.

While these three US play development programs are noteworthy, often playwrights will set up their own play development projects, getting actors and audiences to read, hear and provide feedback on the work at various stages in the play's development. Following the play's initial development phase, a script should be in better shape for publication and performance in theatre venues.

The New Victory Theater in New York City is a prominent venue to showcase such plays from playwrights around the globe. Edie Demas was director of education for the New Victory Theater from 2001 until 2010. Prior to 2001 Demas worked in Ireland as education officer at the Graffiti Theatre County Cork and as an associate artist for education and outreach at the Abbey, Ireland's national theatre. In the following interview, Demas echoes and elaborates on some of the ideas discussed by Fitzgibbon, O'Neill and Swortzell.

> Currently TYA has really expanded in terms of both older and younger kids, and there's been a lot of focus on Infant or Baby Drama in Europe. Scandinavia, Britain and Holland are pioneering this work, some literally for babies, and others for toddlers. At the New Victory we presented the show from Scotland, *My House,* which was geared for 18 months to four-year-old audiences. A huge amount of research into child development went into the needs of that particular audience, but this research didn't interfere with the artistic quality and the artistic aims of the piece. And I think that's what we're seeing in TYA – real aspirations towards marrying those things.
>
> Similarly, I think there's a real interest in developing work specifically for teens – work that is original in content and not just Shakespeare or classic novels adapted for the stage. Also, there's been a kind of blurring of lines for teenagers between Youth Theatre and TYA. We had an example of this at the New Victory with a piece called *Once And For All We're Gonna Tell You Who We Are So Shut Up And Listen* from Belgium. It is a play by teens for teens, and it really pushed buttons and boundaries, just like the title says it does. It was not a cautionary tale or message driven. It was open-ended, non-linear and practically non-verbal.[40]

According to Demas in the past few years 'the most exciting direction in TYA is that the best of it is really messing with the forms of theatre.'[41] It appears this is particularly true outside the US. Similarly Carol Korty, a distinguished playwright and teacher who was featured in the 1982 *Handbook,* said, 'European children's theatre seems to be focused on a search for new forms', but added that it is 'often for shock value'.[42] Korty's work is influenced by her professional years as a dancer and her interest in world cultures. She enjoyed years of touring theatre and helping young people create theatre pieces of their own. In an interview she talked further about the changes she has seen in US TYA, both positive and problematic:

> The change I've seen in American theatre for youth since the mid-1960s is the huge improvement in artistic quality. There is less reliance on simply dramatizing familiar European folktales, certainly among professional companies. Unfortunately, there is heavy reliance on dramatizing award-winning novels. Much of this trend can be attributed to catering to schools' preferences for plays based on books from their reading lists. It is difficult to convince them to book a play, or bus their students to a play, with an unfamiliar title. In the old days, producers would literally say, 'I don't care what you do, darling, as long as you call it Snow White.' Today that seems to have been replaced by a title that won a Newbery Medal for literature.
>
> There is more concern now with addressing social issues in children's theatre than there was in the 60s and 70s. However works tend to play it safe by raising such topics as racism, sexism and discrimination, but in the context of earlier periods of history rather than the present. Sexuality is still pretty much off the table and religious issues are carefully avoided as well. In the US it's hard for our diverse society to reach consensus on these issues.[43]

It has always been difficult for society to reach a consensus on social issues, but during the Great Depression the Federal Theatre Project (FTP) launched and delivered the country's most concerted effort to provide children's theatre programming in the US, much of which was related to social and political realities of the time. While the Depression was the catalyst, organizing the FTP Children's Theatre repertory was an example of praxis on a grand scale, with multiple artists coming together to create a children's theatre for change based in a mix of theory and pedagogical practice, and pointing toward social change.

## The Federal Theatre Project

The Works Progress Administration (WPA) was a government program launched by President Franklin Roosevelt in 1935 to help ease the fallout from the Great Depression. The WPA offered work to the unemployed on an unprecedented scale by spending money on a wide variety of programs. One was the Federal Theatre Project (FTP). 'Eventually employing over 30,000 people in regional and state centers, the FTP kept alive theatrical careers that otherwise would have ended in soup lines, and concurrently provided opportunities for young artists to launch careers that would establish them among the next generation's leading actors, directors, and designers,' wrote Lowell Swortzell.[44]

Hallie Flanagan, an artist who made her reputation as director of Vassar College's Experimental Theatre, was appointed national director of FTP.[45] Previously Flanagan authored *Shifting Scenes*, a book with reflections about theatre practices she observed on a 1927 visit to Europe. In Russia Flanagan was impressed by the significant value the Soviet Union placed on arts education. Likewise throughout her travels she observed the work of heavyweight theatre practitioners like Constantine Stanislavski, Vsevolod Meyerhold and Max Reinhardt.[46] Their innovative ideas impacted Flanagan in directing the FTP.

FTP children's theatre productions were acted by adult performers playing all roles, including child characters. This policy was in place to provide employment for theatre professionals, the main goal of FTP, not because of any artistic stand against child performers.[47]

The first New York production was Charlotte Chorpenning's dramatization of Hans Christian Anderson's *The Emperor's New Clothes*.[48] Many of Chorpenning's plays were based on fairy tales. Yet the fairy tale frame provided a metaphor that 'reflected current fears of war and aggression abroad, while others examined effects of the Depression at home,' noted Swortzell.[49]

As an example *Letters to Santa Claus* by Charlotte Chorpenning, which opened in Chicago in 1938, presented a dark story line, gloomy social commentary and 'disturbing subtext' to young people.[50] The moral of sustaining goodwill during the Christmas season was evident, but the national disillusionment of the period was also conveyed, demonstrating theatre's ability to show how politics impact people's everyday lives.

Among the more political offerings of the FTP was *The Revolt of the Beavers*, by Oscar Saul and Lois Lantz, which stirred great political passion when it premiered in New York City in 1937.[51] Its plot concerns two small children who are transported to 'Beaverland', a society run by a mean beaver chief who forces other beavers to work incessantly on the 'busy wheel', turning bark into food and clothing.[52] He then stockpiles everything for himself and his close friends. With the children's assistance, a beaver named Oakleaf organizes his fellow workers to remove the chief from power and launch a society where everything is shared. For stressing the importance of political power in the labor and work force, theatre critic Brooks Atkinson labeled the play 'Marxism à la Mother Goose'.[53] The city closed the show suddenly after the controversy about the play grew in the press.

In his analysis of *Beavers*, Drew Chappelle notes how historical research has drawn attention to two opposing factions, the FTP and anti-communist members and writers, but has neglected to include other voices that reveal 'more nuanced stories'.[54] Not choosing sides in the debate, these voices include reviewers, audience members and actors who significantly add to the discourse around the project 'through their own constructions of the material'.[55] Their stories raise questions about 'art aimed at young people as a site of ideological struggle'.[56]

In Moscow we find similar examples of the ways in which the cultural position of TYA adapted to cultural and political shifts in society. Van De Water notes that after the October Revolution of 1917, TYA in the Soviet Union functioned 'as an instrument of the totalitarian regime reflecting and perpetuating the official ideology of Marxism-Leninism'.[57] 'However, the rapid changes in material circumstances – political, social, cultural, and economic – that started in the mid-1980s with the launch of Glasnost and Perestroika, significantly challenged traditional Soviet ideology.'[58] These changes in the function of TYA led to 'A collective state of awareness involving a plurality of cultural expressions.'[59] As such culture in post-totalitarian Russia became a site for self-reflection. This change was exemplified by a play called *Pitfall*, which dealt with themes of peer pressure, loneliness, love and cruelty.[60] The play posed questions without giving answers and was less moralizing than previous plays.[61]

After the dissolution of the Soviet Union in 1991, TYA playwrights responded by producing more traditional plays such as *Bérénice* by Jean Racine and Frances Hodgson Burnett's *Little Lord Fauntleroy*.[63] 'Particularly in the first half of the decade the theatre continued to distance itself from the "outside" world by emphasizing humanitarian content and universal values in classical productions,' writes Van De Water.[64]

While TYA comments on culture, politics and society in various ways, Shifra Schonmann laments, 'The power of the didactic approach in TYA is still unshaken.'[65] Indeed moralizing theatre that aims to change social behavior is alive and well. Researcher Jeanne Kleine points out that viewing theatre in itself does not cause social changes in behavior: 'Just because children can distinguish moral from immoral behaviors does not necessarily mean that they will transfer such "learning" to their own future behaviors.'[66] Kleine advocates a model of aesthetic processing where questions of framing devices, perceived reality, satire and irony are 'tackled during production conferences and rehearsal processes from children's perspectives to communicate intended choices best'.[67] With this model, which is similar to that of the Bonderman Symposium, Kleine advocates theatre makers to predict responses of young people from a more informed knowledge base.[68] With improved understanding of responses, productions can be better tailored for transferring learning to future behaviors.

While understanding student responses is important, oftentimes it is the unplanned and unexpected outcomes that lead to positive change, as the following vignette demonstrates. The vignette describes how a theatre for young people with multiple learning disabilities emerged after the Oily Cart British Theatre Company finished and reflected on earlier theatre work with youth.

### ❖ Case vignette: Oily Cart Theatre Company

Oily Cart was created in 1981 and their mission is to provide inventive, communal and multi-stimulatory theatre for young audiences and children with mild to severe learning disabilities throughout the UK.[69] What led Oily Cart to this mission? It started after the company performed one of its under-five shows for an audience of four- to 19-year-olds at a special needs school in west London. It was 1988, and the company discovered that the highly interactive and multisensory performance styles they were utilizing appealed to young people with learning disabilities. Further reflection and examination brought Artistic Director Tim Webb to realize that their shows were 'so interactive, so dependant on one-to-one work, in which the individual performer could continuously adapt their performance to the requirements of each participant, that a meaningful theatrical experience could transpire for young people with autism'.[70]

Consequently in 1996 Oily Cart introduced its first series of performances expressly for children with PMLD (profound and multiple learning disabilities). The company has since expanded its performances to include young people with ASD (autism spectrum disorders), reaching their audiences using one-on-one interaction and artistically adaptable performance. Never exceeding 30 people in total, Oily Cart audiences include a caretaker for each child as each person is provided a unique experience that reflects his or her own way of communicating.[71] The company incorporates non-conventional means to engage its audience, including hydrotherapy pools, trampolines, aromatherapy, video projection and puppetry.[72] Oily Cart's productions resist the conventional relationship between performer and audience and use fantastical settings that welcome their audiences.

### Perspectives from the field

Oily Cart's success substantiates a great need for their specialized work. Like-minded TYA artists substantiate the reputation of the entire field. In this section we highlight the views of two well established TYA practitioners, the playwright José Cruz González, and the director Tony Graham.

## TYA Playwright José Cruz González

José Cruz González's plays include, among many others, *The Blue House*, *Earth Songs*, *Salt and Pepper* and *Harvest Moon*.[73] González wrote for *PAZ*, the Emmy Award-nominated television series, and he teaches theatre at California State University, Los Angeles.

González discussed collaborations and influences that led him to write plays for young people, many of which speak to Latina/Latino experiences.

> I really admired Luis Valdez and El Teatro Campesino for the brilliant social-political theatre work they did during the 1960 through 1980s.[74] El Teatro Campesino brought the Chicano/Mexican-American on to the stage, capturing the imagination and representing our community in ways we had never seen before. *Zoot Suit* is a perfect example of this. During my university studies I was able to intern with El Teatro Campesino, interact with Jerzy Grotowski at UC Irvine, tour internationally and explore new theatre work at South Coast Repertory. During my professional years it was at South Coast Repertory where we created the Hispanic Playwrights Project. The goal of the program was to develop new plays by Latino/Latina playwrights from across the country.
>
> One of the positive trends I have seen over the past 30 years is more Latino/a artists entering into the mainstream of theatre. This also applies to theatre for youth. It is still small but growing. I've also seen more Latino/a theatre artists now teaching at colleges and universities across the country.
>
> Creating new work for children rewards me because it is direct, personal and honest. I entered into the professional world of Theatre for Youth starting with New Vision/New Voices at the Kennedy Center in 1996. There I met David Saar, artistic director of Childsplay and Carol North of Metro Theater in St Louis, and my publisher Gayle Sergel of Dramatic Publishing. At Childsplay, David Saar made me a part of his company which I have been with for 13 years as playwright-in-residence. I am grateful also to Carol North at Metro Theater for allowing me to explore and produce work that is non-traditional, such as *Earth Songs*, a winter solstice piece that premiered in 2004 bringing together many different artistic communities throughout St Louis. Another compelling

person I worked with is Dorothy Webb at the Bonderman. Dorothy has continued to involve me as a playwright over the years. Her work involving children on new play development is brilliant and I now apply her techniques to my own process.

Bill Rauch and Cornerstone Theater in Los Angeles introduced me to community-based work. Creating work with people that know nothing about the art form is significant to me, and with the Cornerstone Theater, I spent eight months interviewing people in a small town in central California, creating a play about them, for them and with them. This experience changed me personally.[75]

González's mentors in El Teatro Campesino also influenced the emergence of Chicano youth theatres and TYA productions in the 1970s, 80s and 90s.[76] Despite this movement, according to Cecilia Aragón, today there are no professional TYA companies focusing on Chicano youth, and it is difficult to find professional adult theatres that include Chicano children's plays.[77] However Aragón applauds the few professional TYA theatre companies 'that have made efforts to produce plays for and by Chicano children and youth', including Childsplay and the Kennedy Center.[78] In line with González's observations, Aragón notes that these efforts have not only led to 'an outgrowth of Chicana/o TYA interest, but also a new Chicana/o generation of playwrights and scholars such as Josefina López, C. C. Casas, Lorenzo Garcia, Christina Marín,' and Cecilia Aragón herself.[79]

Incorporating adolescent characters in their plays, other diverse Latino/a playwrights include Silvia González, Milcha Sanchez Scott, Cheerie Moraga, Migdalia Cruz and Nilo Cruz.[80] Lorenzo Garcia states that 'the public performance of adolescent memory as practiced through the writing of these adult playwrights powerfully challenges the imperative to portray Latina/o youth as violent, outlaw, marginal identity jeopardizing the integrity of the US culture.'[81]

In one example Garcia analyzes the cultural significance of the play *Night Train to Bolina* by Nilo Cruz,[82] revealing how it breaks down the stereotype of Mexican migration to the US. Garcia notes that in the play, 'What is particularly significant is that migration is not portrayed solely in terms of coercion and loss, or life-long obligation to return to the homeland before losing identity and morality. Instead, it is tied to a search for a safer world within which to shape their lives into something vibrant and triumphant.'[83]

From the interview we discover that González cherished the experience of working with non-professional community members to create a play. And we learn that González thrived with the support of mentors and TYA companies. His experience highlights the need for theatres and university programs to support emerging artists.

## TYA director Tony Graham

Founded in 1947 the Unicorn Theatre is the oldest professional theatre for children in the UK. In addition to creating their own productions, they bring in theatre companies from around the world.[84] The artistic director of the Unicorn from 2000 to 2010 was Tony Graham.

Tony Graham initially trained to be a social studies teacher. He learned to teach drama through in-service courses at the now-closed Drama and Tape Centre, the headquarters of the drama advisory to the Inner London Education Authority (ILEA).[85]

After teaching for more than ten years, and stints with the ILEA Drama Advisory team and TAG Theatre Company in Glasgow, he became artistic director of the Unicorn Theatre in London. Graham describes the journey that led him from teaching social studies to working in TYA:

> I trained to be a drama teacher for one outstanding reason. My teaching wasn't working. I recall one overcast afternoon in the late 70s trying to teach town planning to a group of bored 14-year-old girls. In our resources cupboard was a once shiny-covered box-set containing a simulation exercise about town planning. It looked dusty, old-fashioned and uninviting. The girls were required to take on various roles as councillors, planners, tenants, politicians and so on. I asked the girls to shift their traditionally-arranged desks in order to represent a council room. From that point on, the girls woke up. I didn't anticipate that changing the space might prove to be so dynamic. But it awoke a hope, an expectation and a change in perspective. By entering into various roles, the girls' previously undirected energies were released and increasingly focused. The staid classroom had borrowed the magical language and potential of theatre.[86]

This educational drama experience stayed with Graham as he moved into a professional theatre career. Graham contrasts drama and theatre:

> A drama presupposes a virtual, imaginary world peopled by characters who remind us of people we know. To be dramatic, something has to change. This can only happen when those virtual people do something. So it's always reassuring when we see characters doing something. It tends

to help if they get into a mess. The messier the better. Along the way, choices need to be made in front of our eyes. Real choices that will have serious implications. Will Hamlet do what the Ghost tells him to do? Will Ranyevskaya act to save her precious orchard? Will Peter Pan ever (choose to) grow up? A drama will often feature an unfolding and a revelation. But heaven forefend that we use drama to teach a lesson, or preach morality, or reveal what we already know. Great drama is always ambiguous, open and complex. All of which is easier to say than to realize.

Theatre requires an audience and an actor or two and, ideally, but not necessarily, a drama. It does not always involve a theatre, a stage, curtains, lights, or even an all-singing, all-dancing chorus line, although in my experience this can really help lift one's spirits. The opening sentence to Peter Brook's *The Empty Space* answers this question so beautifully: 'I can take any empty space and call it a bare stage. A man walks across this empty space whilst someone else is watching him, and this is all that is needed for an act of theatre to be engaged.'[87]

Finally Graham provided insights regarding shifts in TYA that he sees driving the work forward:

> Often it's the 'marginal' areas such as work for the very young or work for mixed ability audiences that are driving us all forward. There is much more of an international exchange than ever. The advanced cohort of Europeans has raised the stakes in the search for quality, and, for example, forced us to relook at the all-important nature of the transaction between the act of theatre and our young audiences.[88]

While Graham identifies positive trends in TYA here, some argue that what keeps it from becoming a major art form is its tendency to put education ahead of aesthetics and entertainment. Others believe that education must be integral to Children's Theatre. Generalizing the field, James Kincaid critically asserts that TYA is a training lesson in what adults want children to be.[89] Indeed overly didactic TYA fuels Kincaid's case. However values of education are found in all sorts of plays, as Landy noted:

> Even those who would claim that didacticism and teaching have no place in theatre for young audiences must be mindful that no piece of theatre is value-free, and that audiences are very much involved in the everyday process of clarifying values and making sense of the world they live in, all experience in acting or viewing potential evidence to affirm or challenge their understanding and awareness.[90]

Undoubtedly different contexts will dictate the degree to which a play is explicit in teaching its message. When a religious play is performed to affirm the faith of its viewers, as we shall see below, it aims to deliver an explicit message. Nevertheless whether a TYA production is didactic or entertaining or both, the performance must engage young people. Quite often this is achieved through strong aesthetic elements in the acting and design of the play.

Another significant way to engage young audiences is through the incorporation of youth voices, as Aurand Harris advocated and Dorothy Webb continues to endorse with playwrights at the Bonderman. For Laurie Brooks, acclaimed TYA playwright, it's important to capture the voices of young people so that audiences hear themselves represented accurately on stage.[91] Undoubtedly young people's insights will lead to more authentic portraits of their stories.

## Theatre in education

TIE is an example of intentional issue-based young people's theatre. The emphasis is on education as much as, or in some cases, more than entertainment, to the detriment of aesthetic production.[92] For funders looking to address a specific issue, this thematic approach is appealing.

## History and development of TIE

TIE programs started in the UK. The first TIE team was at the Belgrade Theatre in Coventry, England, in 1965. Progressive British governments of that time were willing to support the arts, but only if the art was based in communities. Money was not the only impetus for TIE's development. The influence of political and popular theatre movements, most notably Brechtian Epic Theatre, also played a role. Likewise the work of Augusto Boal in the 1970s impacted the growth of TIE. The Standing Council of Young People's Theatre (SCYPT) was a key supporter of TIE's development in Britain.[93]

TIE is a labor-intensive and highly collaborative form of Educational Drama. It requires an additional set of skills beyond the regular training of professional actors. As such, the team members are called actor-teachers to reflect the addition of a pedagogical approach to their acting work.

To create a TIE program, actor-teachers conduct research in a chosen subject area and collaboratively devise a play which includes ways for students to participate in the performance. Actor-teachers not only learn their lines and develop their characters, but also prepare themselves for improving within the work based on the questions from the participating audience of young people. Additionally TIE teams provide professional development workshops for teachers so that they can both prepare their students and follow-up on learning afterwards.

Unlike DIE, TIE is not tied to a specific school curriculum. Companies devise new scripts and work with teachers, but are not based in schools. John O'Toole notes:

> First, the material is usually specially devised, tailor-made to the needs of the children and the strengths of the team. Secondly, the children are often asked to participate; endowed with roles, they learn skills, make decisions, and solve problems. Thirdly, teams are usually aware of the importance of the teaching context, and try to prepare suggestions for follow-up work, or to hold preliminary workshops for the class teachers.[94]

The TIE work O'Toole describes sounds similar to contemporary Process Drama and Mantle of the Expert work. It requires time – both in preparation and implementation, and willingness on the part of the school for companies to come into classrooms and disrupt the usual routine for one or more days.

O'Toole paints a rich picture of TIE and identifies its roots in Children's Theatre groups that performed in schools, luring young people away from television.[95] Additionally progressive educational ideas of the 1960s influenced TIE, which took off when both fields of theatre and education saw the value in collaboration.

TIE did not start out with fully developed models. Each theatre company put its own spin on the work based on the skills of its members and the needs of the school. Jeremy Turner of the Welsh Arad Goch Theatre Company noted, 'I don't think there is any more such a thing as traditional TIE. I'm not sure that there ever was. There was a way of working that some companies used. But I don't think that that is the only TIE pattern. There were other patterns even in the early days.'[96]

While the work started off as a 'one-off', TIE teams saw the pedagogical value in spending more time in schools, thus adding more days to their programs. The level of participation varied from including students as characters to asking them to make decisions on how a play should end.

As the British government became more conservative, its focus shifted away from the arts in education to more quantifiably measured forms of learning. Consequently the money for TIE in the UK dried up. To stay afloat some performed their plays for much larger audiences and without the participatory component. Less time was spent on professional development. Reflection, that was a key component of TIE, was replaced by study guides or shortened post-performance reflection periods. In response Roger Wooster argued that TIE teams need to respond to the needs of children, not the educators.[97]

## Changes in TIE: Identity crisis?

TIE's evolution occurred naturally from its very inception as new drama strategies developed. In Britain international influences such as Boal's Theatre of the Oppressed made their way into the work of such groups as the Greenwich Young People's Theatre under the direction of Chris Vine.[98] Outside the UK theatre companies in Australia, the US and other parts of the world added their own stamp to TIE. As John O'Toole and Penny Bundy noted, TIE that developed outside of England needed to find its own way within the educational settings, political leanings, interests and financial considerations of its place.[99]

Despite the changes and valiant efforts of TIE teams, TIE waned as the 1980s unfolded. However fresh collaboration gave it renewed life in the late 1980s and early 1990s. As the AIDS/HIV crisis grew, TIE found a new collaborator in Health Education.[100] Rather than limiting itself to its traditional place in the classroom, TIE found space in health care settings. This marked a shift in TIE as it moved into the realm of Applied Theatre, discussed in Chapter 4.

## Pitfalls in practice

O'Toole noted that TIE was not universally embraced nor was it always well done. Some TIE teams were diligent about developing their pedagogy and creating sound work while others put forth theatre that was poorly produced, unrelated to children's interests and, in some cases, exploitative. Turner noted, '[O]ur emphasis is on the theatrical: if the theatre's good, the education's good. If the theatre's crap, the education will be crap.'[101] Emelie Fitzgibbon agreed: 'You have to honor the art form ... for there's no point in having bad theatre and making it work because it is educational.'[102]

In a paper exploring the application of TIE to HIV/AIDS in a mining community in South Africa, Maritz cautioned theatre educators, especially those working outside of their own communities, to be aware not only of their goals, but also whose interests are driving it.[103] He noted a failure on the part of TIE teams to understand socio-cultural aspects of South African life and believed that many TIE programs attack symptoms rather than actual problems. Additionally while the educational information imparted may appear helpful on the surface, neglecting to consider cultural issues can lead to misperceptions.

Similar to Turner and Fitzgibbon, Lowell Swortzell identified an aesthetic flaw within TIE, specifically with TIE scripts, 'Often sounding like the assembly-job construction they were, texts tended to lack individual dramatic voices that audiences could hear in performance or later could recall.'[104] Swortzell contended that TYA playwrights offer a better product than those devised by TIE companies because 'they can plot stories step-by-step and thereby gain the dramatic weight needed to support an issue which gives the play a life of its own'.[105]

To better understand where TIE is today, we go further into the field and see what work is being done.

The first thing to notice is the lack of TIE companies. Many professional TYA theatres such as the Metro Theater Company (St Louis, MO), the Seattle Children's Theatre (Seattle, WA) and the Polka Theatre (London) refer to doing school residencies or workshops, but they do not engage in TIE.[106] In contrast, at Western Carolina University, their TIE program both trains the next generation of TIE artist teachers while providing TIE experiences for the community. As noted on their website, 'the mission of TIE is to present programs that are artistically excellent, educationally relevant, and socially, culturally, and environmentally literate'.[107]

Other groups, such as arepp:Theatre for Life based in South Africa, refer to their work as Applied Theatre.[108] This is also true of the Creative Arts Team (CAT), based in the City University of New York (CUNY), which was featured in the 1982 *Handbook* as a TIE team and now refers to itself as 'the international leader in Applied Theatre – interactive drama for learning and change'.[109] Is this change of title due to a fundamental difference in their work or is it more of a cultural shift? Wooster notes that in Wales at least two TIE companies no longer refer to their work as such, while others 'question the relevance of the term to their work'.[110]

While it would be comforting to applaud the ability of TIE teams to survive financial cut-backs and other struggles, through the many changes made to the traditional TIE format which allowed that survival, Wooster provides a somber reminder of what TIE was and how it has changed,

It has been TIE's ability to hybridize the worlds of play, reflection, personal development, and self-education together with theatrical constructs that gave it its value. If this is now being ignored, then TIE may be regarded as little more than a spectator activity in schools that could be easily replaced by theatre visits or even video, supported by teaching materials.[111]

In considering Wooster's argument, we take a look at an organization that demonstrates how TIE has responded to the educational, financial and technological challenges of the early 21st century.

### ❖  Case vignette: Living voices theatre

Living Voices is a national performance arts organization that uses theatre, video and live interaction with storytelling to enable young audiences to engage with historical events and characters.[112] Using highly skilled and dynamic actors who travel around the US, Living Voices helps fulfill the curricula of countless schools. Natalie Burgess, a former actor-teacher for the organization, explains:

> Before beginning the show, we presented a quick overview of the pertinent history and what the show was about. I did two shows about immigration, one about the Holocaust and another play that dealt with women's suffrage.
>
> Each actor really used her own skills as an educator in that introductory time. After the introduction we pressed play on a DVD or a video [...] And next to us on the screen was the archival photography and film footage from that particular time period telling that specific story. It was either a new picture coming that illustrated the spoken word, or the actor interacted with the voices coming through the video. That became our set and our other characters. After the performance, out of character, we discussed the themes of the play and our characters with the kids, facilitating a sharing of their observations.[113]

But is this TIE? Have the additions of new Educational Drama forms such as Process Drama and Applied Theatre rendered TIE redundant? Is TIE so burdened with misperceptions and alterations that the name is meaningless? Have the needs of schools and the lack of financial support altered the landscape for professional theatres so that they no longer can do TIE? The answer appears to be a combination of factors. While TIE developed at a time when theatricality and progressive educational thought were an ideal marriage of theory and practice, education is more outcome-based today. Live theatre struggles to maintain legitimacy and appeal in a communications environment saturated by the Internet, video games, television and film. While TIE may still have the power to effectively work in some areas of the world, Applied Theatre has supplanted TIE as the preferred method of educating through theatre. We explore this in some depth in the next chapter.

## Youth theatre

The relatively new term Youth Theatre describes a wide variety of organizations that engage young people of all ages in theatre-related activities. Many Youth Theatres focus on introducing young people to theatre arts and developing theatre skills that culminate in performance. Others emphasize the young person's personal development through performances that might be studio-based or presented at a theatre. The Pennsylvania Youth Theatre (PYT) is inspired by the notion that 'process and product are one; and that art and education can skillfully and sensitively conspire to share a common soul'.[114]

Youth Theatre activities involve devising, creating and staging work. PYT's Performing Arts School maintains a comprehensive after-school performing arts curriculum, which includes Creative Drama, acting, dance and voice instruction.

Some artists and teachers work in Youth Theatre to explore social issues with young people, including themes of racism, intolerance and discrimination. Some stay away from such charged and challenging topics. Others may even feel racism is no longer a pressing topic. Indeed social activist and author bell hooks notes that 'while it is a positive aspect of our culture that folks want to see racism end; paradoxically, it is this heartfelt longing that underlies the persistence of the false assumption that racism has ended'.[115] Undoubtedly minority youth still face racial discrimination regularly, and Youth Theatre is one place outside schools where such topics can be explored.

Christina Marín worked with a bilingual Youth Theatre group called Teatro Movimiento Ollin: Una Fuerza Lateen@ (TeMO) to explore how 'social institutions such as schools, mass media, and popular culture represent and perpetuate negative stereotypes of Latinas'.[116] Based in her knowledge of the group, Marín developed a research protocol to study how youth '"read the world" as a result of their social interactions in various cultural and educational settings'.[117]

Marín incorporated several techniques outlined by Boal, including Newspaper Theatre and Image Theatre, and had the young people work with 'numerous formats of popular culture and media, including song lyrics, magazine images and articles, movies, and Internet sites'.[118] Through this process, 'the participants developed a theatrical representation of their negotiation with the story as they "performed" their reading of an unjust world that creates barriers for immigrants, like themselves, who are affected by education policies'.[119]

Many Youth Theatre companies emphasize creating and sharing young people's stories. The viBe Theater Experience, based in New York City, is a non-profit organization dedicated to empowering teenage girls through the creation of original, uncensored performances. ViBe serves teenage girls who write and perform collaborative pieces about real-life issues. The girls are encouraged to express their unique voices, take on challenges and gain the self-confidence to succeed personally, socially and academically.[120] Former viBe director and co-founder, Dana Edell notes, 'As a way to counter the potential for racial discrimination to lower adolescents' self-esteem, the girls of color in viBe push messages of ethnic pride and present themselves as confident and strong.'[121]

To critically examine and build theory around her teaching practice, Edell conducted qualitative research on viBe and was able to find the critical distance needed to honestly scrutinize the organization she co-founded. This included a candid examination of the dangers and challenges of devising original, uncensored theatre with teenage girls.

Edell's findings illuminate the ways in which girls can perpetuate destructive stereotypes, and in fact reproduce clichés in their attempts to empower themselves. Edell's study provides examples of viBe girls who were influenced by 'male-dominated cultural narratives that are a part of their habitus' during their creation of shows.[122] Edell's research questions whether theatre arts programs that claim to empower youth are sometimes doing the opposite and actually silencing authentic stories through celebrating predictable 'safe' stories.

### ❖ Case vignette: The Unusual Suspects Theatre Company

The Unusual Suspects is a Youth Theatre organization based in Los Angeles that uses an instructional program of story development, script writing, improvisation and performance to assist young people in underserved and at-risk environments. Their goals are to promote expression and examine troubling personal and social conflicts. The company was established in response to deteriorated community relations resulting from the 1992 Los Angeles riots and has demonstrated success in a variety of settings including foster care, low income neighborhoods, juvenile correction facilities and gangs. To engender sustainable solutions to problems of gang violence and school dropout, The Unusual Suspects takes a collaborative approach, partnering with the city's Gang Reduction and Youth Development (GRYD) program and the county's Prevention Initiative Demonstration Project, two local programs dedicated to this cause.[123]

The Unusual Suspect's methodology focuses on guiding middle and high school students to create and write plays that are rehearsed and performed for audiences. They work through two separate residencies in playwriting and theatre production. The plays to be produced are developed in the playwriting residency. The Unusual Suspects casts professional actors at the end of each playwriting residency for a public staged reading of the play. After the reading students reverse roles with the actors and participate in a talk-back with the audience.

The following two examples demonstrate the praxis of The Unusual Suspects in their privileging of reflection throughout the developmental process.

## Pacoima Middle School

Montgomery attended a playwriting residency workshop with middle school students in urban Pacoima, California, a community known for gang activity. This residency was under the auspices of the GRYD program. There were four TAs and two volunteers to facilitate the lesson. The executive director of The Unusual Suspects, Sally Fairman, also came to observe the work.

The Unusual Suspects requires all their teaching artists to meet half an hour before workshops to go over the lesson plan and prepare materials. One of the TAs is designated as the workshop coordinator, responsible for keeping the workshop on track.

After the students entered, they were told to make a circle and introduce themselves by expressing how they were feeling on a scale from one to ten. Students were also asked to respond to the question: 'If you were a sport, what would you be?' This checking in, and later a similar checking out process, is a reflective ritual that transpires in every Unusual Suspects setting.

For the main activity of the workshop the participants worked on a character profile. After verbally unpacking the meaning of a character profile, a TA generated ideas from the group on developing one character profile based on an object. The group ended up developing Raul the Coffin who lived underground near a tree in a cemetery. They also came to agreement about Raul's age, other members of his family, how he moved physically, his greatest wish, his greatest fear and his motto for life.

The kids then broke out into smaller groups and began working on creating their own individual character profiles. Afterwards, volunteers acted in role as the characters they had created, fielding questions about themselves from the rest of the class. This was initially modeled by the TA.

Throughout the workshop Montgomery observed a team of teachers who worked together exceedingly well. This was undoubtedly due to their training, knowledge of the population and pre-workshop preparation.

At the conclusion of the workshop the youth once again assigned a number between one and ten that expressed their feelings. After the young people left each member of the team re-capped their challenges and successes, reflecting upon the content of the workshop and the expression of individual students. For example, one TA's challenge was with a male student who was disruptive at various moments in the workshop, while for another TA, this same student was a success because he followed through with the character profile task and shared his role in front of the class. A discussion ensued that compelled each TA to consider the student from varying perspectives.

The TAs explained to Montgomery that when they first started, both the young people and their community distrusted The Unusual Suspects. Compounding the issue, the youth didn't know how to interact positively, and one even ran away during the first day of work. Over time, as TAs and group members got to know each other and the youth realized that their opinions in the workshops mattered, a greater sense of trust emerged. Only then was the group able to accept the clear structures set by the leaders. For The Unusual Suspects, it is the hard work of theatre and constant, ongoing reflection that leads to group ensemble, trust, and personal expression.

This philosophy is in keeping with Dorothy Heathcote's views. In her interview for this book, she advised against delving into the young people's private lives. 'They will use their private understandings,' she said, 'but you are not there to tell them what to dig into or bring to the creative work they do.'[124] Instead you have to 'protect people into looking into human nature,' she stated.[125] The Unusual Suspects participants look at human nature through the protection of creating theatre that is about their lives but within a distanced frame.

Executive Director Sally Fairman shared a success story that revealed how the process of creating and performing a play impacted a young girl and her community:

> In a show called *Love has no Gender*, the reading was done with the professional actors, and it was based on a story of one of the girls who was coming out as a lesbian. The kids rallied behind the girl and her story.

They didn't care if she was gay or not. At the play reading not everyone in the community was ready for that, however. At the end, the father of this girl angrily raised his hand and said, 'I want to know the message of this play.' In a show of support, one of the other young playwrights said, 'This is a play about unity.' Today the kids continue to perform this play and the audience goes nuts. During a more recent talkback, students asked the audience, 'Parents, how did you feel about this play?' And this girl's dad was in the audience, raised his hand and this time offered, 'I just want my daughter to know that I love her very much.' It was electric. And her father has been a champion for us ever since then.[126]

From their participation in The Unusual Suspects, students become aware that they can succeed, develop a new identity and receive the respect they so often lack.

### TA Reflections on Camp David Gonzalez Youth Theatre

At another Unusual Suspects site, a juvenile detention camp called Camp David Gonzalez, the TAs shared with Montgomery some of their overall challenges which included a broken governmental system set up for failure and unchanged home environments.[127] An anecdote was shared about a time when this team of TAs had just finished up a residency. After the final reflection of the final class, 'we left feeling really good about the process, the boys' work and the final production,' said the TA. 'But as we were leaving, one of our boys from the previous residency, a kid who did really well with us, was being processed to come back in to the camp.' He recollected, 'We were feeling good, but that was a sobering sight that brought us back to reality.'

Another TA reflection highlights for us the importance of training all teaching artists in therapeutic matters, 'The teaching artist works to help the boys find and share their voices, and the teaching artist has to try to inspire the boys' he shared. 'However, we can't save the boys. We can simply give them the tools to succeed.' Another TA stated, 'The work fills your heart, but you can't lead with that.'

These sorts of issues always emerge when working in challenging environments. This is a moment where Drama Therapy training is useful, even for those who are not fully trained to be therapists. Because of this lack of training, however, TAs often feel incomplete. We believe that training in therapeutic matters like this is not offered to practitioners nearly as often as it should be, and that such training should be required in university degree programs.

In their Youth Theatre workshops, reflection for students and amongst teachers is a major component of The Unusual Suspects' ethos, one supporting Friere's aim of critical consciousness.[128] In both observed workshops whole group and small group discussions provided varied formats for students to share their insights, discuss concepts about theatre activities and assess their learning. For TAs before and after workshops it was the same. 'This system that works comes from not having worked,' remarked one TA. The shared dialogical spaces assisted everyone to make meaning of their own learning, as well as understand the learning of others, within the process of creating youth theatre.

## The process of production: TYA praxis in practice

Drama in Education practice can be utilized in conjunction with TYA, TIE and Youth Theatre. TYA plays can serve as a pretext for Process Drama work, and Process Drama can feed into the TYA production during rehearsals. Whenever there is a need or desire in rehearsals to explore concepts, assist with skill development, generate aesthetic knowledge and build community, DIE practices can be of great assistance, as the following vignette demonstrates.

### ❖ Case vignette: Process Drama for TYA play rehearsal

During the development of the TYA play *Nasty*, written by Ramon Esquivel, Process Drama was facilitated in rehearsal by Cecily O'Neill, who served as the dramaturg for NYU's New Plays for Young Audiences in 2009.[129] *Nasty* explores friendships, identity and bullying in the context of social networking sites, chat rooms, blogs, tweets, videos and role-playing games on the Internet. The objective of the Process Drama was to help the actors understand the context of the play and more fully realize what was at stake as their middle school characters engaged in various forms of cyber bullying. For Esquivel, the objective of the Process Drama was similarly to clarify the stakes, but also to explore and more fully flesh out the main characters of the piece. In the play, the actors would enact the role of middle school students, but in this Process Drama, they assumed the role of teachers.

In the first rehearsal O'Neill went into role as the school principal to explore with teachers, played by the actors, the cyber bullying problems within the school portrayed in the world of the play. O'Neill facilitated an encounter where overall worries at the fictional school, as well concerns about specific students, were urgently debated. The students that O'Neill referred to in the improvised discussion were characters in the play itself. As teachers, actors gave input regarding the academic and emotional problems they had experienced with their students. They were also compelled to offer solutions for how to deal with the students' problems.

What resulted was a dramatic encounter where the role reversal allowed the actors to take on new perspectives regarding the content and characters in the play, as well as the larger social issue of bullying represented in the play. Esquivel was able to observe and incorporate elements of the improvisation into his script as it continued to be developed throughout rehearsals. This was a dynamic and illuminating improvised drama that fed the playwright's praxis of action, observation, reflection and re-action.

### ❖ Case vignette: Holocaust theatre for young audiences

Plays about the Holocaust and descendants of Holocaust survivors have generated their own genre. Indeed Holocaust education is more important than ever, as survivors die, as deniers find a more global platform upon which to rant and as fascism proliferates in new forms. Unlike film, theatre provides a space for interaction, allowing viewers a space to share their experience with others in the moment. Even an older piece like the children's opera *Brundibár*, first performed in the Theresienstadt concentration camp (Terezin), is mounted regularly.[130] We refer to Tony Kushner's 2006 adaptation in the Introduction.

When Montgomery directed *Kindertransport*, by Diane Samuels, at NYU, he wondered the extent to which he should take responsibility for the education of young people in the audience about Holocaust events.[131] While an accompanying teacher resource guide full of pertinent historical information would be provided, did the play itself provide sufficient history for contemporary students?

He also sat with several questions raised in print by noted scholar Claude Schumacher: 'Can theatre provide the artefacts that will help the spectator towards a better "grasp" of the Holocaust?'[132] Can actors portray Holocaust oppressors or victims 'without glamorizing or demonizing the former and belittling or sanctifying the latter?'[133]

To set the stage for the vignette, *Kindertransport* is about a rescue mission that took place nine months prior to the outbreak of World War II, when the UK took in nearly 10,000 predominantly Jewish children from Nazi occupied territories.[134] As visas became impossible to obtain, a delegation of British Jewish leaders appealed to the Prime Minister of the UK and requested that the government permit the temporary admission of Jewish children and teenagers into the country who would later

**Photograph 3.2** *Kindertransport* (actors Derek Nason and Jessica Schechter), photo by Chianan Yen, courtesy NYU Steinhardt

re-emigrate. Children traveled to the UK on a train that became known as the Kindertransport.

Upon arrival to the UK children were placed in British foster homes, hostels and farms. It is this remarkable rescue mission that provides the context for Samuel's play, which endeavors to unpack the participants' experiences and compels audiences to do the same.

The following reflection was written by Jonathan Shmidt, assistant director of education at the New Victory Theater and an instructor of TYA at NYU. Shmidt describes how a group of Holocaust survivors got involved in the project and in doing so made an enormous impact on the actors and audiences:

Following a performance of Diane Samuels' *Kindertransport*, an audience of high school students faces a panel of Holocaust survivors. In a room full of inner-city teens, a single hand is raised: 'Can you tell me what war this is? Where did this happen?' As the survivors began telling their emotional stories, I watched the faces of the students as they intently listened to a history that seemed completely foreign to them. In that moment, I fully realized the importance of finding new ways to keep these stories alive.

David Montgomery shared my passion to introduce youth to this history, and asked me to serve as his assistant director and dramaturg. We entered this project with our own baggage. While touring as an actor on another Holocaust play, *And Then They Came for Me*, David came into contact with several youth audiences who had little understanding of the Holocaust.[135] As the grandchild of Holocaust survivors, this history has always been a part of my culture. Although David and I felt that we had enough experience to begin our work, we knew that we needed help to ensure our production was culturally sensitive and rich with authenticity.

I began by going directly to the primary source: I contacted the Kindertransport Association (KTA), an organization dedicated to reuniting those who experienced the Kindertransport as children and educating the community on their past.

At first, David and I had hoped to speak with several survivors of the Kindertransport to inform our own understanding of the text. We soon realized that we were given an amazing opportunity through this newfound relationship with the KTA. I arranged meetings between several members of the KTA, their children and the cast of NYU's *Kindertransport*. Before their work on the play began, the company had the rare opportunity to spend time with individuals whose lives were the inspiration for Samuels' play. On the stage of the Provincetown Playhouse, the group sat in a circle and listened to their stories. These individuals gave our cast and crew insight into their experiences as children, as well as the long lasting effects of these events throughout their lives.

Understanding the educational potential of our work, several of the KTA agreed to participate in talkbacks with our audiences following the performances. These incredible moments of conversation and sharing between the audience, the cast and the Kinder proved to be a thought provoking and emotional dialogue for all. The live performance provided the foundation and the spark of engagement for these rich discussions to take place. For this particular production, we were fortunate enough to have the guidance and support of those who experienced these horrors first-hand. However, as the grandchild of survivors, I have always been very aware of the fact that my generation is the last that will have the opportunity to know living survivors of the Holocaust. When the primary sources no longer exist, what happens to the story?

In order to achieve this effect when survivors no longer exist, the artist and the educator must find a way to create a personal connection between the subject material and the student.

Shmidt's vignette reveals how the involvement of the KTA enabled the actors, directors and audience to deeply reflect on the Holocaust, bringing immediacy and weight to the overall theatrical event. It developed through a process of careful research, analysis and art-making. This opened up dialogues among the artists, between the artists and the subjects of their art, between the actors and viewers, and further into the mind and society of all involved. Dramatic and personal interactions such as this educate in a holistic way, provoking feeling and thought and, in some cases, action in a world that continues to perpetrate oppressive acts.

## TYA and religion

Another use of TYA geared toward young people and their families concerns religion. For such theatre, the intended changes for audience members vary. Later on, in Chapter 4, we will look at a specific form we call Theatre of Faith as a subset of Applied Theatre, intended to instill faith within an audience of seekers. Many religiously-based forms of TYA are also about faith, as producers use entertaining forms of spectacle, song and storytelling to preach a faith-based message.

### ❖ Case vignette: Noah the Musical

As an example, Montgomery witnessed a production of *Noah the Musical*, performed by Sight and Sound Theatre in Branson, Missouri. Advertising themselves as the 'Christian Broadway', the production told the biblical story with highly theatrical and entertaining light and sound effects in a brand new, state-of-the-art, 2000 seat theatre.[136]

Act I ended with joyful, tuneful music and voiced exultation to God's greatness while animals paraded down the aisles of the large theatre. In Act II, however, the flood came. The sound of pounding rain began, the thunder cracked at an earsplitting level, the theatre went pitch black and the animals screeched and howled. Characters in the story, including Noah's relatives, who had doubted Noah now begged him from offstage to be allowed to come on board the ark. But Noah could not make room. For God had made it clear that it would be impossible for any non-believers to come on board. Terrible screams of begging, pleading and chaos ensued until eventually the voices ceased. Everyone outside the ark was dead.

This scene was designed to scare the audience. For many the realism of the scene was shocking, for it came in such sharp contrast to the fairy tale quality of Act I. Some adults were likely reminded of real life tragedies involving mass deaths.

After Noah hit dry land and his family promised to repopulate the species, they exited to make room for Jesus to enter through the door of the ark.

The message trumped all the stage effects: accept Christ as your personal savior or you will be damned in your own metaphorical flood.

*Noah the Musical* is unlike TYA shows that seek to raise questions, spark discussion and present multiple perspectives. The message is explicit, didactic and repetitive. In its mix of grisly realism, joyful fantasy, dazzling spectacle and unambiguous message, it lures audiences into experiencing a heavy-handed lesson.

❖ **Case vignette: God Lives in Glass**

In contrast to *Noah the Musical*, a perspective of critical reflection frames *God Lives in Glass*, a musical theatre piece written by Robert Landy and composed by Keith Thompson.[137] The project was conceived around a dinner table when Landy's seven-year-old daughter proclaimed that a Christian classmate accused her, a Jewish girl, of killing Christ. After a long discussion with his daughter and younger son, informing them about the history and legacy of religious intolerance, Landy noticed that his children became bored and began to draw pictures. His daughter created an image of the crucified Christ tormented by a figure looking surprisingly like her. She told her father: 'That isn't me.' His five-year-old son drew a blob behind bars with a sad expression, surrounded by small figures of the crucified Christ. When asked to tell a story about his drawing, he said: 'The Jew is in jail.'

After realizing that his children were reacting to the story of Jews as Christ-killers through art, Landy wondered how other children might depict their relationship to God. He wondered whether there was a way to better understand the seeds of religious intolerance through the drawings and stories of children.

Throughout the late 1990s, Landy developed an arts-based research methodology, asking children to draw pictures, tell stories and role-play in response to a series of questions regarding their views of God. He traveled widely and trained interviewers throughout the world to implement the research protocol with children in various economic, cultural and political conditions. Some lived in war zones; others in relatively secure locales. He collected hundreds of drawings and stories and descriptions of the role-plays, analyzed the data and wrote two books about his research.[138]

In 2002 Landy adapted his book *God Lives in Glass* into a play. It was performed as part of a storytelling series at the Provincetown Playhouse

**Illustration 3.1   Jew in Jail, drawing by Mackey Landy, 2001, courtesy of Robert Landy**

through the Program in Educational Theatre at NYU. As expected there was a family audience in attendance, with children from pre-school through adolescence. Following the performance, Landy worked with director Greg Ganakas and composer Keith Thompson to create a musical theatre piece. All songs were written and composed in collaboration, as Landy and Thompson reflected upon the pictures and stories created by the children from all around the world.

Over a period of eight years, the musical play *God Lives in Glass* has itself been part of a developmental praxis, as each performance has led to further reflection and change. All those involved in the creative process, including audience members, have offered their commentary and the creators responded by re-shaping the form and content. The piece has been performed in concert version with a large chorus of mostly adults. The piece has also been performed in play version by young performers to young audiences in schools, theatres and camps.

In 2010 it was produced by Broadway Bound in Seattle, Washington, with a cast of adolescent actors. By way of introduction:

> Broadway Bound Children's Theatre transforms the lives of children, ages 5–18, through active participation in theatre arts combining a fun and supportive atmosphere with professional standards. Children of all skill levels and backgrounds are challenged and supported while developing their mental, physical, emotional, social and creative potential through the joy and discipline of live theatre.[139]

Broadway Bound's production featured a cast of mostly young people of color who performed to family audiences and created a theatrical experience reflecting the cultural traditions of the performers as well as those of the children whose stories inspired the piece.

The intention of the creators of *God Lives in Glass* is similar to that of others we feature in this chapter, and indeed to that of most engaging theatre artists – to offer an aesthetically-pleasing window onto the world. In this case, two worlds are explored – that of the child, and that of the spiritual beyond or within the child.

**Photograph 3.3   Overture, *God Lives in Glass*, photo by Nigel Cooper, courtesy of Broadway Bound Children's Theatre**

As representative of theatre for young audiences, *God Lives in Glass* seeks to pose questions to audiences, in this case about the nature of God and about religious tolerance and cultural diversity. The questions, as noted in an early song, are presented through the eyes of a child.

The title song is taken from an interview with a seven-year-old girl from South Africa, who reflected upon her drawing of God, looking suspiciously like herself, encased in a shimmering diamond, as follows: 'God lives in glass and is shaped by the wind.' The lyrics to the song point to the relationship between self and God as seen through the refracted images of mirrors and windows:

> God lives in glass and is shaped by the wind,
> I don't know where God ends and where I begin,
> When I look out through the glass I see the sky
> When I look in the mirror, There am I,
> There am I.[140]

As to tolerance, another song, 'Missiles and Stars', features two young people looking up at the sky. One, who lives in a battle zone similar to Iraq in 2003, sees deadly missiles flying overhead. The other, who lives in a peaceful village, watches the shooting stars late at night. In chorus they both ask:

> Look at the missiles, look at the stars,
> See the destruction, see the creation,
> How could this happen, there's just one sky above us,
> Didn't the maker of missiles and stars
> Equally love us,
> Equally love us,
> Equally love us?[141]

As in most plays for young audiences, and in keeping with the spirit of the arts-based research, there is abundant humor. When one 11-year-old girl from Northern Ireland was asked in an interview to tell a story about God, she said: 'Not everyone goes straight to heaven. You can go to hell or puberty or something.' From that remark came the song 'Puberty', which begins with the verse:

> It's often said that when you die,
> Your soul will leave you by and by,
> Some folks go straight to Heaven, some to Hell

But wouldn't it be swell, when I'm dead,
If I could go to Puberty instead.[142]

*God Lives in Glass* focuses upon many phases of childhood as young people develop images of themselves within their material and spiritual worlds, shaped very much by the winds of culture, politics and psychology. Based in a research process that was itself based in a random dinner table conversation, it suggests a praxis that raises unanswered questions. Although audiences, young and old, do not leave the theatre with closure as to the nature of God or religious tolerance, many have reported a need to draw their own pictures and tell their own stories to those willing to listen.

Each theatre project involving young people is profoundly influenced by social, cultural, educational, political and financial policies that either facilitate or hinder progress. Politics play a part in TYA, TIE and Youth Theatre when creative decisions are based upon a reading of community values. Many organizations identify themselves by their target audiences, whether families, young children or teens.

To be as inclusive as possible, youth theatres may utilize large casts, or when financial constraints or requirements by a professional organization like LORT are in play, theatres may require a small cast to tour schools. Some will be commercially driven and need to produce familiar crowd pleasers. However, even where commercial theatre drives ticket sales, new work is produced. 'David Saar at Childsplay has opportunities for perhaps two plays per season to take risks' noted Johnny Saldaña.[143]

Whether young people are the target audience, participants or creators of theatre, it is important that their ideas become part of the theatre-making process. As we saw in Chapters 1 and 2, best practice involves young people reflecting upon their experiences in drama and theatre. Without their creative contributions to a Youth Theatre production, a new TYA play or a TIE piece, there is less likelihood that the experience will be relevant and vital. With their input, the praxis of theatre for, by and with young people will continue to strive toward excellence.

# PART II   DRAMA AND THEATRE IN SOCIAL ACTION

Theatre for Change has deep roots in the community, which, over the past 30 years, has become as significant a site for praxis as the school. In fact, as many DIE and TIE programs lost their funding due to austerity budgets and back-to-basics agendas, the field has grown in other directions, including Applied Theatre, Playback Theatre and Drama Therapy practiced within many community venues. In this section we will look at the dramatic activities and theatre performances within a variety of community spaces, all of which serve to realize the aims of social awareness and change.

In speaking about drama and theatre in social action, we focus upon community organizations, with the recognition that such organizations serve to enhance or, in some cases, to restrict the quality of life of individuals. Although we discussed schools in Chapters 1 and 2, we shall see that many forms of Applied Theatre occur in schools. However, as these activities are most often extracurricular, they offer an enhanced approach to teaching and learning quite different from the standard academic curriculum.

In 2009 Palgrave Macmillan initiated a series called *Theatre &,* several short books on the relationship between theatre and key issues. Within the series many of the authors write of theatre's connection to the community. In one, *Theatre & Globalization,* Rebellato helps to contextualize performance within the community by addressing issues of globalization.[1] In viewing globalization from an economic perspective, Rebellato speaks about theatre as a commodity, giving examples of internationally franchised mega-hits such as Disney's *The Lion King* and *Beauty and the Beast.* He also warns against the exploitation of culture-specific experience by, for example, Western theatre artists who make use of exotic Eastern or African cultural forms to serve their own aesthetic and economic ends back home. Rebellato gives as an example Peter Brook's use of a sacred Hindu text, the *Mahabharata,* as a pretext to create a highly acclaimed production popular within Western theatres.

However Rebellato also argues for the positive influence of globalization upon theatre, as previously isolated forms of performance become available to wider audiences. He gives a classic example of Artaud's first experience of the power of Balinese theatre at the 1931 Paris Colonial Exposition, which influenced his first manifesto of the Theatre of Cruelty. For our purposes, we focus upon the cultural and aesthetic qualities of a globalized world, where cross-cultural experience provides a rich source of fertilization. As an example, Boal's work in Theatre of the Oppressed (TO) has taken deep root in several cultures, including India, where the movement Jana Sanskriti has organized around Boal's praxis within rural Indian communities.[2]

Conversely, Jan Cohen-Cruz, in her book Local Acts, argues for a more grassroots applied form of theatre, looking at the model of Community-based Theatre.[3] For Cohen-Cruz, globalization has deprived communities of the value of creating theatre that pertains to their lives. She argues for localization in performance. The work of Jana Sanskriti also supports her point of view, as it clearly translates the ideas of TO into the local cultural idioms of rural India.

In the cultural life of communities worldwide, the performing arts are most clearly visible in the media of television, film, theatre and the Internet. In fact, one major cultural shift in the past 30 years has been the presentation of self through the Internet. On sites such as Facebook, people present themselves in various desirable roles, as individuals and as part of a wide social network of friends. Local and global communities become instantly visible on Facebook. On YouTube virtually anybody with a computer and webcam can perform virtually any dramatic action that, once posted, becomes available to a global audience. In addition, with the immense popularity of role-playing games, such as World of Warcraft, which boasted upwards of 11 million international subscribers in 2008, the global community is linked through vast networks of players.[4]

With the new technologies people participate dramatically in global communities simply by logging onto their computers. In doing so, they engage in a virtual community even as they are isolated from actual ones. In many ways this state of affairs is antithetical to the more social, political and therapeutic purposes of drama and theatre, as it represents engagement through disengagement. And yet these dramas serve a purpose in the lives of the players, not too dissimilar from that of actual dramas – to take meaningful, often risky action into a mysterious world in the hope of discovering something new.

Most applied forms of community drama, however, are very low-tech and interpersonal. In his 1982 *Handbook*, Landy focused upon several community organizations including the museum, the church, the police department, schools with special programs for inner city youth and organizations for people with disabilities. Over the past 30 years, these and similar organizations continue to provide drama and theatre opportunities for the purpose of education, rehabilitation, recreation and therapy. However, as we shall see, many practices have expanded, most notably Applied Theatre, which will be discussed in Chapter 4.

As previously stated, the examples we choose of praxis in Applied Theatre are based upon our personal experience, field research and review of the published literature. There are several venues reviewed in the previous *Handbook* that we omit, such as the museum. Although drama and theatre in this venue is not as prominent as it once was, specialists continue to work within museums, underscoring the ongoing relationship between culture, cultural artifacts and performance.[5]

Further, we debated how to speak about the application of drama and theatre to religion. We decided to discuss examples of theatre designed to promote a particular faith, an unorthodox choice as these forms of performance tend to be more doctrinaire than dialogical. And yet we made our choice with an understanding that the roots of theatre are firmly planted in the soil of ritual and religion. Also, we recognized that in religious proselytizing, theatre is often used to facilitate change from doubt to dedication, a change that is personal, but that requires social action.

In considering Theatre of Faith, we became aware of a more general connection between theatre, culture and worship. An example follows:

### ❖ Case vignette: When in Rome – The church-museum–theatre axis

When in Rome, researching the connection between Social Theatre and Drama Therapy, Landy noted the link between church and museum on visits to the Vatican and many Renaissance churches housing some of the great Western artworks. The dramas depicted by Michelangelo in the Sistine Chapel are legend, not just because of the subject matter of creation and punishment, paradise lost and found, but also of the dramatically ambiguous images of struggle between flesh and spirit, eroticism and celibacy, subjects especially contemporary in the second decade of the 21st century as the church fathers were confronted with hundreds of allegations of pedophilia.

After viewing an extraordinary exhibition of Caravaggio's major paintings in the Scuderie del Quirinale museum in early 2011, many depicting religious subjects erotically and mundane subjects spiritually, Landy attended a new play called *The Last Words of Caravaggio*, which attempted to speak to these very contradictions through performance.

While walking through the ancient Roman Coliseum, and noting the many complex levels of architecture, history, narrative and myth, Landy became aware of the nature of the cultural spectacles performed during the Roman Empire. This was a theatre of cruelty surpassing the imagination of Artaud, and at the same time, a ritual celebration in praise of beauty and athleticism. Not only were thousands of animals slaughtered for sport, but also humans. Further, in theatrical performance, when the text of an ancient myth called for death, those unfortunate enough to be cast in the role of victim were killed on stage.

In certain stylized dance performances, the producers had more concern with titillating stage effects than verisimilitude. At times the dancers were set on fire to create aesthetically pleasing movements of flaying bodies burning to death. This was a cruel form of catharsis for the amusement and horror of the audience beyond the imagination of Aristotle. As in contemporary bullfights and boxing matches, the performances in the Roman Coliseum satisfied the cultural needs of many for violent spectacle. It also satisfied people's spiritual needs as it presented rituals intensely more active than those that would be developed in the Roman Catholic Church, which offered its own narrative of torture and redemption, but through highly symbolic means.

In locating their greatest artworks within churches, the ancient Romans sanctified their spiritual institutions through art, intuiting that art is a liminal space between the holy and the profane. The presentation of gruesome spectacles for the entertainment of the community also suggests a dialectic implicit in theatrical performance, which electrifies the passions even as it seeks, in Artaud's sense, a purification, revealing new possibilities of being.[6]

Applied Theatre appears to lie on the other side of brutal and cruel forms of theatre. It leans more on the politics and aesthetics of Bertolt Brecht, whose theatre of artifice promoted distance between passion and reason, actor and audience. And yet Brecht's aim of political transformation is not that far from Artaud's aim of revealing the *mythos* of a community.

In using drama and theatre for social change, Applied Theatre artists seek to create performances for the common good of audiences. As such they must consider the thorny question of ethics – for whose good is the performance and at what cost? If the price of a stunning performance is the death of a slave or the denigration of a group, then what does that say about the values of the producers and consumers? How far removed are the spectacles in the Roman Coliseum from that of the ritual burning of Joan of Arc during the Inquisition, the subject of numerous plays throughout theatre history; or the staging by Joseph Goebbels in 1933 of the burning of non-Aryan books by the Nazis in Berlin; or the public executions in too many repressive states in the second decade of the 21st century?[7]

In the following chapter we present examples of drama and theatre praxis for the purpose of social change. We enter into this territory well aware of the history and the hard questions that frame our quest toward creating more humane, socially aware communities through the art form of performance.

# 4    Applied Theatre

### ❖ Case vignette one

Several months after 9/11, a youth theatre company and a drama therapist worked with nine- and ten-year-old children who witnessed the attacks on the World Trade Center towers from their classroom window. Their aim was to help the children find a way to speak about and reflect upon their experience. They engaged in a four-month process, developing characters and stories within a fictional community. Their roles and stories became part of a play that they performed to their local community. Following the performance, the children and adults shared stories about their experiences on 9/11.

### ❖ Case vignette two

To raise awareness of the conditions of exploited child workers in the sugarcane fields of rural Philippines, a Theatre for Development company produced a play based in local cultural art forms and traditions. The play was performed in village squares and theatres by children, many of whom had worked in the fields and were homeless. Based on audience response, several influential people re-examined laws and raised funds to support the education of children of poverty.

### ❖ Case vignette three

To give voice to a cultural group marginalized within Taiwanese society, a Theatre for Reminiscence group performed a play about the lives of Hakka women, a sizable ethnic minority within Taiwan. The actors were elderly Hakka women who felt strong and proud when dramatizing their stories of displacement and abandonment.

### ❖ Case vignette four

In a medium security prison in Israel, a young Jewish woman, highly suspicious of Muslim culture, engaged in a series of role-plays with an incarcerated Arab man, himself highly suspicious of Jews. As part of a group of

Jewish and Arab Israelis, they created a play about their encounters, and shared personal reflections of their fears of the other and their discoveries while encountering the other through drama.

### ❖ Case vignette five

Fifty international fellows at the World Economic Forum, based in Geneva, Switzerland, met to engage in innovative methods to help them better prepare for their imminent roles as world economic leaders. In doing so, they took classes in improvisation, voice and movement, as well as Theatre of the Oppressed. Although many felt pushed beyond their comfort zone, they discovered that drama and theatre helped them discover new ways to conceive of themselves in relationship to others, and more creative ways to think about social and economic issues.

### ❖ Case vignette six

Each Halloween in Temple, Texas, and other locales in the US and abroad, a church-sponsored group of actors performs Hell House, an inversion of the carnival favorite, the haunted house. In the church performance, scenes of contemporary sins, as defined by the church, are portrayed – abortion, extra-marital sex, homosexuality, drug abuse and mass murder among others. At the conclusion of the performance, audience members are asked to renounce sin and accept Christ as their personal savior.

### ❖ Case vignette seven

A group of citizens is summoned, by music and words broadcast over a loud speaker attached to a car, to a barren hill in Yuson, North Korea. They gather to witness the trial, conviction and immediate execution of a man by a firing squad of three riflemen. Following the execution, the voice over the loud speaker proclaims to the citizens: 'You have witnessed how miserable fools end up, traitors who betray the nation and end up like this.' The execution is secretly filmed and posted to the internet via YouTube, witnessed by a virtual audience of millions.[1]

These are examples of drama and theatre applied to the exploration of social issues and, in some cases, resolution of social problems within particular communities. In some examples a praxis framed the process and performance. In others the process and product were performed within an uncritical frame of faith in an infallible church or state. Some of these cases will be expanded to exemplify particular applications of drama and theatre within community venues. Additional examples will also illustrate the range of Applied Theatre activities throughout the world.

As the subject matter is so vast, we limit our choices to examples that we found most compelling in our research and field experience. Our main goal is to provide an overview of Applied Theatre as a change agent within communities.

## What Is Applied Theatre?

Applied Theatre in many ways grew out of the earlier work in TIE in its political orientation and attention to social change in schools. It is a controversial term that ignites dialogue in the literature and at professional conferences because of its forays into politics and social activism, and because of its challenge to the more established fields of Drama in Education and TIE.[2] To further contextualize its origins, we look at intellectual developments in related fields.

In the years 1982–2012 the conception of performance has expanded, moving theatre aesthetics into the social, cultural and political domains. There are numerous examples. In the 1960s and 70s, the aesthete Jerzy Grotowski abandoned theatre space and form altogether, leading his actors into the forest of Brzezinka, Poland, to create para-theatrical forms. During that time radical theatre groups such as the Living Theatre, the Open Theatre and the Bread and Puppet Theatre deconstructed classical dramatic elements of form, space and text in presenting a critical view of politics and culture.

In the 1970s Richard Schechner, like Grotowski and Peter Brook, questioned the primacy of the Western canon of dramatic literature and turned to the East for inspiration, as Brecht had done years before.[3] In researching forms of Indian, African and Chinese theatre, these theatre artists collaborated with anthropologists to help them better understand the cultural dimensions of performance. Brook collaborated with Colin Turnbull to transform Turnbull's study of a Ugandan minority culture, the Ik, into performance.[4] Schechner collaborated with Victor Turner whose studies of ritual practices and liminality influenced the development of Performance Studies.[5]

Early 20th-century sociologists discovered a powerful metaphor in theatre.[6] Several conceived of social interactions in terms of roles and performances, an idea solidified in the highly influential 1959 study by Erving Goffman *The Presentation of Self in Everyday Life*.[7] In the following decades, Goffman and his colleagues analyzed aspects of family, work and institutional life through the frame of performance.

Since 1980 new critical theory deconstructed modern conceptions of self and sexuality, gender, race and culture, infusing much scholarship in the field of Performance Studies and inspiring radical performances that in turn informed the scholarship.[8] Applied Theatre grew out of these shifting conceptions of performance.

Given the above case vignettes as examples, we can begin to understand the scope of Applied Theatre. Since the latter decades of the 20th century, a wide variety of Applied Theatre projects have been undertaken throughout the world, followed by numerous publications. In their 2009 publication *Applied Theatre*, collecting case studies from international venues, Prendergast and Saxton organize the field within nine categories: TIE, Popular Theatre, Theatre of the Oppressed, Theatre in Health Education, Theatre for Development, Prison Theatre, Community-based Theatre, Museum Theatre and Reminiscence Theatre.[9] To that list, we also add: Action Theatre, Bibliodrama, Engaged Theatre, Ethnodrama, Grassroots Theatre, Playback Theatre, Social Theatre and Sociodrama.[10]

It may be a stretch to think of applying theatre to the training of future world economic leaders and public executions, but even these examples point to the complexity of form, content and ethos of a relatively new discipline. These examples are about the possibilities of change, where future world leaders are encouraged to think about their role in facilitating the common good, and the repercussions of change, where the community is reminded about the dire consequences of personal reflection and social action.

At the heart of the experience of Applied Theatre is a simple idea – this is a theatre for change that exists to question and challenge the given order. Although as we shall see, some forms of Applied Theatre serve the hegemony of church and state, they do so in a critical way, implying that the given culture needs to be changed because it is too permissive and diverse, lacking in some essential object of allegiance.

Applied Theatre is a hybrid form and can be conceptualized as theatre plus something else, as in *Theatre &*, the title of the Palgrave Macmillan series of short books that attempt to capture the interdisciplinary links of theatre and key issues in society.

Helen Nicholson speaks of the field's hybridity as it connects to the disciplines of philosophy and social sciences.[11] Nicholson also speaks of the intentionality of Applied Theatre workers to 'develop new possibilities for everyday living rather than segregating theatre-going from other aspects of life'.[12] This does not separate Applied Theatre from aesthetic theatre, but rather provides the link between theatre and politics, ethics, globalization and community, at the center of Applied Theatre praxis.

Nicholson cites several published definitions of Applied Theatre. The Central School of Speech and Drama in London speaks to the aims of Applied Theatre as: 'intervention, communication, development, empowerment and expression when working with individuals or specific communities'.[13] It is important to note in that statement the reference to work with individuals, as many Applied Theatre researchers think of their form as solely social.

Nicholson also refers to the description within the Australian online journal *Applied Theatre Researcher*: 'theatre and drama in non-traditional contexts, theatre in the community, theatre in business and industry, theatre in political debate and action, theatre in lifelong education and learning'.[14] This echoes the definition on the website for the University of Manchester, Centre for Applied Theatre Research:

> Applied Theatre refers to the practice of theatre and drama in non-traditional settings. It refers to theatre practice that engages with areas of social and cultural policy such as public health, education, criminal justice, heritage site interpretation and development.[15]

Philip Taylor makes similar claims for Applied Theatre as performed in non-theatrical settings, and as 'raising awareness about how we are situated in the world and what we as individuals and as communities might do to make the world a better place'.[16] Beginning with raising awareness, Taylor goes on to specify other objectives: to pose alternatives to embedded problems, to heal psychological wounds or barriers, to challenge contemporary discourses and to voice the views of the silent and the marginal.[17] Prentki and Preston add that Applied Theatre concerns 'ordinary people and their stories, local settings and priorities' and that its purpose is to 'effect changes in the world outside of the theatrical discourse [...] In many examples of Applied Theatre there is no audience, only participants'.[18]

Much publication and performance in Applied Theatre relies upon the ideas and aesthetics of the theatre artists Brecht and Boal. Given these sources, we find an aesthetic that is anchored in the politics of the left, influenced by the sociological ideas of Marx and the pedagogical ideas of Freire. Brecht's stylized Epic Theatre form drew on images of popular entertainment such as film, boxing and clowning to distance the viewer from a direct emotional connection to the characters, thereby encouraging a critical response to the political content. Brecht paid special homage to Marxist philosophy in his early Learning Plays, such as *The Measures Taken* and *The Exception and the Rule*, where the goal is revolutionary and the means to the end of class struggle is through a dialectical relationship between actor and text, audience and actor.[19]

Likewise, Freire looked to create dialectical relationships between text and student, student and student, student and teacher, through a pedagogy based in *conscientização*, which, as we have seen earlier, is an understanding of social conditions through the development of a critical consciousness.[20] This occurs through repeated dialogue between the oppressed and the oppressor.

Boal, in turn, applied the same methodology to theatre performance, seeking to question and ultimately overcome oppression. In developing Forum Theatre, he sought to provoke audience members out of their safe passivity as viewers. In Forum Theatre, the spectator becomes a spect-actor by switching roles with the protagonist and entering directly into the action. In doing so, she seeks to play out a new ending and propose alternative solutions to embedded problems. For Boal there is not a single solution to a significant social or personal problem, only alternatives.

Boal's theatre concerns several kinds of oppression – social, personal and political. In his last developed form, called Legislative Theatre, he sought to create alternative laws within the system through performance.[21] Boal presented a practice steeped in specific theatre games and

**Photograph 4.1  Augusto Boal with jokers (left to right) Olivar Bendelak, Helen Sarapeck, Boal, Claudete Felix, Barbara Santos and Geo Britto, photo courtesy of CTO-Rio**

**Photograph 4.2 Theatre of the Oppressed at CTO-Rio (left to right – Aminisha Ferdinand, Edmund Chow, James Webb, Emily Bolton Ditkovski, Gretchen Peters), photo by Alex Sarian**

clearly schematized structures. This practice was grounded in theory that paid homage to his mentor, Freire.

Boal acknowledged as theoretical mentors Brecht, J. L. Moreno and even Stanislavski, whose ideas influenced him as a student in New York City in the 1950s. For the most part, however, Boal preferred to develop his own culturally specific theory. In Boalian praxis, the theory and practice inform each other and lead, optimally, to effective social action within the society.

In breaking down barriers between audience and performer, stage and society, and in posing alternatives to embedded problems, Brecht and Boal exemplify an ethos based in political and sociological principles calling for a reversal of the dynamics of oppression. This ethos permeates much of the work in Applied Theatre.

## Theatre of faith

A different Applied Theatre ethos is framed by an alternative radical consciousness. This alternative comes primarily from the right of the political spectrum and within the ideology of religious and political dogma, the kind that fed the radicalism of Brecht and Boal. Many world religions win converts, assert their authority and affirm community among their congregants through the performance of religious rituals and pageants. These performances offer another way to think about theatre as an applied form. In this instance the application is to a religious institution and to the spiritual needs of its congregants.

We refer to this form of Applied Theatre as Theatre of Faith, which we define as the enactment of stories of the suffering, death, and re-birth of iconic spiritual figures to affirm the faith of a community of celebrants. We referred to an example in Chapter 3 of *Noah, the Musical*, in our discussion of Theatre for Young Audiences and religion. The earliest known form of Theatre of Faith is the Abydos passion play, discovered on an ancient Egyptian tablet, dated before the year 2000 BC. The play is about the heroic and transformational struggles of the god Osiris. The purpose of the performance, like other passion plays, is both to inform an audience of celebrants and to reconnect them to a community of the faithful.

In tenth-century Europe, Christian passion plays were performed in churches by clergymen to teach Bible stories to an illiterate population. Two centuries later, the plays moved into local communities and were performed in village squares by actors and laypeople. Some of the old mystery plays are still produced in their original settings, such as York and Canterbury, England.[22]

In the 17th century, as the plague (Black Death) raged through many communities of central Europe, people within the small Alpine village of Oberammergau were terrified. They pledged that if they were spared, they would perform the story of Christ's passion once every ten years as an act of devotion. Miraculously the villagers were spared and remained true to their word. The Oberammergau passion play, last performed in 2010, is centered on the final five days in the life of Jesus Christ.[23] For each performance since the 17th century, the villagers revise the script, build the sets, assume all the biblical roles, and transform the village of Oberammergau into the setting for their performance. As such, this performance is not only Theatre of Faith, but also Community-based, Grassroots Theatre. Unlike the models of Brecht and Boal, however, this is a performance about faith, not about *conscientização*.

We find another example of Theatre of Faith in Muslim culture in the Persian Shi'ite passion play commemorating the martyrdom of Imam Hussein, an ancient expression of faith in the Iranian-Shi'ite culture.[24] In telling the story the play, called *Taziyeh* ('Condolence Theatre'), recapitulates the ancient narratives of the sufferings and martyrdom of Osiris and Christ. The performance is unusual in that the Muslim faith prohibits the figural depiction of holy characters. And yet, through a shift in the form of presentation, actors read their lines from visible scripts to make clear that they are actors, not to be mistaken with actual spiritual figures. Even in Theatre of Faith, there is a touch of the Brechtian.

Theatre of Faith serves both a religious and social function. Like more political forms of Applied Theatre, this form has a deep impact on those needing to affirm their commitment to a community of like-minded souls. But in doing so these forms have also served politically- and morally-divisive purposes, perpetuating ideology at the expense of non-believers. For example, in 16th-century Rome, passion plays had to be discontinued because audience members, inspired after watching performances to revenge the killing of Christ, entered and sacked the Jewish ghettos.[25] This is an ironic commentary on the later aims of Brecht and Boal who insisted upon a theatre of social action.

Further, the Oberammergau version of the passion play was historically and openly anti-Semitic. Hitler attended two productions and was quoted as saying that the play was accurate in portraying the 'whole muck and mire of Jewry'.[26] Young children often took on roles of the Jewish mob jeering Jesus and proclaiming that the blood curse of the Jews will live on in perpetuity. Until very recent times Jews were often portrayed in performance with horns and exaggerated features.

But these examples of Theatre of Faith are hardly static. As praxis they were subject to criticism, some of which led to change. Responsive to critiques of anti-Semitism, the creators of the 2010 Oberammergau passion play modified its text. Roman Catholic Archbishop Timothy Dolan of New York City and Rabbi Gary Greenebaum of the American Jewish Committee proclaimed the 2010 version of the play as 'a paradigm for the friendship of Jews and Catholics'.[27]

Numerous examples of Theatre of Faith can be found in several religious traditions. The traditional Hindu performance of *Ramman*, for example, tells the epic story of Rama told through music, dance and mask. *Ramman* can be viewed on YouTube.[28] The global Internet technology was helpful in rescuing this near extinct Himalayan performance from obscurity, although the most robust support came from the local community and its relationship with the Indira Gandhi National Centre for Arts, which successfully lobbied the state of India to preserve and protect the performance.

## ❖ Case vignette: Hell House

A final example of Theatre of Faith is that of Hell House, referred to in the opening case vignettes. Hell House came into existence on Halloween

1990 in a community near Dallas, Texas, at the Trinity Assembly of God Church.[29] Supposedly the event was inspired by the evangelical minister Jerry Falwell.

Hell House was packaged and exported to hundreds of evangelical churches by Pastor Keenan Roberts, who sells Hell House Outreach kits, franchising this product like a Broadway 'McTheatre' package.[30] Hell House uses performance to shock people into accepting Christ as their savior. It transforms the entertainment goals of the carnival funhouse into realistic gut-wrenching scenes of incest, infidelity, abortion, suicide, drug addition and mass murder. Included in Pastor Roberts' kit are directions on how to use an abundance of stage blood as well as raw animal parts to represent the appendages of an aborted fetus.

In the premiere run of Hell House in Texas, all the roles were played by congregants within the Trinity Church community, making this experience akin to Grassroots or Community-based Theatre. In performance, audiences are guided through the rooms of the house by ghouls. A scene of sin is enacted in each room. Then they are taken to hell to view eternally tortured souls, with the implicit message that anyone who has experienced incest or abortion or homosexuality will be condemned to everlasting damnation. The final moment is the most powerful as audience members are led by small groups into a waiting room. At one end is a door. A minister in plain clothes enters the room and tells the audience: 'There are people in the next room waiting to pray with you should you walk through that door. By walking through that door you are saying: "I want to get right with the Lord." If this is you, I want you to step through that door now. You have six seconds.'[31] It is unclear whether this man is an actor.

Another man in plain clothes opens the door. Some enter, some do not. Those who do are immediately transformed from observers to actors, taking actions that, according to the producers of the event, have the direst consequences. Although with a radically different intent – conversion rather than problem posing – this moment is evocative of the intentions of Brecht and Boal to transform spectators into actors on the political stage. Many who have trained in the praxis of Brecht and Boal realize that it is difficult to take direct action in the world following a performance, as there are real oppressors with real power blocking all attempts to storm the barricades. But those who conceived of Hell House knew that although the decision to walk through the door is difficult, once made the action that follows is fully supported by the community on the other side of the door.

In the room, the artifice of theatre is gone. Real people trained in the doctrine of the church comfort, lecture, implore and pray, sometimes speaking in tongues, until the sinner has let go and accepted the spirit.

The process and production of Hell House is very theatrical. The directorial concept is superbly realized. This is a theatre that ultimately matters for the producers and some in the audience. Souls are at stake. And yet, for non-believers and for the mainstream of Applied Theatre artists, the question arises: is this theatre or propaganda, a manipulation and distortion of the theatrical ethos? If this is theatre, is it Applied Theatre? Can the intentions of Pastor Roberts sit comfortably within an aesthetic and ethos of Brecht and Boal?

In partial response to these questions, an experimental theatre company called Les Freres Corbusier took Roberts' text and performed it to a decidedly non-evangelical and skeptical audience in New York City around the time of Halloween in 2006. Following Roberts' text, director Alex Timbers devised scenes of rape, suicide, botched abortion, AIDS, school shootings, suicide bombing, and hell and heaven. In the final room of the house, he staged a post-performance Christian hoe-down.

Reflecting upon the performance, critic Theresa Smalec commented on the fact that Timbers' production was not a spoof but a straight rendering of Roberts' text.[32] Smalec noted the pop culture participatory nature of the performance, comparing it to reality television. She referred to a scene where the audience is privy to the aborted fetus of a cheerleader. The ghoul looks at the audience and says sarcastically: 'It isn't a *complete* waste,

Photograph 4.3 *Hell/House*, photo by Richard Termine

though. Soon, we'll be harvesting her body for stem cells!' Spontaneously, one woman in the audience responded: 'Yay!'

Despite the expected cynicism, Smalec found herself and the audience unexpectedly engaged. A scene of a Muslim suicide bomber, wearing a dynamite vest, drew a noticeable gasp from the audience. And yet, as the play moved toward its theatricalized heaven, the glibness of the audience was re-kindled. When the minister of the doors appeared and asked audience members to renew their faith, there were no takers.

But something shifted in the final scene, the Gospel hoe-down. The woman who applauded stem cell research seemed to make fun of the band with hand gestures. The lead singer invited her onstage, and Smalec became aware that she was partially deaf, communicating in American Sign Language, not in parody but in praise as she signed every phrase of Rich Mullins' signature Christian rock anthem, *Awesome God*.[33] She became caught up in the moment, eyes tearing, aware of the contradictory signals coming from the hoe-down audience.

Smalec realized that she, too, was caught up in this liminal moment, identifying with the young woman on stage. She recalled Anne Bogart's statement that: 'Theatre is [...] an act of memory and description. There are plays and people and moments of history to revisit. [...] And our journeys will change us – make us better, bigger and more connected.'[34]

Smalec experienced a call to memory, a yearning for purity and 'a seeker's humbling rebirth'.[35] She wondered whether the band was authentically Christian. Going home, she Googled the band and there on YouTube was their latest praise song. And she realized that the young woman, too, was not an actor, 'but a conflicted spectator like the rest of us'; and she thought: 'This is my true, perverse act of faith.'[36]

Even if the original intention of Jerry Falwell and Keenan Roberts was evangelical rather than dialogical, in the hands of Les Freres Corbusier that intention shifted back to the key aims of Applied Theatre – to expose contradictions, raise questions and transform passive viewers into active actors on the stage of everyday life. Hell House is religion and it is theatre and it is Applied Theatre in the several hands of those who perform it and witness it in performance.

Theatre of Faith is absent from Applied Theatre scholarship, as it is politically incorrect for those who adhere to progressive viewpoints. We include it as it is ubiquitous and speaks to a powerful form of performance that deeply affects life in communities. Although it is primarily about maintaining the status quo, it also serves a transformational purpose, with a focus on spiritual life. Although thinking of this form as praxis seems contradictory, we saw in the preceding vignette how it can be applied to even a skeptical audience, whose responses might lead to some surprising conclusions.

## Applied Theatre in schools

Applied Theatre is used in schools internationally to address many community issues including bullying, cultural identity, racism, health and wellness.[37] For example, Catalyst, a Theatre in Health Education (THE) group in England, has been effective in devising a program of anti-drug education in 11 secondary schools.[38] The California-based group Fringe Benefits has worked on a number of social justice issues with public school students. Among their offerings is *Cootie Shots*, a performance of 54 plays, songs and poems designed for grades K–six designed to explore issues of diversity and tolerance.[39]

Three long-standing Educational Theatre companies in New York City – ENACT, CANY (Creative Alternatives of New York) and CAT (Creative Arts Team) – implement Applied Theatre in schools.[40] CAT works primarily through DIE, TIE and Youth Theatre. ENACT and CANY combine aspects of DIE with Drama Therapy. All work in special and public education facilities in economically depressed communities.

The ENACT method, focusing on developing social and emotional skills, was developed by Diana Feldman and is informed by models of Developmental and Cognitive Psychology, Creative Drama and Drama Therapy. ENACT works with such issues as dropping out of school, bullying and peer pressure. Their process includes initial discussions with classroom teachers followed by discussions of the issues with students. The teaching artists facilitate enactment of the issues and end with a closing ritual and discussion.

In addition to classroom workshops, ENACT developed a theatre component for primary and secondary grades that focuses on making positive life choices. Unlike Boal who said that theatre is not safe, ENACT's facilitators work through the concepts of safety and distance with young people who live in unsafe communities. Their participatory theatre work, although similar to Forum Theatre, is more about personal growth than political change.

Like ENACT, CANY works with young people who are at risk for mental illness, drug addiction and crime. CANY was started in 1969 by a small group of theatre artists determined to enhance the quality of life of institutionalized individuals. Shifting focus in recent years, CANY is now more clearly aligned with the principles of Drama Therapy. As such they also work with women and child survivors of domestic violence, mentally ill individuals in psychiatric hospitals, disabled veterans, individuals living with HIV/AIDS, and seniors in outpatient mental health programs.

Like ENACT, CANY utilizes a specific method, developed by Emily Nash, that combines the aims and techniques of Improvisational Theatre, Psychodrama, Drama Therapy, and group analysis. CANY tends to be overtly therapeutic in its process, attempting to create what Nash calls conscious communities, groups working toward developing awareness, empathy and dialogue. Its praxis includes post-workshop critiques and frequent supervision to address issues of personal and group process.

### ❖ Case vignette: The Creative Arts Team

CAT evolved from the early tradition of British TIE in the 1960s and 1970s. The original group was trained in Educational Theatre at NYU and at Bretton Hall College, England, under the tutelage of John Hodgson and other British DIE specialists.[41] In the 1982 *Handbook*, Landy featured their work in TIE, especially the performances of social issues like racism, multiculturalism, violence and vandalism. In addition to devising TIE, CAT worked through DIE methods in inner city classrooms to address academic and social issues.

Within the past 30 years, CAT has retained its commitment to serving children at risk and to working through a methodology based in TIE and DIE. However, its programs and its praxis have expanded. With the hiring of Chris Vine as artistic and educational director, and Helen White as the director of the Youth Theatre in 1993, the group has shifted more into the arena of Applied Theatre, incorporating many ideas of Freire and Boal. Given this focus, in combination with its on-going mission, CAT views drama and theatre both as a catalyst for social change and as a medium for learning academic and social skills.

Although CAT is primarily focused on children in the New York City area, it has begun to work abroad. Vine and White brought their methodology to Rwanda in 2010, engaging in a project called Theatre and Drama Education for Reconciliation and Development. Vine reflected:

Our work in Rwanda focused on offering new drama strategies to be used in educational contexts. The emphasis was on drama as a means to promote critical thinking. We offered new forms – Process Drama, TIE models, play-building strategies – with universal and potentially metaphorical content, in relationship to the Rwandan context. The contemporary themes came from our participants: poverty, corruption, HIV/AIDS, orphans, the abuse of house girls, the sex trade, gender roles, educational opportunity and many more – serious themes but approached in an extraordinary spirit of playfulness. It was certainly not difficult to encourage debate; there were many points of view and serious disagreements. Interestingly, while the genocide remained a point of reference, it was seldom the main focus. Many of the students […] were orphans themselves, or had certainly lost the majority of their families, and were not shy to tell you this, but they were much more interested in looking forward.[42]

CAT also collaborated with United Arab Emirates University (UAEU). This began as James Mirrione, a founding member of CAT and current professor at UAEU, brought a group of his students, all female, to New York to train with CAT and learn about both Applied Theatre and American culture.

Mirrione has been working to develop an Educational Theatre program in the United Arab Emirates (UAE) within a culture that does not have much of a tradition of theatre, due to the religious prohibition against depicting images of the divine, and cultural prohibition against any form of mixed gender public performance. According to Mirrione, a radical act of theatre in the UAE would be to have men and women performing on the same stage. He speculated that if a performance of Ibsen's *Doll's House*, which was so profoundly controversial when first presented in Copenhagen in 1879, were to occur on a stage in the UAE, it would be even more startling, perhaps significant enough to change Emirati society.[43]

Mirrione took this thesis even further by producing a play in the UAE called *18 Days*, based upon the events in the Arab Spring rebellions of 2011. The play was acted by female students with male faculty in auxiliary roles. Although careful to avoid controversial commentary, the production was bold not only in depicting some of the events, but in mixing male and female actors on stage.

Building upon his training with CAT in TIE, Mirrione conducted a research project with his female students.[44] He asked them to reflect on the figure of Kate from Shakespeare's *The Taming of the Shrew*, whose 16th-century Elizabethan dilemma recapitulates 21st-century cultural issues of arranged marriage, marital obligations and patriarchy in the UAE.

In analyzing 75 student responses to Kate's final monologue, where she appears to renounce her rebelliousness and capitulate to the patriarchal demands of Petruchio, Mirrione discovered that the vast majority, 45, responded in a traditional way, agreeing with Kate that 'Thy husband is thy lord'. Thirteen responded in a more nuanced way, offering an emotional appeal that both accepted the male patriarchy but respected the female's wish for equality.

In the final category, 17 women rejected Kate's conversion and offered the most critical commentary on cultural patriarchy. The boldest response called for the power of education to change the identity and status of women in Emirati society. We agree with Mirrione that when an engagement with theatre leads to a change in consciousness, anything is possible.

In shadowing the CAT workshops for the Emirati women in the summer of 2010, Landy noted Mirrione's cultural as well as educational goals. Following a day of workshops Mirrione led the women, all in *sheylas*, traditional head coverings, on a 45-minute subway ride through Manhattan into Brooklyn where they encountered Hassidic Jews, Somalis, African-Americans and Chinese. Their destination was Bensonhurst, a very traditional Italian neighborhood. After a meal in a local Sicilian restaurant, the 20 young women and their Lebanese chaperone sat under a fig tree in the tiny urban backyard of the home where Mirrione was raised and shared stories about their daily lives with Mirrione's mother, just months shy of her 100th birthday.

### ❖ Case vignette: *Standing Tall*: Youth theatre and drama therapy after a crisis in the community

Although there are many excellent examples of Applied Theatre praxis in schools, some arise from a moment of need within a community. This was the case for the project *Standing Tall*. There was an immediate crisis in New York City on September 11, 2001, when two planes crashed into the World Trade Center towers. Not only were there substantial deaths and injuries, but the blatant attacks were witnessed by thousands on the ground and millions on the media broadcasts. New York City, and indeed, the US, was in crisis.

Shortly after 9/11, the *New York Times* Foundation School Arts Rescue Initiative donated money to selected arts organizations to help children in schools situated near the attacks recover from their experience. When City Lights Youth Theatre was selected, it called upon a drama therapist to devise a program for a class of nine- and ten-year-olds, all of whom witnessed the attacks from their classroom window on the fourth day of the new school year. Landy, the drama therapist, developed the program *Standing Tall*, in collaboration with City Lights Youth Theatre.

Although *Standing Tall* occurred in an elementary school, it also concerned the relationship of the school to its local community. In form *Standing Tall* is a hybrid, a mix of DIE, Youth Theatre and Drama Therapy. The model of working with role types and fictional narratives is part of

Landy's role theory in Drama Therapy. The model of devising student-based texts for performance is standard in many forms of DIE, TIE and devised theatre.

The group worked together each Friday for three months. In these workshops, led by a drama therapist and a teaching artist, the group engaged with three role types – Heroes, Villains and Victims. The first two were offered by the drama therapist, consistent with his role theory. The third, that of Victim, was suggested by the children, some of whom had family members victimized by the attacks. Through role-play and improvisation, writing and storytelling, the students constructed and deconstructed these character types.

Throughout the process, the facilitators and teacher had ongoing dialogues, questioning the choices made in the workshops. In one, for example, the teacher felt that the dramatic improvisations were too farcical and that the children stereotyped the villains. She cited a particular moment when the drama therapist asked the children to imagine the wishes of the parents of Osama bin Laden just before his birth, and then the wishes of Osama himself, as a child. In playing out these scenes, children enacted moments where the baby is born with a machine gun in his hand and where the young Osama plays with his first toy, again a machine gun. "Were the children in their play making fun of Muslims?" wondered the teacher.

The drama therapist responded by speaking about the need of the children to release their fears playfully. In their play, he said, the children were actually working through their own questions about the nature of evil. They wondered: 'Are people who engage in destructive acts born evil?' At one point, seeking to humanize the 'bad guys', he asked the children whether they thought that villains stand tall, that is, feel a sense of pride. Many answered in the affirmative, noting that evil is a complex issue that sometimes arises from familial or cultural circumstances. One girl, favoring nature over nurture, humorously responded: 'Maybe when he [Osama bin Laden] was born, he fell on his head!' This and many other moments were met by great peals of laughter from the group.

Throughout the process, the facilitators asked the children to reflect upon their roles and stories. In responding to the same issue of the nature of evil, a boy said that now he understood the true value of comedy. When the facilitator asked him to explain, he said that it is fun; it helps the group find a way to lighten up, especially in the face of a disaster.

Eight weeks into the dramatic process the drama therapist, in consultation with the teaching artist and classroom teacher, wrote a play called *Standing Tall* that contained, verbatim, the students' character sketches and stories. The teaching artist directed the play with all the students playing roles of heroes, villains and victims. The play was performed to an audience of peers, teachers, parents and community members.

Following the performance by the students, the full community reflected on the play. It was surprising to hear that it was the first time some talked about their experiences openly. For parents, it was an opportunity to address their concerns for the emotional well being of their children. For many children, it became a time to speak out and to be witnessed within their community. For all, this was a clear example of how theatre can perform a vital purpose – holding a community together and creating a forum for addressing an essential issue within that community.

In several follow-up meetings including the teacher, drama therapist and teaching artist, the children reflected upon the experience, some saying that it changed their perceptions of the attack. And yet there was not enough hard evidence to evaluate just how the play affected the children's thinking and feeling. Did some students hold onto the stereotypes played out in the improvisations? Did some think that Osama bin Laden, and by association, all Muslims, were natural-born killers who propagate random acts of violence? Did some students understand, as one articulated in a workshop, that heroes are often regular people, like mothers who dare to listen to their young children? Or that victims are sometimes cast in their roles by chance? Or that villains stand tall? These questions remain unanswered, as do many such questions following an Applied Theatre experience in communities.

On the other hand, the art process itself often provides evidence of outcomes. In this case, a film was made of the experience and the film-maker, Peggy Stern, interviewed several children and their parents in their homes.[45] She learned that even some of the overtly stoic children had nightmares and that the experience of *Standing Tall* helped them deal with their fears. She learned that at least for one girl, the experience of *Standing Tall* changed her way of thinking about life. When asked to reflect upon the experience, the girl told Stern: 'I don't know what I'd do without the drama. ... Without the drama, I would just be ... dead in my mind.'[46]

The process of work through improvisation and role-play, the product of performance, and the reflective conversations with the audience and the children were all important aspects of this Applied Theatre praxis. The group of children was diverse in terms of culture, ethnicity and academic achievement, with exceptionally high achievers as well as special needs children. But just as all were witness to the attacks on their city, all were equally active players in a drama that both reflected a crisis in the

**Photograph 4.4** *Standing Tall*, **photo courtesy of Peggy Stern**

community and looked ahead toward a renewed sense of community.[47]
The final lines of the play articulate this hope:

CHRISTA:    And so the children began to rebuild, one story at a time, not with bricks and mortar, but with words and images, until the city of darkness was once again a city of light and hope.

GARRETH:    We are the artists.

ROBERT:    Our city is a place called New York, New York where buildings stand tall.

ANNA:    Our city is a place where we stand tall. This play is our memorial.

## Theatre for development

In too many communities throughout the world, crisis is a reality of daily living. This reality has not changed much in 30 years, despite the change of locales. In some cases the issues and locales persist – religious and political intolerance, occupation and oppression, cold and hot wars, oil spills and natural disasters, prospects for peace and reconciliation in the Middle East, Africa, South Asia. Applied Theatre groups have worked within these and other cultures in crisis for many years.

The HIV/AIDS crisis, virtually unknown when the 1982 *Handbook* was published, was instrumental in mobilizing a number of Theatre for Development (TfD) groups in Africa. So, too, were political and military struggles as many African countries worked to transcend their colonial histories. Kenya, Ghana and Uganda, among others, have long histories of Applied Theatre that go back to the 1930s.[48] At that time, colonial teachers, agricultural and health workers made use of theatre to spread messages of modernity concerning new ways to educate, farm and care for families. Their work took a top-down approach and exempted local populations from the devising process.

In the 1950s, as talk of independence was in the air, colonial governments in such countries as Ghana and Uganda organized tours of Applied Theatre skits as a form of mass education in villages.[49] The actors were development workers who combined the didactic skits, concerning issues such as controlling the spread of malaria, with practical demonstrations of, for example, how to kill mosquitoes. These efforts had mixed results, especially as the legacy of colonialism played out and as nations struggled to form independent states with leaders who regularly changed the cultural and economic rules.

In the aftermath of apartheid in South Africa and genocide in Rwanda, a number of Applied Theatre groups worked with citizens for the purpose of reconciliation. But the main focus for so many TfD groups continues to be on the devastation caused by the HIV/AIDS pandemic.

In his extensive study, Christopher Odhiambo Joseph discusses the effectiveness of several TfD groups.[50] To provide context, Odhiambo is a professor of literature and theatre at Moi University in Kenya. Like others in Applied Theatre, he views Freire and Boal as mentors. And as one living in a traditional culture, he is also mentored by non-Western theorists, such as the Kenyan post-colonial critics Opiyo Mumma and Ngugi wa Thiong'o.

Theatre for Development involves the creating and performing of plays addressing important issues in developing communities. The term applies especially to work in Africa and is often used in place of the term Applied Theatre.[51] Much of TfD uses processes and terminology from the work of Freire and Boal. Odhiambo speaks to 'the heightened and interactive audience participation and the anticipated resultant empowerment of the target audience'.[52]

In most discussions of TfD, we find reference to dialogue, interaction, participation, codification, empowerment, problem-solving and problem posing.

Dale Byam views TfD as aiming toward Freire's notion of *conscientização*.[53] For Byam, TfD is a form of codification for citizens to explore, analyze and discuss their history. Codification is a term coined by Freire that refers to non-verbal codes of expression and communication through such mediums as drawings and radio.[54] When working with rural peasants in Brazil, for example, Freire encouraged them to express themselves by drawing with sticks in the sand.

Byam also sees TfD as a praxis, a means of challenging traditional ways of thinking about development and of working with a targeted population to create the performance, to critique the issues performed and to decide how best to take action within the community. For Byam, the use of codification in TfD is culturally appropriate when it recapitulates traditional features of African cultural expression, including the use of mask, dance and visual imagery.

TfD targets citizens in given communities and works often outdoors in village squares and community centers. Let us look at two examples, one from Kenya, addressing the spread of HIV/AIDS within a traditional culture; the other from the Philippines, addressing the exploitation of child workers.

### ❖ Case vignette: PET in performance

The project called Participatory Educational Theatre (PET) was created by the efforts of an NGO, CARE-Kenya, and two amateur theatre groups, Kama Kazi and Apondo.[55] Their goal was to help people become more aware of HIV/AIDS and discuss ways of taking action. PET begins by targeting a particular community, choosing members to work with the facilitators and then collectively devising a play. The devising process includes creating a narrative through the use of tableaux, myths, songs, photographs and stories from the local press.[56]

The performance is presented by actors in brief scenes. Each one is followed by a participatory scene that engages the responses of the audience. The audience participation occurs through the mediation of a facilitator. A storyboard appears within the performance space and includes names of scenes as well as ideas that come from the audience.

In the performance of *Red Ribbons for You? Sigand Tom – Ngimani gi Thoni*, the protagonist, Tom Omondi, is infected with HIV while a university student and eventually dies from the virus at age 23.[57] Others among his family and friends are also infected. Tom's father plays a central role as he spreads the virus among many of the figures in the play. The story is told in nine scenes, each one noted on the storyboard by the title of the scene and by a question. An example is the title: 'The Triangle', and the question: What is Tom suffering from? Is it demons? Is it AIDS? Is it *chiraa*?[58]

The play begins as the facilitators specify the beginning and concluding scene to provide a basic structure. Then, following the performance of the first scene, they invite a member of the audience to choose another scene to be performed, until all the scenes are enacted. In doing so, the facilitators allow the group to control the chronology and thematic content of the performance.

Following the performance of a scene, a discussion ensues based upon the question within that scene. Although the performance of each scene is intentionally brief, the discussion can last long into the day. During the discussion audience members are asked to take on roles through which they can dialogue with the actors and find ways to respond to the questions or to raise new ones.

As an example, one person needed to speak with Tom's father, a rather traditional man firm in his opinions. She assumed the role of an AIDS counselor and informed the father that his son was sick with a medical disease, not with *chiraa*, and required immediate medical attention. Her role-play was so effective, that the actor playing Tom's father accepted that his son was sick with the virus.

In performance PET works with cultural assumptions and rituals, such as that of wife inheritance, concerning the obligation of a younger brother to marry the wife of an elder brother who has died. In one example, set in a small village, a group of actors playing HIV/AIDS counselors tell stories, based in actual stories taken from local villagers. From the audience, one elder, drawn to a particular story, makes clear that he is skeptical about the existence of AIDS. But he listens to the story about a village carpenter whose elder brother committed suicide when he discovered that he had the virus. The carpenter was compelled to marry the wife of his older brother, as is customary. But since that time, he became infected with the virus, as did his first wife and their child, as well as the wife he inherited from his brother, who was probably the original carrier of the virus.

Following the story a teenage boy from the audience raised questions about the tradition of wife inheritance. A heated debate took place between the young man and the village elder. At a high point, a woman wished to be heard and was invited into the play space. This was an unusual moment as women are generally reserved within community gatherings. She spoke of the contradictions between supporting tradition and recognizing the realities of deadly infections. She continued to speak firmly about the need for women to have more say in issues like marriage and ownership of land.

The debate continued with various points of view raised and argued. The discussion and enactment concluded, to great applause, when the elder who denied the existence of AIDS spoke out, telling the villagers that he was finally convinced that AIDS is a real and present medical concern.[59]

At the conclusion of his study on TfD in Kenya, Odhiambo raises the question: 'How can theatre as a codification be used effectively in the process of change?'[60] Considering Freire and Boal's aims, Odhiambo thinks about change as taking place both within the consciousness of the audience and within the community, as spect-actors engage in the theatrical action as a rehearsal for real action.[61]

Odhiambo concludes that despite some compelling attempts to deal with issues like HIV/AIDS, wife inheritance, family planning and female genital mutilation, TfD in Kenya, although plentiful, has not met the criteria for effective change. He argues that Kenyan facilitators have not developed clear procedures and methodologies to both devise the performance and engage in pre-performance research and post-performance reflection. He calls for further training of facilitators based in research and exchange through the sharing of knowledge in conferences and seminars. And, echoing the admonitions of Prentki and Preston, he calls for radical discourse among theatre workers to debate issues of culture, globalization and the aesthetics and ethics of performance within developing nations.[62]

These critiques lead us to several questions: If TfD groups in Kenya and elsewhere use the codes of action embedded in local cultural rituals as well as Applied Theatre, and if they spark the kinds of dialogues as given in the previous example, has not change occurred? And what is the best way to measure that change? In attempting to answer, we turn to a second example of TfD in another culture, that of the Philippines.

## ❖ Case vignette: Theatre for Development in the Philippines

The Philippine Educational Theatre Association (PETA) is an example of a group that successfully works through local socio-cultural traditions and art forms to facilitate social awareness and change.[63] It was founded in 1967 and has developed more than 300 performances. Influenced by Boal, PETA urges its audiences to not only interact with the performers, but also to take action to improve the conditions of oppressed people within Philippine society. As a praxis, PETA engages in a continuous process of self-reflection during and after productions. Through documenting their reflections, they seek to understand the theatre's impact upon artist-teachers, child actors, and audiences within targeted communities.[64]

In PETA the performers are children, many of whom are child laborers from a background of poverty, abuse and homelessness. In a recent play, *Mga Batang Hurnal* ('Children Working in the Sugarcane Plantations'), the young actors presented the conditions of their lives in the sugarcane fields.[65] The play begins with a traditional folksong, with words written by the child laborers:

> Come to Ormoc Leyte
> Poor children holding a machete,
> Vast tracks of land,
> Tall coconut trees you will find,
> Child laborers you will see,
> Our woes you will hear,
> So come swiftly,
> Be one with us,
> Hear our stories.

In the play the stories of poverty and harsh living conditions raise many questions for audiences. As this is Theatre for Development, the facilitators sought to 'mobilize the children, parents, communities, schools and ally with local government units, and even landlords ... to support and/or participate in the project'.[66]

The children presented this play in 2007 in seven schools and five communities in rural Philippines, with the goal of increasing social awareness among students and their parents, some of whom were landowners, as to the plight of the young sugarcane workers.

At the conclusion of *Mga Batang Hurnal*, the young actors express their wishes for the future:

I wish I could provide for the good health of my parents and siblings, that we could eat three times a day.

I wish my parents would have higher income so that children like me will have more chances to play instead of working in the fields.

I hope that children can have a choice of what they want to do: to concentrate on schooling, to play with other children, to eat delicious food.

No more hungry children. No more kids recruited and sent to Manila to work. No more batang hurnal.[67]

After expressing these wishes, they reach out to the audience to ask for help in realizing these dreams. Although their reach sometimes exceeds their grasp, PETA has indeed been successful in raising awareness and in some cases changing behavior within communities that tolerated the abuses of children in the sugarcane fields. Many in the audience were deeply moved and some provided funds for school scholarships and for further PETA programs. In several rural communities the production led local politicians to adopt councils and enact laws to protect the rights of children.

In their work on child labor, PETA responds to our questions above but only anecdotally. The example suggests that their form of Applied Theatre can change embedded cultural attitudes. Although the change can be measured in the amount of money raised and laws enacted, its deeper effects are harder to quantify – the change of consciousness among performers and viewers, which is the central aim of those working in the field of Theatre for Development.

## Applied Theatre in prisons

Theatre in prisons has a very long history. Early examples include the incarceration of Marquis de Sade in Charenton Prison in France in the 18th century, where he presumably directed the inmates in plays. That moment in history is poignantly imagined by the playwright, Peter Weiss, in *The Persecution and Assassination of Jean-Paul Marat as Performed by the Inmates of the Asylum of Charenton under the Direction of the Marquis de Sade*.[68] We can even stretch the timeline back to the spectacles in the ancient Roman Coliseum, performed often to the death by imprisoned slaves.

In the same vein, throughout history there are tens of thousands of examples of public executions of prisoners, a bizarre and moralistic form of performance that combined the producers' needs for justice, moral education and brutal control, with the public's need for revenge, catharsis and spectacle. A very recent example is given at the beginning of the chapter of a public execution by firing squad in North Korea. It might be a stretch to call a public execution Applied Theatre. And yet it has some of the earmarks – an engaging performance within a local community venue; a collaboration between the state and its citizens who focus their rapt attention on a rarefied protagonist; an application of the performance to the lives of citizens; a form of moral education in the service of a particular ideology; an act of performance that raises moral and mortal questions for the viewers; an audience that participates fully, though vicariously, with a combination of exaltation and revulsion.

If this is Applied Theatre, however, it is a cynical and cruel commentary on the intentions of Brecht and Boal, who called for performance that provokes criticism of injustice and cruelty. Looking back over history, it might be fair to say that there has been as much reality-based cruel theatre as expressionistic theatre of cruelty, as much ideological performance as dialogical performance.[69] These thoughts are particularly relevant in a discussion of Prison Theatre, as prisons have historically served the contradictory goals of punishment and rehabilitation.

Theatre in prisons is of the non-fatal, rehabilitative kind, even in the historical example of Marquis de Sade at Charenton. In the 20th century, the Applied Theatre practice began in 1957 with Herb Blau's production of Beckett's *Waiting for Godot* at San Quentin Prison in California, to an audience of 1400 inmates.

In a subsequent production of Beckett's symbolic piece at Florida State Prison, the director, Sidney Homan, noted that the audience of inmates so deeply identified with the characters and theme of waiting that they spoke directly to the actors on stage, as if the fourth wall were absent. This was spontaneous Forum Theatre, informed by an audience that was less interested in the aesthetics of theatre than in its immediate message. Reflecting on his experience, Homan writes:

> Here was an audience, these men waiting, who demanded to be part of the production, who took what we said so seriously that they could not remain silent. ... These inmates were Brecht's alert spectator taken to the extreme. ... Their presence and interjections demystified the theatrical experience. By the second act the audience was collaborating with us, both in performing and in thinking about the performance.[70]

In the 1982 *Handbook*, Landy wrote about a number of groups that worked mostly by performing plays in prisons to an audience of inmates. These included Cell Block Theatre, the Family, Theatre for the Forgotten and Theatre Without Bars. None of these groups are still in operation, as their funding dried up and the political climate changed. However, within the past 30 years, several new initiatives appeared. The newer work is part production by civilian actors for audiences of inmates, part production by inmates and part drama-based workshops for and sometimes by inmates. This theatre work, which has expanded internationally, is facilitated by theatre artists, Applied Theatre practitioners and drama therapists.

Rick Cluchey, an ex-offender influenced by the San Quentin production of *Waiting for Godot*, founded the San Quentin Drama Workshop, which produced many plays performed by inmates. In recent years Cluchey established a website, Theatre In Prisons.org, which is a clearinghouse for many such experiences worldwide.[71] For Cluchey this work is valuable for helping incarcerated people develop social skills, self-confidence, positive pro-social attitudes and personal change.

Other groups formed by theatre artists and criminal justice professionals discovered a profundity in the physical environment of the prison and in the psychological and cultural terrain of the prisoners. The goals of many who work in prisons are similar to those of most Applied Theatre professionals – to build cohesive and critical communities, to raise consciousness of oppressive conditions and to work toward change.

One such group is Rehabilitation through the Arts (RTA), founded by Katherine Volkins at Sing Sing Correctional Facility in 1996. Volkins has been assisted by scores of volunteers from criminal justice, theatre, Educational Theatre and Drama Therapy.[72] Specializing both in Applied Drama workshops and Applied Theatre performances, RTA has expanded into several other men's and women's prisons throughout New York State.

Philip Taylor and Nancy Smithner, both professors of Educational Theatre at NYU, led Applied Theatre groups in prison exploring social issues through the use of Brechtian Epic Theatre, Boalian Forum Theatre and popular theatre forms, including clowning. A number of directors helped to realize RTA's ambitious production agenda, including plays written and performed by inmates as well as classical and modern dramas such as *Oedipus Rex* and *Of Mice and Men*.

In writing about *Oedipus* at Sing Sing, *The New York Times* reviewer Lawrence Downes observed:

> As I watched, I wondered what it would be like to be defined by my own worst sins. It struck me that when people are locked up for horrible crimes, a lot of goodness and beauty necessarily get locked up too. It also seemed that the Theban society onstage, though afflicted by plague, vengeance and divine cruelty, was probably gentler and saner than the one the inmates knew. Its members clearly cared for one another, and were not numb to grief.[73]

Along with the many new groups devoted to theatre in prisons, a critical literature has also developed, much of it coming out of Applied Theatre. Examples include a volume by Philip Taylor, *Theatre Behind Bars – Can the Arts Rehabilitate?*, which documents Taylor's action research in a New York state prison, applying Forum Theatre, Process Drama and public performance of plays created by the inmates.[74] Focusing upon praxis, Taylor grounds his work in the theories of Foucault and Freire, among others.

Laurence Tocci also published three case studies of Prison Theatre groups in *The Proscenium Cage: Critical Case Studies in US Prison Theatre Programs*, grounded in theory from Performance Studies and Criminology.[75] In his book *Performing New Lives: Prison Theatre* Jonathon Shailor and others discuss 14 exemplary prison theatre programs, including RTA. In a review of the book, Jefe Von Stanley writes:

> Despite my deep passion for theatre I've often quoted the cynical aphorism, *Theatre changes nothing, but at least it changes that*, and I have believed it to be true. I stand corrected thanks to the new book, *Performing New Lives: Prison Theatre*.[76]

For Von Stanley, like so many others who have worked in prisons, theatre is a force for change.

Of practical value is *The Geese Theatre Handbook*, which provides exercises and workshop experiences used by this international theatre in prisons company since its inception in 1987.[77] A further volume is *Challenging Experience: An Experiential Approach to the Treatment of Serious Offenders* by John Bergman and Saul Hewish, both founding members and directors of Geese Theatre.[78] The later volume focuses upon work with sexual offenders.

Bergman, who began work in prisons as a theatre artist, has since become a drama therapist and in his work combines elements of drama/ theatre, Applied Theatre and Drama Therapy. He specialized for many years in working internationally with incarcerated sex offenders. His later research centered in neuroscience as he worked to discover a more precise language in which to explain the nature of forensically based illness and why such a condition responds so effectively to theatrical interventions.

James Thompson, co-founder of the Theatre in Prisons and Probation (TIPP) Centre and professor of applied and social theatre at the University of Manchester, was one of the first to critically survey the field. In his anthology *Prison Theatre: Practices and Perspectives*, he documents a number of experiments in the UK as well as Brazil.[79] He also makes the point that within such community venues as prisons, theatre serves a complex of purposes, including education, rehabilitation and therapy.

Of special note in Thompson's study is the chapter by the psychiatrist Murray Cox, who was instrumental in bringing theatre and Drama Therapy to Broadmoor Hospital in England. Cox used Shakespearian text to prompt the imaginations of inmates, especially seriously mentally ill offenders.[80] He imported the Royal Shakespeare Company to perform classical plays, such as *Hamlet*, to the inmates, and invited drama therapists such as Sue Jennings to facilitate workshops.

Shakespeare's plays have been the spark for several Prison Theatre companies. Shakespeare Behind Bars was founded in1995 by the director

Curt L. Tofteland, in collaboration with psychologist Julie Barto, at the Luther Luckett Correctional Complex in LaGrange, Kentucky. Tofteland sees his mission as restorative justice, a way for inmates to explore personal and social issues through theatre. The group aims to help inmates develop positive interpersonal life skills that will carry over to their lives as civilians. Their work is featured in the film *Shakespeare Behind Bars*, an exploration of a year-long process on a production of *The Tempest*.[81] Tofteland chose *The Tempest* due to its themes of violence, vengeance and forgiveness. In the film the inmates grapple with these themes as parallel elements of the play and of their personal lives. At the end of the film one inmate raises the question: 'When is a man forgiven?' As praxis, the work centers on exploring this question in performance and in life.

### ❖ Case Vignette: Mickey B

Another organization that works with Shakespearian drama is the Educational Shakespeare Company (ESC), based in Belfast, Northern Ireland.

The company was founded by Tom Magill in 1999 to develop drama and film with prisoners and ex-prisoners. ESC is an arts education charity empowering marginalized people to find their voice and tell their stories through film.[82] Magill studied with Boal who made him his representative in Northern Ireland and became a patron of ESC.

Magill directed *Mickey B*, an award-winning film adaptation of *Macbeth*. *Mickey B* was adapted and acted by inmates of Maghaberry maximum-security prison near Belfast who set the piece in a fictional prison. The actors speak in prison vernacular and transform the Shakespearian settings and characters into those familiar to the prisoners. Birnam Wood becomes Burnam Jail. Macbeth is Mickey B and Lady Macbeth is Ladyboy, Mickey B's bitch; the witches are bookies and Macduff is Duffer. On the experience of directing *Mickey B*, Magill states: '*Mickey B* gives prisoners an opportunity to express the guilt they feel about the crimes they have committed in a safe environment through the mask of classical fiction. This creative expression is the first step towards healing the wound that crime inflicts on perpetrators.'[83]

Magill is unique among Applied Theatre professionals in equating the aims of Boalian praxis with healing. Although he is not a drama therapist, he recognizes the therapeutic value of his work. In fact, he speaks openly about his own struggles with violence and the law, serving time in prison where he experienced a profound change leading to a career as an Applied Theatre artist devoted to serving others in similar circumstances.[84]

As for the prisoners who wrote and performed *Mickey B*, here are some of their reflections:

There is no real violence in the film, it's just acting.

We're not just doing the people doing the violence, we're acting the victims as well.

The story of Mickey B shows that if you use violence to get what you want, then it comes back at you.

[Our] involvement in fictional violence gives convicted men the opportunity to question their own violence in a way which is usually impossible in the prison environment.[85]

John Davies, a senior prison officer, was highly skeptical of the project. But after its completion, he said the following: 'If there's one less victim because of this film, then it was worth it.'[86]

*Mickey B* has drawn international acclaim, serving as a catalyst toward change within other cultures. In Korea, where Magill screened the film, an officer at the Kimcheon Juvenile Training School reflected: 'Through diverse programs offered in correctional institutions in Korea, the inmates and youngsters will be able to integrate back into society more easily. And I also think that Tom Magill's experiences will help us further develop methods of rehabilitating the marginalized through the arts.'[87]

### ❖ Case vignette: Theatre in prisons in Israel

A final example is of an Applied Theatre experience in a medium security prison in Israel. The experience was facilitated by Peter Harris, director of the Community Theatre Program at Tel Aviv University. Harris' work, like Magill's, is heavily influenced by Boal, especially in Boal's concerns for fostering dialogue between oppressors and oppressed people.

In his research Harris initiated a series of weekly collaborations between students and prisoners, culminating in a performance. His aim was to explore the dynamics of prejudice and devise dramatic material for collaborative performance, based in dialogues around questions of morality and justice as expressed in culturally specific ways.

When asked to define his work in Applied and Community Theatre, Harris referred to the following statement by Shulamith Lev-Aladgem:

Community-based Theatre in Israel is a local, non-professional theatre which articulates the life experiences of a given marginalised group with

the intention of generating personal and collective empowerment. ...
The theatre project provides an opportunity to articulate repressed and
forbidden life materials that resist, challenge or negotiate in some way
with the status quo.[88]

The actors in Harris' devised performance were students, all Jewish Israelis,
and prisoners, primarily Arab Israelis. In one scene of the performance
Ofra, a secular, middle-class Jewish student, and Ali, a young incarcerated
man from an Arab village in Israel, confront their biases of the other. The
theme was the way each sub-group, Arabs/Jews, men/women, dealt with
the concepts of honor and respect. The scene follows:

ALI:    In the Quran it is written that a woman must be chaste, in order
to keep her dignity and honor. We do not behave like animals as
you think. We don't 'lock her up.' We respect our parents and take
care of them. We need to get their approval for everything, who to
marry, where to live. Our tradition is very important. It preserves
our unity in this world. Look, life is a test. If you walk a straight
path with prayer and charity, you get peace of mind and then go to
heaven. Our goal is to get to heaven and what it says in the Quran
will bring us there, and also helps us to maintain boundaries.

OFRA:    You know that until I came to this project in the jail, I had known
only two Arabs all my life. One was a cook at a restaurant where
I worked. Wow, was he a moron, but I had to be nice to him,
because he who gives respect gets respect... And a contractor at
my mother's work, who invited us for a meal. Four women worked
and cooked this meal for three days. I've never eaten anything
so delicious. When we were in their house I complimented the
glasses we were drinking from. Before the end of the meal they
had wrapped up two sets of these glasses for us. I was in shock!
My boyfriend fought against the Arabs. Once when we went to the
Dead Sea, we passed through some Arab villages; he started shak-
ing. He was a big man who didn't scare easily. I laughed at him,
as if to say: 'What could happen to us?' And there are those who
planted explosives in Gaza and killed a friend of mine. This was
my familiarity with the Arabs.

ALI:    I noticed that at first you were afraid to make eye contact. You'd
pass near a prisoner at the door and press yourself against the
doorpost, not to touch by mistake, maybe you'd catch something.
I saw you with the students, laughing and nice, not the way you
treated us prisoners. I wanted to change that, I decided to invest

in you. You'll see we're not so scary after all. I started sharing with you, talking to you about my daily life, to try to bring you into our world and see it's not so different from yours. The other prisoners told me: 'What are you doing? You courting her? You'll get in trouble!' But it was important for me to continue the process. And look what happened. You opened up, connected. You've gotten to really know us, without the stigmas that were in your head before you got here. I achieved my goal.

OFRA:  You know at first I was not ready to feel anything. I did not want you to look at me, talk to me and certainly not the personal stuff! And you know what I discovered? I discovered that you are people with feelings, warm and loving, angry, offended, funny and exciting. The difference between us is in the way we define our identity – I consider myself Russian, Jewish, an artist, but with you it's one thing, no matter what else, it's the honor, the pride. This honor put you in jail and dictates your relationships with everyone, even me. I do not understand how a person can take the life of his sister for damaging the family honor. And then a friend from our group said: 'Just as you have blue eyes, for them it's honor, it's in the blood.' I'm really trying to accept it. Sometimes it even seems beautiful to me – the politeness, no swearing because it's disrespectful. On the other hand, I do not really understand how someone chooses to go to jail or die for honor. It makes me so sad that you who are really amazing, could find yourself in prison because of this honor.

Following the performance, all involved were asked to reflect upon the process. Ali spoke of the power of performing on stage and how he came to understand Ofra's point of view. He said: 'When a person comes and throws words at you, it's possible to talk things through. … Before, I didn't think that way. I'd get hurt, wouldn't think twice, go straight at people.'

Ofra, likewise, reflected: 'I went way beyond my comfort zone, I fully extended myself, which is something I don't usually do. I wanted it to be good … for them, and for me.'

Ali was imprisoned because of his cultural beliefs and actions. Through the drama work, he became aware of alternative ways of thinking about his crime and found a way to humanize a former enemy. Ofra was imprisoned in her own limited set of beliefs, one that demonized a large sub-group of others within her society. In the work, she indeed pushed beyond her comfort zone. In playing out the cultural role of other, Ofra began to accept its cultural bounty.

# The community as a performance space

Applied Theatre, as we have seen, occurs in various community venues – churches, schools, village squares, theatres, prisons, places of judgement and execution. Applied Theatre also occurs in corporations, centers for the disabled, marginalized and elderly, and, as we shall see in the next chapter, in hospitals and clinics. In the following example, we look at an experience in Applied Theatre in which the community itself becomes the stage. With this example, we again raise the question of identity: What is Applied Theatre, and is it different in form from ancient ritual and spectacle and more contemporary political and para-theatrical experiments? And is it different in content from the kinds of plays championed by Brecht, Kushner and many other socially conscious theatre artists? After our discussion, we turn to an interview with Jan Cohen-Cruz to further examine the nature of Applied Theatre and its relationship to both theatre and the community.

### ❖ Case vignette: Sojourn Theatre

Sojourn Theatre is a multi-ethnic company based in Portland, Oregon. Its mission is to create theatre that raises questions about social and political issues. The company creates original work and adaptations of classic plays to challenge the traditional performer/spectator relationship. It is committed to honoring multiple perspectives and, according to Artistic Director Michael Rohd, to exploring the intersection of theatre and democracy.[89]

In summer 2010 Sojourn Theatre in partnership with the cities of Portland and Molalla performed *On the Table,* a site-specific theatre piece about issues of identity and values in urban/rural Oregon.

The piece was set in two simultaneous performance spaces. In one space in urban Portland, the audience sat in a circle of folding chairs in a church. In the second, a barn in rural Molalla 40 miles away, the audience sat on hay bales placed in a circle on a dirt floor. Sojourn chose Molalla because its small population offered a distinct contrast to Portland.

The play began as Michael Rohd in Portland spoke to his counterpart, Bob, in Molalla, on cell phones. They spoke about their research and rehearsal process in using place as a way to explore difference.

In both spaces, the actors engaged in a memorial service. In Molalla the service was held for George, and in Portland, for Bess. Both died in 1980. In the scenes, audiences learned about their histories and ties to their families and communities. At times the actors interrupted the narrative to explain how the theatre project compelled them to think about their own dilemmas regarding place. Throughout Act I the narrative was driven by questions posed by the actors.

Act II began as each audience group boarded a school bus to Oregon City, a median point between urban Portland and rural Molalla. On the way, they watched two videos of stories of Bess and George's families. Part of the videos included debates concerning local political issues like immigration and taxes. Sometimes a character on one screen talked to another character on the other screen, enhancing the debate and focusing the viewers on the issues. The Portland audience learned that most Molalla people worked in the timber industry, and that many lost their jobs to technology.

A televised actor on the bus from Portland instructed everyone to turn on their cell phones. They were informed: 'You are about to get a call from people coming from a barn in Molalla. This is your chance to talk to them about what you just saw, and ask them about what they just saw.' Phones all over the bus rang simultaneously, and dialogue ensued.

The bus stopped at a train station, and on the platform a bride and groom appeared. The bride from Molalla boarded the Portland bus, and the groom from Portland boarded the Molalla bus. The bus pulled into a parking lot for the wedding intended to unite the two families, descendants of Bess and George. All were assigned to tables of mixed groups from Molalla and Portland. A fusion meal was served, representing different cultures in the region. Actors seated at different tables called out a variety of questions, such as:

> What if someone here lost their timber industry job and they are sitting next to an environmental activist?
> What if someone here is an anti-war activist seated next to three families with loved ones in Afghanistan.
> What if somebody here is gay and they are worried that somebody here is going to judge them?

The final question was: 'What do you think their odds are of staying together?' This question prompted deeper discussion amongst the characters.

George, the groom, a construction worker, and Bess, the bride, an advocate for migrant workers' rights, presented themselves as a caring couple who, nonetheless, differed politically. After presenting themselves, Rohd, as MC, spoke directly to audience:

> When two people agree to commit, there's quite a lot of intentionality, thoughtfulness and agreement. But when large numbers of us find

ourselves bound, we don't necessarily come at it with the same intentionality. So George and Bess want you to spend a few minutes thinking and talking about what would we need to do to give that giant relationship a chance for success?

An actor was placed at each table to facilitate conversation and summarize all the ideas. Then, the actor gave a toast, raising such questions as: How do we learn to see change not as an invasion but as an opportunity? How do we respond to the changing Oregonian identity?

After eating and dancing, people were led out of the parking lot to contemplate the magnificent view across the Oregon City Bridge. A recording played:

Find something beautiful.
Find something your eye is drawn to
Find something that is not what it seems
Find something that has been there a very long time
Find something that will change.

Unexpectedly, all eight actors appeared on the street below, far off in the distance. They walked together toward the bridge in the near distance. As they did so, a final text played, signalling the end of the play:

What if I were here and you were there and time and place and
    community were a shared meal, no different than walking across the
    street together at the same time towards the same bridge.
Welcome to the moment after the state came together.
Welcome to the moment we hurdled towards the future with the same
    five senses.
Welcome to what comes next!

*On the Table* is an experience in Applied Theatre praxis. It involved 18 months of research and interviews in Portland and Molalla that led to the creation of characters and stories.[90] The group intended to portray a variety of figures that captured the essence of the two communities. As part of their research process, the actors engaged with members of the community in developing their character sketches and interpretations, always seeking feedback as to the authenticity of their portrayals. This dialogue fully informed the creation of characters and text. At the same time, the research process allowed citizens to think about important issues within their communities.

The performers recognized the possibility of opening up painful memories, such as the eruption of the volcano Mount Saint Helen, near Portland, or the loss of timber jobs in Molalla. And yet local people embraced the value of shared reflection to shape the collective identity of the community.

During the bus ride, video, audio and cellular phones were used to bridge the two communities and highlight the idea that: 'Actions that happen far apart from each other are not necessarily distinct in their impact and meaning.'[91]

The wedding served to integrate two communities, providing a ritual enabling the audience to reflect on the present and past, and to contemplate the future. As Jan Cohen-Cruz writes: 'The ritual dimension of fusing past, present, and future signals spirituality's marshalling of strength from those with shared values who have come before and striving toward something that has yet to be.'[92]

Sojourn exemplifies a theatre of interrogation and debate, one that strives to build community and encourage audience members to take action. As Rohd stated: 'One thing that gets said a lot about theatre is that a bunch of people come into a room and they laugh and they cry together in the dark, and that builds community. But [...] people crave something that involves more than sitting and watching.'[93]

Is that additional involvement the stuff that distinguishes Applied Theatre from theatre, or one form of theatre that is socially conscious from another that is not? Is theatre simply a shared catharsis among strangers in a dark auditorium, who experience a fleeting connection and then go home? Rohd's work is provocative in that it raises these questions. His work deconstructs the Aristotelian elements of plot and character, sound and sense and is resonant of the theoretical framework of Brecht and Boal.

We turn again to the questions that frame this chapter, and in many ways this book – What is the nature of drama and theatre when applied to social action within communities? Can it subsist under a single umbrella, such as Applied Theatre? And is this term broad enough to encapsulate all of the disparate places and aspects of performance? To explore these and related issues further, we feature part of an interview with Jan Cohen-Cruz, a scholar and activist whose work is about building communities of citizens through forms of interactive performance. Cohen-Cruz trained with Boal, collaborated with many Grassroots and Community Theatre organizations, directed the Applied Theatre minor at NYU Tisch School of the Arts, and directs Imagining America at Syracuse University, a consortium of university and community organizations pooling resources in the arts, humanities and design to conceive a more equitable and civil society.[94]

LANDY: I wonder if there is an umbrella term for all the applied uses of drama and theatre? In the past I called it Educational Drama and Theatre.

COHEN-CRUZ: You should think twice about that term.

LANDY: What do you think about Applied Theatre?

COHEN-CRUZ: The problem with Applied Theatre is that it is often understood as being too operational. You learn it and then you apply it to a situation. It's treated as the second cousin of real knowledge. And the notion of application doesn't communicate how reciprocal such relationships tend to be. I see how it could be misinterpreted by a lot of people.

LANDY: You mean from people in theatre?

COHEN-CRUZ: Some of the people who understand Applied Theatre the least are in theatre, but their goal in theatre is more product than process. The term I used for my new book is Engaging Performance. It has two meanings: performance is being engaged as part of a process, and it's fun, it holds your attention. I went back to the tradition of Sartre who talks about the engaged artist. To me it's about relationships and sometimes the product is fantastic.

LANDY: So you don't make a separation between someone who is trained in traditional theatre and someone trained in Educational Theatre?

COHEN-CRUZ: Well, I look at what they do. When people were calling AIDS 'gay cancer,' there was Kushner, and it's not by chance that he's gay and he was losing a lot of friends and he wrote *Angels in America*. He reached people in a way that other plays and other processes did not. To me, that was very engaged performance.

LANDY: There are also people in Educational Theatre and Drama Therapy creating engaged theatre.

COHEN-CRUZ: I would count Drama Therapy and Educational Theatre in all of this, absolutely.

LANDY: I recently interviewed Ela Weissberger, a survivor of the Nazi camp, Terezin. She was in the original children's opera *Brundibár*, a thinly disguised parody of Hitler's brutality. Tony Kushner wrote an adaptation of *Brundibár*.

Weissberger was aware that at the end of Kushner's version, he changed the final lyrics. The original says something like: 'We got rid of the tyrant, and everything will be better'. But he changed it to add: 'Just remember that more tyrants will come again'. This upset Ms. Weissberger. For her, theatre was about envisioning a more hopeful future. She felt Kushner reminded the audience of children that evil persists. What are your thoughts about that?

COHEN-CRUZ: I think it depends on the issue, because look at how *Angels in America* ends. There's this unlikely group – this Mormon mother, the gay former lover with AIDS, but he's still alive and they're all under the angel. To me there was just a beautiful sense of who can end up connecting and the fact that we are all interconnected. With *Brundibar*, I think Kushner needed to communicate that we have to talk with each other, but in the case of the legacy of the Holocaust, we should know that the potential for tyranny isn't over. That seems an important thing to say right now.

LANDY: Can you speak about your current work? Are you in theatre? In cultural studies?

COHEN-CRUZ: I'm a scholar and an organizer, working with *Imaging America: Artist's and Scholars in Public Life* at Syracuse University. If I had to put it in one sentence, I would say that I'm in engaged scholarship through the cultural disciplines. My belief is that the arts and humanities contribute deeply to our lives, and my job is to articulate and point to a full range of how that happens so as to be coherent in higher education. The national leverage can support lots of local efforts. We often work locally because we want to have actual contact with people.

LANDY: The term praxis is becoming popular in Applied Theatre. In our book we focus on praxis to identify theatre groups that not only do the work, but also reflect upon the work and use that reflection to work toward change.

COHEN-CRUZ: I find a lot of practitioners are hungry to reflect, but they don't always have the time. Look at those companies in the 60s, like the Living Theatre, that spent endless hours in discussion. Some still do.

LANDY: And what about the term, theatre? Should there be a pure theatre and an Applied Theatre?

COHEN-CRUZ: I think there is a form of theatre that has a lot in common with what we call Applied Theatre. One of the reasons why I think it's important to connect the two has to do with aesthetics. If you're going to use the theatre, you want to use it well. But people assume if it's applied, it's not going to be good.

LANDY: And some people in Applied Theatre assume that if it's done in the commercial theatre, it's not going to be good. *Angels in America* was done on Broadway.

COHEN-CRUZ: Exactly, so it causes a rift.

LANDY: Terminology is really important to this discussion.

COHEN-CRUZ: I think it is important because it ends up shaping how people's work is perceived. ... There's an amazing potential right now, because there is more responsibility put on universities to prepare graduates for jobs. The place of Applied Theatre is becoming a way that you can still be trained as a theatre artist and also be prepared to work in the community – in prisons, with old people, with children.

The title of Cohen-Cruz' 2010 book, *Engaging Performance: Theatre as Call and Response*, suggests an image of dialogue between speakers and listeners, actors and audiences.[95] It also suggests a cultural form of expression steeped in tradition, as call and response refers to musical expression within African and African-American cultures with roots in religious ritual and political debate.

Most forms of Applied Theatre are noted for their dialogical structures as audience members become activated by the events presented on the stage. Cohen-Cruz, in search of language to hold the many forms of community-based drama and theatre, prefers the term Engaging Performance. This term and concept seems to be more inclusive than Applied Theatre, in that it contains compelling theatrical plays performed for general audiences within conventional theatre spaces. Such plays share the values and functions of many forms of Applied Theatre in that they raise questions, provoke dialogue, offer a critique of the status quo and inspire action in the world. Cohen-Cruz gave the example of Kushner's *Angels in America*, which, like the work of TfD organizations in Africa, addresses the scourge of HIV/AIDS as it is played out within a society of denial.[96]

Applied Theatre, as it appears on stage and page, is a praxis when all involved agree to reflect upon both the process and the product and in doing so, consider its capacity to impact the lives of people within their communities. As such it functions to raise awareness within communities as to various personal, social and political realities.

Although Applied Theatre is most often a form of dialogical expression and debate, it can also be a form of repression, based in a political system that seeks to control the behavior of its citizens. Public executions are one glaring example. But there are other less lethal performances, such as the shaming parades popular in China until very recently, where prostitutes and other undesirables were shackled and marched through the streets of a community – a warning to the populace to obey the law.

Applied Theatre can serve a spiritual function, affirming the faith of celebrants and attempting to convert the agnostic. On the secular side, Applied Theatre is also used within corporations to educate future and current workers and managers in methods of communication, socialization and creative problem solving. One company in Taiwan, Smart Orange, with members trained in improvisation, Educational Theatre and Drama Therapy, is committed to corporate training and does so by encouraging tired workers to get on their feet, bang a drum and use their bodies and voices playfully. Even Chicago's famous comedy troupe Second City is in on the act, working within corporate culture to lighten up the very serious business of business.

Applied Theatre is a complex form that serves several goals and populations, that occurs within multiple cultures and community spaces, and that exists in a somewhat ambivalent relationship to the art form of drama/theatre. In the next chapter we will focus upon, arguably, yet another form of Applied Theatre, that of Drama Therapy. Like much of Applied Theatre, Drama Therapy attempts to raise consciousness and raise questions. Like Applied Theatre, it is practiced within communities. And yet it is rarely mentioned within the literature and thus remains isolated from the fold. We explore why, and attempt to raise the question of whether these two strange bedfellows can indeed co-habit a common nesting place: a theatre for change.

# PART III    DRAMA AND
#                     THEATRE IN THERAPY

The premise of this book is that an engagement in the metaphorical world of applied forms of drama and theatre is potentially transformational. By becoming who we are not, we become more of who we are and who we can be as individual, social and spiritual beings. In Parts I and II, we looked at drama and theatre as agents for changing learning in schools and social life in communities. In this section we address therapeutic applications of the art form.

Change in this case is similar to the others in terms of aims. It is about developing a critical consciousness, an awareness of options, and the capacity to take action through a modification of thought, feeling and behavior. Like leaders in Educational and Applied Theatre, drama therapists apply the aesthetic forms of role-play and storytelling, improvisation and formal theatre to realize these aims. And like their colleagues, they explore such compelling issues as human growth and development, conflict resolution, HIV/AIDS, incarceration and child abuse.

All applied forms of drama and theatre are similar in their nature as hybrids, but different in the kinds of attachments made. In this case, the hybrid is a mix of the art form and the therapeutic form, implying a uniqueness in training and contract. Drama Therapy is a praxis, unlike other therapeutic models, where action precedes reflection. And it is a praxis, like the models discussed in the previous chapters, where thoughts are embodied and where reflection leads to action.

A major training program in Drama Therapy at NYU begins with a question: How is performance healing? We respond with a vignette set in the ancient Hellenic world.

### ❖  Case vignette: The ancient theatre of healing

In researching the relationship between theatre and healing, Landy visited various Asclepions in Greece and Turkey, healing centers in the classical world. As Asclepius was the god of healing, ancient peoples erected temples to engage in healing rites. In the Greek tradition, the temples to Asclepius were built near theatres as performance was considered part of the therapeutic cure of the sick. This is clear in Epidavros and Delphi in Greece and in Pergamon in Turkey. As part of the healing, the patients were required to witness performances and sometimes participate as actors in the Chorus.[1]

In Pergamon, the Asclepion is quite intact. In its ancient incarnation, patients were invited into tunnels to spend the night. Streams of water flowed on both sides of the tunnels, and above, circular windows were cut out of the roof. The priests chanted over the openings throughout the night and burned incense whose fragrance wafted down upon the sleepers. In the morning, the patients recounted their dreams to the priests who interpreted them and diagnosed their patients according to the dream imagery. Then, the priests escorted the patients to the amphitheatre, several hundred meters away, where they experienced a cathartic reaction to the characters' dilemmas, an emotional purging intended to enhance their cure.

In these sites, the temple was built not only near the theatre, but also near the sports stadium. In the Asclepion at Delphi, the theatre stands between the temple and the sports stadium, implying that theatre is the link between the body and the spirit. As an historical footnote, the Greek playwright Sophocles kept a shrine to Asclepius in his home.[2]

In standing between body and spirit, the theatre is not just about healing, but also about liminality.[3] Theatre becomes a threshold through whose portals pass the human need for groundedness and transcendence. As an applied form of discourse, theatre facilitates the dynamic flow of ideas, bodily sensations and images, and as such serves as a powerful exemplar of holistic education and wellness.

In locating their greatest artworks within churches, the ancient Romans sanctified their spiritual institutions through art, intuiting that art is a liminal space between the holy and the profane. In locating their theatres between sports stadiums and temples, the ancient Greeks sanctified essential functions of the art form of performance. One way of thinking about those functions is to imagine the theatre as a place that can hold together the great polarities of body and spirit, of competition and communion, of ignorance and wisdom. As such, this is a theatre of healing. Let us now look at contemporary examples that continue to respond to the question: how is performance healing?

# 5     Drama Therapy

### ❖   Case vignette one

Georgie at three-years-old is sitting in her mother's lap in the morning. She opens the front of her mother's nightgown and exposes her breast. She examines it attentively and touches it in a very serious way, paying particular attention to the nipple. Her mother says: 'Do you remember when you were a baby and you had your milk from Mommy breasts?'

Georgie replies: 'When I am a Mommy and you are a baby then I will feed you on my breasts.'[1]

### ❖   Case vignette two

Caitlin at six-years-old is so frail that she can barely walk or talk. She is hospitalized and dependent upon constant medical treatment to sustain her bodily functions. In working with her drama therapist, she creates the role of a soaring bird. For the first time in her brief life, she is able to transcend her physical limitations and soar unencumbered through a beautiful expansive sky, with limited movement but unlimited imagination.[2]

### ❖   Case vignette three

An American drama therapist collaborates with colleagues in Japan to organize an encounter between a group of Japanese students and professionals and their counterparts in Nanjing, China. The purpose is to create a ritual to begin to heal the pain of the past. In 1937 the Japanese army slaughtered and raped many thousands of Chinese civilians in Nanjing. The encounter is held at the Memorial to the Nanjing Massacre. Through this experience in Drama Therapy, Japanese and Chinese participants are able to express their deep feelings of loss and shame, address the wounds of their common historical trauma, and understand how it continues to be played out in present generations.[3]

### ❖ Case vignette four

Shortly after the assassination of John F. Kennedy, J. L. Moreno directed a Sociodrama representing the event and its aftermath. Trained Psychodrama auxiliaries played the roles of JFK and Jackie Kennedy. Others were chosen from the audience to play Lee Harvey Oswald and Jack Ruby. The Sociodrama was held during the annual conference of the American Psychiatric Association and 400 people attended. Moreno said to those gathered: 'We are all suffering from a tremendous amount of unresolved guilt and confusion over what happened to President Kennedy. After all, if you can "kill the father", anything goes.'[4] The full group experienced an intense moment of connection and catharsis in their shared grieving.

### ❖ Case vignette five

In a Drama Therapy group in Greece, a woman arrives very late. The participants debate whether or not to allow her to remain in the group. The therapist asks the group to imagine the latecomer as a role type. The group names her: the intruder. The therapist asks members of the group to create stories about intruders. One woman tells a story about an idyllic isolated island where an intruder suddenly appears and terrorizes the population with displays of aggression and sexuality. The group dramatizes her story, and she becomes aware of her need for a figure that can inject passion into her cloistered, tradition-bound life. Although this figure is an intruder, it is one whose qualities can help her live a more fully integrated existence.[5]

### ❖ Case vignette six

In a Playback Theatre group a Japanese man tells a story about experiencing the atomic bomb blast as a young boy in Hiroshima. He recalls thinking: 'It was the day that the sun fell out of the sky.' The man witnesses the group of actors play back his story in a stylized, respectful way. He is very moved, as is the audience.[6]

### ❖ Case vignette seven

In a Psychodrama group a black woman recalls a story from her childhood where her white teacher insisted that she color in a drawing of her hand in white flesh colors. Through the Psychodrama the woman dialogues with the teacher and with herself as a little girl, releasing her shame and anger and moving toward reparation of the past injury.[7]

These examples are taken from published cases of Drama Therapy, Psychodrama and Sociodrama. The first is an example of a spontaneous process of parenting a young child as viewed through the lens of Drama Therapy.

Like Applied Theatre, Drama Therapy occurs within community settings and concerns the exploration of social issues and the implementation of actions intended to ameliorate distress and oppression. Although drama therapists most frequently work in groups, they also treat individuals, helping them to identify problematic issues in their lives and to discover effective ways to move through their distress.

The above examples are of praxis, where practice, theory and reflection inform each other and lead toward some form of change. As in Chapter 4, some of these cases will be discussed in greater depth to elucidate the scope of Drama Therapy with individuals and groups. And as before, other examples of praxis will be given to highlight exemplary work throughout the world. Of note will be our continuing search for commonalities among the various forms of drama and theatre in their pure and applied manifestations.

## What is Drama Therapy?

We are aware that professionals in Applied Theatre use the term health rather than therapy in speaking about treatments of illness through drama and theatre. Examples of professional conferences include: *Health Acts: Applied Theatre, Health and Well-being* at the University of Exeter, and *Forum on Theatre for Public Health* at NYU, both in spring 2011. Further, a major journal published by Intellect in the UK is called *Journal of Applied Arts and Health*.

It is our opinion that Drama Therapy derives more from traditions of psychotherapy and traditional healing practices than from medicine and public health. Additionally, in establishing itself as an independent therapy profession, it has distanced itself from the medical model of diagnosis and illness, embracing holistic models of wellness and an alternative notion of assessing clients (rather than patients) through the art form. It is a therapy, a term that is often suspect to those Applied Theatre practitioners who view change as political rather than therapeutic.

Drama Therapy is the application of one or more forms of drama and theatre to people who choose to explore personal and collective problems and to take action toward change. The facilitator is a trained and licensed drama therapist, and all involved enter into a contract of confidentiality and safety. The forms of drama and theatre can include, but are not limited to: free play, improvisation, storytelling and story-making, role-playing, puppetry and mask, and theatre performance.

Drama Therapy, like Applied Theatre, is not at all monolithic. It has many forms and many related approaches. The best known is Psychodrama, a form initiated by J. L. Moreno in the 1920s in Europe and later developed by him and his wife, Zerka Toeman Moreno, in the US. For many this form is a precursor and thus source of Drama Therapy, which was only fully recognized as an academic discipline in the 1970s with the founding of professional organizations in the UK and the US.[8]

And yet Drama Therapy has other sources that pre-date Psychodrama, in some cases by thousands of years. Drama Therapy, like other forms of Theatre for Change, is a hybrid in that it integrates drama/theatre and psychotherapy. And it is a chameleon as its techniques and theories slip comfortably within pure and applied forms of drama and theatre as well as counseling and clinical psychology. It is also viewed by many as a subset of Creative Arts Therapy or Expressive Therapy, fields that include therapeutic work in art, music, dance/movement and poetry.

In naming this chapter Drama Therapy, we are aware again of the problematic nature of naming so many of the pieces of this very flavorful pie.

**Photograph 5.1   J. L. and Zerka Toeman Moreno, photo courtesy of Zerka T. Moreno**

In the book *The Couch and the Stage*, Landy situates the field within several healing practices. He begins with the traditional healing form of shamanism, which has a venerable history throughout the world and is still widely practiced, often alongside Western medicine.[9] A shaman is a healer who not only works through the application of traditional medicine, but also through engaging the spirit world to procure its powerful medicines. The shaman invokes the spirits in the guise of an actor, through trance, dance, song, storytelling, impersonation and role-play.

In addition to shamanism, we note that forms of healing theatre are at least as old as the ancient Greek rituals performed in the Asclepions. As many aspects of African Applied Theatre are based in traditional cultural practices, so too are many aspects of African and Asian Drama Therapy.

Landy also speaks about the Western roots of Drama Therapy within the early theory and practice of psychoanalysis, giving special attention to the early disciples of Freud who later broke from the master's orthodoxy, at great risk to their reputations. They did so, in part, because they believed that the talking cure was a limited path to traverse in order to access the unconscious and transform ingrained patterns of psychological distress.

For Jung the journey toward awareness was through expressive imagery that revealed universal archetypes and motifs.[10] Rank and Ferenczi considered an action-based approach toward awareness and change.[11] Ferenczi went so far as to enact scenes from the patient's life and reverse roles with his patients in a controversial form called mutual analysis.[12] The most daring of all of Freud's fallen angels was Wilhelm Reich, who believed that neurotic patterns were armored within the musculature of the body. To unlock these patterns, Reich utilized forms of role-play and dramatic action.[13]

Throughout the history of Western psychotherapy, many others developed approaches to treat patients through forms of dramatic action. For example, behaviorists used behavior rehearsal to help patients practice new and more useful behaviors.[14] Constructivists used fixed role therapy to help patients change their cognitive schemas.[15]

In addition to these more conventional therapies alternative practices arose, especially during the liberation and self-help movements of the 1960s. During that time, J. L. Moreno's popularity grew as he presented trainings internationally. Fritz Perls, who trained with Moreno but did not acknowledge his mentor, developed his own approach to action treatment called Gestalt therapy.[16]

The timeline of drama and theatre in therapy in Western cultures stretches back hundreds of years to Marquis de Sade's performances with mental patients in Charenton Prison, France, in the 18th century. Throughout Europe in the 19th and 20th centuries, many psychiatric and medical personnel experimented with theatre performances by, with and for institutionalized mental patients.[17] And in Russia in the early part of the 20th century, the theatre directors Vladimir Iljine and Nicholas Evreinoff experimented widely with Therapeutic Theatre.[18]

Throughout the 1960s and 70s theatre itself was rapidly changing with many forms of avant-garde and later post-modern theatre that challenged classical structures. A number of early drama therapists came from this movement, training with members of the Living Theatre, the Performance Group and the Polish Lab Theatre.

During this time there were also radical changes in the field of education. While seeking to create a transformative pedagogy, drama educators developed ways to frame their practice theoretically. As noted in Part I, leading figures coming out of the 1960s included Slade, Heathcote, Bolton, Way and Courtney. All became aware of parallel developments in Drama Therapy and some, like Slade and Courtney, pioneered early forms of Drama Therapy.[19] Gavin Bolton wrote the Foreword to Landy's 1996 book: *Essays in Drama Therapy: The Double Life.*[20]

Although Drama Therapy is similar to Applied Theatre in terms of theory, practice and communities served, there are essential differences in contract, training, leadership and purpose. As mentioned above drama therapists are trained and licensed as therapists, guided by ethical issues of informed consent, confidentiality and the edict to do no harm. Drama therapists learn to work with a range of clinical populations, and they learn how to both encourage and contain emotional expression. They also engage in a process of their own therapy and supervision, learning how best to use their own personalities in the service of their clients.

Drama Therapy students, most of whom enter graduate training with a strong background in drama and theatre, continue their immersion in the art form. For the most part, however, this study is about learning how to integrate an aesthetic process and a therapeutic one. In addition students study theories of abnormal psychology, personality and psychological development, as well as the theory and practice of individual and group therapy.

In terms of leadership, drama therapists are called facilitators, therapists, leaders and even teachers, depending upon where they work. In Playback Theatre they are called conductors. In Psychodrama they are called directors.

There is a range of names for leaders widely used in Applied Theatre, including: facilitator, teaching artist, animator or joker. The term joker, derived from the wild card in a deck of playing cards, is used in Theatre of the Oppressed to highlight the variable and flexible quality of leadership.

Both Applied Theatre and Drama Therapy practitioners aim for change in individuals and groups. However Applied Theatre artists focus more on cognitive, social and political change. Ironically, although theatre is so often about emotional expression and the inner life of actors and characters, modeled on years of interpretation of Stanislavki's classic text *An Actor Prepares*, most Educational and Applied Theatre artists stay clear of psychological processes and uncontained emotional expression, some accepting Boal's idea that catharsis, which he once called Aristotle's coercive system, deadens reflective action.[21] Drama therapists most often work toward psychological change, but even when engaging emotional expression, do so through the distance of theatrical fiction.

In noting these differences, we also point to the many similarities between Drama Therapy and Applied Theatre. Although all drama therapists are trained to work with psychological change, most are also skilled at facilitating change within communities. Thus drama therapists are required to learn about the ethical and political realities of social systems. The majority of jobs in Drama Therapy are in community institutions that serve people challenged by conditions of poverty, disease and disability, oppression, racism, homelessness and trauma. Such placements and populations are familiar to many Applied Theatre practitioners.

Drama therapists and Applied Theatre artists both use the full range of drama and theatre techniques, from play to performance. They both make use of similar theoretical orientations, including those of Brecht and Boal. Drama therapists also take considerable theoretical substance from Moreno as well as psychologists and sociologists not very prominent in the Applied Theatre literature. Both fields serve similar communities of oppressed peoples, with some differences noted.

Most essentially both Applied Theatre and Drama Therapy are versions of a dramatic praxis and of a theatre for change. Practitioners in both fields aim toward helping clients develop awareness and take positive action toward change. In fact one component of the Drama Therapy Program at California Institute for Integral Studies is called Theatre for Change and serves to raise awareness about the effects of racism and other forms of oppression through the performance of original plays. The rehearsal and performance process involves a mix of Drama Therapy and Theatre of the Oppressed methods.[22]

Given the similarities, why is there not more reciprocity and less divisiveness between the two fields, at least in the published literature? We will address that question and also attempt to redress the lack of trust and dialogue below.

## Splits within splits

In the early days of human history, performance was a sure way to ritualize the yearnings within communities for power and protection, for propagating the species, for health and long life. Through an impersonation of the powerful forces of nature and the superhuman qualities of spirits, people could at least temporarily satisfy their yearnings. Given the evolution of civilization and the migration of peoples throughout the world, ritual performance separated out from its distinctive place in the life of communities. With the development of systems of religion, medicine, sport and art, performance became one of several ways to satisfy the human yearning for immortality.

In the Asclepions at Epidavros, Delphi and Pergamon, we find a separation of temple, sports stadium, hospital and theatre. Although related, they are housed in separate buildings, a long way from the simple circle of celebration extant in many ancient villages. Since the 19th century in the commercial and fringe theatres of major cities throughout the world, the theatre is even further removed from institutions of worship, healing and sport. If anything, urban planners situate theatre spaces among other arts centers.

In ancient Greece theatre was part of a festival in praise of the gods, a contest among celebrated writers. And through the Renaissance theatre artists built a popular following among the growing masses of working citizens who desired diversion from the day's labor. The skills of theatre were learned through apprenticeship. With the exception of the church that applied theatre to the teaching of Bible stories, theatre was about art and entertainment.

By the end of the 20th century theatre academies and departments within universities developed throughout the world, some embedded in the related fields of education, speech, communications and media. Further, there was variation in the names of the departments, that is, Theatre Arts, Performing Arts, Communication Arts, Speech and Performance Studies.

As the profession of Educational Theatre achieved some prominence, it too entered academia, first as a subset of theatre and then as a split-off part, meriting the status of an academic department. Lagging behind by some 20 years, Drama Therapy also found its way into academia. But because of splits within splits, it too struggled to find its identity within such departments as Performing Arts, Counseling Psychology and Creative Arts Therapy.

In the scrambling to maintain a professional identity, a clientele and sufficient funding, competition arose among the theatre forms. Many theatre academics set up arbitrary hierarchies with the pure theatre programs at the top and applied ones at the bottom.

As Drama Therapy began to separate out from Educational Theatre, both in the US and the UK, a similar hierarchy appeared. Academics and theatre workers felt the need to protect their turf. Additionally, members of each group made assumptions about the other that were based upon limited knowledge of the practice and, indeed, the praxis.

At yet another level, many splits erupted within the field of Drama Therapy. Some needed to assert their independence from Psychodrama. Others looked to separate from the more interdisciplinary Expressive Therapies. Even when those separations appeared to work, drama therapists created internal splits and drew lines between various forms of Drama Therapy, to the extent that the 2009 book *Current Approaches in Drama Therapy* features 18 different forms.[23]

While acknowledging the many splits within splits, here we attempt to envision a greater whole which is a mix of Educational Theatre, Applied Theatre and Drama Therapy. Holding the pieces together, however, is challenging.

In recent Applied Theatre publications, writers make distinctions between the social/political aims of Applied Theatre artists and the personal/psychological aims of drama therapists. For example, Prentki and Preston state:

> Drama therapy [...] grew out of the expanding fields of psychology and psychiatry in the 1960s as a way of using drama processes to assist with the recovery of patients from mental illness. Today many practitioners of applied theatre are usually quick to assert that they are not therapists, either by training or inclination, and are concerned with social transformation rather than individual pathologies of rehabilitation.[24]

And yet Drama Therapy also grew out of Moreno's work in Sociometry and Sociodrama. In working with a range of clients from war veterans hospitalized with post-traumatic stress to incarcerated felons, drama therapists, like Applied Theatre workers, focus as much on social transformation as on rehabilitation.

In an early publication James Thompson cites the work of Role Theory in Drama Therapy pejoratively, arguing that it is 'reductive and assumes that role is personally held when it is in fact socially constructed and situated'[25]

A closer reading of Landy's *Persona and Performance*, which serves as Thompson's source material, reveals that role is in large part socially constructed, based in the work of Charles Cooley, George Herbert Mead, Erving Goffman and others.[26] As to role's reductive nature, Landy and others point to its archetypal nature, akin to Jungian and post-Jungian understanding of archetypes and myths.[27]

In beginning to stitch the splits, we find it more useful to acknowledge differences while focusing upon the commonalities. What if in the training of Applied Theatre artists and drama therapists, there were core courses and experiences? What if key concepts, such as role and narrative, could be understood in their many complex iterations? Students and practitioners would be privy to a broad conception of the psychological, social and political aspects of essential theatrical concepts.

There are many examples of collaborations between drama therapists and Applied Theatre artists as noted in an earlier discussion of *Standing Tall*.[28] In Africa there are strong signs of collaboration. Drama for Life, based at the University of Witwatersrand, offers trainings and courses in both Applied Theatre and Drama Therapy. Originally intended to battle HIV and AIDS, the program expanded to include issues of social justice, peace building and environmental sustainability. It fosters dialogue and collaborative research among many prominent theatre workers in several African countries. Their third yearly conference in 2010, 'Arts Activism, Education and Therapies: Transforming Communities across Africa,' initiated a dialogue whose purpose was

> to ask questions about the relationship between activism, education and therapies; to acknowledge the role of traditional healing arts in Africa; to find relationships between African and western notions of healing through the arts and to acknowledge that education – as we have historically known it – has to change fundamentally to embrace the profound human crises throughout the continent.[29]

Warren Nebe, the director of Drama for Life, is a theatre and Applied Theatre artist, as well as a drama therapist, trained at New York University. Other efforts in South Africa include developments at the University of Natal, Pietermaritzburg, to pilot a project called Kwazulu-Natal Programme for Survivors of Violence.[30] This program explores the use of various art-forms to facilitate the social, psychological and career development necessary for sustainable recovery from trauma. The project seeks to facilitate personal and community stories and to transform the stories into performance.[31]

In a recent interview Hazel Barnes, Drama for Life Research Professor, was asked how she envisions the future of the field of Applied Theatre. She responded:

> There is an increasing awareness of the therapeutic possibilities of drama and theatre. I see a move away from purely development

issues towards a more holistic approach to social problems which takes into account the psychological impacts of disease, poverty and violence.[32]

Another attempt to integrate Applied Theatre and Drama Therapy comes from an unlikely source, Augusto Boal. Boal often proclaimed that he was not a therapist and that his work was not therapy. Yet his technique of Rainbow of Desire (ROD) was intended to help individuals deal with inner figures of oppression, which Boal called 'cops in the head'. Boal shifted to this form when in exile in Paris. There Boal saw that people's struggles stemmed from more personal sources – unresolved conflicts between parents and children, struggles within the home and work environment, or internal struggles with loneliness, emptiness and miscommunication. The impetus for writing his book *Rainbow of Desire* came from an invitation in 1989 to address the International Association of Group Psychotherapists, an organization founded by J. L. Moreno.[33]

Rainbow of Desire is a group process. Although it utilizes warm-up games and stylized modes of presentation, it primarily involves the telling of stories within a group and the choice of protagonists from the group whose stories are dramatized by the group members and directed by the joker. The stories involve episodes of unresolved conflicts between the storyteller and an oppressor who might be a boss, a friend, a lover, a parent.

In the dramatization there are a number of techniques, all involving a series of sculpts depicting a range of emotions that the protagonist experiences in relationship to the oppressor. The spect-actors in the group help the protagonist by sculpting the desires and expressing their own feelings in role through monologue and dialogue, consistent with the needs of the protagonist. Throughout the process the protagonist is led to experience the rainbow of her desires, that is, the full emotional range relevant to her relationship with her oppressor. In the end there is no resolution, only a moment of *conscientização*, a deeper awareness of the complex nature of the conflict. Often both protagonists and spect-actors experience catharsis, which Boal sees as a moment that purifies the spect-actors and removes detrimental blocks.[34] In nearing the conclusion a discussion can ensue, which Boal characterizes as follows:

> All the actors must tell what they felt or noticed from within the scene, while the other participants express what they felt or noticed observing the scene. The director must coordinate the discussion, without ever trying to 'interpret' or 'discover the truth.'[35]

In some ways ROD is similar in structure to Psychodrama and other forms of Drama Therapy, as a conflict between protagonist and antagonist is dramatized before an active group, many of whom play roles in the drama. The drama is led by a joker who helps the protagonist develop awareness. In sessions that we observed led by Boal, there is a clear form that begins with warm-up and proceeds into action. Further, we observed that protagonists and spect-actors experience catharsis, a powerful expression of emotion. These sessions demonstrated less clear evidence of group closure than is the norm in Psychodrama and Drama Therapy, leaving some participants feeling unbalanced.

When discussing catharsis, Boal contrasts his point of view with that of Moreno. However, he misinterprets Moreno by conflating Moreno's catharsis with the Aristotelian purgation of toxins, thereby dulling an individual's capacity to critically examine options.[36] In closely reading Moreno, we learn that he proposed several forms of catharsis. The most fully realized, catharsis of integration, is that which attempts to release feeling while also enhancing the critical ability to become aware of the circumstances leading to that feeling.[37] Moreno's conception, pre-dating Boal's by some 50 years, is close to Boal's understanding of catharsis in the Theatre of the Oppressed.

In *Rainbow of Desire*, Boal gives a number of examples of work in psychiatric facilities, again blurring the line between his praxis and that of drama therapists. Although there are clear differences between ROD and Drama Therapy in training, contract, process and goals, at times Boal appeared to minimize some of those distinctions. Dedicating his book in part to Zerka Moreno and Grete Leutz, a pioneer German psychodramatist, Boal moved toward rapprochement. It should be noted, however, that he first dedicates his book to Paolo Freire and the Workers' Party of Brazil.

When Boal invited a mixed group of Educational Theatre and Drama Therapy students to his center in Rio in 2008 for a joint training in Rainbow of Desire, the experience appeared to be a step toward reconciliation. However it also raised many thorny questions about ROD and challenges inherent in collaboration among the three strands of education, therapy and social action. Such questions include: Is and should theatre be safe for the actors and spect-actors? If so, how safe? What is the impact of catharsis and strongly expressed emotion on the protagonist and the group? How much responsibility should the facilitator/joker take in revealing deeper issues in the individual/group? Should there be time following ROD enactments for verbal processing? How can people with different training and skills in applied forms of theatre work together in building a supportive learning community through a deep experiential process?

The process in Rio was rich and complex but led to some confusion and dismay on the part of many participants. The above questions were not answered, and certainly Boal intended them to be pondered rather than answered. The following reflections from two students, used with permission, raise questions as to safety, collaboration and the effectiveness of Rainbow of Desire.

External oppression was something we all could wrap our heads around. But Boal urged us to push beyond our comfort zones to explore our internally expressed oppressions, noting that theatre is not safe. Unfortunately, internal oppressions are deeply entrenched and harder to express than external oppressors. They develop from people we love and respect just as often as from people we despise and hate. In participating in ROD, I avoided going deeper. Despite Boal's insistence that ROD is not therapy, it asks participants to delve into the same unconscious and emotional areas that one explores in therapy.

While the focus of ROD may be on taking the individual experience and universalizing it, I could not get past the personal to experience a truly communal learning environment. Two worlds – South American and North American, academic and practical, psychological and theatrical – collided that August in Rio. Rather than leaving with clarity on ROD, I left more certain of the importance of appropriate and rigorous training, especially in setting boundaries and creating safe dramatic learning environments for facilitators of Educational Theatre. I also left with sadness at the divide between those worlds. With so much to learn from each other, it was disheartening to realize our differences were easier to grasp than our similarities.

Another student offered this:

There is a certain something that happens when you work with an artist who has proven the willingness to live and die for his craft. Entering a classroom with Augusto Boal in the midst of Brazil is itself a Rainbow of Desire. Perhaps it is simply that the vibrancy of his character will provide you with the hues you are lacking. When our two groups collided – one Drama Therapy, one Educational Theatre – it seemed a perfect match. Theatre, we all agreed, has the power to unlock the richest treasures available: emotion and knowledge. Something, however, seemed amiss during our shared travels. Safety, it seemed, was at the crux of all our disagreements. Drama therapists, after all, are clinicians, trained to create secure environments. Boal, on the other hand, has lived a life without safety, enduring imprisonment and torture for his beliefs. Our fears concerning trust within an acting exercise felt selfish and spoiled. When Boal would say, 'but it ISN'T safe,' he meant it. And we were uncertain how to handle that as therapists. In Brazil swift judgment and a fiery temper can work in one's favor, but when one's perspective is of creating a healthy group culture, these qualities can become impediments. We all sought something, and were all bound to be disappointed. Boal, in his creative work, gives oppressed persons the opportunity to think of alternatives. Our group struggled because it became stagnant, judging wishes inconsistent with our own and mourning each failed fulfillment. We could never embrace the possibility that perhaps each of us were permitted to seek as we saw fit, and reap those benefits we most needed. The Rainbow of Desire simply could not thrive within the context of a collective bathed in grayscale.

The splits within splits are considerable hurdles, especially within fields that are small and poorly funded to begin with. But as realities of academic and occupational life, they need to be acknowledged and questioned. As we have seen, many in the separate fields of Educational Theatre, Applied Theatre and Drama Therapy work collaboratively. We feel this is a positive development, despite the inevitable obstacles and challenges. It seems even more challenging, given the above example, to hold together splits that could not even be effectively contained by Boal.

Having compared ROD with Psychodrama and Drama Therapy, let us turn to the latter two forms and give examples of praxis within a number of community settings. Although we present each as a single entity, we again point to the reality that many practitioners integrate these forms, producing at times a confusing blend, but at other times a brilliant rainbow intended to satisfy a panoply of desires.

## Psychodrama

Psychodrama has not essentially changed in form since the original 1982 *Handbook* was published. Certainly there have been many innovations in technique and in populations served, given a greater emphasis upon work in social justice and trauma.[38] And yet the primary Morenian approach is intact. Moreno is to Psychodrama what Boal is to Applied Theatre. As Boal developed approaches to political and personal oppression through Forum Theatre and Rainbow of Desire, so Moreno developed similar approaches through Sociometry, Psychodrama and Sociodrama. Much of this work was developed in collaboration with his second wife, Zerka Toeman Moreno.

Moreno, a physician, was less interested in practicing conventional medicine than in treating forms of oppression through the healing art of drama. Throughout a long career Moreno worked with, among others, traumatized war veterans, homeless children, mentally-ill adults, prostitutes and prisoners.[39]

Moreno was a larger-than-life personality whose bold experiments captured the imagination and wrath of supporters and critics. Moreno recounts the birth of Psychodrama in a commercial theatre, the Komoedien Haus, in Vienna in 1921. He rented the theatre and invited a distinguished audience of politicians, artists and religious leaders. He describes the event as follows:

> I had no cast of actors and no play. ... When the curtain went up the stage was bare except for a red plush armchair ... like the throne of a king. On the seat of the chair was a gilded crown. ... But psychologically speaking, I had a cast and a play. ... The people in the audience were like a thousand unconscious playwrights. ... If I could only turn the spectators into actors.[40]

This idea was conceived in the 1920s and written about some 50 years before Boal coined the phrase 'spect-actor'. Moreno's intention was to provoke the spectators into taking action by coming on stage to take on the role of the king. For Moreno post-war Europe was leaderless and restless, in search of a cultural identity. If this group of distinguished citizens could take on a leadership role at least in fiction, he reasoned, they might offer solutions to the post-war crisis that eventually erupted in a second world conflagration. Moreno's psychodramatic experiment, 'to treat and purge the audience from a disease, a pathological cultural syndrome which the participants shared',[41] was a failure. No one came up. Many in the audience walked out, and the press wrote scathing editorials the next day.

Moreno persisted in Europe and the US, where he emigrated in the 1930s. He developed many forms of improvisational and participatory theatre with a personal, social and political agenda. One example was the Living Newspaper, where actors improvised the daily political events, taking on individual roles of political figures or collective roles of oppressed groups, all the while attempting to involve the audience in a dialogue. Later Boal developed a similar approach in his Newspaper Theatre, where contemporary news items were dramatized to groups of illiterate people.[42]

For Moreno such theatre forms eventually became centered on specific moments of crisis within communities. The example given earlier in case vignette four is of a dramatization of the assassination of John F. Kennedy within the context of a professional psychiatric conference. Through the dramatization the spectators became spect-actors who experienced a group catharsis of integration, expressing feelings and thoughts previously unexpressed.

The Kennedy dramatization is an example of Sociodrama, a form Moreno innovated for a group in crisis. Sociodramatic enactments are practiced throughout the world, serving a similar purpose as many forms of Social Theatre, Community Theatre, Theatre for Development and, more generally, Applied Theatre. Although Moreno was a physician, most practitioners of Sociodrama and Psychodrama are from mental health professions, education and related fields. Sternberg and Garcia provide a broad range of sociodramatic examples in theatre, education, the workplace and therapy.[43]

Moreno's best-known innovation is that of Psychodrama, the dramatization of an individual's dilemma. Like Sociodrama it developed from Moreno's ideas about a fractured and wounded society, the same historical roots that influenced his contemporary, Brecht, in Germany. Psychodrama and Sociodrama evolved from his theoretical system of Sociometry, the study of human relationships within groups. Moreno's sociometric system was complex and never fully validated through rigorous theoretical writing or research. However it did impact the burgeoning fields of Psychodrama and group psychotherapy that developed internationally throughout the 20th century, and that influenced many other forms of non-medical, arts-based group treatments including Drama Therapy, Expressive Therapy and Gestalt Therapy.

As a praxis Psychodrama attempts to help people expand their role potentials – to play old, familiar roles more spontaneously, and to play new roles with a degree of playfulness and competence. In the praxis of Psychodrama, a group engages in a series of exercises to warm-up to their feelings. A single protagonist emerges from the warm-ups. Protagonists focus upon a particular conflict in their lives. They choose auxiliary roles from the group to represent antagonists within that conflict, and they chose one person to double for them, that is, to express their inner feelings not otherwise available.

As the players engage, the Psychodrama facilitator, called the director, helps the protagonist set the scene and explore in depth the nature of the conflict. Often protagonists experience a catharsis of abreaction (purging of emotion) or integration (balance of feeling and thought). When this happens the scene winds down, and the director leads the protagonist toward a dramatization of unfinished business.

The experience ends as the protagonist reflects upon the experience, and group members share their own experiences related to that of the protagonist. Although the closure is not usually about specific actions to be taken in the world outside, there is an implicit understanding within the group as to changes needed on the part of the protagonist going forward. The psychodramatic goal, according to Moreno, is to increase the spontaneity and creativity of the protagonist and group members. Moreno defined spontaneity as an ability 'to respond with some degree of adequacy to a new situation or with some degree of novelty to an old situation'.[44] He saw creativity as a process of bringing to life something that did not exist before. In his theoretical book *Who Shall Survive?*, Moreno speculated that the best hope for the future of civilization is to train human beings to develop the requisite skills of spontaneity and creativity.[45]

Psychodrama and Sociodrama proceed often toward the reparation of early wounds. Many drama therapists, like Armand Volkas, integrate Psychodrama into their work for that purpose.[46] Volkas also frequently applies Playback Theatre, an approach developed by Jonathan Fox and Jo Salas in the 1970s. Fox trained in Psychodrama with the Morenos. However, in his search for a more theatrical and political form of treatment, he developed a type of improvisational theatre that seeks to recapitulate the ritual qualities of collective storytelling. In Playback Theatre a group gathers within a given community, such as a church in New Orleans just after Hurricane Katrina, or a square in a rural village in Sri Lanka in the midst of sectarian violence. The conductor invites people up to a designated chair to tell a story of concern to the community. Once the story is told, it is enacted by a group of Playback actors who are often accompanied by musicians who riff on the theme of the story.

Following the spontaneous performance, the teller gets the last word, reflecting on the performance. Then another teller comes up, and another, each story building upon the previous one, until a tapestry of stories is woven that paints a picture of community concerns. Playback Theatre, like Drama Therapy, is based upon the telling and enactment of stories. And like Moreno's ideas of Sociodrama and Sociometry, it speaks to the collective needs of a community. As such, it is a bridge between the two. Playback Theatre, with a growing network throughout the west and east, is fully mobile and applicable to many cultures with traditions of storytelling and theatre.

The work of Psychodrama, Sociodrama and Playback Theatre helps people to understand and modify ways that the past intrudes upon the present. As is often the case, the personal explorations of the protagonist are linked to the collective issues of the group within a particular setting.

Let us look at one group that focused upon exploring and healing intergenerational trauma stemming from the conflict between Germans and Jews during the Nazi times. This process was site-specific, that is, it took place in Krakow, Poland, and in the concentration camps of Auschwitz, just outside Krakow. These locations were especially significant as some of the most heinous atrocities of the Holocaust occurred there in the 1940s.

The following is a reflection upon the Psychodrama experience, told from the point of view of co-author Landy, who was a member of the group. Because the experience involved the sharing of so much personally harrowing material, we take care to protect the confidentiality of the group members by changing all names and details. We identify the group leaders, whose work we feel to be exemplary and who continue to lead such groups.

## ❖ Case vignette: Reflections on the Holocaust

The group was co-led by Yaacov Naor, an Israeli Psychodrama director whose parents were Auschwitz survivors, and Hilde Goett, a German Psychodrama director whose family was affiliated with the SS. The experience lasted five days over each of two consecutive summers. The group was comprised of professionals – teachers, therapists, mental health workers, clergy, physicians – some trained in Psychodrama.

The group commenced in a museum in Krakow, where all worked through Psychodrama to explore their relationship to the Holocaust. The group began and ended with a simple ritual, repeated each day. Individuals assembled in a circle and held hands, passing around a greeting. The directors suggested a moment of silent reflection at the end of each day. Several experiences warmed-up the group to the psychodramas. In one, each group member found a partner and in pairs walked through the museum, reflecting upon the photographs of Polish villages scarred by the war.

In a more intensive warm-up, the directors gave everyone a large poster board and instructed them to create a collage representing their view of the Holocaust in the present. The directors brought with them art materials including, most provocatively, copies of images from the concentration camps.

My description follows:

I used a famous image of a Nazi holding a gun to the head of a Jewish boy in short pants, hands raised over his head. I chose another image of a field of dead bodies of concentration camp victims in striped pajamas. Over the image I wrote: 'These are not my bodies.' Over one corpse

I wrote: 'I am not dead.' I glued a small pencil to the collage and wrote: 'My only weapon.' I entitled the picture: 'It's not about the Holocaust.' Irony was everywhere, the meeting place of what I am and what I am not. I wrote a story on the bottom of the page: 'The war is over. Let's forget about it. And so they did. Except the father. The father, being the father, because he cannot tell his father, tells his son. And the son, because he is a child, has no one to tell it to. And so he buried it under the ground for safe keeping. So deep and in such a secret place and without a map so no one can ever find it.

The directors asked the group to tell stories about their artwork and then hang the creations on the wall. I told a story about my father bringing home images of war that deeply tortured him and, unbeknownst to him, his son. Warmed-up, I volunteered to work on the psychodrama stage. My reflection follows:

I chose Silvia, a Polish woman, to be my father. She was so quiet. She sat with me and listened to the child in me recount my rage toward the Nazis and toward my father for dumping his stories on me. She comforted me at the end, singing to me as my father did when I was young. There was one difference. My father sang a song about a condemned man on the gallows, looking down at the crowd and cursing them, blaming them for his misfortunes. But Silvia sang a Polish lullaby. I told her I did not want to carry around my father's pain any more. His war was not mine. I was only a child. What could I do for him? For myself? What can I do now? I realized that now I can let go of the stories. I can see how they helped me become a professional who can hold the stories of others, even though they are sometimes too painful for me to hear. I realized that I am a receptor of painful stories, and I want to be able to listen and to hear them. But how?

After writing this I became aware of why I traveled so far to the Psychodrama group in Poland, where so many in my extended family were raised and where some were killed in the concentration camps. I wrote: 'My aim was to get rid of my near obsession with the Nazis and the Holocaust. Somehow, I intuited that this group of strangers from unknown places could help me do so.'

After an evening of psychodrama enactments, the group left Krakow by train and arrived in Oswiecim where they visited Auschwitz I, entering the camp through an archway marked by the chilling sign, 'Arbeit Macht Frei' (Work Makes You Free). In the evening they engaged in Psychodrama.

The next day they went to Auschwitz II, Birkenau, where they formed sub-groups to create rituals in specific sites in the camp to commemorate the dead and to mark the present.

For me the reality of site-specific Psychodrama performance in Auschwitz was very powerful. But the choice of a particular site within a site was even more so. Our group chose Kanada, the place where the clothing and belongings of the prisoners was deposited and sorted. It was a prize job to work in Kanada, because the workers always found contraband hidden in the clothing and valises – jewelry, silver, money and the greatest of all riches – food. For me Kanada symbolized a flicker of light in the deepest darkness. I wrote:

> The group rituals were presented in the women's barracks, the children's barracks, the railroad tracks, the gate leading to the gas chambers, the crematoria, the pool of ashes, the memorial stones. Our small group chose Kanada. In Kanada, we asked everyone to focus upon the sounds of the body, the camp beyond the body and the town beyond the camp. Then one person at a time entered the circle of the group and recalled the sounds. Each was embraced and incorporated within the circle where all spontaneously created a group sound, strained and solemn, that echoed throughout Kanada.

So much more happened during those five days and the subsequent five days of the next summer, as the group entered deeper and deeper into the morass of telling and dramatizing their stories. The majority of participants were Germans, from families of perpetrators, whose stories of physical and sexual abuse, depression and suicide informed us how the terror of the Nazi times was re-played in the family through the generations. So many tellers removed some 60 years from the war lived their lives as if they were responsible for heinous crimes against humanity. Like the families of the victims, they too carried a legacy of pain.

I questioned often whether the deep cathartic expressions and repeated stories of abuse and denial did more harm than good, re-traumatizing rather than healing. I questioned whether Psychodrama was too reality-based and raw, insufficiently distanced to provide the safety of an aesthetic space. It became clear through follow-up email exchanges that some returned home from those two summers with more rage than calm. Although I often reflected upon Boal's statement that theatre isn't safe, I wondered whether this time the psychodramatic process went too far.

On a more personal level, I wondered whether I went too far. In my riskiest psychodrama, I enrolled some of my peers as Nazis, collaborators and most painfully, as the despised part of myself, born out of Hitler's vile propaganda. In confronting them, I opened up historical and personal wounds without effectively closing them.

After two summers in Poland, had I realized my goal: to get rid of my near obsession with the Nazis and the Holocaust?

As Brecht, Boal and Moreno teach, the hardest questions do not yield easy answers, and the hardest journeys into the heart of darkness require a willingness to take great risks. In retrospect, I did realize my goal. As of this writing I am far less tortured by the past, and less likely to imagine Nazis behind each random act of omission and commission. I feel a greater sense of closure in relationship to my father, and understand clearly, for the first time, that he returned emotionally wounded from the war with no one to share his stories with except his young son, whom he loved as hard as he could. I recognize that the father's legacy to the son was not only pain, but also the ability to listen to stories beneath stories, and to appreciate their complexity.

But I can only speak for myself. I have checked in with the leaders of the group and some of the others who also experienced deep catharses of abreaction and integration. Like others who participate in or, indeed, lead such groups, I cannot know how such an experience affected those who chose to remain silent.

## Site-specific therapeutic performance

There are other examples in the book of therapeutic performance and ritual within significant sites. We referred above to a site-specific healing ritual in Nanjing, China, where a group of Japanese students and professionals joined their Chinese peers in memorializing the death and humiliation of innocent Chinese people at the hands of the invading Japanese army in the 1930s. This and other ritual sites are significant as they are sacred spaces, marked by the blood and suffering of real people, places of painful memory and, in some cases, more painful yet, places of denial. When political figures and governments deny their complicity in sustained brutality and genocide, where do the survivors and the children and grandchildren of victims and perpetrators go to find comfort and closure? And who will lead them there?

In the Holocaust example, the guides had particularly relevant credentials as they came from families of victims and perpetrators. Many who lead such arduous journeys come from similar families, as is the case with Armand Volkas, who is the son of Holocaust survivors and resistance fighters. Yet other facilitators do this work without any direct connection to the historical events.

Why are people drawn to particular sites of historical horror? An easy answer is that human beings have always been aroused by gazing at dramatically riveting and revolting events in everyday life, in history and in fiction. The lines of tourists are very long at the Roman Coliseum, the Mayan sites in Mexico where human beings were sacrificed, the killing fields in Cambodia and Ground Zero in New York City. The history of theatre is rife with plays depicting loathsome human behavior in sometimes graphic detail.

But the thrill seekers are primarily consumers of the drama. What about those who wish to heal the wounds of others by taking them back to the origin of the wounds? Perhaps the larger question is why does one seek a profession in the applied arenas of drama and theatre with people living on the edge? Is living for a time in the rarefied air of a war zone more exciting than the daily rituals of life in an urban apartment or a gated community in the suburbs? Is it because many in the profession are wounded healers and chose to work in concentration camps and homeless shelters to heal their own wounds? Or is it because many approach the work of Applied Theatre and Drama Therapy with a political motivation, to change the world?

When we asked James Thompson, he replied:

Gradually I ... loved this work for the shades of grey it provided – who were the oppressed in this work, whose voice is silenced, whose voice is heard in prisons? I want to work with those communities that have suffered the worst forms of human rights abuses or where action for social justice is most desperately needed. But I think that this must be only part of the story. Maybe it is a very old political argument in my head that questions what the point of theatre is when there are important political campaigns to fight and I'm perhaps trying to prove (to myself) that if theatre feels necessary in these most trying of settings, then it is no luxury but a vital part of our lives.[47]

Performances and rituals in sacred spaces are particularly significant as they evoke not only memory, but also the legacy of the past as it is recapitulated in the present. The space itself offers an opportunity for reconciliation and transformation of past wounds. In its aesthetic nature, the theatre becomes a sacred space. Because of its distance from historical reality, it is presumably safe. And yet an engaging theatre of the sort described by Cohen-Cruz and created by some of the most provocative theatre artists, operates at the borderline of safety and danger.[48] In creating the illusion of the actual scene of the crime, theatre artists, too, evoke images of the concentration camp, the streets of Nanjing, Phnom Penh, Srebrenica, Rwanda. As drama therapists well know, and as many theatre artists recognize, like those who followed Grotowski into the Polish woods, the work within a specific site, in removing some of the aesthetic distance, pushes participants well beyond their comfort zones, into liminal spaces, where anything is possible.

## Drama Therapy

In working with trauma and other pervasive issues, drama therapists proceed somewhat differently than their colleagues in Psychodrama. In general drama therapists work through the more metaphorical aesthetic distance of theatre. Instead of directing a protagonist to play himself in relationship to his father, a drama therapist might first help the protagonist discover a fictional role through which to play a figure who is not the protagonist. If there is a conflict with the father, the therapist might also help the protagonist create a fictional father, more archetype than actuality. Drama Therapy is about theatre and as such, it imposes all theatrical artifice in the service of exploring a fictional reality underneath that of everyday life, one that can illuminate and in some instances transform the actor.

Drama Therapy has changed significantly since 1982. At that time there were a handful of practitioners, most of whom were inventing their practice, extending it from what they knew of the theatre arts, Psychodrama, Psychoanalysis and Educational Theatre. Most worked without a clear critical eye in place to qualify their approach as a praxis.

In the early days of the field's development in the 1960s and 70s, a number of people worked in isolation. Sue Jennings pioneered a practice in the UK called Remedial Drama, based in her training in theatre, dance and Creative Drama, and in her commitment to working with special needs children.[49] Some of Jennings's early ideas were already in play in the work of the early British Educational Drama practitioners, Peter Slade and Brian Way. Slade is widely credited with writing the first piece about Dramatherapy with his monograph *Dramatherapy as an Aid to Becoming a Person*.[50]

Jennings is credited with founding several university-based and training institutes in the UK, Europe and the Middle East. She also played a major role in founding the professional organization the British Association of Dramatherapists (BADTh) in 1976. Since then she has continued to pioneer the field by linking Dramatherapy (one word in the UK) to social anthropology, theatre performance and neuroscience. In support of our notion of commonalities, we note that she collaborated with Applied Theatre and Social Theatre scholars to create the anthology *Dramatherapy and Social Theatre: Necessary Dialogues*.[51]

Marian Lindkvist is a second key figure in the development of British Dramatherapy. Like Jennings, she has a background as a performer and has devoted her career to helping people with various medical and psychological impairments. As a mother of an autistic child, Lindkvist had a very personal motivation to apply her performance training to children in need.[52]

Lindkvist founded the Sesame Institute in 1964. Sesame is devoted to training and offering Dramatherapy services to the community. Further, Sesame has become a center of research and study in the field of Dramatherapy, integrating the ideas of Peter Slade in Child Drama, Rudolf Laban in dance and movement, C. G. Jung in archetypal psychology and Marian Lindkvist in the non-verbal language of Movement with Touch.

Both Jennings and Lindkvist are retired and two generations of their students have continued the work they pioneered. Among those are: Alida Gersie in Therapeutic Story-making; Ann Cattanach (who died in 2009) in Drama and Playtherapy with abused children; Phil Jones in theory and research; John Casson in work with psychotic individuals; Roger Grainger in the spiritual dimensions of Dramatherapy; Anna Seymour in work with theatrical texts; and Ditty Dokter in work with eating-disordered individuals and refugees.[53]

The history of Drama Therapy in the US has similar roots as those in the UK, coming out of Educational Drama, improvisational theatre and theatre performance. Many in the US also trained in Psychodrama and view Moreno as a major influence. However, the first mention of Drama Therapy as a field separate from Psychodrama came in a 1945 publication from Lewis Barbato, an officer in the US Marine Corps.[54] Barbato described treatments through Drama Therapy within a neuropsychiatric clinic of a general hospital in Denver, Colorado. The treatment team consisted of a theatre director and a psychiatric nurse with acting experience. Their aim was to ameliorate symptoms associated with war trauma. Barbato described techniques of role-playing, re-enactment of battlefield stories and role-reversal that are standard in the fields of Psychodrama and Drama Therapy. What is especially note-worthy in this early example was its relationship to cognitive-behavioral therapy, as aspects of behavioral rehearsal were applied, helping the veterans discover new ways to play old civilian roles as they re-entered society.[55]

The professional organization National Association for Drama Therapy was founded in the US in 1979, barely three years after its counterpart was founded in England. The first president was Gertrud Schattner, a former Viennese actress who, like Barbato, discovered the value of treating war veterans through drama. Schattner, however, worked with concentration camp survivors in Switzerland, using rehearsal and performance techniques to help individuals tell and dramatize their stories. She later settled in New York City and worked with children and then psychiatric patients through theatre games and performance. In collaboration with drama educator Richard Courtney, she co-edited the first American publication in Drama Therapy. But due to Courtney's influence, the co-editors refrained from calling the work Drama Therapy. The title of their two co-edited volumes was *Drama in Therapy*,[56] suggesting an adjunctive role of drama. In these volumes they published chapters by early drama therapists as well as established figures in Playback Theatre and Educational Theatre.

The name Drama Therapy appeared modestly in the clinic and in the research literature in the US in the late 1970s. David Read Johnson used the term to describe his work at the Yale Psychiatric Institute combining elements of clinical psychology, theatre and dance therapy. Renée Emunah, who studied child drama, psychodrama and improvisational theatre, initiated a Drama Therapy Program at Antioch University in San Francisco, then at the California Institute for Integral Studies. And Robert Landy, with a background in theatre performance, English literature, social psychology and Developmental Drama, joined the Educational Theatre faculty at NYU in 1979 to, among other things, initiate a Drama Therapy Program.

Other influences added to the mix. Eleanor Irwin, a former speech therapist and Creative Drama teacher, devoted herself to training in psychoanalysis and integrated her Drama Therapy work within analytical treatment. Ramon Gordon, a theatre director, developed an early program to treat prisoners and ex-offenders through Drama Therapy, called Cell Block Theatre.

In the 30 years since the publication of the 1982 *Handbook*, Drama Therapy has grown broadly. Landy's initial 1986 text, *Drama Therapy – Concepts and Practices*, was expanded in 1994 to incorporate developing theory.[57] As mentioned earlier, the 2009 edition of the US-based anthology *Current Approaches in Drama Therapy*, features 18 models of theory and practice.[58]

When placed side-by-side with its British counterpart, the field is even more inflated. Further, a number of international Drama Therapy experts have established their own culturally based practices. Examples include Mooli Lahad from Israel, who developed an approach called Six Part Story-making; Hsiao-hua Chang from Taiwan, whose mask work has had positive effects on the quality of life of physically disabled children and the elderly; and several psychiatrists from Greece, including Stelios Krassinakis and Lambros Yotis, who have worked effectively with groups of drug addicts and schizophrenics through Drama Therapy.[59] Training programs also exist in Italy, Germany, the Netherlands, Czech Republic, Korea and Japan. Although some of these models exist as a practice, others offer a theoretical framework and point toward a reflective praxis.

Given so many approaches within such a small field, we again raise the issue of splits within splits and wonder whether the foundations of Drama Therapy are solid enough to support so many rooms. In reviewing all the Drama Therapy approaches, however, certain repeated concepts emerge as

**Photograph 5.2   Mask Drama at Pai Ai-hsin Home for Persons with Disabilities, Taipei, photo by Lin, Yi-shiuan, photo courtesy of Hsiao-hua Chang**

**Photograph 5.3 Mask Drama with the Elderly at the County Senior Citizen Home for Compassion, Tapei, photo by Hsieh, Tsai-miao, photo courtesy of Hsiao-hua Chang**

key building blocks. Not surprisingly these concepts are derived from theatre. The two most essential are role and story. In all forms of Drama Therapy, clients take on roles, and while in role they tell and/or enact a story. Role is the indivisible piece, as the dramatic moment begins as an actor slips into the skin of the other. Story, on the other hand, exists in relationship to the role of a storyteller, a figure who breathes life into a given narrative.

Another concept fundamental to the Drama Therapy experience is space, the location of the dramatic action. Moreno called it the *locus nascendi*.[60] Boal called it aesthetic space. Child analyst, D. W. Winnicott, refers to it as transitional space.[61] Drama therapist Mooli Lahad calls it fantastic reality,[62] and David Read Johnson calls it the playspace.[63] Other important concepts include ritual, conflict, resistance, spontaneity, distance and catharsis.[64]

It could be that the field of Drama Therapy is not mature enough to fully embrace its commonalities. Suffice it to say at this point that Drama Therapy is rich in progeny even as it is conflicted as to its attachments to its forebears. Before looking at several examples of exemplary praxis, we raise another issue that speaks to the private and confidential nature of Drama Therapy.

Unlike the public nature of Applied Theatre praxis, Drama Therapy is a private practice. The model of action–observation–reflection–re-action is still intact. However, the nature of the group as a whole is different. In Applied Theatre the group consists of performers, facilitators and spectators. Audience members are generally viewed as participants and thus are often characterized as spect-actors. Many performances are public, open to a given community.

In Drama Therapy the clients within the therapeutic process are both the performers and the spectators. At times only one client is in treatment, but more often than not, there is a group process than ranges in size from two to several hundred. A more usual number is six to ten, especially if the group takes place in an institutional setting.

The one exception is in Therapeutic Theatre, a more public form of performance where a particular population of, for example, psychiatric patients or Iraqi war veterans perform for an invited audience.[65] The case of Therapeutic Theatre blurs the lines between Applied Theatre and Drama Therapy.

Further, James Thompson makes the point that even the distinction between private and public becomes unclear and in some instances dangerous when a leader assumes that her group is private, only later to discover the public implications of the process when implemented within a contentious political environment. For Thompson that awareness came from his Applied Theatre work in Sri Lanka at a time of continuing civil and military conflict. In thinking through the implications of a massacre of young men following his work, Thompson became aware of the ambiguity of a private process within a broader context of the politics of civil war.[66]

Because of the confidential nature of Drama Therapy, the groups are generally closed to outside observers and thus the reflective part of the praxis comes solely from within. Given the contract of confidentiality, drama, like other forms of therapy, remains shielded from the kind of criticism taken for granted in theatre performance and Applied Theatre. Even writing up case studies, as we will do below, raises the specter of confidentiality. If therapy is indeed confidential, how can the profession justify the public presentation of cases? And if no outside eye is present to reflect on the process, how can the therapist/writer achieve objectivity and reliability? Is the presentation of a clinical case, then, a valid document or is it more in the realm of fiction, as Hillman suggests in his provocative book *Healing Fiction*?[67] Such rich questions continue to challenge not only Drama Therapy, but all clinical fields that present their findings phenomenologically.

## Small epiphanies

Much of the actual practice of Drama Therapy is not very dramatic, in the sense of being exciting. Progress can appear to be very slow and resistance very high. The kinds of cathartic breakthroughs that regularly occur in training sessions, workshops and professional conferences do not necessarily match the reality of a group process within an inner city psychiatric hospital where therapeutic moments might be telling a simple story or recognizing the difference between self and role; or within an after school group of autistic children where the therapeutic objective might be the establishment of eye contact for a brief moment.

The sites of such interaction are not remarkable concentration camps or war memorials, but drab day rooms within psychiatric units of metropolitan hospitals where interruptions are frequent, drama therapists are low on the pecking order, and burn-out is the norm. To further complicate matters, the newly initiated drama therapists are more often than not white middle-class women treating people, often male, of color, poverty and disability. Having said this, the small moments of connection between therapist and client, client and client, can be quietly profound.

Drama therapist Maria Hodermarska openly describes the disgust that she and others experience when working with babies who have been neglected and abused by their mothers. In one passage she expresses a moment when she cleansed a malodorous infant's feet, an ambivalent moment of revulsion and love. In another she describes a colleague fearlessly playing with a two-month-old HIV positive baby:

> I watch him approach this little girl without fear. He does not wear gloves. He nuzzles her. She sucks on his checks and drools on his shiny, bald head. He knows no fear because I think he knows that the world turns on a dime. This girl needs human contact now. ... They literally dance in a mess of human secretions. ... No gowns, no masks, gloves, no medication. She is giddy and laughing.[68]

In their readiness to engage, to take on the role of mother for a very small individual who has not yet learned how to be a daughter, and in their willingness to confront their own disgust and mortality, these two drama therapists create performative acts that are gently transformational.

In the city's psychiatric hospitals, there are groups of adults who have lived their lives in and out of delusional thoughts and flaccid, medicated bodies. Their imaginative capacities have been maligned and neglected by their keepers whose only recourse is to steer them into solid walls of reality. Drama therapists work with these groups to open the door to the body and the imagination and help the people experience the difference between imagination and delusion.

In one group an actively delusional woman was asked to take on the role of someone she admired. In a moment of clarity, she chose a famous pop singer and modeled her body in an expressive gesture. The cynical medical staff present in the day room was impressed. But as the group continued she decompensated, stuck in the role with no way out. The other group members were able to enact their roles in the playspace and then let them go, returning to the present of the dayroom. Almost discouraged the drama therapist turned to her one more time as the group was closing and asked: 'Can you either show or tell me one way that you are different from the pop star?' Unexpectedly she ran her fingers through her hair and responded: 'She wears her hair in a pony-tail. I do not.' The group broke out in spontaneous applause.

### ❖ Case vignette: Three approaches to Drama Therapy

As an example of a full praxis, we turn to a film made by Landy in 2005, *Three Approaches to Drama Therapy*.[69] The film was made as a research piece, intended to compare and contrast three well-known Drama Therapy approaches: Role Theory and Method, Psychodrama, and Developmental Transformations. The idea was modeled on a project filmed in 1965, 'Three Approaches to Psychotherapy', featuring one client, named Gloria, working with three prominent psychotherapists: Fritz Perls, founder of Gestalt Therapy; Carl Rogers, founder of Person-Centered Psychotherapy; and Albert Ellis, founder of Rational Emotive Behavioral Therapy.[70]

In Landy's film a single client called Derek (fictional name) works with three major figures within their specializations: Landy in Role Method, Nina Garcia in Psychodrama and David Read Johnson in Developmental Transformations. The work is structured as a praxis. Each section begins with a discussion of theory, followed by a demonstration of the practice in a 45-minute therapy session. The therapist then reflects upon the session. Next Derek, the client, is interviewed by a panel of graduate students who are present throughout the session. After that the panel interviews the therapist. The question of whether or not the process of action–observation–reflection leads to change is addressed in the several interviews following the session. Derek, over time, has the final word.

We present these cases as examples of individual treatment which, although less prevalent than group treatment in Drama Therapy, is effective for exploring embedded personal issues.

At the time of the filming Derek had completed all his coursework toward an MA in Drama Therapy, and had previously studied with all of the therapists. He was chosen by his peers, and gave his informed consent. His peers and teachers felt that his awareness of the therapies, therapists and peers would keep the sessions relatively safe.

As context Derek is an African-American man, from an inner city working-class family. All the therapists are Caucasian from middle-class families. Two are male, one is female. In preparation for the process, Landy asked Derek to bring in an issue to work on with all three therapists.

## Role Method

Landy began the first session on Role Theory and Role Method, which he described as follows:

> I believe that an individual is not one thing, a core self, but a multitude of character traits and alter-egos, which I call roles. The term is essential to theatre as actors in plays take on roles that are different from themselves. My aim is to help people identify roles that are difficult in their lives, to explore them, to discover and explore counterroles on the other side that can help move them toward a more balanced state, and to find a way to work toward that balance. The figure of the balancer, I call the Guide.
>
> My work in Role Method is indirect. I try to help clients express their issues in a distanced way. The distance of fictional roles and fictional stories provides perspective, a way of viewing the roles and stories as if they belonged to somebody else. Rather than asking clients to tell me about their real life situation, I ask them to make up a story.
>
> Following the storytelling and fictional role-playing, I ask the clients to reflect upon their roles and stories. Who are they and what do they want? What is the story about? And then I ask them to relate the fiction to their everyday lives. Consistent with many forms of verbal therapy, I feel it is important to include a verbal, reflective piece. It gives the client a way to engage the brain in its dual function of taking action and making sense of the action, of feeling and thinking. From my point of view, Drama Therapy is a form of reflective action.
>
> Role Method is a way to help clients identify their strengths and work through problematic roles, locate their counterparts and, through the means of a guide, find a way to accept the contradictions and tensions caused by living a complex life.

Drama Therapy is a journey taken by the most dramatic of all journeyers, the hero, who searches for some elusive truth about him or herself and about the world. Like all profound journeys, this one is difficult and challenging. There are obstacles along the way – villains, deceivers, seducers, demons and sometimes gods, real and false. Because the journey is so arduous, the hero needs a guide. In Drama Therapy the journey is the full course of treatment. The hero is the client. The counterparts of the hero are all the wounds, resistances, fears, confusions and hidden parts of the psyche. The guide is, first, the therapist and. finally, the client herself, who dares to hold together the contradictions she has uncovered without fear of disintegration.

The aim of Role Method is to help individuals and groups live a full and balanced life, accepting and working through the natural struggles with emptiness and imbalance. Wholeness springs from the ability to play many roles, to tell and enact many stories and, in the end, to discover value not only in one role or story that is most authentic, but in all.

In the first session Derek expressed discomfort, fearing the camera would exaggerate the darkness of his skin and the whiteness of his teeth. Landy asked Derek to take on the role of the camera and to speak:

DEREK:     I am a camera. I am here to shoot Derek. ... My job is to make him look as unflattering as possible ...
ROBERT:   Why would you want to make him look as bad as possible?
DEREK:     Because that's the way he already feels.

Working in and out of the role of the camera, Derek realizes that he wants to discover a way to feel more comfortable about himself as a man of color. Landy asks:

ROBERT:   So what can you tell him, camera, to make him more at ease?
DEREK:     Be yourself. ... Take pride in your teeth. They can be as white and shiny as possible. Take pride in the sheen that comes off your skin. Chill. Relax. I'm gonna make you look good.

Landy asked Derek to make up a story with three characters, representing the personal issue he brought to the session. Derek identified the characters as the Father, the Son and Pain. To distance the story from reality, Landy suggested he begin: 'Once upon a time.'

The story is about a boy who tries to make his father happy. But because the Father is under the relentless influence of Pain, 'the bad guy from the neighborhood', the Father is abusive. As the Son grows up, he realizes that it is time for him to climb a mountain and prove himself a man. But as he does so, he is pursued by Pain who tells him that he is worthless. In persisting the Son makes it to the top, feeling nothing but fatigue. On the mountain top he hears the sound of a hissing radiator, an actual fixture he recalls from his childhood tenement apartment. The sound calms him. Over time the Father relents and urges the Son to keep climbing. The story ends with:

DEREK:   He was waiting for those couple of words. All he needed was two words from the Father. He never got them, so the Son keeps climbing up that mountain and falling down but he keeps getting back up.
ROBERT:  What are the two words?
DEREK:   I'm sorry.

In the remainder of the session Landy helps Derek devise a dramatic frame in which to give and receive the apology. Landy engaged in role-play with Derek, playing both Father and Son. Not incidentally, through the role-play Derek was also able to confront Pain for the harm he caused the Father and the Son, and dramatically break him up into little pieces. Derek was also able to accept Pain's gift – the courage to keep climbing the mountain.

Toward the end of the dramatic enactment Derek, enrolled as the Son, listens to the Father, played by Landy, speak the full apology created earlier by Derek: 'I'm sorry, my son, for bringing pain in our home. All of it. P.S. I'm proud of you and you're a good man and I mean it. I mean it. Please forgive me.' Derek responds: 'You ain't getting me to cry here.'

Having said this Derek laughs, and Landy invites him to let go of all the roles that he played in the session – Son, Father, Pain. Together they reflect on the fictional roles.

Derek's final comment is: 'The Son now has to hold on to all that pain that the Father brought that he never got rid of. So now the Son is gonna have a hard time trying to grow up to be a man and trying to climb the mountain.'

## Therapist's reflections

Following the session, Landy reflected on the process:

When Derek identified the problem as a father and son issue and even came up with the third role as pain, I thought of the Son as the hero going on the journey. In the story the Son goes on the journey up the mountain. The counterrole I saw as the Father, and Pain in some ways I saw as the guide, even though he is a negative figure. I stood pretty close to Derek, wanting to guide him on the journey in a less fearful way. I thought it was hard for him to say the words that needed to be said – I'm sorry. I was hoping that the balance would come if he could, as the Father, say those words to the Son. And if the Son could take in those words, and if Pain could stand between them. It was interesting because Derek did not banish Pain forever from the mountain, but he broke it into pieces and he held onto a piece as if it had a guiding energy. ... At the very end when we were processing the work, he came up with another guide figure, which was the image of the radiator and the hissing sound, which was comforting to him. It gave me a sense of hope that Derek does have an internal guide figure, a way of soothing himself and making peace with the fact that Pain is not gone forever, but it's a part of him. At the end I did feel a certain integration among more than three roles – Son, Father, Pain and Radiator.

## Post-session dialogue with graduate students and therapist

In a dialogue with the graduate students, Derek was asked what he gained from the session. He responded:

> I got to confront my father. Something I can't do being me. ... It was also good, as painful as it was, to actually hear the words come – especially from another man. When Robert was standing there and said [those words] it kind of [was] like oxygen couldn't get through to my heart because I couldn't believe what I was actually hearing. I almost broke down but I didn't.

When asked whether the session might lead him to take action, he replied, 'I'd like to. But to say that I'm actually going to do it, that's not realistic. I know at this time my father's not ready to hear that. ... But doing this actually gives me a voice to say something.'

When asked whether there was something else he'd like to work on going forward, he responded, 'I think I need to deal with the race issue ... the color complex is still there and that is to me almost directly related to the father/son issue.'

In a dialogue between the students and Landy, the issue of race was raised and Landy acknowledged the challenge of being a white therapist working with a black client and how that reality raises implicit issues of power dynamics and racism. He reflected upon how the choice of working dramatically with the camera as metaphor foregrounded Derek's negative self-image as a black man. By encouraging Derek to find an alternative way of playing the camera, Landy led Derek to a counter-perception – of his blackness as beautiful. As such, for Landy, the camera was an early guide figure leading the protagonist to a more balanced place, ready to work.

## Psychodrama

Nina Garcia led the second session on Psychodrama, which she described as follows:

> In Psychodrama people enact scenes from their lives, dreams or fantasies in an effort to express unexpressed feelings, gain new insights and understandings, and practice new and more satisfying ways to behave in their lives. Moreno also was a great believer in the here and now. Thus he designed a form of psychotherapy where everything enacted happens in the present. By moving fluidly between past, present and future, Psychodrama collapses time and brings everything into the present.
>
> Based on the principles of spontaneity and creativity, Psychodrama focuses on strengths. Of the several techniques, one is the empty chair technique. Another is the double. Doubling occurs when the psychodramatist expresses unexpressed thoughts or feelings that the client may be experiencing. The third technique is role-reversal in which the client changes places and changes role, putting himself in the other's shoes. Role-reversal develops empathy and understanding for the other's position.

When the session begins Derek tells Nina that he wants to work on his relationship with his father. He describes a recurring dream, where 'my father is looking at me and all I can remember is him pointing at me and seeing his gold teeth with a scowling look on his face. Then he turns to my mother and he spits in her face. ... And I just remember her crying. And I always remember her spitting back into his face.'

Nina asked Derek to set up the scene from the dream. She provided many colored scarves to represent aspects and characters in the scene. As Derek speaks about his mother, Nina picks up a physical cue in Derek's smile and asks him about it. He responds that his mother 'was the man in the family. ... But she couldn't quite teach me how to become a man. I always tried to look to my father to do that but that wasn't going to happen.'

Through further dramatization and discussion we learn that the father was physically abusive to the mother, once knocking her out in public. Following each argument the young Derek was left feeling helpless. Nina asks him: 'So you're ready to be done with this dream?' He responds: 'Yeah. I'm tired.'

As they work on the dream, Derek plays a scene where his mother is attempting to divert the father from hitting Derek. Nina asks Derek to take on the role of the Mother, and says to him as Mother: 'I see it hurts you when he does that. You love your boy.'

When Nina asks Derek to reverse roles, and take on the role of the Father, he cannot. He says: 'Right now I'm feeling quite desperate.'

NINA:     You as Derek are feeling desperate?
DEREK:    Yeah. I'll try my best not to cry.

With Nina's encouragement, Derek begins to cry, then to sob. Nina asks Derek to put his feelings into words. As he struggles, she doubles for him, speaking to the father: 'I hate what you did to me. ... You have made it so hard for me to become a man. ... You sapped my strength.'

Through his tears Derek expresses his great sense of abandonment and pain. As the scene comes to a close he tells Nina: 'He just needs to see me cry, that's all.'

Nina then invites Derek to take on the role of the Father. Derek agrees but decides to play his dad in the present, as a religious person who has modified his aggression toward his son. Nina questions the father:

| NINA: | Dad, you've seen your son today. What do you want to say to him? |
|---|---|
| DEREK (as Father): | That I'm sorry. |
| NINA: | And I don't want you to say anything that's not really in your heart, because he will know if you're lying to him. |
| DEREK: | I know he's really intelligent. |
| NINA: | Tell him that. Don't tell me. |
| DEREK: | Ok. I won't lie to you, because I know you're a very intelligent young man. |
| NINA (Doubling for Derek as Father): | And I want to tell you how it feels to see the damage I've done. |

DEREK:     And I want to tell you that I see how much damage I've caused and …

NINA:      So tell Derek some of those things. Here's a moment to own up and make amends.

DEREK:     I see my wrongs now. They're … well, you turned out to be a good man. Got a lovely dedicated wife just like your mother is to me and...

NINA:      (Doubling) But you're a better man than I … (to Derek) If that's right, repeat, if not correct it.

DEREK:     But you're a better man now than I was when I was your age. I'm just learning how, and if it wasn't for seeing you turning your life around I wouldn't have changed mine.

NINA:      (Doubling) So in some ways you were almost my father.

DEREK:     So in some ways you were almost like my father.

NINA:      Let's switch roles. And respond to Dad. In some way you were almost like my father.

DEREK:     That's kinda crappy.

NINA:      Yeah tell him. That stinks!

DEREK:     I actually needed to see you be a father so I would know to take the right steps in life and instead I tried to find it elsewhere.

NINA:      (Doubling) You failed me in a lot of ways, Dad.

DEREK:     You failed me in a lot of ways and …

NINA:      (Doubling) And it's good to hear you're sorry, but I'm not ready to completely forgive you yet.

DEREK:     It's good to hear you say that you're sorry and I'm working on forgiveness.

NINA:      (Doubling) Don't rush me.

NINA:      I want to ask you something, Dad, as a special gift to your boy today. What can you say to him so that when he gets stressed he doesn't have to have this dream to make him more stressed?

DEREK:     Don't take life as seriously as I did. … Be honorable, the person I know that you are and take things easily. Do the opposite of me.

In the end Nina asks Derek to set up a dialogue between the young, emotionally wounded Derek and the adult in the present. The young Derek tells the adult to take good care of himself and to listen to the feelings of the young boy. Intuiting one more step to be taken, Nina asks Derek: 'Do you pray? Would you be willing at some point in your prayer life to bring him in?'

DEREK:     Sure.

NINA:      Could you tell him that, please.

DEREK:   Little Derek, I promise to say a prayer for you, to put you inside of my prayers every day.

NINA:   Does that feel complete for now?

DEREK:   Yeah, Thank you.

NINA:   What I'm going to ask you to do is ... clear the scene.

## Therapist's reflections

Following the session, Nina reflected on the process:

> At the beginning of the session, it was wonderful to see Derek so warmed up to the dream and to hear from him early on how he felt it was related to his waking life. The first moment that I noticed he had some feelings was when he spoke about his mother in relation to the dream, and I wanted to take a moment [for him] to express those feelings. ... The reason that at the end I asked him to connect with his eight-year-old self is that. ... the integration of that eight-year-old self is absolutely essential to the healing. And at that moment when Derek made the promise to bring the child with him in his prayers, there was literally a change in his physiology that was about the internal shift that had taken place. That's one of the ways that the psychodramatist knows that the work has taken root and has begun to be integrated into the experience life of the person.

## Post-session dialogue with graduate students and therapist

Following the Psychodrama the graduate students asked Derek about his moment of catharsis:

DEREK:   Last week the same thing was about to happen because the male/male relationship that I have with the therapist stirred up a lot of emotion, but I was able to put up my wall and not do it. It was just ready to come out this week. ... When I had to speak for my mother, it was devastating for me...I felt it. I tried to have my eyes suck up the tears, but I was present. ... If I had held it in anymore I think I would've hit something, so it's better to express it.

INTERVIEWER: I know that when asked last week how much this session affected you, you said you'd know a little bit later. Can you reflect on how this session has affected you?

DEREK: Last week I know I said I'd feel it when I'd get home. And I did. I spent more time reading about father/son relationships or lack thereof and it was quite new. I was more conscious about people I was working with and now I'm very conscious when I see a father actually with his son or daughter.

INTERVIEWER: What about today?

DEREK: Today is just ... I'm just ... I'm at a loss of words. I feel like I had a thousand bricks on my shoulders and they were lifted.

INTERVIEWER: When you couldn't speak you were crying, and Nina was doubling for you. How was that?

DEREK: That was great because I couldn't talk at the time. I needed someone to speak for me. Just like I needed someone to speak for me when I was a kid.

INTERVIEWER: Nina asked your permission to place her hand on your shoulder. What was that like?

DEREK: I appreciated that because I don't want just anyone putting their hand on me. I had that too much as a child so I'm conscious about touching people.

INTERVIEWER: Did becoming the younger child help you?

DEREK: It helped me at the end. He was ready to speak to the adult me and he finally had a voice and someone who could actually listen to him.

INTERVIEWER: Could you say something about that moment of the prayer?

DEREK: It was a silent prayer to myself almost like my soul was at ease and it was just peaceful.

In the final dialogue with the students, Nina responded to a question about whether the moment that Derek offered a prayer to the young Derek was healing:

The idea in Psychodrama is that you're able to have a fundamental shift as a result of the work. And that was a moment where I could tell he had a lot of feeling. That's called a catharsis of integration – when we can shift how we experience the world, when we can shift how we experience the people in our world.

## Developmental Transformations

The third session was led by David Read Johnson, the founder of Developmental Transformations (DvT). He describes his work as follows:

> The basis of Developmental Transformations is the creation and maintenance of the playspace between the client and the therapist. This is an imaginative space, a state of playfulness that exists between the client and the therapist. There are three main conditions of this playspace. First, both parties understand that no actual harm will take place within the play. Second, the boundary of reality and fantasy is represented simultaneously. Third is a sense of mutual agreement that the work takes place within the playspace. A unique element of Developmental Transformations is that the therapist puts himself in the therapeutic playspace and allows his body to be available for play with the client. The role of the therapist is modeled on the role of the actor, whereas in many forms of Drama Therapy, the role of the therapist is modeled after the theatrical director. As this process unfolds the therapist applies various techniques to try to loosen the grip of the client on various forms that they have attached themselves to, such as relationships, issues, roles, stories. We believe that sickness is often associated with trying to hold on to previous forms that are no longer working. So the therapist basically is going to try to encourage the client to move from a state of seriousness about themselves to a state of play. Essentially the work comes down to this moment of trying to allow the person to take aspects of their world that they view as solid and to give it up for a moment and place those solid, serious things within the confines of the playspace and allow them to transform.

In beginning his scene with Derek, Johnson explains:

> We'll begin a scene. As the scene proceeds you're going to have thoughts and feelings that will come inside of you. I want you to use those thoughts and feelings to transform the scene into another scene. If you transform the scene into a new scene, I will take a role in the new scene and follow along. If I transform a scene to another scene you need to flow along with me. Every once in a while during our work I'm going to go over to the witnessing circle and I'll sit there and watch you and you will continue to play alone. You can ignore me, you can look at me, you can make me into whatever you want to, just don't come over and

pull me into the play. And I will return and continue. At the end I will tell you to take a minute. I will de-role, and you take a moment to sit with your thoughts.

Before beginning Johnson asks Derek what he intends to work on. He responds: 'My father and I.'

DAVID:   And the issue with your father is basically…

DEREK:   Abuse.

DAVID:   Abuse. Alright. I want you to put me in a position or a statue of some kind.

DEREK:   Turn around. Hands up. Hands like claws. Bend over just a little bit. *(He sculpts David)*

DAVID:   Something like that?

DEREK:   Yeah. You have to be meaner.

DAVID:   Meaner?

DEREK:   Yeah. And turn around.

DAVID:   Now I want you to place yourself in relationship to me with one part of your body touching one part of my body. We'll begin from here. Take your time developing the scene. *(Derek puts one hand on David's chest as if trying to stop an attack.)*

The scene proceeds as Derek and David push each other in an intimidating manner. Derek and David face off with their bodies. David attacks Derek, playfully. Derek gets on all fours on the floor.

DAVID:   Where's my victim. I had a victim here and now my victim's gone.

DEREK:   Your victim is gone.

DAVID:   I can't abuse without a victim. I need a victim. Where'd he go?

DEREK:   Grrrr.

DAVID:   There he is.

DEREK:   Grrr.

DAVID:   You know what I like best? Kicking the dog. I come in, I work hard all day, I swing open that door and I say: 'What the fuck are you doing?'

DEREK:   Grrr. Dogs can fight back.

DAVID:   Oh yeah? The dogs I know hid in the corner. Dogs don't cause any real trouble. Because you know what happens when the trouble starts.

DEREK:   Grrr.

DAVID: Am I being mean enough? What are you laughing about? I have to be meaner. I'm just a pushover. You know what? I'm not going to be able to match up to your Dad. I'm not going to be able to be as abusive as he was. You know why? I'm a nice guy. I'm a nice white man. I'm a nice white mentor man. A nice white father figure.

DEREK: I don't need a father figure.

DAVID: They're really nice people. Nice white men. Father figure mentors.

DEREK: I was told that in high school. Lots of nice white men in high school.

DAVID: We have a problem here.

DEREK: Yeah, we do have a problem.

DAVID: A big problem

DEREK: Because you're a nice white man. *(Bowing to David and taking on the role of a slave)* Massah. What you need, Massah? What you need me to do?

DAVID: I need you to get my bedclothes and my mattress. And I want you to set everything up for me.

DEREK: Alright, Massah. I'll clean up the shit. Let me get the toilet bowl. Whatever the Massah told him to do, he did.

DAVID: It's a long tradition. A long tradition.

DEREK: There's a whole lot of white Massahs.

DAVID: I could use you, you know. My wife, you know, she's on me all the time about equal relationship. I need someone who could really be a servant. I think you would be fine.

DEREK: Ok, Massah, whatever you say. There's one thing though, Massah.

DAVID: What's that?

DEREK: Don't let me get near your white wife. You know what they say about that.

DAVID: I'm not worried about that because we have ways to deal with that. Very quickly.

DEREK: Oh yeah. I won't get out of order. I promise you, Massah. My dad didn't get out of order.

DAVID: You're pretty comfortable with this issue. This race thing.

DEREK: Oh my daddy used to come home and call me a nigger many times.

DAVID: Nigger. The N word.

DEREK: You can't say that word

DAVID: I can't say that word?

DEREK: No.

DAVID: But this is Developmental Transformations. I can say whatever I want to. This is just play. It's not real, so I can say nigger.

DEREK:   Yeah. Honky.

DAVID:   I can say nigger and you can call me honky.

DEREK:   That's not the same.

DAVID:   But here in the play space it's not really nigger.

DEREK:   Oh, it's something else.

DAVID:   It's play. Right?

DEREK:   Right.

DAVID:   It's play ... Nigger.

DEREK:   *(Whipping David)* You wanna say it again?

DAVID:   Yeah. Nigger. You fucking black, fucking weak, scared... *(Derek whips David again).* Ow. Ow. Ow.

David continues to play with the racial stereotypes and throw Derek off balance just enough so that he can in turn play with the old forms and allow them to transform. As harsh and transgressive as his words are, David intuits Derek's need to play out the unplayable issue of racism. The play between them is very physical, but always stylized within the playspace.

As the play develops, the scenes change spontaneously. Moving more deeply into exploring how abuse compromises one's ability to be intimate, David asks if they can play a love scene. Derek responds: 'Who's going to be the aggressor?'

DAVID:   I'm gonna be the lover and you're going to be the lover. Just love. Between one human being and another. Not black or white. Not dominant or submissive.

DEREK:   No. I have problems with loving people.

Playfully, David compliments Derek on his appearance and his authenticity. Derek replies: 'Ok. Love me. It's time that somebody loved me.' David counteracts with: 'Can I touch? I'll do it very lightly.' Derek agrees and David puts an arm around Derek's shoulder. As this scene develops, David begins to dance with Derek. Although the playing is exaggerated, the scene is edgy. They struggle physically, pulling each other back and forth.

David urges Derek to trust him and Derek responds: 'I'm tired of trusting.' David grabs Derek's arm and they begin to walk around the playspace. Although Derek implores him to let go, David holds on. Finally letting go, he helps Derek sit down, offering to serve him food. Sensing Derek's resistance, he acts as if he does not have enough to satisfy Derek's needs. As a final gesture, Derek puts his head in his hands and becomes very quiet. As the session ends, David walks to the witnessing circle and says: 'Take a minute.' There is no verbal reflection. Both men leave the space.

## Therapist's reflections

Following the session, David offered these reflections:

> Well right now I'm filled up with a whole bunch of images, thoughts and feelings. It's hard to sort them out. Derek was very much present with me, and we did a lot of playing with issues that he has been obviously thinking about – racial issues, his family. The image that I'm sitting on was when we were walking around at the end hand in hand. I ended up holding just his thumb so I couldn't even get his hand or he wouldn't give me his hand. And that said several things – I'm not able to, I don't want to, and also, come get me. There was a sadness that I started to feel at the end about whether I could either in the play or in reality reach across some divide to be with him. There's a feeling that the divide is too wide. Not just between us, but within him. And I started to feel it within myself, too. So at the end I was filled up with the phrase: 'I'm sorry'. I started to feel: 'I'm sorry', although I'm not sure what I'm sorry for. You know, it's not about race; it's about something more intimate than that. I mean, it's about race, but it's not about race. But I feel his presence around me at this point.

We should add that neither Nina nor David was aware of the previous sessions. David did not know that Derek had already worked with the fantasy of his father saying: 'I'm sorry'. In his reflection, David sees himself in the role of the perpetrator, the one who has some apologizing to do. We question whether DvT as a method allows him the optimal distance to separate himself from such intractable issues as race and intimacy? Has David identified with the aggressor in the thorny dance of race and intimacy? David's complex reflection adds richness to the process.

## Post-session dialogue with graduate students and therapist

In a dialogue with the graduate students, Derek was asked to compare the three sessions.

INTERVIEWER: The one thing that sticks out in my mind in the Psychodrama was the crying, a deep, deep catharsis. This week was different. It seemed cathartic but in a very different way. Could you respond?

DEREK:        In the Psychodrama session I was dealing with the issue of speaking to my father so I had to go back and picture myself as that kid. That brought up a lot of feelings that led to what I like to call my break-up. This week, I could just play around with issues and laugh at certain things that I couldn't laugh at when I was doing Psychodrama.

INTERVIEWER:  [Were you] comfortable with David's touch?

DEREK:        I was caught off guard by it. It stems from my own issues with men and not wanting any men that close to me. The love scene wasn't necessarily in a sexual way. It was more emotional. I'm sure a couple days will pass and I'll look back and see that I appreciate it. But right now I don't trust any man to say they love me.

INTERVIEWER:  So what allowed you to tolerate the boundary that was broken for you in some way?

DEREK:        The deep need that I've always wanted a man to love me. Like a father.

When asked about working on the issue of race, Derek responded: 'That's when I felt more comfortable than father/son. Yeah, just playing with the taboo stuff. That for me was important. Just playing with the "N" word.'

David responded to several questions from the students who were especially uncomfortable about David's use of touch:

DAVID:  We use touch because it's a natural human activity. It would be impossible for example to play with your kids with the restriction of not touching them. It doesn't mean that there can't be appropriate touch or inappropriate touch. But touch is a part of the human condition. I don't initiate touch unless I'm reading that in the client. In the very beginning, I requested that he touch one part of his body to me, but it was how he touched me that let me know something about his comfort with touch. And the way that he put his finger on my chest I knew he would respond to my pushing him. So in this work I am an actor and my text is the client so I'm reading what I'm seeing in the client and then feeding it back to him. When he was kicking or hitting he was more comfortable in miming it and pretending to hit me. There are other clients who don't actually hit you, but would like that physical contact. That doesn't mean I can't make an error about it, but my intention is never do anything unless I've just seen it in the client.

INTERVIEWER:   At one point you said: 'We're having too much fun.' Can you talk about the function of laughter in the playspace?

DAVID:   Yes, laughter is a very important emotion. It's a form of catharsis. Laughter occurs when there are two contradictory streams and the person sees the irony in that situation. Laughter is very important but we're not trying to get laughter; laughter occurs. Just like touch. We're not trying to have touch. We're not trying to have insight. These are things that are produced from the work.

## Reflections

The three approaches are different in terms of the role of the therapist, the theory that informs the treatment, the techniques and the varying levels of emotion and distance. Psychodrama is different from the others in that it is less theatrical and more reality-based. Further it more directly aims at evoking catharsis, both as an abreaction and as an integration.

The role of the therapist is most unique in DvT, as he serves more as actor than director, engaging in continuous play with the client. Role Method and Psychodrama are both based in role theory. DvT is more eclectic, based in part on theories of psychological development, on the performance theory of Grotowski and on the philosophy of Buddhism.[71]

Unlike Psychodrama, Role Method and DvT both work with fictional stories and roles to emotionally distance the client from the demands of everyday reality. The techniques of DvT are based in play and improvisation, the free flow of action in the moment. Role Method uses the same at times, but relies more directly upon projective techniques such as storytelling and story-making. Psychodrama has its own set of techniques, such as role-reversal and doubling, but also incorporates aspects of play and story-making.

In Role Method the action is followed by verbal reflection. Catharsis is viewed as a moment of aesthetic distance, where feeling and thought are accessible but not overwhelming. The goal is balance, a state of living among contradictory thoughts and feelings, rather than transformation, a push beyond the given circumstances. In Role Method nothing is pushed away. Rather the shadow side of existence, 'the Pain' in Derek's words, is integrated with its counterparts, and given a valued place within the psyche. The Psychodrama session ends with a closing discussion, intended to frame the dramatized issue as somewhat universal. In DvT there is no ending discussion as such, as the therapy is intended to occur fully through the play. Reflective moments, according to Johnson, occur within the playspace.[72]

As ethical practice all three approaches subscribe to a similar code of professional ethics, established by their professional organizations. The film has been viewed by numerous students and professionals in the fields of Drama Therapy and Psychodrama internationally. Of the three approaches, DvT has sparked the most lively and sometimes acrimonious ethical debate, especially around issues of race and touch. The Western cultural taboo surrounding 'the N word' cuts deep, prohibiting many in the fields of education, social action and therapy from uttering the word, no less addressing racism directly. DvT, though certainly provocative, offers one way to do so as it invites clients to openly address their taboos in action, in the presumed safety of the playspace, and in the service of working toward change.

If Johnson is correct in thinking that Derek's session was as much about intimacy as about race, then he raises another ethical dilemma – how much and what form of touch is acceptable in a therapeutic drama without crossing a psychologically and culturally unacceptable boundary?

On balance all three approaches share basic similarities. They all are dramatic, proceeding through action and role and stories told in role. They all work through a similar spectrum of emotion and distance. They all begin with the ancient assumption that performance is healing. And they all subscribe to Moreno's notion that change occurs through helping people enhance their spontaneity and creativity.

As time passed in Derek's life, he came to perceive the three approaches as confluent and integrated. In reflecting upon the change he experienced, in part as a result of participating in the film, he wrote:

Overall, each method individually contributed to healing the wounds in my personality and relationships, and together they functioned in a complimentary fashion, one preparing me for the next. In a perfect world, one would hopefully have access to multiple methods like I was fortunate to have in this experience. The different methods used are like unique musical instruments that sound exceptional by themselves but when put together work like a well-coordinated orchestra, capable of much more intricate and beautiful music.[73]

## The Peripatetic Drama Therapist

Over the years 1982–2012 Drama Therapy pioneers have conducted numerous training groups. Like many in DIE and Applied Theatre, they are peripatetic. They travel to forge new paths for Drama Therapy and to respond to invitations from those living in cultures that embrace the new discipline.

There are reasons why certain cultures are drawn to Drama Therapy. Greece and Italy both have deep historical roots in dramatic literature. In addition both ancient cultures present examples of a healing theatre. We have already seen that in the Asclepions of ancient Greece. The Roman Coliseum has a more nefarious place in the history of healing theatre, as it was the locus of brutal spectacle: catharsis for the spectators; death for scores of unfortunate actors. On the other side, the ancient Roman physician Soranus, advocated a dramatic cure for depression and other mental illnesses.[74] Also, in the fifth century, Caelius Aurelianus advocated the viewing of comedy as an effective cure for depression, and tragedy as an effective cure for hysteria.[75]

Contemporary Greek culture has welcomed Drama Therapy since the mid-1980s, with invitations to such peripatetic trainers as Sue Jennings, Alida Gersie, Phil Jones, Robert Landy and Renée Emunah. Several Greek and Cypriot training institutes have developed in those years, two of which are headed by psychiatrists, Stelios Krassinakis and Demys Kyriacou.

At the beginning of this chapter we refer to a Drama Therapy group experience in Greece, where an actual intruder to the group became the catalyst for the group to create stories about intruders. One woman told a story of an isolated island and an aggressive intruder from far away. In dramatizing the story the storyteller discovered the value of the role of the Intruder. This figure, with the power to boldly rattle the established order, indicated a need for change in her life. At the end of the session several pointed out that Landy, the leader, was a foreigner who came from far away. He too was an intruder who had the power, in the eyes of the group, to shake things up.[76]

Italy has also been active in initiating Drama Therapy institutes. Salvo Pitruzzella began the Dramatherapy School at the Arts Therapies Training Centre in Lecco in 1998 and has sought out mentors such as Roger Granger, Sue Jennings and Robert Landy.[77] Further, a new program in Dramatherapy and Social Theatre began in 2010 at the University of Rome, La Sapienza. Landy was in residence for a brief time and worked with the faculty and students on Role Theory and Role Method. At one point, in the midst of a Drama Therapy group, Landy, sensing a lull, inquired about a shared form of cultural expression. The group spontaneously sang 'Bella Ciao,' a powerful song popular among the resistance fighters during World War II and still emblematic of political struggles for freedom. It was, for example, translated into Persian and sung in Iran following the rigged elections of June 2009.[78] In a reversal of the above story, the intruder in 'Bella Ciao' is the enemy. The partisan is the hero who bids goodbye to beauty and dies for the sake of freedom.

At the end of the training session in Rome, the group collectively created a poem about their journey through the Role Method. Echoing the story of Moreno's performance with an empty throne on a stage in post-World War I Vienna, the group questioned whether there was a leader powerful enough to take them forward on their journey: 'We need a guide who is able to really help us.' Through the process they made a discovery, written in the final verse of their poem, which they performed in the group:

> The eyes of the storyteller are wide
> Love is the destination,
> Love is the companion for the journey,
> Love for small things, for nature's details,
> There is a large window and there is risk,
> The hero proves herself,
> As the day arrives,
> By opening the drawer of her heart.[79]

Chinese culture, too, has ancient roots in healing performance based in the philosophical tradition of Taoism and the ancient practice of Chinese medicine. In both cases existence is viewed through the interplay of polarities, represented by *yin* and *yang* energies. The polarities, while seeking balance, cannot be fully reconciled. Balance is a matter of discovering a way to live within the paradox of the polarities. Healing obtains by internalizing the optimal mix of elements, which, in Chinese medicine, are wood, fire, earth, metal and water.

This point of view is very much recapitulated in Landy's Role Theory and his creation of a taxonomy of roles, a typology of archetypal roles derived from the history of Western dramatic literature. In his journeys to Taiwan, Hong Kong and China, Landy worked to integrate his Western notion of Role Theory within Chinese cultural traditions.[80] While in Taiwan he worked with a group of performers, educators and therapists to create a Therapeutic Theatre performance based upon the stories of the Buddhist trickster god, Ji-gon.[81] In China he worked with a group of theatre professionals and students to examine the cultural and personal complexities of expressing anger in the family and in the workplace.

There are many other examples of international programs and trainings. During the past 30 years, Israel developed three Drama Therapy training programs. In the West Bank city of Nazareth, peripatetic drama therapist

**Photograph 5.4   Drama Therapy Group in China, photo courtesy of Sai Ye**

Sue Jennings has been working with a group of Palestinians to develop a form called Theatre of Resilience.

In neighboring Lebanon, drama therapist Zeina Daccache, mentored by Sally Bailey in the US, directed a group of maximum security prisoners in a therapeutic rendering of the play *Twelve Angry Men*. Their version, *Twelve Angry Lebanese*, caught the attention of prison guards and officials and led to productive discussion about changing the conditions and terms of imprisonment.[82] In its raw passion, the film version of *Twelve Angry Lebanese* recapitulates the energy and power of Tom Magill's *Mickey B*, referred to in Chapter 4.

Peripatetic drama therapists tend to travel alone, isolated from their colleagues in Drama Therapy and other applied forms of theatre. If these wanderers could pause for a moment and recognize their common practice and history, many productive dialogues might occur, challenging the ethos of isolation and splitting. In such an exchange the pitfalls of colonialism, paternalism and parochialism might be avoided, or at least revealed.

Like Applied Theatre artists, drama therapists strive to help individuals and groups move toward change. In a recent interview we asked Nisha

Sanjani, Applied Theatre artist and drama therapist, about the possibility of dialogue between the two fields. She responded:

> At every conference I have ever presented at, as soon as I reveal myself to be a therapist, I get a cold shoulder. So I play that card very carefully because I want to form alliances and I think it's particularly necessary now ... [If Applied Theatre artists do not embrace Drama Therapy], they are going to be missing out on a very important piece of the puzzle. It has to do with the emotional geography of change.[83]

The divisiveness is historical and systemic. It comes with the territory not only in theatre, but in many academic and aesthetic disciplines that focus on intellectual hegemony. We write this book, in part, to move forward the discussion of integrations. We write this book in the name of dialogue and change.

# PART IV    REFLECTIONS

When Landy published the 1982 *Handbook of Educational Drama and Theatre*, the title suggested a name for the field, which, according to Landy, included: DIE, TIE, Puppetry-in-Education, Children's Theatre and Theatre for Young Audiences. In addition, the umbrella term Educational Drama and Theatre included various forays into community life as represented by the museum, church, school, prison, police academy and various organizations specializing in work with the physically disabled, mentally ill and elderly. The terms Drama Therapy and Applied Drama were mentioned, the former in some detail, the latter in passing.

Near the end of the book Landy speculated as to future directions, drawing from the wisdom of such experts as Geraldine Brain Siks, Nellie McCaslin and Ann Shaw. He spoke of a future burdened by government cutbacks but committed to growth and change. Of note was his concern for the clarity of terminology and parameters of the field. He saw growth needed 'in clarifying the field through relevant research and experimentation and through constructive dialogue with colleagues within educational drama and theatre and related disciplines such as psychology, special education, and the language arts.'[1]

This book is the future, some 30 years on. It is a response to the need for clarity and constructive dialogue. Throughout, we have drawn attention to a number of people creating a praxis that is theoretically grounded, action-oriented and reflective of on-going dialogue. We have seen that some of these people move easily between drama/theatre, education and the social sciences. Others find more synergy with politics and philosophy. As evidenced in the preceding chapters, the field has broadened, if not blossomed. We see this especially in the growth of Applied Theatre and Drama Therapy. In the concluding chapter we assemble a collage of diverse voices heard in the book to address many of the questions raised throughout. This imaginary dialogue echoes a conceit used in the 1982 *Handbook*, when Landy took on dual roles of interviewer and expert and engaged in a self-interview to review a number of central issues raised in the book.

Imaginary dialogue suggests a conversation constructed imaginatively. This notion reflects an earlier understanding of praxis as a creative process.[2]

Further, it highlights our perspective that effective change in education, social action and therapy can be facilitated through the art forms of drama and theatre.

The collage design of the imaginary dialogue presents a view of the field as a patchwork quilt of images and ideas, each patch an intact form that when juxtaposed with others reveals a richly dynamic tapestry.

# 6    Imaginary Dialogue

The dialogue that follows actually occurred in the course of our research face-to-face and via email, with the addition of brief cameos from Bertolt Brecht, Paulo Freire and Augusto Boal. Some of it found its way into our text. It is imaginary in its juxtapositions, as if all these people were sitting together on well-worn chairs, engaging long into the night on the applications of drama and theatre to education, social action, therapy and religion.

As much as we tried to create a cross-cultural and diverse view of the world of Theatre for Change, we recognize that the majority of prominent figures in the field are white, middle-class Westerners. We also acknowledge that although the majority of drama and theatre workers are female, we find a predominance of men in positions of leadership and publication. Many practitioners, especially in Theatre for Development and Drama Therapy, work often with people of color and people of poverty. These realities are represented in the following dialogue. The field has certainly grown more diverse over the past 30 years, as noted in the preceding chapters. It is our hope that an even greater diversity not only of clients, but also of practitioners will subsist well into the future.

| PHILIP TAYLOR: | The *Handbook* from 1982 is such a rich resource of Educational Theatre and kind of fascinating to talk about in relation to where we are now 30 years on. I actually have a copy of the original book by Richard Courtney, *Play, Drama & Thought*, which I know must have had a huge impact on you, Robert.[1] |
| --- | --- |
| ROBERT LANDY: | Courtney was my mentor in Developmental Drama. |
| TAYLOR: | Courtney's real contribution was bringing drama into interdisciplinary perspectives, opening it to psychology, philosophy, sociology. In his Foreword to the 1982 *Handbook*, which he called 'Robes, Roles & Realities', he says that its great contribution is threefold.[2] Firstly, it pushes |

drama outside of schools into community contexts, whereas most books about Creative Drama up until then really had been located in the world of education. The second is that this is a serious intellectual approach based on evidence. And the third is that there are diverse viewpoints in this text, and he defines diverse as based upon multiple viewpoints. Courtney was quite influential in setting up a drama resource center in Melbourne. When I began working at the University of Melbourne in 1992, Courtney's influence was profound.

LANDY: He died in 1997, having lost a good deal of his influence. Not many read his books anymore.

TAYLOR: We're now in 2010. If you were going to track the major texts that influenced your new book, what titles come to mind?

DAVID MONTGOMERY: Nellie McCaslin's *Creative Drama in the Classroom and Beyond.* In multiple editions. Gavin Bolton was beginning to write when the *Handbook* originally came out, and since then added *Acting in Classroom Drama* and *Biography of Dorothy Heathcote.* Cecily O'Neill's books are very important and you, Philip, wrote a number of influential texts including *Redcoats and Patriots, The Drama Classroom* and *Researching Drama and Arts Education: Paradigms and Possibilities.* I also think of the work of Helen Nicholson, James Thompson, many more in Applied Theatre.[3]

TAYLOR: I would add Cecily O'Neill's *Drama Structures* which came out in 1982. It treated teachers as intellectuals, having the capacity to change things in groups. I thought *Theory of Creative Drama Education* by David Hornbrook was a great book. I would also put Hornbrook's *Education in Dramatic Art* as a text much reviled, but it certainly got people talking. For all the people who were studying with Heathcote and Bolton, it was seen as very disrespectful to their legacy. You just don't hear much about him now.

MONTGOMERY: I remember hearing Cecily O'Neill say that David Hornbrook had some really good points to make. But she also felt that he was biased in promoting the Western theatre canon, and teaching theatre skills and plays. But he did not recognize that this can happen alongside the work of Dorothy, Gavin, Cecily and others. I would put *Researching Drama and Arts Education* on the list, because it was dealing with really new territory, talking about qualitative research as a legitimate scholarly activity.

TAYLOR: In terms of North Americans, you'd put David Booth on the list.

MONTGOMERY: Yes, David Booth for *Story Drama* and Manon Van de Water writing about TYA. Johnny Saldaña's texts come to mind, and Michael Rohd's *Theatre for Community Conflict and Dialogue*.

LANDY: Really groundbreaking work came from TIE.

TAYLOR: There was Tony Jackson's *Learning Through Theatre*.

LANDY: And that was followed by Applied Theatre in the early 2000s. Your text, Philip, *Applied Theatre: Creating Transformative Encounters in the Community,* was very important, as was James Thompson's.

TAYLOR: That was 2003. But in the original *Handbook*, there is Applied Theatre work being done. In fact, Robert, you use the term Applied Drama. You pre-date Helen Nicholson. But you don't actually flesh it out.

LANDY: That's right.

TAYLOR: And when you used the term Applied Drama, you really meant adapting this methodology to community sites. And particularly therapeutic settings.

LANDY: I began to flesh out its therapeutic implications in my 1986 text, *Drama Therapy: Concepts and Practices.* The second edition in 1994 was called: *Drama Therapy: Concepts, Theories and Practices.*

TAYLOR: It's like *Play, Drama, and Thought,* don't you think?

LANDY: Yes, because I look at the psychological, sociological, theatrical and pedagogical roots of Drama Therapy. My subsequent books are on Role Theory and on viewing the relationship of Drama Therapy to psychoanalysis and the psychological traditions that incorporate action. Other important books in Drama Therapy were written by Sue Jennings, Alida Gersie and Phil Jones in the UK. Italian drama therapist Salvo Pitruzzella wrote an important text called *Introduction to Dramatherapy: Person and Threshold*. In the US, *Acting for Real* by Renée Emunah is quite influential, as is the widely read anthology edited by Johnson and Emunah, *Current Approaches in Drama Therapy*, reissued in 2009.

TAYLOR: When Courtney says in his Foreword to the *Handbook* that one of the strengths is the diverse viewpoints, he's referencing multiple voices. Whereas today, if you use this term 'diversity' we're talking about aspects of race, ethnicity, religion, sexuality, gender. Those concepts apply to the whole movement of critical pedagogy, which really took off in the eighties, prior to publication of the *Handbook*.

LANDY: I agree. I think the social justice agenda is implicit in the 1982 *Handbook*. It is more explicit in this book.

TAYLOR: So who are the key people?

LANDY: James Thompson is a key voice. Helen Nicholson in Applied Drama.

TAYLOR: Helen Nicolson's great contribution is that she provided an intellectual context for that kind of thinking.

LANDY: In Theatre for Development we're looking at work in South Africa, Kenya, Rwanda and Uganda. I see three major influences in Applied Theatre.

BERTOLT BRECHT: Change the world, it needs it.[4]

PAOLO FREIRE: Liberation is a praxis: the action and reflection of men and women upon their world in order to transform it.[5]

AUGUSTO BOAL: Theatre is a rehearsal for the revolution.[6]

TAYLOR: But these are all white people.

LANDY: That has changed somewhat and will change even more. Christopher Odhiambo Joseph is an important voice in Theatre for Development.

TAYLOR: And Dale Byam.

LANDY: I admire Dale's work in TfD.

TAYLOR: And also Johnny Saldaña's book *Drama of Color*. That was one of the first texts that really encouraged

|  |  |
|---|---|
|  | teachers to grapple with the issues of race and economics and whose voice is being privileged. |
| SALDAÑA: | I was educated in the mid-1970s. When you look at that time today, you had stories like Little Black Sambo and few female protagonists.[7] |
| LANDY: | For me, the two most important developments in the field over 30 years are the inclusion of drama and theatre in social justice and in therapy. It's a move from a pedagogical model to therapeutic and political ones. These two major strands have moved the field out from its conservative, non-critical agenda in Children's Theatre and classroom drama. |
| SALDAÑA: | I agree that is what's happening, but I think these transitions have also occurred in the literature in education, anthropology, ethnography. We also hear about the things coming out in research in brain-based learning, and that too is something we need to be informed by. |
| LANDY: | That work is on the rise in Drama Therapy. John Bergmann is researching Drama Therapy and neuroscience. The psychiatrist and neuroscience researcher Bessel van der Kolk is doing research in drama and theatre with children from traumatic environments.[8] Sue Jennings has a book out called *Healthy Attachments and Neuro-Dramatic-Play*. I took part in a seminar on Acting and Mirror Neurons at the New York Psychoanalytic Society in 2007.[9] This research has applicability to education and social justice, as Johnny suggests. |
| TAYLOR: | David, you say that the field has many problems of definition and unresolved issues. Now 30 years on, would you say that those problems of definition have dissipated somewhat? Or have they become more problematic? |
| MONTGOMERY: | I think they're more complicated. |
| TAYLOR: | Why's that? |
| MONTGOMERY: | Because of the Applied Theatre movement. Likewise, within school settings we've always had Creative Drama, Process Drama and Story Drama. And now we have more which require more definitions, for example, Theatre for the Very Young. |

227

NANCY SWORTZELL: Drama in Education has become a diverse and yet hybrid forum because within that classification you have Sociodrama, art drama, Psychodrama, Drama Therapy.[10]

TONY GRAHAM: Educational Drama and Theatre is akin to Children's Theatre in that they are inadequate, potentially misleading terms. At one end of the spectrum we find Process Drama, at the other, theatre. Between the two lies a range of possibilities, crossovers and emergent forms. Theatre in Education, for example, in its orthodox guise, manages to reconcile the best of both. One of the drawbacks in talking about theatre and education is that we don't share a common understanding of 'education' (let alone theatre). Today's educational zeitgeist has reduced learning to a set of instrumental objectives. No wonder people are often suspicious of anything in the arts that invokes the idea of education.[11]

GAVIN BOLTON: In the 1950s onwards, pioneers in the 'new' kind of drama sought to find labels that distinguished it from stage plays. Ward chose 'Creative Dramatics'; Slade chose 'Child Drama'; Way chose 'Creative Drama'; and Heathcote, eager to separate from Slade and Way, chose 'Drama in Education'. Performances by actors for children battled with two conflicting titles of 'Children's Theatre' and 'Theatre-in-Education'. Since then all sorts of terminology have taken over – 'Theatre of the Oppressed', 'Process Drama', 'Applied Theatre', 'Theatre for Young Audiences'. Now my choice of terminology would be 'Drama Education' as a broad label covering all drama/theatre activities linked with education. Such a collective term allows us all to feel we are working together – while accepting that within that term we branch out along different routes.[12]

PETER HARRIS: I think the title Educational Drama and Theatre excludes community, political activism and all that has developed from Boal's work. You need a broader and more provocative title I believe.[13]

| | |
|---|---|
| TAYLOR: | I would say that TIE is a subset of Applied Theatre, like Process Drama is a subset of Applied Theatre. O'Toole started to talk about how the term Applied Theatre is exclusionary and is blocking out Drama in Education. |
| HARRIS: | Applied Theatre seems to be a good term as it can be inclusive of all the above and again places the application of theatre for social means before the sanctity of the art-form. |
| JAN COHEN-CRUZ: | Well, the problem with Applied Theatre is that it is often understood as being too operational. If I had to put it in one sentence, I would say that I'm in engaged scholarship through the cultural disciplines.[14] |
| NISHA SANJANI: | As a field itself I believe we have to be forming bridges across cultural studies, not just across theatre.[15] |
| O'NEILL: | It seems to me people would object to Educational Theatre as somehow being less than theatre. But Applied Theatre seems to be even more instrumental than Drama in Education was. And we're seeing this in teaching literacy, exploring history and in saying: 'I'm doing this to get a message across, to teach people how not to catch AIDS, or to help people acquire self-esteem.' They're all very worthy, but it's an agenda driven by instrumentality rather than aesthetics. You know, we became so issue-based that eventually theatre was kind of the tail that wagged the dog.[16] |
| EMELIE FITZGIBBON: | As a practitioner I find that the term Applied Theatre puts us into a corner. And it somehow implies that it is not theatre. By putting an adjective before it, it implies that it is theatre of a different order. It doesn't help bring the elements of the art form into any explanation that is valuable.[17] |
| SALDAÑA: | We [at ASU] do Applied Drama but we don't call it that officially. We call it Community-based Drama, Theatre for Social Change. If you want to use devised work, we'll call it that, too. There are other terms—the British use the term Verbatim Theatre. The qualitative researchers |

229

|  |  |
|---|---|
|  | call it Performance Ethnography. I prefer the compound word Ethnodrama. Sally Bailey calls it Non-fiction Playwriting. |
| HARRIS: | My personal practice can best be described as Community Action Theatre, as my belief is that the purpose of all theatre should be to agitate and promote new critical thinking catalyzing action for change. |
| HAZEL BARNES: | My experience has been in educating students to use drama and theatre in educational contexts but also predominantly in developmental contexts. So I tend to think of the field as broad and diverse with many voices contributing. The practice in Africa, north of South Africa, has been strongly focused on Theatre for Development, while my... work with students and experienced practitioners in Africa, has been to develop an eclectic range of praxis which can be varied according to the context. So I see the field as a continuum moving from loosely structured improvisatory Process Drama through Boalian techniques towards more structured theatre creation. With the AIDS pandemic the move has been away from message carrying to more holistic investigation of the psychological impact of disease and loss. I feel that a more umbrella term such as Applied Drama and Theatre is now more appropriate.[18] |
| JAMES THOMPSON: | What's in a name, eh? I try to avoid the debates about this name at the moment because it is one of those clichés about academics – arguing about the name and not the actual work. But I think the name Applied Theatre appealed to me first because it implied hard work. That is you had to apply yourself to a problem, and theatre had to apply itself to its context, social problem, setting, community and make itself relevant. I liked the term because it permitted conversations under the umbrella. In the UK when the Theatre in Education folk and the Theatre for Development practitioners were conceived of as belonging under the same umbrella, their points of contact |

and differences could be explored quite pro-
ductively. I hope that similarly Applied Theatre
could permit discussions with drama therapists
without insisting anyone has to be entirely happy
with the term. At the moment one of my worries
about the term is that it has become a shorthand
for a set of techniques and practices. It should
not become *an* approach, *an* orthodoxy. Helen
Nicholson says it is a discourse not a practice. I've
said it is an attitude rather than a field, an ethos
of practice, trying to make theatre that responds
to urgent social/personal needs with communities that might not usually make theatre.[19]

SANJANI:      Applied Theatre implies something about one's intention. Drama Therapy belongs under the umbrella
term of Applied Theatre as does Educational Theatre
or other forms like Theatre of the Oppressed or
Playback Theatre. Some of these practices yield
performances that are about trying to shift the
perception of the audience. We have an intention
of hoping for some progressive change.

CHRIS VINE:   I find Applied Theatre a very useful term because
it suggests intentionality while remaining neu-
tral. It does not wear its heart on its sleeve by
invoking any given cause, be it social justice,
social change or healing, but it can be used to
encompass them all. It should also be noted that
it can include work that many of us might prefer
to avoid. I have former colleagues and friends
who are making very comfortable livings in the
world of management training, and the military
uses role-play and simulation in its war games.
I don't think we should assume that the name
automatically conjures a set of shared values – or
even attitudes, as James Thompson suggests.
Theatre does not innately enjoy an ethical orientation. Many of the terms we use are problematic:
Process Drama, Theatre in Education, Drama
in Education and of course Applied Theatre.
I think they all beg questions, frequently about
the unspoken opposite that the names suggest.

But for the time being, I find the term Applied Theatre as good as any, and better than most. I like its ability to be inclusive and yet, as James suggests, to promote discussion about similarities and differences between practices. Perhaps new, more useful terms will emerge. But if and when they do, I hope it is because they are really needed to move us forward, not because someone wants a catchy new book title.[20]

LANDY: Like Theatre for Change. In our book we propose that this can be an umbrella for the field. I think change is the essence of the theatre experience, applied or not. In speaking to people and engaging with their work in education, social action, therapy, the word change kept coming up over and over.

THOMPSON: I like Theatre for Change, with a worry that change is often the object of theatre, the instrument, rather than a sense that through collaborative, theatrical endeavor, changes can be made possible – or imagined. A youth theatre director in UK recently said, to paraphrase, 'I'm not interested in theatre that changes young people, but in young people creating theatre that expresses the changes they would like to see.' They don't need to change, society's response to them does.

CHRISTOPHER
ODHIAMBO JOSEPH: Changes have taken place in a number of nations in the Third World as a result of consciousness-raising dramas and theatre. The awareness about the risks of HIV/AIDS was highlighted through Applied Drama/Theatre activities. A lot of transformation in South Africa regarding the past injustices has been addressed through drama. The case of Educational Drama as part of a change agenda is exemplary in the HIV/AIDS work in Uganda.[21]

HEATHCOTE: I am not interested in changing the person. What I am interested in is the drama. We are interested in formulating ideas so all of us together are not saying: 'What sort of a person are you?' What we can say is: 'I wonder what's motivating this man?' And I don't assume I can change character or personality. I have seen change in attitude to doing things well or becoming involved in understanding the form we are after. I am not there to reform people in reform schools; I am there to give them an opportunity to make a relationship, not only with me, but with each other within the context of the drama.[22]

LANDY: One way I think about change through drama is in the making of relationships.

BARNES: I think drama can change people, but only very slowly through sustained interventions. I think its primary value is in encouraging participants to think critically and to align their thinking with an empathetic understanding of people and circumstances within a widened worldview.

TAYLOR: One of the criticisms of my book *Applied Theatre: Creating Transformative Encounters,* was the use of the term transformation. Do you mean Transformation when you say Change? Because people interested in evidence-based learning are saying, how are you documenting that change? Where is the evidence for it?

MONTGOMERY: Empirical research is possible, but in our field it is not broadly applied or conclusive in any way. You, Philip, have spearheaded qualitative approaches to research. Johnny Saldaña has written about ethnographic approaches. Barone and others have written extensively on arts-based research. Beyond that, I think the evidence for change is in the kinds of actions taken as a result of drama/theatre experience, if any. We have given many examples in the book from education, social action and therapy. Even in Theatre for Faith change is marked by some kind of conversion.

TAYLOR: My book on prisons is all about documenting the shifts in people's thinking, perspective.[23] And what they write in their journals and scripts and how the audience interfaces with the material in the prison. It is a challenge, particularly in this neo-positivist era where we have to constantly justify our existence.

LANDY:          Could you tell us, Philip, about your mentors in Educational Theatre?

TAYLOR:         Cecily O'Neill has been the principle mentor to me stemming from reading *Drama Structures* in 1982 as a student. I get jazzed by Brecht myself. Boal wasn't a mentor to me, but I can see that his work had a powerful impact on my practice, translating some of those rich participatory theatre techniques into educational drama. But Gavin had also written about this in the early eighties, and I love reading Bolton's *Essential Writings*. Critical pedagogy strongly influenced me as a teacher. It was rich reading Henry Giroux's book about teachers as intellectuals.

MONTGOMERY:     Robert Landy, Philip Taylor and Nancy Swortzell are great mentors to me at NYU. Nancy Swortzell introduced me to the world of TYA in New York and Process Drama in London, where I got to see the work in action of Jonothan Neelands, Emelie Fitzgibbon, Warwick Dobson and especially Cecily O'Neill. Her book *Drama Worlds* has been the most significant text in the work that I do. I got to know and admire Gavin Bolton and Dorothy Heathcote, who became mentors. The first time I saw *Three Looms Waiting*, the documentary about Heathcote's teaching of drama, I was moved to tears. Finally, I consider drama teacher John McEneny to be a mentor. In observing his work on a regular basis in a Brooklyn middle school, I am excited by the variety of drama approaches in his classroom and the depth of thought and emotion he pulls from students.

HEATHCOTE:      From a master weaver you learn an awful lot about which things they do that help you and which things they do that don't. I am not saying I worked these out, but now when I am planning I often have a picture of me and Emily Carr standing in front of a loom and her saying, 'No, don't do that, Dorothy. Now, you just remember: work it out, watch your head, you know you've only got one brain and that kicking stick will hit you.' She didn't talk about safety at work, she talked about looking after your brain.

BOLTON:         Dorothy Heathcote stands out as my mentor. She changed my conception of drama education. Slade and Way enticed me into specializing in the subject. But the most influential people have been my own students. I was lucky in having as my students some of the most respected figures in drama education today: Professors David Booth, David Davis, Mike Fleming, Cecily O'Neill and John O'Toole. But the person who helped me most to gain confidence in my often clumsy attempt to write about breaking new ground was Norah Morgan of Ontario.

VINE: I would have to begin with Brecht, especially his influence on my formative theatre going years. I would not typically use this word, mentor. Boal comes close. He was extremely important in my development, but I still have an ambivalent attitude towards much of his work. I first encountered him in Austria in 1982. Gavin Bolton played my oppressed mother's head teacher in my first-ever Forum Theatre experience. I introduced his work to the TIE movement [where he] led his first-ever workshops in the UK in 1984. Long before we ever heard Augusto's name, many of us were shaping our pedagogical practices under the explicit influence of Paulo Freire. Indeed, it is *his* work, rather than Augusto's, that has had the most *far-reaching* influence on mine. As to my beginnings as an artist, I guess my 'mentors', rather than individuals, were the *fields* of TIE/DIE and small-scale political/community theatre. Much of the strategies I have used for years evolved with the TIE movement, or were learned and incorporated from DIE practitioners like Dorothy Heathcote, Gavin Bolton and, a little later, Cecily O'Neill.

THOMPSON: I think the first clear mentor for me was Paul Heritage. He was my tutor at university and then we set up the Theatre in Prisons and Probation Centre together. I learnt from him a form of commitment to engaged theatre practice that was both pragmatic and idealistic. Perhaps all the things I've written on Applied Theatre have been an extended conversation with the work of Boal. My last book almost has no reference to Boal so I think I may have at last exorcised that ghost. Mentors today – I have always enjoyed and learnt from Richard Schechner's work.

TOM MAGILL: At 19 I was imprisoned for three years for violence. I wanted to give some other poor bastard
a taste of what I felt. And that release of violence
felt good. My cell in Bedford prison was next to
an IRA hunger striker. Here was an excuse to vent
my hatred again. I had a dilemma – should I stab
him or scald him? When I saw him he weighed
five stones. He was like a child in a man's clothes.
My hatred turned to compassion. I wanted to
save his life, not hurt him. He told me to educate
myself and not waste my life. Frank Stagg, my
enemy, became my mentor. Later when I worked
in prisons, Paulo Friere's *Pedagogy of the Oppressed*
was an educational bible so the fit with Boal was an
easy step.[24]

ODHIAMBO: My mentors are Opiyo Mumma, Ngugi wa Thiong'o,
Augusto Boal and Paulo Freire. I admire Boal's work
most as his work collapses the dichotomies of theory
and practice and is applicable in diverse contexts:
community, classroom, industry, prison.

ZEINA DACCACHE: In Drama Therapy, it's Sally Bailey who's been following up and supervising my work since 2005. In
theatre, I coordinate much with Armando Punzo,
the Italian director who has been doing theatre
in Italian prisons for 22 years. He also visits our
work in Roumieh Prison, Lebanon, once every
year.[25]

RENÉE EMUNAH: The people who have inspired me and my work
come from multiple disciplines – some from
Educational Theatre, including Peter Slade and
Dorothy Heathcote; also from England, Brian Bates'
work on the psychological process of acting. From
theatre, Grotowski, Stanislavski, Chaiken; from psychology, humanistic and existentialist theorists.
And of course Moreno.[26]

ARMAND VOLKAS: The work of Stanislavski and Lee Strasberg taught
me how to recognize and value authenticity when
I see it on stage and in everyday life and how to
bring it out in myself and my clients. Eric Berne,
the creator of Transactional Analysis, taught me

how to uncover the toxic scripts that people live by and help them change. Joseph Chaiken and the Open Theatre taught me that theatre can have a goal of social change and also be brilliant theatre. Joseph Moreno taught me that, 'A truly therapeutic procedure cannot have less an objective than the whole of mankind.' Psychodrama trainer Dorothy Satten taught me how to hold trauma, deep grief and pain and that it is disrespectful to take on someone else's pain. It belongs to them. Jonathan Fox taught me the art of witnessing someone's story through the Playback Theatre form and profoundly validating their experience. Victor Frankel taught me how to help people make meaning out of suffering. My parents, who were resistance fighters and survivors of Auschwitz, taught me that it is important to hold on to hope, resist and keep striving to make a better world even in the face of overwhelming odds.[27]

JONATHAN FOX: Albert Lord at Harvard, author of *Singer of Tales*, deepened my understanding of history and performance, and the Morenos, J. L. and Zerka, taught me about group process, especially techniques of inclusion. What excited me most, however, was contemporary non-scripted theatre. As a budding Applied Theatre practitioner, I worked with experimental theatre groups, including Andre Gregory's and Richard Schechner's. The early Playback Theatre short forms were inspired by ideas and images from the Open Theatre and Alwin Nikolais' Dance Theatre. Dare I also say Nepal? Two years living in a tiny village marked me deeply. After Nepal, I wanted a theatre that was intimate, communal, close to the sun and stars. I wanted performers who were highly skilled when on stage and ordinary villagers when not. That is, I wanted my modern troupe to be comprised of citizen actors rather than urbanite theatre pros.[28]

ZERKA MORENO: Moreno was my only mentor, but he and I were familiar with the work of Ibsen and Shakespeare.[29]

| | |
|---|---|
| WILLIAM SUN: | Richard Schechner. After Richard read my first paper on The Peasant's Theatre Experiment, he told me about Boal. I think that's still the only new discovery I made since I went to the States. I think most Chinese know about Boal because of my introduction and writing. But now I think it will only work for trainings for professionals, not for schoolchildren. They cannot handle it. And the authorities would be very wary of rehearsal for revolution. Even our acting students are not completely comfortable. Forum Theatre takes forever. I asked colleagues in the US if they had ever seen Forum Theatre with a happy ending. No they hadn't. There is something in the Chinese culture that avoids nasty conflicts as presented in Greek tragedy. In the States, actors would never want a happy ending. They want to show their individuality. But there are many Chinese who think if you reach agreement, that's great. This should be learned by the Chinese officials. But government would not buy this theory, because it could be revolution, you never know.[30] |
| HSIAO-HUA CHANG: | My mentors are Nellie McCaslin and Robert Landy. Professor McCaslin led me into the teaching of Creative Drama, and Professor Landy led me to combine Creative Drama with Role Method in the field of Drama Therapy.[31] |
| BARNES: | My own experience has been one of little mentorship within the academic environment – one was expected to simply get on with it and learn as you went along. This was exacerbated by the marginal status of drama departments within the South African universities where there has been little understanding of the interrogative nature of our praxis. There have been significant changes with the democratization of South African universities. Since 1994 contact and partnership with other universities worldwide has meant an opening up of opportunities for meaningful collaboration. However I have |

found incredible inspiration through my first teacher, Joan Little, and also in the writings of a number of experts, such as: Dorothy Heathcote, Gavin Bolton, Brain Way, Cecily O'Neill, Richard Courtney, Philip Taylor, Helen Nicholson, Paolo Freire, Augusto Boal, Zakes Mda, Sue Jennings, Alida Gersie, Robert Landy and Roger Grainger.

COHEN-CRUZ: Brecht was someone who, as a young person, gave me a vision of what theatre could be. I don't want to be part of a field that doesn't include Tony Kushner. In terms of Boal, he really made me feel more connected to a world movement. Barbara Meyerhoff, the anthropologist, had been really important to me. Also, M. C. Richards, a potter. She had a real sense of how art is part of the world we live in. And Brooks McNamara. He reframed the whole field of popular theatre. I realized how inspiring that was and I know that's one of my strategies, reframing a kind of theatre that's undervalued by showing parallels with other kinds of theatre.

LANDY: Richard Courtney, Dorothy and Gavin. In theatre, Brecht, whose plays I directed and songs I sang in cabaret. Samuel Beckett's aesthetic touched me deeply. And in the 60s: the Living Theatre, the Open Theatre, the Bread and Puppet Theatre. In psychology, Jung, Rank and Ferenczi. In sociology, Erving Goffman and Tom Scheff. In Psychodrama, Zerka and J. L. Moreno, Lew[is] Yablonsky and Jim Sacks.

MONTGOMERY: Let's shift into a conversation about the goals of our work.

COHEN-CRUZ: In the classroom you are generating knowledge, you're not just passing it on. A major goal is rebuilding community through the arts.

HEATHCOTE: Drama engages everyone, because it's based in the thing we all have in common – we're all human. It's a question of we, and us and our. It engages the total person, the whole experience, empathy and intelligence.

JOSÉ CRUZ GONZÁLEZ:  Drama is a place where we come together to share our common humanity. To educate, question and inspire. To be transported to another place, time or world.[32]

BOOTH:  The goal of Educational Drama is to teach and reach all students, regardless of natural talent or particular dispositions to this art form. Personal involvement at deep levels of artistic experience; cooperative and collaborative growth within the work, resulting in creating an ensemble; an exploration of topics and issues that can surprise and shock the participants into deeper awareness at every level.[33]

BARNES:  I do, as do many others, attempt to find appropriate ways of adapting Western praxis for an African but multicultural context. My goals are: increased self-knowledge and growing self-actualization; increased knowledge of and concern for others along with a greater ability to work co-operatively; and an increased sense of responsibility for positive action in the world.

SUN:  I realized we should develop a new model for Educational Theatre, because so far all the Chinese writings or translations are basically copying the Western model based on the philosophy of individualism, which is the belief that every individual has the potential to be a writer, director, performer, everybody's story can be staged. In theory, of course that's great. I hope in the future we can do that. But our urgent task is to put theatre into the curriculum of all kinds of schools. In order to do that, we have to convince them that this is going to be beneficial to all children, not only a few of the smartest and most outspoken students. And this is not only going to improve our education, but it would also help the government. We want the government to see drama as a 'revolutionary' tool, which the Communist Party used to like before 1949. It could be a

|  |  |
|---|---|
|  | harmonizing element now. On the other hand, the need to create a Chinese brand of Drama Therapy or Educational Drama is only based on the fact that most Chinese students are not used to spelling out their individual stories, let alone enacting them in public. |
| HEATHCOTE: | I have a word I keep in mind, I don't even know if it's a proper word: praxis. Praxis is doing to understand it. So all the tasks, any part I play in keeping the tasks going or initiating them, is doing so they understand the doing of it and I learn what I realize I didn't know when I started. |
| FITZGIBBON: | I've always worked on the basis to create the best aesthetic product that you possibly can. You have to honor the art form. There's no point in having bad theatre and making it work because it is educational. |
| BOLTON: | The first goal is the training of students to examine and question their cultural values and to respect differences in people. Second, gaining a sense of the aesthetic and a love of theatre. Third, gaining confidence in oneself and skills in communication. |
| LANDY: | What do you see as some significant changes in the field in the past 30 years? |
| GRAHAM: | There is now an aesthetic shift in TYA which involves everything from new writing, object theatre, music theatre, experiments in work for the very young, site specific work, promenade theatre, circus and on and on. The sectarian divisions between theatre for children and teenagers have been superseded by something much more interesting. |
| SWORTZELL: | Many more forms are included, such as the musical, the opera, the play with über-marionettes. And the topics change from predominantly fairy tale, goody-goody plays to serious plays, even for younger children. It's a total expansion and a new concept of the child. And who is the child? And who is the young adult? |

EDIE DEMAS:   In the last few years, some of the most exciting directions in Theatre for Young Audiences are messing with the form of theatre. In some cases it's being influenced by adult theatre, and in other cases it's influencing adult theatre. I think it's particularly true outside the US.[34]

O'NEILL:   The youth theatre movement in England is very, very strong – and it's very strong in Ireland – and doing very exciting and innovative work.

TAYLOR:   Another interesting shift took place. The Process Drama people now say that what we're doing is theatre. Gavin wrote his book *Acting in Classroom Drama*, and Cecily O'Neill talked about how there's always theatre in drama and drama in theatre. There's always process in product, product in process.

LANDY:   Gavin, what changes have you seen over time in the field?

BOLTON:   Over time is two generations. If you think of the UK: the 1950s witnessed a battle against traditional drama as 'speech-training' or 'stage performance'; the 1960s/70s: a battle between Heathcote's 'teacher-in-role', Slade's 'free expression' and Way's 'exercises'; 1980s: the resurrection of drama as literature or stage performance in opposition to Heathcote's and my emphasis on 'Learning through Drama'; 1990s: drama as a subject for national examinations took over. From the 1980s onwards, there has been a quiet development. I am referring to the impressive input of Augusto Boal. What a pity he and Dorothy Heathcote never put their heads together!

LANDY:   They both envisioned drama as centered in posing problems, and as centered in the group process. I believe they both saw theatre as a place to challenge, to reason through, as is the literal meaning of dialogue. And they both were formidable presences. Their influence dominated the field during the past 30 years.

GRAHAM:   There is much more international exchange than ever. The advanced cohort of European TYA has raised the stakes in the search for quality and forced us to re-look at the all-important nature of the transaction between the act of theatre and our young audiences. And here's the weird thing – as old Europe breaks up and new nations are forged, so too is the quest for language and identity.

Participatory drama is being rediscovered by new generations as a unique way of making fresh connections between old and new cultures. Another symptom of this shift is the appearance of young and old alike alongside professional actors on our main stages.

ODHIAMBO: I see a shift from enclosed spaces to more open performance spaces, more interactive approaches and the privileging of theory in the reading of educational drama/theatre and site specific performances.

BARNES: Since 1994 there has been an attempt to find a bridge between Western theory and practice and indigenous African modes of education, development and therapy. Prior to that, a shift from traditional theatre creation to broadening the field to include first avant-garde European and American practice and then postmodern and post-colonial perceptions and methods and to embrace all the different forms of applying drama and theatre.

GONZÁLEZ: I've seen more Latino/Latina artists enter into the mainstream of theatre. This also applies in Theatre for Youth. It is still small but growing. I've also seen Latino/a theatre artists now teaching at colleges and universities across the country.

THOMPSON: The changes I see include the fragmentation of the groups – DIE is no longer focused on schools/education but in an amazing diversity of contexts; the popularity in universities in these areas; the 'professionalisation' of many practices; the funding that became available, particularly under 'New Labour' in the UK; the level of critical writing and debate in the field. The link to politics has become more complicated. The TIE movement here was closely associated with particular left movements, and the Applied Theatre movement perhaps started with a radical view of social change, but I think Applied Theatre has a range of political perspectives and rationales. Baz Kershaw sees the fragmentation of theatre into lots of special interest groups and communities as an example of the influence of postmodernism and identity politics. No longer class, but the elderly, disabled, people of color.

LANDY: What do you see as the future of the field?

THOMPSON: In *RiDE: The Journal of Applied Theatre*, there are some new really impressive voices emerging, particularly those writing about theatre and disability. So one orientation is that the scholarship is improving and I would hope that from this there is a positive dialogue with practice. The Uni [University] here started an Applied Theatre Professional Doctorate program in 2010. What I would like to see is also a more sophisticated understanding of theatre as well as the contexts that people work in. The interdisciplinarity of practice and theory has been and I hope will continue to be strong, but we should start to think again about working as artists.

COHEN-CRUZ: I think it would be exciting if there were a very interdisciplinary department where one could take a body of courses in order to develop some expertise in what we are talking about.

BOOTH: I feel that it will be the arts that hold the future of drama in schools. As technology becomes the norm, we will need personal interaction as a medium for socialization, and the arts can offer these experiences.

COHEN-CRUZ: Eighty-five to ninety-five percent of the students who graduate from theatre departments are not going to work in the arts as it is traditionally conceived. But if you add jobs that draw on theatre in related fields, a lot more people are going to work.

JAMES MIRRIONE: We are not at the stage in Emirati society where women are given license to think about a career, much less a vocation. A job, yes. And, in the field of Educational Theatre, the only program in the whole of the Emirates that can train women to be professionals in the field is through the work I do at the United Arab Emirates University and its connection with the Creative Arts Team in New York. The struggle now is to keep these women interested in this field and not have them get short circuited by the cultural tradition that when you're married, usually in an arranged marriage, the husband will determine whether you can work outside the home.[35]

BOLTON: World-wide, the main development will be in different forms of Applied Theatre, offering learning experience for a group with personal or social problems. There will also be an increased respect for academic research, which may or may not lead us back into the classroom.

ODHIAMBO: The field has a bright future as more people are beginning to appreciate the role of Entertainment Education.[36] In the classroom it is both a subject and a pedagogic strategy and methodology. It provides a site for negotiation of issues which cannot be confronted in other situations.

BARNES: There is an increasing awareness of the therapeutic possibilities of drama and theatre. I see a move away from purely development issues towards a more holistic approach to social problems which takes into account the psychological impacts of disease, poverty and violence.

MORENO: I envision a greater spread of our [psychodrama] work, as is happening now in Taiwan, China, India and Bangladesh, Turkey and Greece, besides former Marxist countries in Eastern Europe.

FOX: My hope for the future for Playback Theatre. ... So many people deserve and need to tell their stories. I want the Playback practitioners to succeed much more than they have to date in connecting with established social institutions. On another level, you might ask me what is my fear for Playback Theatre's future? There is a danger with Playback Theatre that it becomes sentimental and superficially positive, you know, building empathy and community come hell or high water. Thus recent initiatives to unpack stories, insist on multiple viewpoints, and court discord in the name of true dialogue have my full support. At the same time, I would regret it if Playback Theatre retreated from its allegiance to personhood and the basic idea of bearing witness.

MONTGOMERY: I also have fears for the future of drama in schools where arts education continues to remain very low on our national priority list. There's been a decline in student exposure to the arts since 1997, which is not surprising when you consider schools' obsessive focus on standardized testing. In the UK they are currently experiencing massive arts funding cuts within higher education and primary education, as well as within arts organizations. At the same time, we've seen more Educational Drama and Theatre programs in higher education emerge. New Applied Theatre programs are cropping up around the world. The number of undergraduate and graduate students at NYU Program in Educational Theatre's has probably doubled since the 1982 *Handbook* came out. What makes me feel positive about the future is that most of our graduating certified teachers are getting jobs in schools and community settings. And they will create positive change for the future. I believe that drama and theatre will survive and flourish in schools and various community settings despite our economic downturns.

SALDAÑA: I am not the barometer for the metric of where the field is going. I see it pretty much the same for the next five years. After five years, I also want to see what goes on in education and the economy. There is questioning about what really matters. If we follow that same trend we will come to a crisis point where we ask, what's really important at this point. I think there's this need to examine meaning, the simplicity of what we are trying to do.

LANDY: Maybe it's about building a theatre for change. Drama and theatre cannot stop violence or global warming or cure AIDS or mental illness. But drama and theatre workers can address profound personal and social issues by facilitating the transformation of complex realities into vivid, provocative metaphors. And by enabling viewers to engage with the metaphors and to see themselves and their worlds in new ways. And maybe to change those aspects of themselves and their worlds that demand change.

MONTGOMERY: And what about the pageants of Christianity and Hinduism and Islam? What about dogma?

LANDY: Theatre is big in Oberammergau. Change has a completely different meaning in Theatre of Faith. It is about conversion. Or it is not about change at all, but a celebration of the status quo.

MONTGOMERY: And what about spectators who witness public executions?

LANDY: This question reminds me of Tony Kushner's translation of *Brundibar* when he informs the children at the end that although one tyrant is dead, more will follow. Even though Theatre for Change is about questioning oppression, the dramas of master and slave will certainly endure. As for executions as performance, I see that the top court in Atlanta, Georgia ruled in July 2011 to permit the videotaping of the execution by lethal injection of Andrew DeYoung.

SANJANI: We are hoping for some progressive change. Of course, the idea of what that progressive change is or what we assume the good to be, the values we bring to it, all have to do with the ethics of our practice.

TAYLOR: Robert, when you talk about future directions in the 1982 *Handbook*, you essentially close the book with: *The field must engage in a constructive dialogue. This means cutting through our tendencies to separate knowledge into impregnable compartments in our minds, and departments on our campuses. That means risking the sharing and debating of our ideas, not to leave us open to exploitation, but rather to the building of the field much in need of clarification and cooperation.* Has that happened?

LANDY: I think we've gone the other way. I think we've split the splits.

SANJANI: At every conference I have ever presented at, as soon as I reveal myself to be a therapist, I get a cold shoulder. So I play that card very carefully because I want to form alliances and I think it's particularly necessary now. If Applied Theatre artists do not embrace Drama Therapy, they are going to be missing out on a very important piece of the puzzle. It has to do with the emotional geography of change.

LANDY: Why can't we all get along? Isn't it possible that the personal and the political are compatible, an idea promoted by feminists for some 50 years?

EMUNAH: I see a great opportunity for dialogue, as there is so much overlap, and ways we can inform each others' work. I don't know that we can't get along; I think our separateness is largely based on practicalities – there is so much to explore within our individual disciplines, we each have our own conferences and organizations, and there is limited time. Each field is so rich, complex and vast that an in depth immersion in one takes decades.

FOX: Of course I think it would be a good idea to talk to each other more. My struggle to bring Playback Theatre into the world forced onto me a kind of solitary road. When established institutions did not easily accept our work, I had to forge ahead anyway. The students became the colleagues. Looking back, I wish I did have more contact with other theatre practitioners, and do today. Of course I share a deep ambivalence as well about being thrown in with this lot or that lot. Playback Theatre is boundary crossing, and while there are some people in Therapeutic Theatre, Educational Theatre, Theatre for Development, Experimental Theatre and TO with whom I would have a great deal to share, it is also true that in all those sectors, there are many people with whom I cringe to be identified. It is not easy to pull my focus up from my own practice, which has been such a joy and struggle over the years. Perhaps we theatre practitioners need you and other academics to seed the ground for a common field.

LANDY: In my 1982 *Handbook* I said: 'We must work at least to find a common rhetoric if we are to communicate more fully. In the future, this rhetoric must be inclusive rather than exclusive of current work in the field.'

MORENO: We should encourage greater interweaving with all trends and forms of drama.

EMUNAH: Given that your project is called Theatre for Change, I would have reservations of a common field with that title, given that our program at California Institute for Integral Studies initiated and rapidly developed a project called Theatre for Change about seven years ago. But the idea of a common field is an interesting proposition. I could more easily envision it as a coalition, under which there are separate fields. The main obstacle I see at this point is that there are other related disciplines that each field is also closely connected to, for example, Drama Therapy to other creative arts therapies.

TAYLOR: Wouldn't we want to say that with the critical peda-gogy movement, that this notion of commonality, of heteronormative renderings, is somewhat redundant when we're talking about teaching pluralistic under-standings? And when people talk about a common rhetoric, they tend to be referencing Euro-centrism. What's your view on that?

MONTGOMERY: We embrace the multiple and diverse viewpoints. They are what tie us all together. In fact, when I think about the future, I see some exciting practice and research.

LANDY: Back to Jonathan Fox – everywhere that I travel, East and West, I find an abundance of Playback Theatre, not all of equal quality, but some quite stunning and culturally-relevant. In Drama Therapy there is new and exciting work internationally. For example, Zeina Daccache's work in the prisons of Lebanon; and in Montreal, a mix of Drama Therapy and Social Theatre.

SANJANI: In Montreal I work with a multi-disciplinary research initiative called *Life Stories of Montrealers: Displaced by War, Genocide, and other Human Rights Violations*. That involves working in a Haitian community group, Rwandan community group and Cambodian. I am spe-cifically looking at performative approaches that might have something to contribute, not only to the process of healing from mass atrocity, but the reintegration into society at large; how we speak about ourselves as a Canadian society, a Montreal community.

MONTGOMERY: I think about the new contributions in theatre educa-tion and social action of Javier Cardona, Daphnie Sicre, Alex Santiago-Jirau, Kayhan Irani and Christina Marín.

LANDY: I wrote a song called 'Jewel Blues' as part of my musi-cal, *God Lives in Glass*. The lyrics are based upon a story about God told to me by a young Indian girl. The song begins: 'God does not need jewels/He's got them in his heart.' When I made the film, *Three Approaches to Drama Therapy*, I added the song at the end, as the credits are rolling. In a training group several African-Americans expressed discomfort with the song, feeling that it sounded like an old Negro spiritual and was demeaning. Some heard the lyrics as: 'God does not need Jews/He's got them in his heart.' This led to a troubling but open discussion of the tensions between Blacks and Jews within a number of communities. Although no resolution was reached, all agreed that the dialogue was riveting.

TAYLOR: I think of the Applied Theatre and Applied Drama movement in terms of the conferences that bring those disparate communities together. Look at the Theatre Without Borders conference at LaMama in 2010.[37] Twenty-five years ago you wouldn't have found all those people coming together.

LANDY: David and I were there. Theatre artists came from Pakistan, Sudan, Serbia, Sri Lanka, Cambodia, Iran.[38] Globalization has some benefits. I think these people could dialogue well because they were not from specific camps of Applied Theatre or Drama Therapy. They were theatre people with a common social justice agenda. Their interest was in changing the world through theatre. Our interests are the same, although we look at theatre in an applied sense.

VINE: I would hope we are always open to dialogue across this field or fields, whatever we call them. It saddens me when people retreat to fixed positions. But our differences demand rigorous scrutiny. That can be difficult and is harder for some than others. I am uncomfortable in my new academic garb. I am not a natural theoretician nor a good writer, so it can be intimidating to address the necessary questions in company with those for whom these forms and processes hold no fears. It is a word-bound, intellect dominated culture. Sadly, the theoretical facility is still elevated above practical expertise – partly because theory travels so much more easily than practice. But I believe passionately that theory and practice should not be separated in our work, so it is incumbent on us all to find ways of contributing. Fortunately, there are many different ways to dialogue.

This chapter presents one way to dialogue, offering a collage of opinions on the ends and means of drama and theatre in education, social action and therapy. We value difference as much as commonality. We also value the advice of our mentors. For both of us, Dorothy Heathcote was a towering mentor. Apparently the Queen of England agreed, as she honored Dorothy, a humble teacher and a weaver, with the MBE (Member of the Order of the British Empire), for her contributions to drama as education.

In closing, we recall Dorothy's advice to us as we began this project: 'Don't write another textbook'. But we did so, keeping her intent in mind. We believe that intent is to engage our readers in compelling dialogue around the complexity of drama and theatre praxis. Our intent has been to interweave the various strands of this incredibly diverse field. We suspect that Dorothy, a former weaver, would have welcomed our efforts.

# Glossary

## Drama and theatre in education

**Child drama:** A term coined by Peter Slade that refers to drama focused on children as audience and/or as participants. It relies heavily on children's propensity to play. Goals of Child Drama include optimal expression through the body and emotions, as well as building confidence, collaboration and critical thinking.[1]

**Creative drama:** Spontaneous dramatic play for educational ends.[2] It is 'an improvisational, non-exhibitional, process-centered form of drama in which participants are guided by a leader to imagine, enact and reflect upon human experiences. Built on the human impulse and ability to act out perceptions of the world in order to understand it, creative drama requires both logical and intuitive thinking, personalizes knowledge, and yields aesthetic pleasure.'[3] In high school, the term 'improvisation' is often used instead of creative drama.[4] Also known as Informal Drama and Drama in Education.

**Curriculum drama:** School-based drama to teach various subject areas. It 'engages students in the core practice and mindful activity of related fields' in which, through 'the power of student and teacher constructions...class members interact as insiders within a field of practice.'[5] 'Curriculum drama forms a bridge that links the tasks of teaching, learning, and inquiry to the authentic interests, concerns, and energies of the students.'[6] Curriculum Drama is also known as Drama Across the Curriculum.

**Developmental drama:** The study of dramatic play/transformation.[7] It includes five subsets: Educational Drama, Drama Therapy, Personal Drama, Social Drama and Artistic Development.[8] 'Developmental Drama involves the personal growth of the student. It uses dramatic forms and strategies in a dynamic, sequential manner, based on the physical and psychological stages of human development. Stressing personal physical and intellectual growth, Developmental Drama places greater emphasis on affective learning than on cognitive learning and on the learning process than on the product or presentation.'[9]

**Drama in education**: 'the use of drama as a means of teaching a variety of content areas. It is used to expand children's awareness, to enable them to look at reality beyond fantasy, to see below the surface of actions to their meanings. The objective is understanding rather than playmaking, although a play may be made in the process.'[10] There is an emphasis on developing the child's imagination, self-awareness and expressiveness and upon the social skills involved in group work.'[11] Also known as Educational Drama and Drama Education.

**Process drama**: 'proceeds without a script, its outcome is unpredictable, it lacks a separate audience, and the experience is impossible to replicate exactly.'[12] Participants in process drama 'take on roles that are required for the enquiry, investigation or exploration of the subject matter of the drama. The task of the teacher is to find ways in which to connect the pupils with the content and enable them to develop responses to it through active engagement and reflection.'[13]

**Story drama**: the creation of stories through improvisation and used in the classroom to enhance learning. It is 'improvised role play stimulated by a story.' Participants co-construct the story, or part of the story, and the characters within it.[14]

## Drama and theatre in social action

**Bibliodrama**: A form of dramatization in which the roles played are taken from Bible stories. The goal of Bibliodrama is to help people reconnect with stories in the Bible so those stories can guide, heal and comfort people.[1] A subset of this form is called Playback Bibliodrama.[2]

**Community-based theatre**: emphases the creating and performing of people within their local communities. These stories may be celebratory or critical, or a combination of both.[3] The process emphasizes participation on the part of actors and audiences and leads to philosophical and ethical inquiry into the forging of identity.[4] May also be referred to as Theatre for Communities and Theatre by Communities. See also Grassroots Theatre.

**Engaged theatre**: Used by Jan Cohen-Cruz to speak of drama activities and theatre performances that focus upon social and political issues within communities. It is also known as socially engaged performance and covers not only alternative forms of theatre, but also commercial forms that address social and political concerns. As a generic term, it is similar to Applied Theatre as well as Grassroots Theatre, Non-scripted Theatre,

Social Theatre, Community-based Theatre, Theatre of the Oppressed and Popular Theatre.

**Epic theatre**: A type of narrative theatre developed in the early 20th century and popularized by Bertolt Brecht. Brecht's Epic Theatre intended to distance spectators from sentimental attachments to characters and provoke them to critically examine and question societal injustices. Through Epic Theatre, Brecht aimed toward social change. The expressionistic style of performance helped to achieve the desired alienation effect.

**Ethnodrama**: Stems from ethnography, the study of human culture, adding the element of performance to the presentation of the ethnographic research. Ethnotheatre is the performance of the ethnodrama.[5] Ethnodrama 'consists of dramatized, significant selections of narrative collected through interviews, participant observation field notes, journal entries, and/or print and media artifacts such as diaries, television broadcasts, newspaper articles, and court proceedings.'[6]

**Grassroots theatre**: Was developed by Dudley Cocke, Harry Newman, and Janet-Salmons-Rue and concerns a commitment to local issues within specific communities.[7] Grassroots Theatre values work with traditional cultures and indigenous populations. It is linked to the struggles for cultural, social, economic and political equity for all people.[8] See also Popular Theatre.

**Museum theatre**: Engages visitors in drama and theatre activities to enhance the educational experience within a museum. It includes storytelling and living-history interpretation, musical and theatrical presentations, creative drama, puppetry and mime. First used by only a few institutions, museum theatre has grown significantly, leading to a number of evaluation studies.[9]

**Playback theatre**: An original form of improvisational theatre in which audience members tell stories from their lives and watch them enacted on the spot by actors and musicians.[10] 'Although the performances often focus on a theme of interest or concern to the group, the performers follow no set narrative agenda, but bring their dramatic skills and their humanity to embodying on the stage the concerns and experiences of audience members.'[11]

**Popular theatre**: Uses popular forms of entertainment such as dance, song, puppetry and mime to develop awareness of social and political issues within communities. To do so it points out contradictions, leaving the audience with unanswered questions upon which to reflect and seek answers. Popular Theatre draws on participants' experiences to collectively create theatre and engage in discussion of issues.[12] See also Grassroots Theatre.

**Prison theatre**: Refers to drama and theatre workshops and performances created by, with and for incarcerated people worldwide. The aims of the work include entertainment, play, rehabilitation, transformation and therapy.[13]

**Reminiscence theatre**: Designed by, with and for older populations. The participants are encouraged to recall memories around a particular moment in personal and cultural history and to tell their stories.[14] Many of the stories are developed into plays performed by the elderly themselves or professional actors. There is an intergenerational form of Reminiscence Theatre.[15] Reminiscence Theatre is also known as Theatre for the Elderly.

**Social theatre**: Often used synonymously with Applied Theatre. Social Theatre is a theatre for change.[16] Derived from Performance Studies, it is a participatory form intended to 'empower differences and create solidarity ... to question society, with the living presence of its differences, rather than to be purified and be brought back to a "normal" value system or social code.'[17]

**Sociodrama**: Was coined by J. L. Moreno as 'based upon the tacit assumption that the group formed by the audience is already organized by the social and cultural roles which in some degree all the carriers of the culture share.'[18] It is 'an action method in which individuals enact an agreed upon social situation spontaneously.'[19]

**Theatre of the oppressed**: Was developed by Brazilian director Augusto Boal and codified in his text of the same name, partly in response to the work of educator Paolo Freire and his book *Pedagogy of the Oppressed*, and also in response to the social and political turmoil in Brazil in the 1970s.[20] TO consists of theatre games and activities which generate dialogue in communities and rehearse action toward real social change. The best known TO strategy is Forum Theatre. See also Invisible Theatre, Rainbow of Desire and Legislative Theatre.

**Theatre of faith**: Throughout history and culture, many religions sponsored performances of scripture and myth, as well as stories from the lives of saints and martyrs. Of note were the performances of the suffering, death, and re-birth of such iconic spiritual figures as: Osiris, Christ, Rama, and Imam Hussein. Theatre of Faith is the enactment of such stories in religious settings to affirm the faith of a community of celebrants.

The performances may also be created with a focus on religious principles and practices rather than directly tied to religious texts.

**Theatre in health education**: Uses drama and theatre as media for learning about health.[21] It combines the principles and practices of Theatre in Education and health education to address issues of health, safety, and well-being. It arose largely in response to the HIV/AIDS crisis in the late 1980s and early 1990s, but is now used with a variety of health issues including drug abuse, child abuse, effective parenting, safe driving, safe/clean water and organ donation.[22]

**Theatre for development**: The creating and performing of plays addressing important issues in developing communities worldwide, although the bulk of research on this topic is focused in various African countries. Originally a force that supported many of the aims and interests of colonizers, TfD now focuses on locally driven issues that are facilitated by outside specialists and agencies, but with control of the process in the hands of those within a given community.[23]

**Theatre in education**: Originally a British concept, TIE is the use of theatre by professional actor-teachers mostly within school environments to create thought-provoking content for young audiences for educational purposes.[24] In TIE, plays are followed by a workshop and include participatory events.[25] TIE makes use of curricular material or social problems as themes.

## Drama and theatre in therapy

**Creative arts therapy**: The application of one or more forms of art, dance, music, poetry, drama and theatre to people in need of help in exploring personal and collective problems and in taking of action toward change. Creative arts therapists usually specialize in a one expressive form, for example, Art Therapy, Dance and Movement Therapy, Drama Therapy, Psychodrama, Music Therapy or Poetry Therapy.[1]

**Developmental Transformations** (DvT): A form of Drama Therapy defined by David Read Johnson, its founder, as 'embodied encounters in the playspace.'[2] Johnson bases his work on an understanding and application of free play. DvT is an improvisational approach that seeks to facilitate flow. The therapist is an active participant and the work is intended to deconstruct 'psychic structures that inhibit the client(s) from accessing primary experiences of Being.'[3]

**Expressive therapy**: A collective form that engages clients in a healing process through the therapeutic use of the arts. Expressive therapists integrate the modalities of dance, drama, literature, music, poetry and the visual arts with the practice of psychotherapy.[4]

**Narradrama**: An eclectic approach, innovated by Pam Dunne, that combines aspects of Narrative Therapy and Drama Therapy to treat a variety children and adults through several forms of art-making, story-making and drama.[5]

**Playback theatre**: An original form of improvisational theatre in which audience or group members tell stories from their lives and watch them enacted on the spot.[6] 'Performances are carried out by a team of actors, emcee (called the conductor), and musician.'[7] 'Although the performances often focus on a theme of interest or concern to the group, the performers follow no set narrative agenda, but bring their dramatic skills and their humanity to embodying on the stage the concerns and experiences of audience members.'[8]

**Psychodrama**: A therapeutic process, conceived by Jacob L. Moreno, that centers on exploring individuals' issues through role-playing in a group setting. Protagonists play themselves in relationship to significant others in their lives, played by other group members. 'Psychodrama facilitates insight, personal growth, and integration on cognitive, affective, and behavioral levels. It clarifies issues, increases physical and emotional well being, enhances learning and develops new skills.'[9]

**Remedial drama**: Was coined by Sue Jennings to describe dramatic activities, based in improvisational theatre and Creative Drama, to help remediate various cognitive and emotional handicaps as well as physical disabilities. For Jennings, Remedial Drama was a precursor to Drama Therapy.[10]

**Rainbow of desire**: One of several approaches developed by Augusto Boal, where the oppression to be dramatized is based upon an oppressor. In this approach, single protagonists tell stories about their actual life circumstances in relationship to an antagonist. The stories are then dramatized to explore the issues.[11]

**Role-playing**: A basic procedure in everyday life and in drama and theatre that occurs when individuals put themselves in the shoes of others. It involves a process of de-centering, imagination and action. In therapy, role-playing is used to rehash an unresolved episode from the past, to rehearse a future possibility and to learn to live more fully in the present.

**Site-specific theatre**: Theatre in any of its several modes of education, social action and/or therapy conducted within a particular location. 'Site-specific theatre is a performance which overtly uses the properties, qualities, and meanings found at/on a given site, be it a landscape, a city, a building or a room. This form of theatre emphasizes particular images, stories, and events that reveal the complex relationship between ourselves and our physical environment.'[12]

**Sociodrama**: See definition above.

**Sociometry**: The study of human relationships within groups. It is a term attributed to J. L. Moreno who studied corporate, military, educational, recreational and therapy groups. Moreno sought to help people understand how and why they choose to connect with and isolate from others, thereby improving the group dynamics.[13]

**Therapeutic story-making**: Was developed in the 1980s by Alida Gersie, who used stories in her work as a drama therapist and organizational consultant to identify and work through problems in the life of an individual or group. Through the story-making, Gersie helped clients and organizations discover new ways to conceptualize problems and develop strategies toward change.[14]

**Therapeutic theatre**: A form of theatre production by, with and for a particular population in need of expressing their issues and sharing them with a group. A process of research and rehearsal precedes the performance, and a process of reflection follows the performance. Groups associated with therapeutic performance include war veterans, addicts, developmentally disabled people and mentally ill people, among many others.

# Notes

## Foreword

1. P. Weiss (2001) *Marat/Sade* (London: Marion Boyars).
2. H. G. Barker (1922) *Exemplary Theatre* (Boston, MA: Little, Brown, and Company).
3. R. J. Landy (1982) *Handbook of Educational Drama and Theatre* (Westport, CT: Greenwood Press).

## Introduction

1. Aristotle (330 BC; 1997) *Poetics* (Mineola, NY: Dover Publications).
2. P. Freire (1970/2000) *Pedagogy of the Oppressed* (New York: The Continuum International Publishing Group, Inc.), p. 79. See also P. Taylor (1993) *The Texts of Paulo Freire* (Buckingham: Open University Press).
3. R. J. Landy (1982) *Handbook of Educational Drama and Theatre* (Westport, CT: Greenwood Press).
4. R. Landy (Writer, Host) (1980) 'Drama in Education' (USA: CBS-TV).
5. Blizzard Entertainment (2011) 'World of Warcraft: Cataclysm.' http://us.battle. net/wow/en/, date accessed 12 August 2011.
6. See R. Landy (2008) *The Couch and the Stage* (Lanham, MD: Jason Aronson).
7. Pedagogy and Theatre of the Oppressed (1999) 'A Brief Biography of Paulo Freire', http://www.ptoweb.org/freire.html, date accessed 12 August 2011.
8. H. Giroux (ed.) (1997) *Pedagogy and the Politics of Hope. Theory, Culture, and Schooling: A Critical Reader* (Boulder, CO: Westview Press). J. Kincheloe and P. McLaren (1994) 'Rethinking Critical Theory and Qualitative Research' in N. Denzin and Y. Lincoln (eds), *Handbook of Qualitative Research* (Thousand Oaks, CA: Sage), pp. 138–57.
9. See, for example, J. Neelands (2010) 'Mirror, Dynamo or Lens? Drama, Children and Social Change' in P. O'Connor (ed.) *Creating Democratic Citizenship through Drama Education: the Writings of Jonothan Neelands* (Stoke on Trent: Trentham Books).
10. See, for example, J. Thompson (2005) *Digging Up Stories*: *Applied Theatre, Performance and War* (Manchester: Manchester University Press).
11. For praxis, see J. Thompson (2009) *Performance Affects: Applied Theatre and the End of Effect* (Basingstoke: Palgrave Macmillan). For globalization, see H. Nicholson (2011) *Theatre, Education and Performance: The Map and the Story* (Basingstoke: Palgrave Macmillan).
12. See NADT (2007) 'NADT Code of Ethics', revised 2007, http://www.nadt.org/ codeofethics.htm, date accessed 12 August 2011, and British Association of

Dramatherapists (n.d.) 'Standards of Ethical Practice', http://www.badth.org. uk/code/supcode.html, date accessed 12 August 2011.

13. See B. Brecht (1977) *The Measures Taken and Other Lehrstucke*. (London: Eyre Methuen).

14. For more information, visit CTO's website, Center Theater of the Oppressed (2009) 'Center Theater of the Oppressed', http://ctorio.org.br/novosite/, date accessed 12 August 2011.

15. For a description of this experience, see Y. Naor and H. Goett (2010) 'Towards Healing: Confronting the Holocaust through Psychodrama, Sociodrama and Rituals', *Australian and New Zealand Psychodrama Association Journal*, 19, 38–45.

16. H. Volavkova (1993) *I Never Saw another Butterfly*, 2nd edn (New York: Schocken).

17. H. Krása (composer) and A. Hoffmeister (libretto) (1993) *Brundibár* (opera) (Amersterdam: Channel Classics Records).

18. B. Brecht (1949) *Three Penny Opera* (New York: Grove Press). B. Brecht (lyrics) and K. Weill (music) (1928) 'What Keeps Mankind Alive?' (song) (New York: European American Music Corporation).

19. H. Krása and Adolf Hoffmeister (1938) *Brundibár* (opera) (Berlin: Tempo Praha). See also, T. Kushner and M. Sendak (2003) *Brundibar* (New York: Hyperion Books).

20. J. Bor (2006) in V. Blodig, et al. *Art Against Death* (Terezin, Czech Republic: Oswald), p. 21.

21. Interview conducted with Ela Weissberger, 15 December 2009.

22. T. Kushner and M. Sendak (2003) *Brundibar* (New York: Michael di Capua Books/Hyperion Books for Children).

23. Interview conducted with Ela Weissberger, 15 December 2009.

24. A. Boal (1995) *The Rainbow of Desire: The Boal Method of Theatre and Therapy* (London; New York: Routledge).

# Part I   Drama and Theatre in Education

1. Y. Chan and L. P. Chan (2009) 'In their own words: how do students relate drama pedagogy to their learning in curriculum subjects?', *RiDE: The Journal Of Applied Theatre and Performance*, 14, 2, 196.

2. Ibid., p. 204.

3. Ibid., p. 204.

4. Ibid., p. 204.

5. Voices in Conflict (n.d.) 'Voices in Conflict,' http://voicesinconflict.com/, date accessed 18 September 2010.

6. A. L. Cowan (12 April 2007) 'Canceled by Principal, Student Play is Headed to Off Broadway,' *New York Times*, http://query.nytimes.com/gst/fullpage.html?res=9A0 5EFD9123FF931A25757C0A9619C8B63, date accessed 15 September 2010.

7. M. Ryzik (14 June 2007) 'Unwelcome at Home, Student Play is a Hit in New York,' *New York Times*, http://www.voicesinconflict.com/nytimes4.html, date accessed 16 September 2010.

8. Ibid.

9. C. O'Neill (1996) 'Into the Labyrinth: Theory and Research in Drama' in P. Taylor (ed.) *Researching Drama and Arts Education: Paradigms and Possibilities* (London: The Falmer Press), p. 140.

10. C. O'Neill (2006) 'Foreword,' in J. J. Schneider and T.P. Crumpler, and T. Rogers (eds) *Process Drama and Multiple Literacies: Addressing Social, Cultural, and Ethical Issues* (Portsmouth, NH: Heinemann), p. xi.

11. M. Kaufman and the Members of the Tectonic Theater Project (2001) *The Laramie Project* (New York: Dramatists Play Service).

12. R. Landy (1982) *Handbook of Educational Drama and Theatre* (Westport, CT and London: Greenwood Press), p. 7

13. C. O'Neill and A. Lambert (1982) *Drama Structures: A Practical Handbook for Teachers* (Cheltenham, Stanley Thornes; Portsmouth, NH: Heinemann Educational Books), p. 141.

14. G. Bolton (2003) *Dorothy Heathcote's Story: Biography of a Remarkable Drama Teacher* (Stoke on Kent, UK; Sterling, VA: Trentham), p. 60.

15. S. Grady (1996) 'Toward the Practice of Theory in Practice' in P. Taylor (ed.) *Researching Drama and Arts Education: Paradigms and Possibilities* (London and New York: Routledge, Falmer), p. 70.

16. S. Brecht (1988) *Peter Schumann's Bread and Puppet Theatre*, vol. 2 (London: Methuen). E. Blumenthal (2005) *Puppetry and Puppets: An Illustrated World Survey* (London: Thames and Hudson). D. Currell (2007) *Puppets and Puppet Theatre* (Marlborough, Wiltshire: Crowood Press). S. Tillis (1992) *Toward an Aesthetics of the Puppet* (Santa Barbara, CA: Greenwood Publishing Group). R. T. E. Hanford and T. Enik (1981) *The Complete Book of Puppets and Puppeteering* (New York: Sterling Publishing Company). Websites: Union Internationale de la Marionnette: http://www.unima.org/; Center for Puppetry Arts: http://www.puppet.org/; Puppet Centre Trust: http://www.puppetcentre.org.uk/; Puppetry in India: http://www.puppetryindia.org/; Handspring Puppet Company (for adults), South Africa, http://www.handspringpuppet.co.za/.

17. Scottish Arts Council (n.d.) 'Starcatchers', http://www.scottisharts.org.uk/1/artsinscotland/drama/projects/starcatchers.aspx, date accessed 10 October 2010.

18. Big Brum TIE Company (2010) 'Company: About Us', http://www.bigbrum.org.uk/archives/cat_company.html, date accessed 16 October 2010.

19. Ibid.

20. F. Chowdhury (2010) 'Dubai youth theatre fest to boost national talent', http://www.khaleejtimes.com/DisplayArticle09.asp?xfile=data/theuae/2010/July/theuae_July337.xmlandsection=theuae, date accessed 10 October 2010.

21. Dubai Culture (2010) 'Eight plays by UAE talent at Dubai Festival for Youth Theatre showcase compelling tales from the Arab world', http://www.dubaiculture.ae/en/media-center/press-releases/festival-play.html, date accessed 15 October 2010.

22. From the Weatherhead School of Management at Case Western Reserve University, http://weatherhead.case.edu/, date accessed 6 September 2010. To see the ad, http://adsoftheworld.com/media/print/case_western_reserve_university_cool?size=_original, date accessed 6 September 2010.

23. Interview conducted with Johnny Saldaña, 16 March 2010.

# 1   Educational Drama in the Elementary School

1. J. Dewey (1934) *Art as Experience* (New York: Penguin Group).
2. V. Spolin (1963) *Improvisation for the Theater: A Handbook of Teaching and Directing Techniques* (Evanston, IL: Northwestern University Press).
3. W. Ward (1930) *Creative Dramatics* (New York: D. Appleton-Century Company). W. Ward (1947) *Playmaking with Children* (New York: D. Appleton-Century Company).
4. The organization is now called the American Alliance for Theatre and Education (AATE) and is based in Bethesda, MD. Their website is: http://www. aate.com/.
5. W. Ward (1930) *Creative Dramatics* (New York: D. Appleton-Century Company), p. 1.
6. H. Finlay-Johnson (1911) *The Dramatic Method of Teaching*, (London: Nisbet Self-Help Sereis, James Nisbet).
7. C. Cook (1917) *The Play Way* (New York: Frederick A. Stokes Company), p. 31.
8. Ibid., p. 31.
9. McCaslin's numerous articles and pioneering texts include (1971/1997) *Theatre for Children in the United States: A History* (Studio City, CA: Player's Press), (1975/2001) *Children and Drama* (Studio City, CA: Player's Press), (1978) *Theatre for Young Audiences* (New York: Longman), and (2006) *Creative Drama in the Classroom and Beyond* (New York: Allyn and Bacon).
10. N. McCaslin (2006) *Creative Drama in the Classroom and Beyond* (New York: Allyn and Bacon), p. 7.
11. See G. B. Siks (1958) *Creative Dramatics, an Art for Children* (New York: Harper); G. B. Siks and H. B. Dunnington (1961) *Children's Theatre and Creative Dramatics* (Seattle, WA: University of Washington Press).
12. R. Landy (1982) *Handbook of Educational Drama and Theatre* (Westport, CT: Greenwood Press), p. 21.
13. W. Ward (1939) *Theater for Children* (New York: D. Appleton-Century Company); W. Ward (1947) *Playmaking With Children* (New York: D. Appleton-Century Company); and W. Ward (1952/1981) *Stories to Dramatize* (Louisville, KY: Anchorage Press).
14. W. Ward (1952/1981) *Stories to Dramatize* (Louisville, KY: Anchorage Press), p. 5.
15. Ibid., p. 6.
16. Ibid., p. 12.
17. Ibid., p. 12.
18. N. McCaslin (2006) *Creative Drama in the Classroom and Beyond* (New York: Allyn and Bacon), p. 7.
19. Interview conducted with Philip Taylor, 22 March 2010.
20. P. Slade (1954) *Child Drama* (London: University of London Press), p. 105.
21. C. Stanislavski (1936) *An Actor Prepares* (New York: Theatre Arts).
22. P. Slade (1954) *Child Drama* (London: University of London Press), p. 127.
23. Ibid., p. 136.
24. G. Bolton (1999) *Acting in Classroom Drama: A Critical Analysis* (Portland, ME: Calendar Island Publishers, LLC), p. 138.
25. Ibid., p. 141.

26. B. Way (1967/1998) *Development through Drama* (Amherst, NY: Humanity Books), p. 6.
27. Ibid.
28. Ibid., p. 7.
29. Ibid.
30. G. Bolton (1999) *Acting in Classroom Drama: A Critical Analysis* (Portland, ME: Calendar Island Publishers, LLC), p. 159.
31. B. Way (1967/1998) *Development through Drama* (Amherst, NY: Humanity Books), p. 268.
32. Ibid., p. 268.
33. Ibid., p. 268.
34. G. Bolton (1999) *Acting in Classroom Drama: A Critical Analysis* (Portland, ME: Calendar Island Publishers, LLC), p. 154.
35. Ibid., p. 164.
36. N. McCaslin (2006) *Creative Drama in the Classroom and Beyond* (New York: Allyn and Bacon), p. 346.
37. Ibid.
38. Ibid., p. 346.
39. Interview conducted with David Booth, 22 February 2010.
40. Ibid.
41. Ibid.
42. D. Booth (2005) *Story Drama* (Markham, Ontario: Pembroke Publishers).
43. Ibid., pp. 55–6.
44. L. Rosenblatt (1938/1968) *Literature as Exploration* (New York: D. Appleton-Century Company).
45. Ibid, p. 227. Citing J. Dewey (1922), *Democracy and Education,* revised (New York: Macmillan).
46. See J. Dewey (1934) *Arts as Experience* (New York: Perigee Books); P. F. Carini (2001) *Starting Strong: A Different Look at Children, Schools, and Standards* (New York: Teachers College Press); E. R. Duckworth (1987) *The Having of Wonderful Ideas and Other Essays on Teaching and Learning* (New York: Teachers College).
47. Interview conducted with David Booth, 22 February 2010.
48. Ibid.
49. Ibid.
50. B. Haseman (1991) 'Improvisation, Process Drama and Dramatic Art', *The Drama Magazine*, July 20.
51. C. O'Neill (2005) *Drama Worlds: A Framework for Process Drama* (Portsmouth, NH: Heinemann), pp. xvii–xviii.
52. P. Taylor (1998) *Redcoats and Patriots: Reflective Practice in Drama and Social Studies* (Portsmouth, NH: Heinemann), p. 14.
53. C. O'Neill (1995) *Drama Worlds: A Framework for Process Drama* (Portsmouth, NH: Heinemann).
54. Ibid., p. 19.
55. S. M. Kao and C. O'Neill (1998) *World into Worlds: Learning a Second Language through Process Drama* (Stamford, CT: Ablex Publishing Corporation), p. 13.
56. B. J. Wagner (1976) *Dorothy Heathcote: Drama as a Learning Medium* (West Haven, CT: National Education Association).

57. J. Kase-Polisini (1988) *Drama as Meaning Maker* (Lanham, MD: University Press of America); D. Hornbrook (1991) *Education in Drama: Casting the Dramatic Curriculum* (London; New York: Falmer).

58. D. Hornbrook (1991) *Education in Drama: Casting the Dramatic Curriculum* (London; New York: Falmer); D. Hornbrook (1998) *Education and Dramatic Art* (London; New York: Routledge); D. Hornbrook (1998) *On the Subject of Drama* (London; New York: Routledge).

59. D. Hornbrook (1998) *Education and Dramatic Art* (London; New York: Routledge), p. 12.

60. Ibid., p. 49.

61. Interview conducted with Philip Taylor, 22 March 2010.

62. P. Taylor and C. D. Warner (eds) (2006) *Structure and Spontaneity: The Process Drama of Cecily O'Neill* (Stoke on Trent; Sterling, VA: Trentham).

63. C. O'Neill (1976) *Drama Guidelines* (London: Heinemann Educational Books in association with London Drama); C. O'Neill (1991) *Drama Structures: A Practical Handbook for Teachers* (Cheltenham, Stanley Thornes; Portsmouth, NH: Heinemann Educational Books); C. O'Neill (1995) *Drama Worlds: A Framework for Process Drama* (Portsmouth, NH: Heinemann); D. Heathcote, L. Johnson, and C. O'Neill (1984) *Dorothy Heathcote: Collected Writings on Education and Drama.* (London: Hutchinson); M. Kao and C. O'Neill (1998) *World into Worlds: Learning a Second Language through Process Drama* (Stamford, CT: Ablex Publishing Corporation).

64. Interview conducted with Cecily O'Neill, Emelie Fitzgibbon, and Nancy Swortzell, 15 June 2010.

65. J. Neelands (2000) 'In the Hands of Living People,' *Drama Research: The Research Journal of National Drama*, 1, 1. Neelands also presented the article as a paper in April 2000, in York, UK, as the keynote address at the National Drama Conference. A copy of that text is available online at http://www.theatroedu.gr/main/images/stories/files/Magazine/EandT_e-mag_June2002_EN_06.pdf, date accessed 07 September 2010. The page numbers cited refer to the text of the speech, p. 3 (p. 49 in journal article).

66. Ibid., p. 2.

67. Ibid., p. 3.

68. D. Heathcote, L. Johnson, and C. O'Neill (1984) *Dorothy Heathcote: Collected Writings on Education and Drama* (London: Hutchinson).

69. J. Neelands (2000) 'In the Hands of Living People,' *Drama Research: The Research Journal of National Drama*, 1, 1. Neelands also presented the article as a paper in April, 2000, in York, UK, as the keynote address at the National Drama Conference. A copy of that text is available online at http://www.theatroedu.gr/main/images/stories/files/Magazine/EandT_e-mag_June2002_EN_06.pdf, date accessed 07 September 2010. The page numbers cited refer to the text of the speech, p. 3 (pp. 49–50 in journal article).

70. J. Neelands and T. Goode (2000) *Structuring Drama Work: A Handbook of Available Forms in Theatre and Drama* (Cambridge; New York: Cambridge University Press).

71. See P. Taylor and C. D. Warner (eds) (2006) *Structure and Spontaneity: The Process Drama of Cecily O'Neill* (Stoke on Trent; Sterling, VA: Trentham). J. Neelands (1984) *Making Sense of Drama: A Guide to Classroom Practice* (Oxford; Portsmouth, NH: Heinemann Educational Books published in association with *2D Magazine*).

C. O'Neill (1995) *Drama Worlds: A Framework for Process Drama* (Portsmouth, NH: Heinemann). M. Kao and C. O'Neill (1998) *World into Worlds: Learning a Second Language through Process Drama* (Stamford, CT: Ablex Publishing Corporation). T. Rogers (ed.) (2006) *Process Drama and Multiple Literacies: Addressing Social, Cultural, and Ethical Issues* (Portsmouth, NH: Heinemann). P. Bowell and B. Heap (2001) *Planning Process Drama* (London: David Fulton). G.M. Bolton (1998) *Acting in Classroom Drama: A Critical Analysis* (Stoke on Trent: Trentham Books in association with the University of Central England).

72. J. Ackroyd (2004) *Role Reconsidered: A Re-evaluation of the Relationship between Teacher-in-role and Acting* (Stoke-on-Trent; Sterling, VA: Trentham), p. 166.

73. N. Toye and F. Prendiville (2000) *Drama and Traditional Story for the Early Years* (New York: Routledge), p. 51.

74. D. Montgomery (2007) 'Living an Arts Partnership: The Experience of Three Middle School Classroom Teachers in a Drama Residency,' Dissertation, New York University.

75. R. Philbrick (2000) *The Last Book in the Universe* (New York: Blue Sky Press).

76. D. Montgomery (2007) 'Living an Arts Partnership: The Experience of Three Middle School Classroom Teachers in a Drama Residency,' Dissertation, New York University, p. 105.

77. Ibid., p. 186.

78. Ibid.

79. C. O'Neill (1995) *Drama Worlds* (Portsmouth, NH: Heinemann), pp. 61–2.

80. Ibid., p. 61.

81. P. Freire (1998) *Pedagogy of Freedom: Ethics, Democracy, and Civic Courage* (New York: Roman and Littlefield Publisher, Inc.), p. 79.

82. G. M. Bolton (2000) 'It's all Theatre,' *Drama Research*, 1, 21–29.

83. Ibid., p. 21.

84. Ibid.

85. Ibid, p. 27.

86. L. Jardin (1995) *Reading Gavin Bolton: A Biography for Education*, a thesis submitted in partial fulfilment of the requirements for the degree of Doctor of Philosophy, University of British Columbia, Vancouver, BC (UBC Retrospective These Digitization Project, http://www.library.ubc.ca/archives/retro_theses, date accessed 24 October 2010).

87. Interview conducted with Gavin Bolton, 12 January 2010.

88. B.R.I.D.G.E Theatre Project, http://www.bridgetheatre.org/, date accessed 25 August 2010.

89. B.R.I.D.G.E Theatre Project, http://www.bridgetheatre.org/whatwedo.htm, date accessed 15 August 2010.

90. B.R.I.D.G.E Theatre Project, http://www.bridgetheatre.org/history.htm, date accessed 20 July 2010.

91. D. Heathcote (1995) *Drama for Learning: Dorothy Heathcote's Mantle of the Expert Approach to Education* (Portsmouth, NH: Heinemann), p. 27.

92. P. Taylor and C. D. Warner (eds) (2006) *Structure and Spontaneity: The Process Drama of Cecily O'Neill* (Stoke on Trent; Sterling, VA: Trentham), p. 121.

93. T. Fisher and L. Smith (2010) 'First Do No Harm: Informed Consent Principles for Trust and Understanding in Applied Theatre Practice,' *Journal of Applied Arts and Health*, 1, 2, DOI: 10.1386/jaah.1.2.157_1.

94. D. Heathcote (1995) *Drama for Learning: Dorothy Heathcote's Mantle of the Expert Approach to Education* (Portsmouth, NH: Heinemann), p. 84.

95. Interview conducted with Cecily O'Neill, Emelie Fitzgibbon, and Nancy Swortzell, 15 June 2010.

96. D. A. Schön (1983) *The Reflective Practitioner: How Professionals Think in Action* (New York: Basic Books), p. 52.

97. K. Robinson (2001) *Out of Our Minds* (West Sussex: Capstone Publishing Ltd).

## 2  Educational Drama and Theatre in the Middle and Secondary Classroom

1. G. N. Anderson (2010) 'Schools Arts Program Range from Four Star to Nonexistent', *Gotham Gazette,* http://www.gothamgazette.com/article/arts/20100205/1/3175, date accessed 1 June 2010 (New York: Citizens Union Foundation Publication).

2. T. Lewin (21 July 2010) 'Many States Adopt National Standards for their Schools,' *The New York Times,* http://www.nytimes.com/2010/07/21/education/,21standards.htm,l, date accessed 7 December 2011.

3. Common Core State Standards Initiative (2011) 'The Standards,' http://www.corestandards.org/the-standards, date accessed 7 December 2011.

4. The Ontario Curriculum (2009) 'Grades 1–8 | The Arts' rev. See also P. Slade (1954) *Child Drama* (London: University of London Press).

5. Estyn (2003) 'The Arts in Schools: Standards and Quality in Key Stages 2 and 3' (Cardiff: Crown) date accessed 18 September 2010, http://www.estyn.gov.uk/publications/artks2and3.pdf, p. 2.

6. The Department of Education (2010) 'Curriculum Assessment and Reporting,' http://www.det.wa.edu.au/curriculumsupport/arts/detcms/navigation/curriculum-assessment--reporting/?oid=MultiPartArticle-id-9192567, date accessed 9 August 2010.

7. Education, Audiovisual and Culture Executive Agency (2009) 'Arts and Cultural Education at Schools in Europe' (Brussels: EACEA P9 Eurydice), p. 15.

8. D. Siaulytiene (2003) 'Lithuania. Arts Education', http://portal.unesco.org/culture/en/files/40526/12669213133Lithuania.pdf/Lithuania.pdf, date accessed 1 September 2010.

9. Education, Audiovisual and Culture Executive Agency (2009) 'Arts and Cultural Education at Schools in Europe' (Brussels: EACEA P9 Eurydice), Section 1.2.

10. Ibid., p. 30.

11. Ibid., section 1.2

12. National Taiwan College of Performing Arts (2004) '2004 Information for International Applicants', http://edu.tcpa.edu.tw/onweb.jsp?webno=333333332:, date accessed 12 September 2010.

13. RTLB.RU (n.d.) 'Oleg Tabakov's Theatre School', http://www.rtlb.ru/page.php?id=785, date accessed 9 September 2010.

14. Fiorello H. LaGuardia High School (2010) 'Mission' and 'History', http://www.laguardiahs.org/about/mission.html, date accessed 18 September 2010.

15. International Drama/Theatre Education Association (n.d.) 'IDEA International Drama/Theatre and Education Association', http://www.idea-org.net/, date accessed 13 August 2011.
16. Griffith University (2010) *'Applied Theatre Researcher/IDEA Journal'*, http://www.griffith.edu.au/humanities-languages/centre-cultural-research/publications/applied-theatre-researcheridea-journal, date accessed 29 July 2011.
17. Taylor and Francis Group (2011) *'Research in Drama Education: The Journal of Applied Theatre and Performance'*, http://www.tandf.co.uk/journals/ride, date accessed 29 July 2011.
18. Ibid.
19. P. Taylor (1996) 'Preface' in P. Taylor (ed.) *Researching Drama and Arts Education* (London; New York: Falmer Press).
20. IDIERI (2008) 'The 6th International Drama in Education Research Institute, 14–18 July 2009 Sydney Australia: Home', http://www.idieri2009.org/, date accessed 29 July 2011.
21. See AATE's website at http://www.aate.com.
22. AATE (n.d.) 'Publications', http://www.aate.com/content.asp?contentid=21, date accessed 29 July 2011.
23. Ibid.
24. Educational Theatre Association (2010) 'About EdTA', http://schooltheatre.org/about, date accessed 18 September 2010.
25. Educational Theatre Association (2010) 'International Thespian Society', http://schooltheatre.org/society, date accessed 18 September 2010.
26. C. Isherwood (July 13, 2008) 'Talk about your Spring Awakening' (New York: *The New York Times*), http://www.nytimes.com/2008/07/13/theatre/13ishe.html?pagewanted=1, date accessed 18 September 2010.
27. Ibid.
28. University Interscholastic League (n.d.) 'Theatre', http://www.uil.utexas.edu/academics/drama/UILResouces.html, date accessed 1 June 2010.
29. Ibid.
30. University Interscholastic League (2010) 'An Approved List of Short Plays for Contest', http://www.uiltexas.org/theatre/approved-plays, date accessed 18 September 2010.
31. W. L. Shumante (n.d.) 'A Short History of The English-Speaking Union of the United States, 1920–1996', http://www.esuus.org/esu_history.htm, date accessed 18 September 2010.
32. The English-Speaking Union of the United States (n.d.) 'ESU National Shakespeare Project', http://www.esuus.org/programs_shakespeare_competition.htm, date accessed 18 September 2010.
33. NYU (2011) 'Looking for Shakespeare', http://steinhardt.nyu.edu/music/edtheatre/programs/summer/shakespeare, date accessed 13 August 2011.
34. A. Boal (2002) *Games for Actors and Non-Actors* (A. Jackson, trans.) (London; New York: Routledge).
35. D. E. Moffit (n.d.) 'Viola Spolin,' http://www.improvcomedy.org/hall/spolin1.html, date accessed 18 September 2010.
36. V. Spolin (1963, 1983) *Improvisation for the Theater: A Handbook of Teaching and Directing Techniques* (Evanston, IL: Northwestern University Press).
37. Ibid., p. 4.

38. J. Hoetker (1975) *Theater Games: One Way into Drama* (Urbana, IL: National Council of Teachers of English), p. 5.
39. K. Johnstone (1981,1992) *Impro: Improvisation and the Theatre* (New York: Routledge/Theatre Arts Book).
40. Ibid., p. II.
41. C. Poulter (1987) *Playing the Game* (Oxford: Macmillan Education).
42. Interview conducted with Chrissie Poulter, 15 July 2009.
43. P. Freire (2000) *Pedagogy of Freedom* (Lanham, MD: Rowman and Littlefield Publishers).
44. S. Aronowitz (1998) 'Introduction' in P. Freire's *Pedagogy of the Oppressed: Ethics, Democracy, and Civic Courage* (New York: Rowman and Littlefiield Publisher, Inc.), p. 8.
45. D. Israel (2009) 'Staying in School: Arts Education and New York City High School Graduation Rates', New York Center for Arts Education, http://www.cae-nyc.org/staying-in-school/arts-and-graduation-report, date accessed 19 September 2010.
46. F. Ostrower (2005) 'The Reality underneath the Buzz of Partnerships: The Potentials and Pitfall of Partnering' published in *Stanford Innovation Review* (CA: Leland Stanford Jr. University), p. 36.
47. Ibid.
48. Cultural Ministers Council and the Ministerial Council for Education, Employment, Training and Youth Affairs (2005) 'National education and the Arts Statement', http://www.mceecdya.edu.au/verve/_resources/National_Education_Arts_Statement.pdf, date accessed 19 September 2010, p. 7.
49. D. Montgomery (2007) 'Living an Arts Partnership: The Experience of Three Middle School Classroom Teachers in a Drama Residency', Dissertation, New York University.
50. R. Philbrick (2000) *The Last Book in the Universe* (New York: Scholastic).
51. D. Montgomery (2007) 'Living an Arts Partnership: The Experience of Three Middle School Classroom Teachers in a Drama Residency,' Dissertation, New York University, p. 134.
52. Ibid., pp. 136–7.
53. Ibid., p. 223.
54. H. Finley-Johnson (1984) 'Heathcote', in L. Johnson and C. O'Neill's *Dorothy Heathcote: Collected Writings on Education and Drama* (London: Hutchinson), p. 7.
55. G. Bolton (1999) *Acting in Classroom Drama: A Critical Analysis* (London: Heinemann Drama), p. 21.
56. See R. Courtney (1968) *Play, Drama and Thought* (London: Cassell and Collier Macmillian Publishers Ltd) and R. Courtney (1980) *The Dramatic Curriculum* (New York: Drama Book Specialists).
57. R. Courtney (1980) *The Dramatic Curriculum* (New York: Drama Book Specialists), pp. 96–8.
58. E. Forbes (1943) *Johnny Tremain* (New York: Houghton Mifflin).
59. National Council on Social Studies (n.d.) 'About National Council on Social Studies', http://www.socialstudies.org/about, date accessed 5 July 2010.
60. H. Zinn (2005) *Class Dismissed* (documentary), L. Alper (Director and Producer).
61. S. Tanenhaus (March 19, 2010) 'In Texas Curriculum Fight, Identity Politics Lean Right' (*The New York Times*), http://www.nytimes.com/2010/03/21/weekinreview/21tanenhaus.html, date accessed 19 September 2010.

62. (Out)Laws andJustice (n.d.) '(Out)laws and Justice', http://www.outlawsand justice.org/, date accessed 19 September 2010.

63. Interview conducted with Lisa Citron, 2 June 2010.

64. Ibid.

65. Ibid.

66. Ibid.

67. Ibid.

68. A. Boal (1998) *Legislative Theatre: Using Performance to Make Politics* (London: Routledge).

69. R. Payne (2005) *A Framework for Understanding Poverty*, 4th rev. ed. (Highlands, TX: aha! Process, Inc.).

70. Much of Cook's theoretical source material is in R. Landy (2008) *The Couch and the Stage* (Lanham, MD: Jason Aronson).

71. Interview with Judge Helen Ginger Berrigan, conducted 8 November 2010.

72. Ibid. H. Lee (1993) *To Kill a Mockingbird*, 50th anniversary edn (New York: Harper Collins).

73. G. M. Bolton (2003) *Dorothy Heathcote's Story: Biography of a Remarkable Drama Teacher* (Stoke-on-Trent; Sterling, VA: Trentham Books), p. 117.

74. D. Heathcote and G. Bolton (1995) *Drama for Learning: Dorothy Heathcote's Mantle of the Expert Approach to Education* (Portsmouth, NH: Heinemann), p. 16.

75. P. Freire (1988) *Pedagogy of the Oppressed* (trans. M. B. Ramos) (New York: Continuum), p. 81.

76. See National Drama (2011) 'Dorothy Heathcote Honoured', http://www. nationaldrama.org.uk/nd/index.cfm/nd-news/dorothy-heathcote-honoured/, date accessed 20 July 2011.

77. See H. Chang (2008) 'The Policy and Development of Contemporary Drama/ Theatre in Taiwan', in *The International Conference of Drama in Education and Applied Theatre* (Taipei: National Taiwan University of the Arts); H. Chang (2003) *Creative Drama, Theory and Practice for Teachers and Leaders*, revised ed. (Taipei: Healthy Growth foundation); H. Chang (2011) Simplified Chinese Character Edition (Shanghai: Shanghai Bookstore Publishing House).

78. G. M. Bolton (1984) *Drama as Education: An Argument for Placing Drama at the Centre of the Curriculum* (Harlow, Essex: Longman). C. Tarlington and P. Verriour (1991) *Role Drama* (Portsmouth, NH: Heinemann Educational Books). C. O'Neill (1995) *Drama Worlds: A Framework for Process Drama* (Portsmouth, NH: Heinemann). J. Somers (2002) 'Drama Making as a Research Process', *Contemporary Theatre Review*, 12, 4, 97–111; J. Somers (1996) *Drama and Theatre in Education: Contemporary Research* (North York, Ont: Captus Press); J. Somers (1994) *Drama in the Curriculum (Education Matters)* (London: Cassell). D. Heathcote (1995) *Drama for Learning: Dorothy Heathcote's Mantle of the Expert Approach to Education* (Portsmouth, NH: Heinemann). D. Booth (2005) *Story Drama: Creating Stories through Role-playing, Improvising, and Reading Aloud*, 2nd edn. (Ontario: Pembroke Publishers Limited).

79. See R. Landy (2008) *The Couch and the Stage* (Lanham, MD: Rowman and Littlefield).

80. See Y. Chan (2008) 'The Role of Drama in Education in a Drama Project Teaching Model', *Journal of Department of Applied Foreign Languages, Forune Institute of Technology*, l, 2, 37–44.

81. S. Ma (2010), personal communication.
82. Y. Hong (1992) 'Catharsis in ritual and theatre', Doctoral dissertation, New York University.
83. Y. Oh (2010), personal communication.
83. Interview conducted with Akeyo Onoe, 26 February 2010.
84. Interview conducted with Watanabe Jun, 26 February 2010.
85. J. Watanabe and J. Neelands (2009) *Using Drama as a Medium of Instruction* (Tokyo: Bansei Shobo Publications).
86. X. Lu (2004) *Rhetoric of the Chinese Cultural Revolution* (Columbia, SC: University of South California Press), pp. 143–50.
87. Interview conducted with William Sun, 8 March 2010.
88. Interview conducted with Dorothy Heathcote, 19 January 2010.

## 3   Theatre for, by and with Young Audiences

1. R. Steinweg (1976) *Brechts Modell der Lehrstucke. Zeuignissse, Discussionen, Erfahrungen* (Frankfurt am Main: Suhrkamp Verlag).
2. T. Mack (2009) 'What is Theatre for the Very Young?', http://www.ipayweb. org/news/?id=23, date accessed 17 October 2010.
3. Ibid.
4. Goethe Institut (2010) 'Theatre for the Very Young', http://www.goethe.de/kue/ the/ibf/en2740978.htm. date accessed 17 October 2010.
5. ASSITEJ (2009) 'The First eNewsletter', http://www.assitej-international.org/ adorletter/newsletter.aspx?i=2099AE5, date accessed 17 October 2010.
6. Bitef (2008) 'Story', http://www.bitef.rs/en/festival/festival.php, date accessed 18 October 2010.
7. Author unidentified (20 September 2010) 'Serious Play Date: These Critics May Create a Fuss Over a Show', *The Wall Street Journal*, http://online.wsj.com/article/ SB10001424052748704652104575493810115906420.html?KEYWORDS= baby+theater, date accessed 20 November 2010.
8. R. Weinert-Kendt (2010) 'Baby Theatre Comes to Age', *American Theatre*, http://www.faqs.org/periodicals/201009/2143890851.html#ixzz12lk3NizP, date accessed 18 October 2010.
9. R. Bedard (2009) 'The Cultural Construction of Theatre for Children and Young Audiences: A Captive Eddy of Recursive Harmonies', *Youth Theatre Journal*, 23, 1, 27; DOI: 10.1080/08929090902851551.
10. M. Goldberg (1974) *Children's Theatre: A Philosophy and a Method* (Englewood Cliffs, NJ: Prentice-Hall), p. 101.
11. A.L. Manna (1984) 'Instruction and Delight in Moses Goldberg's Plays for the Maturing Child', *Children's Literature Association Quarterly*, 9, 3.
12. C. Jennings (1974) 'The Dramatic Contributions of Aurand Harris to Children's Theatre in the United States', Doctoral dissertation, New York University, p. 290.
13. A. Harris (1991) *Short Plays of Theatre Classics* (Louisville, KY: Anchorage Press Plays).
14. N. McCaslin (1984) 'Aurand Harris: Children's Playwright', *Children's Literature Association Quarterly*, 9, 3, p. 116.

15. A. Harris (1980) *The Arkansaw Bear* (Louisville, KY: Anchorage Press Plays).
16. A. Harris (1966) *Rags to Riches* (Louisville, KY: Anchorage Press Plays).
17. R. Landy (1977) 'Measuring Audience Response to Characters and Scenes in Theatre for Children: A Developmental Approach', *Children's Theatre Review*, XXVI, 3, 10–13.
18. R. Landy (1983) *The Padrone* (Rowayton, CT: New Plays).
19. S. Zeder (1978) *Wiley and the Hairy Man* (Louisville, KY: Anchorage Press Plays).
20. S. Zeder (1985) *Doors* (Louisville, KY: Anchorage Press Plays). S. Zeder (1976) *Step on a Crack* (Louisville, KY: Anchorage Press Plays).
21. S. Zeder (1986) *Mother Hicks* (Louisville, KY: Anchorage Press Plays).
22. S. Zeder (1999) *The Taste of Sunrise* (Louisville, KY: Anchorage Press Plays).
23. S. Zeder (2011) *The Edge of Peace*, unpublished. Commissioned and developed by Seattle Children's Theatre. Performances at Northwestern University, July 28–30, 2011. See AATE (2011) 'The Edge of Peace', http://www.aateconference.com/index.php?option=com_contentandview=articleandid=116:the-edge-of-peaceandcatid=7:eventsandItemid=42, date accessed 29 July 2011. S. Zeder (2008) 'Letter requesting time off to write a third play', http://docs.google.com/viewer?a=vandq=cache:KZwPSPs_hsoJ:www.utexas.edu/ogs/faculty/fdp/pdf/zeder.pdf+suzan+zeder,+The+Edge+of+of+Peace andhl=enandgl=usandpid=blandsrcid=ADGEESiUVJMANET76UBbELdm9sZ C2vPKpm5LkjGPl5av3IfK_rTgw9CxGhxQ4ltBboaRrmSyCkngHFLUMLqHj6 G2CE6bahgIGyuLmxgJmF4Gfk4C1UAt_KpmWW4svih1AupyLBqudJ6Zandsig= AHIEtbQka_3R9er81Cz3iP0z_bF4sEq0FA, date accessed 25 October 2010.
24. J. Dickey (1994) 'The Yellow Boat (Theatre Review)', *Theatre Journal*, 46, 3, 412–413, http://www.accessmylibrary.com/article-1G1-15851679/yellow-boat-temple-music.html, date accessed 12 November 2010.
25. Arizona State University (2007) 'World's Largest Child Drama Collection Turns 30', http://asunews.asu.edu/20071217_childdrama, date accessed 12 November 2010.
26. M. van de Water (2009) 'TYA as Cultural Production: Aesthetics, Meaning, and Material Conditions', *Youth Theatre Journal*, 23, 1, 17; DOI: 10.1080/089290909 02851395.
27. Ibid., p. 21.
28. CTFA (2008) 'Children's Theater Foundation of America', http://www.childrenstheatrefoundation.org/, date accessed 21 September 2010.
29. AATE (2009) 'AATE history', http://www.aate.com/content.asp?pl=2andsl=151 andcontentid=151, date accessed 4 August 2010.
30. Ibid.
31. ASSITEJ (n.d.) 'ASSITEJ International', http://www.assitej-international.org/english/home.aspx, date accessed 21 September 2010.
32. N. Eek, A.M. Shaw, and K. Krzys (2008) *Discovering a New Audience for Theatre: The History of ASSITEJ Volume I* (Santa Fe, NM: Sunstone Press).
33. Ibid., pp. 62–3.
34. ITYARN (n.d.) 'ITYARN Mission and Board', http://www.ityarn.org/organization.htm, date accessed 7 September 2010. IPAY (2009) 'About Us', http://www.ipayweb.org/about/, date accessed 7 September 2010.
35. Interview conducted with Cecily O'Neill, Emelie Fitzgibbon, and Nancy Swortzell, 15 June 2009.

36. Kennedy Center Education (n.d.) 'New Visions New Voices', http://www.kennedy-center.org/education/nvnv.html, date accessed 21 September 2010.

37. Indiana Repertory Theatre (n.d) 'History of the Bonderman Workshop and Symposium', http://www.irtlive.com/artists_information/playwrights/bonderman_history/, date accessed 29 September 2010.

38. Ibid.

39. Ibid.

40. Interview conducted with Edie Demas, 4 September 2009.

41. Ibid.

42. Interview conducted with Carol Korty, 28 November 2009.

43. Ibid.

44. L. Swortzell (1986) *Six Plays for Young People from the Federal Theatre Project (1936–1939): An Introductory Analysis and Six Representative Plays* (New York: Greenwood Press), p. 5.

45. Ibid., p. 5.

46. Ibid., p. 7.

47. Ibid., p. 10.

48. Chorpenning is widely recognized as one of the leading TYA playwrights in US history. In recognition of her influence on TYA, the American Alliance for Theatre and Education (AATE) gives the Charlotte Chorpenning Cup annually to an outstanding Children's Theatre writer. C. B. Chorpenning (1972) *The Emperor's New Clothes*, adapted from the book by H.C. Andersen (New York: Baker's Plays).

49. L. Swortzell (1986) *Six Plays for Young People from the Federal Theatre Project (1936–1939): An Introductory Analysis and Six Representative Plays* (New York: Greenwood Press), p. 12.

50. Ibid., p. 22.

51. Ibid, p. 13-14.

52. O. Saul and L. Lantz (1936) *Revolt of the Beavers* (New York: Dramatists Play Service).

53. Ibid., p. 14. E. W. Trumbull (1998) 'Revolt of the Beavers Poster', http://novaonline.nvcc.edu/eli/spd130et/beavers.htm, date accessed 09 August 2010.

54. D. Chappell (2007) 'Constructions of Revolt of the Beavers and Notions of the Child Audience: Controversy In the Federal Theatre Project', *Youth Theatre Journal*, 21, 41.

55. Ibid.

56. Ibid.

57. M. van de Water (2006) *Moscow Theatre for Young People: A Cultural History of Ideological Coercion and Artistic Innovation, 1917–2000* (New York: Palgrave Macmillan), p. 3.

58. Ibid., p. 1.

59. Ibid., p. 6.

60. Iurii Shchekochikhin, *Pitfall*, premiered 26 December 1985 at the Central Children's Theatre. Information found in M. van de Water (2006) *Moscow Theatre for Young People: a Cultural History of Ideological Coercion and Artistic Innovation, 1917–2000* (New York: Palgrave Macmillan), pp. 114–15.

61. M. van de Water (2006) *Moscow Theatre for Young People: A Cultural History of Ideological Coercion and Artistic Innovation, 1917–2000.* (New York: Palgrave Macmillan), p. 117.

62. Ibid., p. 179.
63. J. Racine. *Bérénice* premiered at the Russian Academic Youth Theatre in 1993. Information found in M. van de Water (2006) *Moscow Theatre for Young People: a Cultural History of Ideological Coercion and Artistic Innovation, 1917–2000* (New York: Palgrave Macmillan), p. 191. F. Hodgson Burnett, *Little Lord Fauntleroy* premiered at the Russian Academy Youth Theatre in 1996. Information found in M. van de Water (2006) *Moscow Theatre for Young People: a Cultural History of Ideological Coercion and Artistic Innovation, 1917–2000* (New York: Palgrave Macmillan), p. 193.
64. M. van de Water (2006) *Moscow Theatre for Young People: A Cultural History of Ideological Coercion and Artistic Innovation, 1917–2000*. (New York: Palgrave Macmillan), p. 205.
65. S. Schonmann (2006) *Theatre as a Medium for Children and Young People* (New York: Springer), p. 3. For examples of a variety of praxis within the scholarly field, see S. Schonmann (ed.) (2010) *Key Concepts in Theatre/Drama Education* (Rotterdam: Sense Publishers).
66. J. Kleine (2005) 'From Children's Perspectives: A Model of Aesthetic Processing in Theatre', *Journal of Aesthetic Education*, 39, 4, 52.
67. Ibid., p. 54.
68. Ibid.
69. Oily Cart (n.d.) 'About Us', http://www.oilycart.org.uk/about_us/, date accessed 23 September 2010.
70. SEN Magazine (2009) 'The Power of Performance', 42, p. 37, http://www.oilycart.org.uk/complex_disabilities/current/downloads/SEN42Oily_Cart.pdf, date accessed 23 September 2010.
71. Ibid., pp. 37–8.
72. Ibid., p. 6.
73. Dramatic Publishing (2010) 'José Cruz González', http://www.dramaticpublishing.com/AuthorBio.php?titlelink=10081, date accessed 23 September 2010.
74. El Teatro Campesino (2010) 'El Teatro Campesino', http://www.elteatrocampesino.com/, date accessed 23 September 2010.
75. Interview conducted with José Cruz González, 28 March 2010.
76. Chicano refers to Americans of Mexican descent. C. A. Aragón (2008) 'Niños y el Teatro: Critical Perspectives of Children in Mexican-American Theatre' in *Youth Theatre Journal*, 22, 10–13.
77. Ibid., p. 13.
78. Ibid., p. 13.
79. Ibid., p. 15.
80. L. Garcia (2008) 'The Serious Game of Love in Nilo Cruz's *Night Train to Bolina*' in *Youth Theatre Journal*, 22, 68.
81. Ibid., p. 68.
82. N. Cruz (1979) *Night Train to Bolina* (New York: Dramatists Play Service).
83. Ibid., p. 80.
84. Unicorn Theatre (2010) 'About Us', http://www.unicorntheatre.com/about_us, date accessed 2 August 2010.
85. Interview conducted with Tony Graham, 12 February 2010.
86. Ibid.
87. Ibid. Also, P. Brooks (1968, 1996) *The Empty Space* (New York: Touchstone), p. 9.

88. Ibid.

89. J. R. Kincaid (2003) 'What's a Young Audience? An Argument', *Youth Theatre Journal*, 17, 53–8.

90. R. Landy (1982) *The Handbook of Educational Drama and Theatre* (Westport, CT: Greenwood Press).

91. Z. Moore (2003) 'Faculty Spotlight ~ Laurie Brooks, NYU Program in Educational Theatre's *EdTh News* (David Montgomery and Zachary Moore, eds.), 1, p. 5.

92. N. McCaslin (2006) *Creative Drama in the Classroom and Beyond*, 8th edn (New York: Pearson Education), p. 12.

93. C. Vine (1993) 'TIE and Theatre of the Oppressed' in T. Jackson (ed.) *Learning through Theatre*, 2nd edn (New York: Routledge), pp. 109–27.

94. J. O'Toole (1976) *Theatre in Education: New Objectives for Theatre, New Techniques in Education* (London: Hodder and Stoughton), p. vii.

95. Ibid.

96. R. Wooster (2007) *Contemporary Theatre in Education* (Bristol and Chicago, IL: Intellect), p. 83.

97. Ibid.

98. C. Vine (1993) 'TIE and the Theatre of the Oppressed' in T. Jackson (ed.) *Learning through Theatre*, 2nd edn (New York: Routledge), pp. 109–30.

99. J. O'Toole and P. Bundy (1993) 'Kites and Magpies: TIE in Australia' in T. Jackson (ed.) *Learning through Theatre*, 2nd edn (New York: Routledge), pp. 133–49.

100. M. Prendergast and J. Saxton (ed.) (2009) *Applied Theatre* (Chicago, IL: Intellect), pp. 31–49. From pages 34–47, they reprint articles from journals by other authors discussing their TIE work. From pages 47–9, they include other reading and suggested activities.

101. R. Wooster (2007) *Contemporary Theatre in Education* (Bristol and Chicago, IL: Intellect), p. 83.

102. Interview conducted with Cecily O'Neill, Emelie Fitzgibbon, and Nancy Swortzell, 15 June 2009.

103. G. Maritz (2004) 'Educational Theatre at the Edge of the Crush: The Use of Theatre as Entertainment-Education in HIV and AIDS Awareness and Prevention in the South African Mining Sector – Opportunities for Change' (Centre for the Study of AIDS, University of Pretoria and Department of Drama, University of Pretoria).

104. L. Swortzell (1993) 'Trying to like TIE: An American critic hopes TIE can be saved' in T. Jackson (ed.) *Learning Through Theatre: New Perspectives on Theatre in Education* (New York: Routledge), p. 241.

105. Ibid., pp. 241, 242–3. L. Swortzell (1997) *Theatre for Young Audiences: Around the World in 21 Plays* (New York: Applause).

106. Metro Theater Company (2010) 'Education', http://metrotheatercompany.org/section/education/, date accessed 10 July 2010. Seattle Children's Theatre (2010) 'Education Outreach', http://www.sct.org/classes/educationoutreach/, date accessed 10 July 2010. Polka Theatre (2010) 'Workshops', http://www.polkatheatre.com/generic.php?p=4andep=49, date accessed 10 July 2010.

107. Western Carolina University (2011) 'Theatre in Education (TIE)', http://wcu.edu/4852.asp, date accessed 9 December 2011.

108. arepp: Theatre for Life (n.d.) 'arepp: Theatre for Life', http://www.arepp.org. za/, date accessed 29 July 2011.

109. Creative Arts Team (2010) 'About CAT', http://www.cuny.edu/academics/k-to-12/cat/about.html, date accessed 10 July 2010.

110. R. Wooster (2007) *Contemporary Theatre in Education* (Bristol and Chicago, IL: Intellect), p. 72.

111. Ibid., p. 65.

112. Living Voices (n.d.) 'Bringing Life to History', http://www.livingvoices.org/main/main.html, date accessed 7 July 2010.

113. Interview conducted with Natalie Burgess, 6 July 2010.

114. Pennsylvania Youth Theatre (n.d.) 'About Us', http://www.123pyt.org/about/, date accessed 22 October 2010.

115. b. hooks (2003) *Teaching Community: A Pedagogy of Hope* (New York, Routledge), p. 29.

116. C. Marín (2007) 'A Methodology Rooted in Praxis: Theatre of the Oppressed (TO) Techniques Employed as Arts-Based Educational Research Methods', *Youth Theatre Journal*, 21, 82.

117. Ibid., p. 82

118. Ibid., pp. 90–1.

119. Ibid., p. 91

120. viBe (2010) 'Say It How It Is: About viBe', http://www.vibetheater.org/about. php, accessed 13 August 2011.

121. D. Edell (2010) 'Say It How It Is: Urban Teenage Girls Challenge And Perpetuate Cultural Narratives Through Writing and Performing Theatre', Dissertation, New York University, p. 287.

122. Ibid., p. 31.

123. The Unusual Suspects Theatre Company (2009) 'The Unusual Suspects Theatre Company', http://www.theunusualsuspects.org/html/mission.php, date accessed 23 July 2010.

124. Interview conducted with Dorothy Heathcote, 19 January 2010.

125. Ibid.

126. Interview conducted with Sally Fairman, 2010.

127. All quotes in this section, unless otherwise noted, come from David Montgomery's interview with the TAs at Camp David Gonzalez. For more information: http://probation.co.la.ca.us/scripts/RTSB.html, date accessed 21 July 2010.

128. P. Freire (1974, 2007) *Education for Critical Consciousness* (New York: The Continuum International Publishing Group, Inc.).

129. R. Esquivel (2011) *Nasty* (Woodstock, IL: Dramatic Publishing).

130. T. Kushner and M. Sendak (2003) *Brundibar* (New York: Michael di Capua Books/Hyperion Books for Children).

131. D. Samuels (2010) *Kindertransport*, 2nd edn (London: Nick Hern Books).

132. C. Schumacher (1998) 'Introduction' in C. Schumacher's *Staging the Holocaust* (Cambridge: Cambridge University Press), p. 3.

133. Ibid., p. 8.

134. D. Samuels (1995, 2000) *Kindertransport* (London: Nick Hearns books).

135. J. Still (1999) *And Then They Came For Me: Remembering the World of Anne Frank* (Woodstock, Ill: Dramatic Publishing).

136. D. N. Dunkle (2007) 'Amish Country, "Christian Broadway" is Big Business', *Adventist Review*, Religion News Service, http://www.adventistreview.org/article.php?id=921, date accessed 8 July 2010.

137. R. Landy (book and lyrics) and K. Thompson (music and additional lyrics) (2002, 2004, 2007, 2010) *God Lives in Glass* (musical), unpublished. R. Landy (2001) *God Lives in Glass* (Woodstock, VT: Sky Light Paths).

138. R. Landy (2001) *How We See God and Why It Matters* (Springfield, IL: Charles C. Thomas). R. Landy (2001) *God Lives in Glass* (Woodstock, VT: Sky Light Paths).

139. From Broadway Bound Kids (n.d.) 'About Us', http://www.broadwaybound.org/about-us, date accessed 13 November 2010.

140. From R. Landy (book and lyrics) and K. Thompson (music and additional lyrics) (2002, 2004, 2007, 2010) *God Lives in Glass* (musical), unpublished.

141. Ibid.

142. Ibid.

143. Interview conducted with Johnny Saldaña, 16 March 2010.

# Part II   Drama and Theatre in Social Action

1. D. Rebellato (2009) *Theatre and Globalization* (Basingstoke: Palgrave Macmillan).

2. S. Ganguly (2010) *Jana Sanskriti: Forum Theatre and Democracy in India* (New York: Routledge).

3. J. Cohen-Cruz (2005) *Local Acts: Community-based Performance in the United States* (New Brunswick, NJ: Rutgers University Press).

4. E. Cavalli (December 23, 2008) 'World of Warcraft Hits 11.5 Million Users', *Wired*, www.wired.com/gamelife/2008/12/world-of-warc-1/, date accessed 11 November 2009.

5. See T. Bridal (2004) *Exploring Museum Theatre* (Walnut Creek, CA: Altamira Press); J. F. Hayes and D. N. Schindel (1994) *Pioneer Journeys: Drama in Museum Education* (Charlottesville, VA: New Plays Books); C. Hughes (1998) *Museum Theatre: Communicating with Visitors through Drama* (Portsmouth, NH: Heinemann); A. Jackson and J. Kidd (2011) *Performing Heritage: Research, Practice and Innovation in Museum Theatre and Live Interpretation* (Manchester: Manchester University Press). See also: United States Holocaust Memorial Museum (2001) *Teaching About the Holocaust: A Resource Book for Educators* (Washington, DC: United States Holocaust Memorial Museum), http://www.ushmm.org/education/foreducators/nesse/pdf/teaching_holcaust.pdf, date accessed 23 September 2010. Also see: the International Museum Theatre Alliance at http://www.imtal.org/home.asp.

6. A. Artaud (1958) *Theatre and its Double* (New York: Grove Press).

7. Today a plaque hangs in the Bebelplaz with an ironic quotation from the poet Heinrich Heine dated 1820: 'where books are burned, in the end people will burn'. Indeed in the 1930s and 1940s the Nazis burned the bodies of millions of people in their crematoria.

# 4 Applied Theatre

1. A link to the video: http://www.youtube.com/watch?v=SAQE7kDwPZY, date accessed on 7 August 2010.
2. See A. Jackson (2007) *Theatre, Education and the Making of Meanings.* (Manchester: Manchester University Press); J. O'Toole, M. Stinson, and T. Moore (2009) *Drama and Curriculum: A Giant at the Door* (New York: Springer).
3. See: R. Schechner (1985) *Between Theater and Anthropology* (Philadelphia, PA: University of Pennsylvania Press); B. Brecht (1964) 'Alienation Effects in Chinese Acting' in J. Willett (trans. and ed.), *Brecht on Theater* (New York: Hill and Wang), p. 99.
4. C. M. Turnball (1972) *The Mountain People* (New York: Simon and Schuster). C. Higgins and D. Cannan (1975) *The Ik.* Directed by Peter Brook, the play premiered in Paris in 1975 and was produced in London in 1976 (http://www.bookrags.com/biography/colin-higgins-dlb/). It also toured the US in 1976.
5. V. Turner (1982) *From Ritual to Theatre: The Human Seriousness of Play* (New York: PAJ Publications).
6. See M. Mead (1953) *Coming of Age in Samoa: A Psychological Study of Primitive Youth for Western Civilization* (New York: Modern Library); C. H. Cooley (1983) *Social Organization: A Study of the Larger Mind* (Piscataway, NJ: Transaction Publishers); E. Goffman (1959) *The Presentation of Self in Everyday Life* (New York: Doubleday).
7. E. Goffman (1959) *The Presentation of Self in Everyday Life* (New York: Doubleday).
8. Intelligence and feeling: see A. Demasio (1995) *Descartes' Error: Emotion, Reason, and the Human Brain* (New York: Harper Perennial); D. Goleman (1997) *Emotional Intelligence* (New York: Bantam). The self: see K. Gergen (2000) *The Saturated Self* (New York: Basic Books). Sexuality: see M. Foucault (1978) *The History of Sexuality Volume 1: An Introduction* (Robert Hurley, trans.) (New York: Pantheon). Family: see D. Elkind (1992) *The Post-modern Family, A New Imbalance* (New York: Knopf ). Language: see J. Derrida (1976) *Of Grammatology* (Baltimore, MD: Johns Hopkins University Press). Colonialism: see F. Fanon (1967) *Studies in a Dying Colonialism* (New York: Grove Press). See J. G. Reinelt and J. R. (eds) (2007) *Critical Theory and Performance,* revised and enlarged edn (Ann Arbor, MI: University of Michigan Press).
9. M. Prendergast and J. Saxton (eds) (2009) *Applied Theatre: International Case Studies and Challenges for Practice* (Chicago, IL: Intellect/University of Chicago Press).
10. See Glossary.
11. H. Nicholson (2005) *Applied Drama: The Gift of Theatre* (New York: Palgrave Macmillan).
12. Ibid., p. 4.
13. Ibid., p. 3.
14. Ibid., p. 3.
15. The Centre for Applied Theatre Research (n.d.) 'About us', http://www.arts.manchester.ac.uk/catr/about/index.htm, date accessed 7 August 2010.
16. P. Taylor (2003) *Applied Theatre: Creating Transformative Encounters in the Community* (Portsmouth, NH: Heinemann), p. xx.

17. Ibid, pp. xxii–xxvi.
18. T. Prentki and S. Preston (2009) 'Applied Theatre: An Introduction' in T. Prentki and S. Preston (eds) *The Applied Theatre Reader* (London, New York: Routledge).
19. P. Liukkonen (2008) 'Bertolt Brecht', http://www.kirjasto.sci.fi/brecht.htm, date accessed 7 August 2010. *The Measures Taken* (*Die Massnahme*, 1930): 'In the play a young Communist is murdered by the Party, his sympathy for the poor and their suffering only postpones the day of the historical showdown between the working class and capitalist class. The lesson is that the freedom of the individual must be suppressed today so that in the future mankind will be able to achieve freedom.' *The Exception and the Rule* (*Die Ausnahme und die Regel*, 1930; translated by E. Bentley, in *New Directions in Prose and Poetry*, 1955).
20. P. Freire (1974, 2007) *Education for Critical Consciousness* (New York: The Continuum International Publishing Group, Inc.).
21. A. Boal (1998) *Legislative Theatre: Using Performance to Make Politics.* (London: Routledge).
22. See Folger Shakespeare Library (n.d.) 'What's the Mystery?: Medieval Miracle Plays', http://www.folger.edu/template.cfm?cid=2514, date accessed 7 August 2010.
23. A website about the *Oberammergau Passion Play*, http://www.oberammergau-passion.com/en-us/home/home.html, date accessed 7 August 2010.
24. J. Malik'pūr (2004) *The Islamic Drama* (London: Frank Cass). *Ta'ziyeh* is the Islamic drama of Iran that commemorates the martyrdom of Imam Hussein. For more information on Imam Hussain's story, see S. H. Akhtar (2009) 'The Martyrdom of Imam Hussain', http://www.irfi.org/articles/articles_51_100/martyrdom_of_imam_hussain.htm, date accessed 7 August 2010. See also, M. C. Riggio (2002) 'Moses and the Wandering Dervish', http://asiasociety.org/arts-culture/performing-arts/theater/moses-and-wandering-dervish, date accessed 7 August 2010.
25. See J. Shapiro (2000) *Oberammergau: The Troubling Story of the World's Most Famous Passion Play* (New York: Pantheon).
26. Ibid.
27. K. Grieshaber (July 6, 2010) 'Passion Play called more balanced', http://www.signonsandiego.com/news/2010/jul/02/ap-interview-passion-play-called-more-balanced/, date accessed 7 August 2010.
28. See 'Ramman: religious festival and ritual theatre of the Garhwal Himalayas, India', http://www.youtube.com/watch?v=TNvPNwOvWOg, date accessed 7 August 2010.
29. See: G. Ratliff (2008) *Hell House* (film), http://hellhousemovie.com/, date accessed on 7 August 2010; B. A. Robinson (2009) 'Halloween Hell Houses', http://www.religioustolerance.org/hallo_he.htm, date accessed 7 August 2010. See also A. S. Lewis (May 3, 2002) 'Better Git Hit in Your Soul: George Ratliff's "Hell House" Examines the Scary Business of Belief', *The Austin Chronicle*, http://www.austinchronicle.com/gyrobase/Issue/story?oid=oid%3A85796, date accessed 7 August 2010.
30. Destiny Christian Center (2010) 'The Hell House Outreach Kit', http://www.godestiny.org/hell_house/HH_kit.cfm, date accessed 7 August 2010.
31. G. Ratliff (2008) *Hell House* (film), Plexigroup, Inc., http://hellhousemovie.com/, date accessed 7 August 2010.

32. T. Smalec (2009) '"Celebrate Like True Believers": Performing Evangelical Christianity in Les Freres Corbusier's *Hell House*', http://hemi.nyu.edu/hemi/en/e-misferica-41/smalec, date accessed 7 August 2010.

33. R. Mullins (1988) 'Awesome God' (song) in *Winds of Heaven, Stuff of Earth* (album) (Brentwood, TN: Reunion Records).

34. A. Bogart (2001) *A Director Prepares: Seven Essays on Art and Theatre* (London and New York: Routledge), pp. 38–9.

35. T. Smalec (2009) '"Celebrate Like True Believers": Performing Evangelical Christianity in Les Freres Corbusier's *Hell House*', http://hemi.nyu.edu/hemi/en/e-misferica-41/smalec, date accessed 7 August 2010.

36. Ibid.

37. Bullying: see H. Cassidy and V. Watts (2002) 'Burn an Image in their Head: Evaluating the Effectiveness of a Play on Bullying', *NJ: Drama Australia Journal*, 26, 3, 5–19; J. O'Toole, B. Burton, and A. Plunkett (2005) *Cooling Conflict: A New Approach to Managing Bullying and Conflict in Schools* (French Forest, NSW: Pearson/Longman); A. Hickson (2009) 'Social Theatre: A Theatre of Empowerment to Address Bullying in Schools' in S. Jennings (ed.) *Dramatherapy and Social Theatre* (East Sussex: Routledge). Cultural identity: see J. Tan (2005) 'One Island: A Theatre-in-Education Approach in Singapore', *NJ: Drama Australia Journal*, 29, 1, 45–50. Health education: see J. Winston (2009) 'Fit for a Child: Artistry and Didacticism in the Theatre in Health Educational Program for Young Children' in T. Prentki and S. Preston (eds) *The Applied Theatre Reader* (London and New York: Routledge). Racism: see K. McCreery (2009) 'Challenging Racism in Sunderland and Newcastle' in T. Prentki and S. Preston (eds) *The Applied Theatre Reader* (London and New York: Routledge).

38. See J. Winston (2001) 'Drug Education through Creating Theatre in Education', *RIDE: Research in Drama Education*, 6, 1, 39–54.

39. See N. Bowles and M. E. Rosenthal (eds) (2000) *Cootie Shots: Theatrical Inoculations Against Bigotry for Kids, Parents and Teachers* (A Fringe Benefits Project) (New York: Theatre Communications Group, Inc.). See also N. Bowles (2005) 'Why Devise? Why Now? Houston, We Have a Problem', *Theatre Topics*, 15, 1, 15–21.

40. See ENACT (n.d.), 'Home', http://enact.org/Home/index.php, date accessed 7 August 2010; CANY (Creative Alternatives of New York) (n.d.) 'Making a Connection', http://www.cany.org/, date accessed 7 August 2010; CAT (Creative Arts Team) (2010) 'Creative Arts Team', http://www.cuny.edu/academics/k-to-12/cat.html, date accessed 7 August 2010.

41. See J. Hodgson and E. Richards (1979) *Improvisation* (New York: Grove Press).

42. Interview conducted with Chris Vine, 9 November 2010. Chris Vine is also Academic Director, MA in Applied Theatre, School of Professional Studies, The City University of New York (CUNY).

43. Interview conducted with James Mirrione, 28 July 2010.

44. J. Mirrione (2011) 'Kiss Me Khatema: An Analysis of Emirati Women's Responses to Kate's Fianl Monologue in Shakespeare's *The Taming of the Shrew*', unpublished paper.

45. See P. Stern (producer) (2003) 'Standing Tall (film)' (peggysternfilms.com). Study Guide and full text of play available from website: peggysternfilms.com.

46. Ibid.

47. See R. Landy (2010) 'Drama as a Means of Preventing Post-traumatic Stress Following Trauma within a Community', *Journal of Applied Arts and Health*, 1, 1, 7–18.

48. C. Odhiambo (2008) *Theatre for Development in Kenya: In Search of an Effective Procedure and Methodology* (Eckersdorf: Pia Thielmann and Eckhard Breitinger).

49. R. Kidd (1984) 'From People's Theatre for Revolution to Popular Theatre for Reconstruction: Diary of a Zimbabwean Workshop', The Hague: CESO.

50. C. J. Odhiambo (2008) *Theatre for Development in Kenya: In Search of an Effective Procedure and Methodology* (Bayreuth: Pia Thielmann and Eckhard Breitinger).

51. M. Prendergast and J. Saxton (ed.) (2009) *Applied Theatre* (Chicago, IL: Intellect), p. 105.

52. C. J. Odhiambo (2008) *Theatre for Development in Kenya: In Search of an Effective Procedure and Methodology* (Bayreuth: Pia Thielmann and Eckhard Breitinger), p. 17.

53. L. D. Byam (1999) *Community in Motion: Theatre for Development in Africa* (London: Bergin and Garvey), p. 23.

54. See P. Freire (1974, 2007) *Education for Critical Consciousness* (New York: The Continuum International Publishing Group, Inc.).

55. R. Chamberlain, M. Chillery, L. Ogolla, and O. Wandera (1995) 'Participatory Educational Theatre for HIV/AIDS Awareness in Kenya', *PLA Notes*, 23, 69–74, http://www.planotes.org/documents/plan_02314.PDF, date accessed 8 August 2010.

56. See C. J. Odhiambo (2008) *Theatre for Development in Kenya: In Search of an Effective Procedure and Methodology* (Bayreuth: Pia Thielmann and Eckhard Breitinger).

57. R. Chamberlain, M. Chillery, L. Ogolla, and O. Wandera (1995) 'Participatory Educational Theatre for HIV/AIDS Awareness in Kenya', *PLA Notes*, 23, 69–74, http://www.planotes.org/documents/plan_02314.PDF, date accessed 8 August 2010.

58. Chiraa is a traditional Luo illness resulting from the breaking of a cultural taboo. If it is not dealt with in time by the performing of certain culturally prescribed rituals, then death will be the certain outcome. Naturally, the HIV/AIDS pandemic in Western Kenya is complicated by such customary beliefs, together with others such as wife inheritance by one brother on the death of another; and Ke, the obligatory performance of sexual intercourse by all immediate members of the family before dispersal following a funeral.

59. R. Chamberlain, M. Chillery, L. Ogolla, and O. Wandera (1995) 'Participatory Educational Theatre for HIV/AIDS Awareness in Kenya', *PLA Notes*, 23, 69–74, http://www.planotes.org/documents/plan_02314.PDF, date accessed 8 August 2010.

60. C. J. Odhiambo (2008) *Theatre for Development in Kenya: In Search of an Effective Procedure and Methodology* (Bayreuth: Pia Thielmann and Eckhard Breitinger), p. 182.

61. A. Boal (1979) *Theatre of the Oppressed* (New York: Theatre Communications Group), p. 142.

62. T. Prentki and S. Preston (eds) (2009) *The Applied Theatre Reader* (London and New York: Routledge).

63. See Philippines Educational Theatre Association (PETA) (n.d.) 'About Us', http://www.petatheater.com/aboutus.html, date accessed 8 August 2010.

64. M. G. Santos-Cabangon (2009) *The International Conference of Drama in Education and Applied Theatre* (Taipei: National Taiwan University of the Arts), pp. 148–61.

65. Ibid., p. 147.

66. Ibid., p. 156.

67. Ibid., p. 160.

68. P. Weiss (1963, 2001) *The Persecution and Assassination of Jean-Paul Marat as Performed by the Inmates of the Asylum of Charenton under the Direction of the Marquis de Sade* (Long Grove, IL: Waveland Press Inc). Often referred to simply as *Marat/Sade*.

69. See A. Artaud (1958) *Theater and its Double* (New York: Grove Press).

70. S. Homan (1991) 'Waiting for Godot: Inmates as Student and – Then – Teachers' in J. Schlueter and E. Brater (eds) *Approaches to Teaching Beckett's Waiting for Godot* (New York: Modern Language Association Press), pp. 156–7.

71. See Theatre in Prisons website, http://web.mac.com/thesqdw/theSQDW.org/theatre_in_prisons.org.html, date accessed 13 August 2011.

72. See Rehabilitation in the Arts (RTA) website, http://www.rta-arts.com/, date accessed 8 August 2010.

73. L. Downes (November 16, 2006) 'Oedipus Max: Four Nights of Anguish and Applause in Sing Sing', *The New York Times*, http://www.nytimes.com/2006/11/16/opinion/16thur4.html?_r=1andscp=1andsq=Oedipus%20Max%20Ossiningandst=cse, date accessed 8 August 2010.

74. P. Taylor (2011) *Theatre Behind Bars – Can the Arts Rehabilitate?* (Stoke-on-Kent: Trentham).

75. L. Tocci (2007) *The Proscenium Cage: Critical Case Studies in U.S. Prison Theatre Programs* (Amherst, NY: Cambria).

76. J. Von Stanley (2010) 'News Flash: Theatre Really *Can* Change Lives', http://brain-on-fire.com/jefeblog/?s=theatre+change+lives, date accessed 25 October 2010.

77. C. Baim, S. Brookes, and A. Mountfound (2002) *The Geese Theatre Handbook* (Sherfield-on-Loddon: Waterside Press).

78. J. Bergman and S. Hewish (2003) *Challenging Experience: An Experiential Approach to the Treatment of Serious Offenders* (Bethany, OK: Wood N Barnes).

79. J. Thompson (1998) *Prison Theatre: Practices and Perspectives* (London: Jessica Kingsley).

80. See M. Cox and A. Theilgaard (1994) *Shakespeare as Prompter* (London: Jessica Kingsley).

81. See *Shakespeare Behind Bars* (film) website, http://www.shakespearebehindbars.com/, date accessed 8 August 2010.

82. See ESC: Understanding through Film, http://www.esc-film.com, date accessed 22 July 2011.

83. Interview conducted with Tom Magill, 26 August 2010.

84. Tom Magill is an ex-prisoner who transformed his life through arts education while in prison for violence. On release, he studied drama and became an award-winning actor and filmmaker. He formed ESC in 1999 to develop drama and film with prisoners and ex-prisoners. ESC is an arts education charity empowering marginalised people to find their voice and tell their stories through film. (http://www.esc-film.com)

85. See *Mickey B* trailer at http://shootingpeople.org/watch/film.php?film_id=81655, date accessed 4 September 2010.
86. Ibid.
87. From: 'Rehabilitation through Arts Education', http://www.arirang.co.kr/News/News_View.asp?nseq=109260andcode=Ne2andcategory=2, date accessed 24 November 2010.
88. S. Lev-Aladgem (2008) 'Between Home and Homeland: Facilitating Theatre with Ethiopian Youth', *Research in Drama Education*, 13, 3, 275–93. All quotes in this section, unless otherwise noted, come from this article.
89. M. Rohd (1998) *Theatre for Community, Conflict, and Dialogue: The Hope is Vital Training Manual* (Portsmouth, NH: Heinemann Drama).
90. M. Blankenship (2010) 'Repast, Present, Future', *American Theatre*, 27, 4, 26–30.
91. Ibid., p. 27.
92. J. Cohen-Cruz (2005) *Local Acts* (Piscataway, NJ: Rutgers University Press), p. 85.
93. M. Blankenship (2010) 'Repast, Present, Future', American Theatre, 27, 4, p. 27.
94. See Imagining America's website, http://www.imaginingamerica.org/, date accessed 8 August 2010.
95. J. Cohen-Cruz (2010) *Engaging Performance: Theatre as Call and Response* (New York: Routledge).
96. T. Kushner (1993) *Angels in America, Part One (Millennium Approaches) and Part Two (Perestroika)* (New York: Theatre Communications Group). In addition to its performances on stage, the play was made into a major motion picture. Part One won the Pulitzer Prize for Drama in 1993. Part Two won a Tony Award.

## Part III   Drama and Theatre in Therapy

1. See K. V. Hartigan (2009) *Performance and Cure: Drama and Healing in Ancient Greece and Contemporary America* (London: Duckworth).
2. Sophocles (1994) *Antigone, Oedipus the King, Electra* (Kitto, trans.) (Oxford University Press).
3. V. Turner (1982) *From Ritual to Theatre: The Human Seriousness of Play* (New York: PAJ Publications).

## 5   Drama Therapy

1. R. Landy (2008) 'The Dramatic World View Revisited: Reflections on the Roles Taken and Played by Young Children and Adolescents', *Dramatherapy*, 30, 2, 1–11.
2. See C. B Bouzoukis (2001) *Pediatric Dramatherapy* (London: Jessica Kingsley).
3. See A. Volkas (2009) 'Healing the Wounds of History: Drama therapy in Collective Trauma and Intercultural Conflict Resolution' in D. Johnson and R. Emunah (eds) *Current Approaches in Drama Therapy* (Springfield, IL: Charles C. Thomas), p. 154.
4. H. Weiner (1975) 'Living Experiences with Death – A Journeyman's View through Psychodrama', *Omega – Journal of Death and Dying*, 6, 3, 251–74.

5. R. Landy (1997) 'Drama therapy – The State of the Art', *The Arts in Psychotherapy*, 24, 5–15.

6. From A. Volkas (2009) 'Healing the Wounds of History: Drama therapy in Collective Trauma and Intercultural Conflict Resolution' in D. Johnson and R. Emunah (eds) *Current Approaches in Drama Therapy* (Springfield, IL: Charles C. Thomas), p. 154.

7. Ibid.

8. The British Association of Dramatherapists was founded in 1977 (See http://www.badth.org.uk/). The US National Association for Drama Therapy was founded in 1979 (See http://www.nadt.org/).

9. R. Landy (2008) *The Couch and the Stage* (Lanham, MD: Jason Aronson).

10. C. Jung (1921, 1971) *Psychological Types: Collected Works*, vol. 6 (Princeton, NJ: Princeton University Press).

11. S. Ferenczi and O. Rank (1925, 1986) *The Development of Psycho-analysis* (Madison, CT: International Universities Press).

12. S. Ferenczi (1955) *Final Contributions to the Problem and Methods of Psychoanalysis* (New York: Basic Books).

13. W. Reich (1949) *Character Analysis*, 3rd edn (New York: Orgone Institute).

14. J. Wolpe and A. Lazarus (1966) *Behavior Therapy Techniques: A Guide to the Treatment of Neuroses* (New York: Pergamon Press).

15. G. A. Kelly (1955) *The Psychology of Personal Constructs*, vols. 1 and 2 (New York: Norton).

16. F. Perls (1969) *Gestalt Therapy Verbatim* (Lafayette, CA: Real People Press).

17. See J. Casson (1997) 'Dramatherapy History in Headlines: Who Did What, When, Where?', *Journal of the British Association for Dramatherapists*, 19, 2, 10–13.

18. Ibid.

19. See P. Slade (1959) *Dramatherapy as an Aid to Becoming a Person* (London: Guild of Pastoral Psychology). See also R. Courtney and G. Schattner (1982) *Drama in Therapy, Two Volumes* (New York: Drama Book Specialists).

20. R. Landy (1996) *Essays in Drama Therapy: The Double Life* (London: Jessica Kingsley).

21. C. Stanislavski (1936) *An Actor Prepares* (New York: Theatre Arts Books). A. Boal (1979) *Theatre of the Oppressed* (New York: Theatre Communications Group).

22. See California Institute of Integral Studies (2009) 'Theatre for Change', http://www.ciis.edu/Academics/Graduate_Programs/Drama_Therapy/Theatre_for_Change.html, date accessed 23 July 2011.

23. D. R. Johnson and R. Emunah (eds) (2009) *Current Approaches in Drama Therapy* (Springfield, IL: Charles C. Thomas Publisher).

24. T. Prentki and S. Preston (eds) (2009) *The Applied Theatre Reader* (New York: Routledge), p. 12.

25. J. Thompson (2008) *Applied Theatre – Bewilderment and Beyond* (Bern: Peter Lang), p. 46.

26. R. Landy (1993) *Persona and Performance-The Meaning of Role in Drama, Therapy, and Everyday Life* (New York: Guilford Press).

27. R. Landy (2008) *The Couch and the Stage: Integrating Words and Action in Psychotherapy* (Lanham, MD: Jason Aronson).

28. See Chapter 4, p. 230.

29. See Drama for Life (2010) 'Drama for Life', http://www.dramaforlife.co.za, date accessed 19 June 2010.

30. KwaZulu-Natal Programme for Survivors of Violence (PSV) is a non-governmental organization established in 1992 to address the consequences of political violence in KwaZulu-Natal. PSV works with groups of children, unemployed youth and adults which are established on request from the communities and, in consultation with leadership. These groups are guided through processes of personal, community and career development. See their website at http://www.survivors.org.za/.

31. H. Barnes and D. Peters (2002) 'Translating trauma: using arts therapies with survivors of violence', South African Theatre Journal, 16, 157–84.

32. Interview conducted with Hazel Barnes, 24 August 2010.

33. A. Boal (1995) The Rainbow of Desire: The Boal Method of Theatre and Therapy (London; New York: Routledge).

34. Ibid., pp. 72–3.

35. Ibid., p. 156.

36. Ibid., pp. 70–3.

37. J. L. Moreno (1971) 'Psychodrama' in H. I. Kaplan, and B. J. Sadock (eds) Comprehensive Group Psychotherapy (Baltimore, MD: Williams and Wilkins), pp. 460–500.

38. See, for example, T. Dayton (2000) Trauma and Addiction: Ending the Cycle of Pain through Emotional Literacy (Deerfield Beach, FL: Health Communications); J. Gershoni (ed.) (2003) Psychodrama in the 21st Century (New York: Springer); P. Holmes, M. Karp, and M. Watson (eds) (1994) Psychodrama since Moreno: Innovations in Theory and Practice (London: Routledge).

39. See J. L. Moreno (1946, 1994) Psychodrama, vol. 1 (New York: Beacon House); J. L. Moreno (1985) The Autobiography of JL Moreno M.D. (abridged) Jonathan Moreno (ed.) Moreno Archives (Cambridge, MA: Harvard University Press); R. Marineau (1989) Jacob Levy Moreno 1889–1974 (New York: Tavistock/Routledge).

40. J. L. Moreno (1946, 1994) Psychodrama, vol. 1 (New York: Beacon House), p. 1.

41. Ibid., p. 1.

42. A. Boal (1979) Theatre of the Oppressed (New York: Urizen Books).

43. P. Sternberg and A. Garcia (2000) Sociodrama: Who's in your Shoes?, 2nd edn (Westport, CT: Praeger).

44. J. L. Moreno (1946, 1994) Psychodrama, vol. 1 (New York: Beacon House), p. xii.

45. J. L. Moreno (1934/1978) Who Shall Survive? (New York: Beacon House).

46. The Center for the Living Arts (2009) 'Healing the Wounds of History', http://www.livingartscenter.org/Healing-Wounds-of-History/Home.htm, date accessed 18 October 2010.

47. Interview conducted with James Thompson, 2010.

48. J. Cohen-Cruz (2010) Engaging Performance: Theatre as Call and Response (New York: Routledge).

49. S. Jennings (1973) Remedial Drama (London: Pitman).

50. P. Slade (1959) Dramatherapy as an Aid to Becoming a Person (London: Guild of Pastoral Psychology).

51. S. Jennings (2009) Dramatherapy and Social Theatre: Necessary Dialogues (London; New York: Routledge).

52. M. Lindkvist (1998) Bring White Beads When You Call on the Healer (New Orleans, LA: Rivendell House).

53. A. Gersie (1991) *Storymaking in Bereavement* (London: Jessica Kingsley); A. Gersie (1997) *Reflections on Therapeutic Storymaking* (London: Jessica Kingsley). A. Cattanach (1993) *Playtherapy with Abused Children* (London: Jessica Kingsley); A. Cattanach (2003) *Introduction to Play Therapy* (New York: Brunner-Routledge). P. Jones (2007) *Drama as Therapy: Theory, Practice and Research* (London: Routledge); P. Jones (2010) *Drama as Therapy, Volume II: Clinical Work and Research into Practice* (London: Routledge). J. Casson (2004) *Drama, Psychotherapy and Psychosis: Dramatherapy and Psychodrama with People Who Hear Voices* (New York: Brunner-Routledge). R. Grainger (1990) *Drama and Healing: The Roots of Dramatherapy* (London: Jessica Kingsley); R. Grainger (1995) *The Glass of Heaven – The Faith of the Dramatherapist* (London: Jessica Kingsley); R. Grainger (2008) *Drama of the Rite: Worship, Liturgy and Theatre Performance* (Sussex: Sussex Academic Press). A. Seymour (2008) 'A Theatre model of Dramatherapy Supervision' (with Madeline Andersen Warren) in P. Jones and D. Dokter (eds) *Supervision of Dramatherapy* (Routledge: London and New York). D. Dokter (ed.) (1994) *Arts Therapies and Clients with Eating Disorders: Fragile Board* (London: Jessica Kingsley); D. Dokter (ed.) (1998) *Arts Therapists, Refugees and Migrants: Reaching across Borders* (London: Jessica Kingsley.).
54. L. Barbato (1945) 'Drama Therapy', *Sociometry*, 8, 396–8.
55. Behavior rehearsal is role-playing technique developed by Joseph Wolpe and Arnold Lazarus, both behavior therapists, to help clients modify their behavior in relationship to life stressors. See J. Wolpe and A. Lazarus (1966) *Behavior Therapy Techniques: A Guide to the Treatment of Neuroses* (New York: Pergamon Press).
56. G. Schatter and R. Courtney (eds) (1981) *Drama in Therapy*, vol. 1 (New York: Drama Books); G. Schatter and R. Courtney (eds) (1982) *Drama in Therapy*, vol. 2 (New York: Drama Books).
57. R. Landy (1986, 1994) *Drama Therapy – Concepts and Practices* (Springfield, IL: CC Thomas Publisher).
58. D. R. Johnson and R. Emunah (eds) (2009) *Current Approaches in Drama Therapy* (Springfield, IL: Charles C. Thomas Publisher).
59. M. Lahad (1992) 'Storymaking: An assessment method of coping with stress' in S. Jennings (ed.) *Dramatherapy, Theory and Practice*, vol. 2 (London: Routledge).
60. J. L. Moreno (1946, 1994) *Psychodrama*, vol. 1 (New York: Beacon House).
61. D. W. Winnicott (1971) *Playing and Reality* (Routledge: London).
62. M. Lahad (2000) *Creative Supervision* (London: Jessica Kingsley).
63. D. Johnson (2009) 'Developmental transformations: Toward the body as presence' in D. Johnson and R. Emunah (eds) *Current Approaches in Drama Therapy*, 2nd edn (Springfield, IL: Charles C Thomas), pp. 89–116.
64. For a fuller discussion of concepts in Drama Therapy, see R. Landy (1994) *Drama Therapy—Concepts, Theories and Practices*, 2nd edn (Springfield, IL: Charles C Thomas); and R. Landy (2008) *The Creative Supervision Couch and the Stage* (Lanham, MD: Jason Aronson).
65. See J. Casson (1997) 'Dramatherapy History in Headlines: Who Did What, When, Where?', *Journal of the British Association for Dramatherapists*, 19, 2, 10–13.
66. J. Thompson (2010) *Performance Affects: Applied theatre and the End of Effect* (London: Palgrave Macmillan).

67. J. Hillman (1983) *Healing Fiction* (Barrytown, NY: Station Hill).

68. M. Hodermarska (2009) 'Perfume: A Meditation on the Countertransferential Drama with Babies Who Smell Bad', *The Arts in Psychotherapy*, 36, 39–46.

69. R. Landy (2005) *Three Approaches to Drama Therapy* (Video and DVD) (New York: New York University). The quotes in this case vignette, unless otherwise indicated, come from the Landy DVD.

70. E. Shostrom (1965) *Three Approaches to Psychotherapy I* (Videorecording) (Corona Del Mar, CA: Psychological Films Inc.). See also: C. Magai and J. Haviland-Jones (2002) *The Hidden Genius of Emotion* (Cambridge: Cambridge University Press).

71. See D. Johnson (2009) 'Developmental Transformations: Toward the Body as Presence' in D. Johnson and R. Emunah (eds) *Current Approaches in Drama Therapy*, 2nd edn (Springfield, IL: Charles C Thomas), pp. 89–116.

72. Ibid.

73. Derek (2006) Personal communication.

74. See W. Cockerham (2000) *Sociology of Mental Disorder* (Englewood Cliffs, NJ: Prentice Hall).

75. C. Aurelianus (1951) *On Acute Diseases and On Chronic Diseases* (Chicago: University of Chicago Press) (London: Cambridge University Press), pp. xxvi, vii, 1019.

76. See R. Landy (1997) 'Drama therapy – The State of the Art', *The Arts in Psychotherapy*, 24, 5–15.

77. See S. Pitruzzella (2004) *Introduction to Dramatherapy: Person and Threshold* (New York: Brunner-Routledge).

78. See Rooz Video (2010) 'Bella ciao, Iran', http://www.roozvideo.com/video/39/bella_ciao_iran/, date accessed 14 October 2010.

79. R. Landy (2010) Workshop in Drama Therapy, University of Rome, La Sapienza, 13 April 2010.

80. R. Landy (1997) 'Drama therapy in Taiwan', *The Arts in Psychotherapy*, 24, 159–73.

81. Ibid.

82. See: Arab Comment (2010) '"12 Angry Lebanese": interview with Zeina Daccache', http://arabcomment.com/2010/12-angry-lebanese-interview-with-zeina-daccache/, date accessed 14 October 2010.

83. Interview conducted with Nisha Sanjani, 21 June 2010.

## Part IV  Reflections

1. R. Landy (1982) *Handbook of Educational Drama and Theatre* (Westport, CT: Greenwood Press), p. 254.

2. P. Taylor (1993) *The Texts of Paulo Freire* (Buckingham: Open University Press).

## 6  Imaginary Dialogue

1. Interview conducted with Philip Taylor, 22 March 2010. All quotes from Taylor in this chapter are from the interview. R. Courtney (1989) *Play, Drama and Thought*, 4th edn rev. (Toronto, Ont: Simon and Pierre Publishing Co. Ltd.).

2. R. Courtney (1982) 'Robes, Roles and Realities' (Forward) in R. Landy's *Handbook of Educational Drama and Theatre* (Westport, CT: Greenwood Press).

3. Unless otherwise noted, see bibliography for publications referenced in this chapter. When only names are given, we leave it to the reader to look up publications.

4. Bertolt Brecht, title of music album released in 1982.

5. P. Freire (2000) *Pedagogy of the Oppressed*, 30th anniversary edn (New York: Continuum International Publishing Group), p. 79.

6. A. Boal (1979) *Theatre of the Oppressed* (New York: Theatre Communications Group), p. 122.

7. Interview conducted with Johnny Saldaña, 16 March 2010. All quotes from Saldaña in this chapter are from the interview.

8. B. van der Kolk, A. C. McFarlane and L. Weisaeth (eds) (2006) *Traumatic Stress: The Effects of Overwhelming Experience on Mind, Body, and Society* (New York: The Guilford Press). C. Kisiel, M. Blaustein, J. Spinazzola, C. S. Schmidt, M. Zucker and B. van der Kolk (2006) 'Evaluation of a Theater-Based Youth Violence Prevention Program for Elementary School Children', *Journal of School Violence*, 5, 2, 19–36, http://www.traumacenter.org/products/pdf_files/JSV5_2_2006.pdf, date accessed 29 July 2011.

9. The Philoctetes Center (2007) 'Acting and Mirror Neurons', philoctetes.org/documents/Acting.pdf, date accessed 4 August 2011.

10. Interview conducted with Cecily O'Neill, Emelie Fitzgibbon, and Nancy Swortzell, 15 June 2010. All quotes from O'Neill, Fitzgibbon, and Swortzell in this chapter are from the interview.

11. Interview conducted with Tony Graham, 12 February 2010. All quotes from Graham in this chapter are from the interview.

12. Interview conducted with Gavin Bolton, 12 January 2010. All quotes from Bolton in this chapter are from the interview.

13. Interview conducted with Peter Harris, 2010. All quotes from Harris in this chapter are from the interview.

14. Interview conducted with Jan Cohen-Cruz, 25 June 2010. All quotes from Cohen-Cruz in this chapter are from the interview.

15. Interview conducted with Nisha Sanjani, 21 June 2010. All quotes from Sanjani in this chapter are from the interview.

16. Interview conducted with Cecily O'Neill, Emelie Fitzgibbon, and Nancy Swortzell, 15 June 2010. All quotes from O'Neill, Fitzgibbon, and Swortzell in this chapter are from the interview.

17. Ibid.

18. Interview conducted with Hazel Barnes, 24 August 2010. All quotes from Barnes in this chapter are from the interview.

19. Interview conducted with James Thompson, 2010. All quotes from Thompson in this chapter are from the interview.

20. Interview conducted with Chris Vine, 9 November 2010. All quotes from Vine in this chapter are from the interview.

21. Interview conducted with Christopher Odhiambo Joseph, 2010. All quotes from Odhiambo in this chapter are from the interview.

22. Interview conducted with Dorothy Heathcote, 19 January 2010. All quotes from Heathcote in this chapter are from the interview.

23. P. Taylor (2011) *Theatre Behind Bars – Can the Arts Rehabilitate?* (Stoke-on-Kent: Trentham).
24. Interview conducted with Tom Magill, 2010. All quotes from Magill in this chapter are from the interview.
25. Interview conducted with Zeina Daccache, 28 November 2010. All quotes from Daccache in this chapter are from the interview.
26. Interview conducted with Renée Emunah, 2010. All quotes from Emunah in this chapter are from the interview.
27. Interview conducted with Armand Volkas, 11 June 2010. All quotes from Volkas in this chapter are from the interview.
28. Interview conducted with Jonathan Fox, 2010. All quotes from Fox in this chapter are from the interview.
29. Interview conducted with Zerka Moreno, 2010. All quotes from Moreno in this chapter are from the interview.
30. Interview conducted with William Sun, 8 March 2010. All quotes from Sun in this chapter are from the interview.
31. Interview conducted with Hsiao-Hua Chang, 2009. All quotes from Chang in this chapter are from the interview.
32. Interview conducted with José Cruz González, 28 March 2010. All quotes from González in this chapter are from the interview.
33. Interview conducted with David Booth, 22 February 2010. All quotes from Booth in this chapter are from the interview.
34. Interview conducted with Edie Demas, 4 September 2009. All quotes from Demas in this chapter are from the interview.
35. Interview conducted with James Mirrione, 28 July 2010. All quotes from Mirrione in this chapter are from the interview.
36. Entertainment Education is also known as edutainment and e-e. It refers to the use of various entertaining strategies to engage learners in educational settings.
37. The conference at LaMama took place 23–26 September 2010, in New York City. It was called: 'Acting Together on the World Stage: A Conference on theatre and Peace Building in Conflict Zones'.
38. See C. Cohen, R. Gutierrez Varea, P. Walkers (eds) (2011) *Acting Together: Performance and Creative Transformation of Conflict*, two volumes (Oakland, CA: New Village Press).

## Glossary

## Drama and theatre in education

1. This definition is compiled from the work of Nellie McCaslin, Peter Slade, and Winifred Ward as well as C. D. MacKay (1915) *How to Produce Children's Plays* (New York: Holt and Company).
2. R. Courtney (1989) *Play, Drama and Thought: The Intellectual Background to Dramatic Education*, 4th edn rev (Ontario: Simon and Pierre), p. 14.
3. R. Landy (1982) *Handbook of Educational Drama and Theatre* (Westport, CT and London: Greenwood Press), p. 4. Citing a definition from the Children's Theatre

Association of America (now the American Alliance of Theatre and Education): J. H. Davis and T. Behm (1978) 'Terminology of Drama/Theatre with and for Children: A Redefinition,' *Children's Theatre Review*, 27, 1, 10–11.

4. N. McCaslin (1996) *Creative Drama in the Classroom* (New York: Longman), p. 8.
5. C. A. Franklin (n.d.) Civic Literacy through Curriculum Drama, Grades 6–12 (Corwin Press), p.2.
6. Ibid., p. 3.
7. R. Courtney (1989) *Play, Drama and Thought: The Intellectual Background to Dramatic Education*, 4th edn rev (Ontario: Simon and Pierre), p. 14.
8. R. Courtney (1987) *Dictionary of Developmental Drama* (Springfield, IL: Charles C Thomas), p. 30.
9. S. Katz and B. Manson (1986, 1989, 1990) *Drama Continuum Grades JK-OAC Across the Curriculum* (Hamilton: Hamilton Board of Education), as cited by S. Katz (2000) 'Drama and Therapy in Education: The Double Mirror', http://www.doublemirror.com/chapter_one.htm, date accessed 13 November 2010.
10. N. McCaslin (1996) *Creative Drama in the Classroom* (New York: Longman), p. 12.
11. T. Jackson (ed.) (1993) *Learning through Theatre*, 2nd edn (New York: Routledge), pp. 8–9.
12. C. O'Neill (1995) *Drama Worlds: A Framework for Process Drama* (Portsmouth, NH: Heinemann), p. xiii.
13. P. Bowell and B. Heap (2001) *Planning Process Drama* (London: David Fulton Publishers), p. 7.
14. D. Booth (2005) *Story Drama: Creating Stories Through Role Playing, Improvising, and Reading Aloud*, 2nd edn (Ontario: Pembroke Publishers), p. 8.

## Drama and theatre in social action

1. P. Pitzele (n.d.) 'Bibliodrama: A Call to the Future', http://bibliodrama.com/bibpurpose.htm, date accessed 1 July 2010.
2. R. Pramann (2006) 'Playback Bibliodrama', http://www.ssccc.com/pbbd.doc, date accessed 1 July 2010.
3. S. Kuftinec (2003) *Staging America: Cornerstone and Community-based Theater* (Carbondale, IL: Southern Illinois University Press), p. xvi.
4. M. Prendergast and J. Saxton (eds) (2009) *Applied Theatre: International Case Studies and Challenges for Practice* (Chicago, IL: Intellect/University of Chicago Press), p 135.
5. J. Saldaña (ed.) (2005) *Ethnodrama: An Anthology of Reality Theatre* (Walnut Creek, CA: AltaMira Press), p. 2.
6. J. Saldaña (ed.) (2005) *Ethnodrama: An Anthology of Reality Theatre* (Walnut Creek, CA: AltaMira Press), p. 2.
7. J. Cohen-Cruz (2005) *Local Acts: Community-based Performance in the United States* (New Brunswick, NJ and London: Rutgers University Press), p. 7.
8. D. Cocke. (1993) 'A Matrix Articulating the Principles of Grassroots Theater' in D. Cocke, H. Newman, and J. Salmons-Rue (eds) *From the Ground Up: Grassroots Theater in Historical and Contemporary Perspective* (Ithaca, NY: Cornell University), http://roadside.org/matrixessay.html, date accessed 1 July 2010.

9. International Museum Theatre Alliance (n.d.) 'Frequently Asked Questions: What is Museum Theatre?', http://www.imtal.org/faqs.asp, date accessed 1 July 2010.

10. Playback Theatre.org (2010) 'Playback Theatre', http://www.playbacktheatre.org/, date accessed 1 July 2010.

11. Playback Theatre.org (2010) 'Playback Theatre', http://www.playbacktheatre.org/about/, date accessed 1 July 2010.

12. D. Conrad (2004) 'Exploring Risky Youth Experiences: Popular Theatre as a Participatory, Performative Research Method,' *IJQM*, 3, 1, 12–25 (13), http://ejournals.library.ualberta.ca/index.php/IJQM/article/view/4482/3787, date accessed 2 July 2010.

13 M. Prendergast and J. Saxton (eds) (2009) *Applied Theatre: International Case Studies and Challenges for Practice* (Chicago, IL: Intellect/University of Chicago Press), p. 119, reflecting on Thompson (2003) *Applied Theatre: Bewilderment and Beyond* (New York: Peter Lang).

14. P. Schweitzer (2006) *Reminiscence Theatre: Making Theatre from Memories* (London: Jessica Kingsley Publishers).

15. M. Prendergast and J. Saxton (eds) (2009) *Applied Theatre: International Case Studies and Challenges for Practice* (Chicago, IL: Intellect/University of Chicago Press), p. 169.

16. G. Schinanà (2009) 'Like Ham in a Temperance Hotel: Healing, Participation, and Education in Social Theatre' in S. Jennings (ed.) *Dramatherapy and Social Theatre* (New York: Routledge), p. 37.

17. Ibid.; G. Schinanà (2004) 'Here We Are: Social Theatre and Some Open Questions about its Development,' *TDR*: 48, 3, 18–33 (24).

18. J. L. Moreno and J. Fox (1987) *The Essential Moreno: Writings on Psychodrama, Group Method, and Spontaneity* (New York: Springer Publishing Company), p. 18.

19. P. Sternberg and A. Garcia (2009) 'Sociodrama' in D. R. Johnson and Renée Emunah (eds) *Current Approaches in Drama Therapy* (Springfield, IL: Charles C. Thomas Publisher), p. 424.

20. A. Boal (1979) *Theatre of the Oppressed* (New York: Theatre Communications Group). P. Freire (1970/2000) *Pedagogy of the Oppressed* (New York: The Continuum International Publishing Group, Inc.).

21. S. Ball (1993) 'Theatre in Health Education' in T. Jackson (ed.) *Learning through Theatre*, 2nd edn (New York: Routledge), p. 227.

22. M. Prendergast and J. Saxton (eds) (2009) *Applied Theatre* (Chicago, IL: Intellect), p. 87. They cite Bury, Popple, and Barker (1998) '"You've Got to Think Really Hard": Children Making Sense of the Aims and Content of Theatre in Health Education', *RIDE: Research in Drama Education*, 3, 1, 13–27 (13).

23. M. Prendergast and J. Saxton (eds) (2009) *Applied Theatre* (Chicago, IL: Intellect), p. 105.

24. T. Jackson (1999) '"I've never been in a story before": Audience Participation and the Theatrical Frame' in N. McCaslin (ed.) *Children and Drama*, 3rd edn (Studio City, CA: Players Press), p. 185.

25. R. Wooster (2007) *Contemporary Theatre in Education* (Chicago, IL: Intellect Books).

## Drama and theatre in therapy

1. See Health Careers Center (2002–2004) 'Creative Arts Therapist', http://www.mshealthcareers.com/careers/creativeartstherapist.htm, date accessed 16 September 2010.
2. D. Johnson (2009) 'Developmental Transformations: Towards the Body as Presence' in D. Johnson and R. Emunah (eds) *Current Approaches in Drama Therapy* (Springfield, IL: Charles C. Thomas), p. 89.
3. Ibid.
4. Lesley University (2010) 'Division of Expressive Therapies', http://www.lesley.edu/gsass/56etp.html, date accessed 16 September 2010.
5. See P. Dunne (2009) 'Narradrama: A Narrative Approach to Drama Therapy' in D. Johnson and R. Emunah (eds) *Current Approaches in Drama Therapy* (Springfield, IL: Charles C. Thomas), p. 89.
6. Playback Theatre.org (2010) 'Playback Theatre', http://www.playbacktheatre.org/, date accessed 1 July 2010.
7. Playback Theatre.org (2010) 'Playback Theatre', http://www.playbacktheatre.org/about/, date accessed 1 July 2010.
8. Ibid.
9. American Society of Group Psychotherapy and Psychodrama (2006) 'General Information about Psychodrama', http://www.asgpp.org/pdrama1.htm, date accessed 16 September 2010.
10. S. Jennings (1973) *Remedial Drama* (London: Pitman).
11. See A. Boal (1995) *The Rainbow of Desire: The Boal Method of Theatre and Therapy* (London; New York: Routledge).
12. The Weyburn Project (n.d.) 'What is Site-Specific Theatre?,' http://uregina.ca/weyburn_project/pages/sitespec.html, date accessed 27 September 2010.
13. J. L. Moreno (1953) *Who Shall Survive?: Foundations of Sociometry, Group Psychotherapy and Sociodrama* (Redlands, CA: Beacon House).
14. A. Gersie (1997) *Reflections on Therapeutic Storymaking: The Use of Stories in Groups* (London: Jessica Kingsley).

# Bibliography

## Drama in schools

J. Ackroyd (2004) *Role Reconsidered: A Re-evaluation of the Relationship between Teacher-in-role and Acting* (Stoke-on-Trent; Sterling, VA: Trentham).

J. Ackroyd, J. Neelands, M. Supple and J. Trowsdale (1998) *Key Shakespeare: English and Drama Activities for Teaching Shakespeare to 10–14 Year Olds Book 1* (London: Hodder Murray).

J. Ackroyd, J. Neelands, M. Supple and J. Trowsdale (1998) *Key Shakespeare: English and Drama Activities for Teaching Shakespeare to 14–16 Year Olds Book 2* (London: Hodder Murray).

J. Allen (1979) *Drama in Schools: Its Theory and Practice* (London: Heinemann Educational).

G. M. Bolton (2003) *Dorothy Heathcote's Story: Biography of a Remarkable Drama Teacher* (Stoke-on-Trent; Sterling, VA: Trentham Books).

G. M. Bolton (1998) *Acting in Classroom Drama: A Critical Analysis* (Stoke on Trent: Trentham Books in association with the University of Central England).

G. M. Bolton (1992) *New Perspectives on Classroom Drama* (Hemel Hempstead, Herts: Simon and Schuster Education).

G. M. Bolton (1984) *Drama as Education: An Argument for Placing Drama at the Centre of the Curriculum* (Harlow, Essex: Longman).

G. M. Bolton (1979) *Towards a Theory of Drama in Education* (London: Longman), pp. 20–5.

G. M. Bolton and D. Heathcote (1999) *So You Want to Use Role-play?: A New Approach in How to Plan* (Stoke-on-Trent: Trentham Books).

G. M. Bolton, D. Davis and C. Lawrence (1986) *Selected Writings [on Drama in Education]* (Harlow, Essex: Longman).

D. Booth (2005) *Story Drama: Creating Stories through Role-playing, Improvising, and Reading Aloud*, 2nd edn (Ontario: Pembroke Publishers Limited).

D. Booth and M. Hachiya (eds) (2004) *The Arts Go to School* (Markham, Ont: Pembroke Publishers).

D. Booth and K. Gallagher (eds) (2003) *How Theatre Educates: Convergences and Counterpoints with Artists, Scholars and Advocates* (Toronto, Ont.: University of Toronto Press).

P. Bowell and B. Heap (2001) *Planning Process Drama* (London: David Fulton).

C. Brown (1929) *Creative Drama in the Lower School* (New York; London: D. Appleton and Company).

K. Byron (1986) *Drama in the English Classroom* (London; New York: Methuen).

H. C. Cook (1917) *The Play Way: An Essay in Educational Method* (New York: Frederick A. Stokes Company).

R. Courtney (1989) *Play, Drama and Thought: The Intellectual Background to Dramatic Education*, 4th edn revised (Ontario: Simon and Pierre).

R. Courtney (1987) *Dictionary of Developmental Drama: The Use of Terminology in Educational Drama, Theatre Education, Creative Dramatics, Children's Theatre, Drama Therapy, and Related Areas* (Springfield, IL: C.C. Thomas).

R. Courtney (1980) *The Dramatic Curriculum* (New York: Drama Book Specialists).

D. Davis (ed.) (1997) *Interactive Research in Drama in Education* (Stoke on Kent: Trentham Books Limited).

R. Dickinson and J. Neelands (2006) *Improving your Primary School through Drama* (London: David Fulton Publishers).

C. R. Duke (1974) *Creative Dramatics and English Teaching*, 3rd print edn (Urbana, IL: National Council of Teachers of English).

F. C. Durland (1952) *Creative Dramatics for Children* (Yellow Springs, OH: Antioch Press).

T. Evans (1984) *Drama in English Teaching* (London; Dover, NH: Croom Helm).

S. M. Fennessey (2000) *History in the Spotlight: Creative Drama and Theatre Practices for the Social Studies Classroom* (Portsmouth, NH: Heinemann).

H. Finlay-Johnson (1912) *The Dramatic Method of Teaching* (Boston, MA: Ginn and Company).

M. Fleming (1994) *Starting Drama Teaching* (London: Fulton).

C. A. Franklin (2008) *Civic Literacy through Curriculum Drama, Grades 6–12* (Thousand Oaks, CA: Corwin Press).

K. Gallagher (2000) *Drama Education in the Lives of Girls: Imagining Possibilities* (Toronto: University of Toronto Press).

H. Gardner (1983, 1993) *Frames of Mind: The Theory of Multiple Intelligences* (New York: Basic).

M. Greene (1995) *Releasing the Imagination: Essays on Education, the Arts, and Social Change* (San Francisco, CA: Jossey-Bass Publishers).

J. J. Hausman and J. Goodlad (1980) *Arts in the Schools* (New York: McGraw Hill).

D. Heathcote (1995) *Drama for Learning: Dorothy Heathcote's Mantle of the Expert Approach to Education* (Portmouth, NH: Heinemann).

D. Heathcote, L. Johnson and C. O'Neill (1984) *Dorothy Heathcote: Collected Writings on Education and Drama.* (London: Hutchinson).

R. B. Heinig (1993) *Creative Drama for the Classroom Teacher* (Englewood Cliffs, NJ: Prentice Hall).

J. Hodgson and E. Richards (1979) *Improvisation* (New York: Grove Press).

J. Hoetker (1975) *Theater Games: One Way into Drama* (Urbana, IL: National Council of Teachers of English).

D. Hornbrook (1991) *Education in Drama: Casting the Dramatic Curriculum* (London; New York: Falmer).

D. Hornbrook (1998) *Education and Dramatic Art* (London; New York: Routledge).

D. Hornbrook (1998) *On the Subject of Drama* (London; New York: Routledge).

M. Hulson (2006) *Schemes for Classroom Drama* (Stoke-on-Trent; Sterling, VA: Trentham).

N. B. Hutson (1968) *Stage: A Handbook for Teachers of Creative Dramatics* (Stevensville, MI: Educational Service).

A. Jackson (2006) *Theatre, Education and the Making of Meanings: Art or Instrument?* (Manchester: Manchester University Press).

K. Johnstone (1992) *Impro: Improvisation and the Theatre* (New York: Routledge/ Theatre Arts Book).

M. Kao and C. O'Neill (1998) *World into Worlds: Learning a Second Language through Process Drama* (Stamford, CT: Ablex Publishing Corporation).

N. Kitson (1997) *Drama 7–11: Developing Primary Teaching Skills* (London; New York: Routledge).

J. Lazarus (2004) *Signs of Change: New Directions in Secondary Theatre Education.* (Portsmouth, NH: Heinemann).

R. Linnell (1982) *Approaching Classroom Drama* (London: E. Arnold).

X. Lu (2004) *Rhetoric of the Chinese Cultural Revolution* (Columbia, SC: University of South Carolina Press).

P. Marson (1989) *Drama 14–16: A Book of Projects and Resources* (London: Thornes).

N. McCaslin (1999) *Children and Drama*, 3rd edn (Studio City, CA: Players Press).

N. McCaslin (1996) *Creative Drama in the Classroom and Beyond* (New York: Longman).

N. McCaslin (1987) *Creative Drama in the Intermediate Grades: A Handbook for Teachers* (New York: Longman).

N. McCaslin (1987) *Creative Drama in the Primary Grades: A Handbook for Teachers* (New York: Longman).

C. D. MacKay (1915) *How to Produce Children's Plays* (New York: Holt and Company).

B. McKean (2006) *A Teaching Artist at Work: Theatre with Young People in Educational Settings* (Portsmouth, NH: Heinemann).

N. Morgan (1987) *Teaching Drama: A Mind of Many Wonders* (London: Hutchinson Education).

N. Morgan and J. Saxton (1994) *Asking Better Questions* (Markham, Ont: Pembroke Publishers).

N. Morgan and J. Saxton (1991) *Teaching, Questioning, and Learning* (London; New York: Routledge).

S. Nachmanovitch (1990) *Free Play: Improvisation in Life and Art* (New York: Penguin Putnam Inc.).

J. Neelands and T. Goode (2000) *Structuring Drama Work: A Handbook of Available Forms in Theatre and Drama* (Cambridge; New York: Cambridge University Press).

J. Neelands and W. Dobson (2000) *Drama and Theatre Studies at AS/A Level* (London: Hodder and Stoughton Ltd).

J. Neelands (1998) *Beginning Drama 11–14* (London: David Fulton Publishers).

J. Neelands (1984) *Making Sense of Drama: A Guide to Classroom Practice* (Oxford; Portsmouth, NH: Heinemann Educational Books published in association with *2D Magazine*).

L. Nelson (2006) *Drama and the Adolescent Journey: Warm-ups and Activities to Address Teen Issues* (Portsmouth, NH: Heinemann).

E. Nighbert (1986) *Learning through Creative Dramatics* (East Aurora, NJ: D.O.K. Publishers).

C. O'Neill (1997) *Dreamseekers: Creative Approaches to the African American Heritage* (Portsmouth, NH: Heinemann).

C. O'Neill (1995) *Drama Worlds: A Framework for Process Drama* (Portsmouth, NH: Heinemann).

C. O'Neill and A. Lambert (1991) *Drama Structures: A Practical Handbook for Teachers* (Cheltenham: Stanley Thornes; Portsmouth, NH: Heinemann Educational Books).

C. O'Neill (1976) *Drama Guidelines* (London: Heinemann Educational Books in association with London Drama).

J. O'Toole (2002) *Pretending to Learn: Helping Children Learn through Drama* (Frenchs Forest, NSW: Longman).

J. O'Toole (1992) *The Process of Drama: Negotiating Art and Meaning* (London; New York: Routledge).

J. O'Toole (1976) *Theatre in Education: New Objectives for Theatre, New Techniques in Education* (London: Hodder and Stoughton).

C. Poulter (1987) *Playing the Game* (Oxford: Macmillan Education).

G. Readman, G. Lamont and British Broadcasting Corporation (1994) *Drama: A Handbook for Primary Teachers* (London: BBC Educational Pub).

S. Renard (1987) *Creative Drama: Enhancing Self-Concepts and Learning* (Minneapolis, MN: Educational Media Corp).

P. Ressler (2002) *Dramatic Changes: Talking about Sexual Orientation and Gender Identity with High School Students through Drama* (Portsmouth, NH: Heinemann).

Riverside Studios (ed.) (1980) *Exploring Theatre and Education* (London: Heinemann).

K. Robinson (ed.) (1980) *Exploring Theatre and Education* (London: Heinemann).

K. Robinson (ed.) (1977) *Learning through Drama: Report of the Schools Council Drama Teaching Project (10–16), Goldsmiths' College, University of London* (London: Heinemann Educational for the Schools Council).

T. Rogers (ed.) (2006) *Process Drama and Multiple Literacies: Addressing Social, Cultural, and Ethical Issues* (Portsmouth, NH: Heinemann).

L. Rosenblatt (1938/1968) *Literature as Exploration* (New York: D. Appleton-Century Company).

G. Schneer (1994) *Movement Improvisation: In the Words of a Teacher and her Students* (Champaign, IL: Human Kinetics).

D. A. Schön (1987) *Educating the Reflective Practitioner* (San Francisco, CA: Jossey-Bass).

D. A. Schön (1983) *The Reflective Practitioner: How Professionals Think in Action* (New York: Basic Books).

G. B. Siks (1958) *Creative Dramatics, an Art for Children* (New York: Harper).

G. B. Siks and H. B. Dunnington (1961) *Children's Theatre and Creative Dramatics* (Seattle, WA: University of Washington Press).

P. Slade (1954) *Child Drama* (London: University of London Press).

J. Somers (1994) *Drama in the Curriculum* (London: Cassell).

V. Spolin (1999) *Improvisation for the Theater: A Handbook of Teaching and Directing Techniques* (Evanston, IL: Northwestern University Press).

V. Spolin (1986) *Theater Games for the Classroom: A Teacher's Handbook* (Evanston, IL: Northwestern University Press).

V. Spolin (1963/1983) *Improvisation for the Theatre* (Chicago, IL: Northwestern University Press).

C. Stanislavski (1936) *An Actor Prepares* (New York: Theatre Arts Books).

P. Sternberg (1998) *Theatre for Conflict Resolution in the Classroom and Beyond* (Portsmouth, NH: Heinemann).

L. Swartz (1995) *Dramathemes* (Portsmouth, NH: Heinemann).

K. Taylor and Islington Drama Teachers (1991) *Drama Strategies: New Ideas from London Drama* (Oxford: Heinemann Educational).

P. Taylor (2000) *The Drama Classroom: Action, Reflection, Transformation* (London; New York: Routledge/Falmer).

P. Taylor (1998) *Redcoats and Patriots: Reflective Practice in Drama and Social Studies* (Portsmouth, NH: Heinemann).

P. Taylor and C. D. Warner (eds) (2006) *Structure and Spontaneity: The Process Drama of Cecily O'Neill* (Stoke on Trent; Sterling, VA: Trentham).

N. Toye and F. Prendiville (2000) *Drama and Traditional Story for the Early Years* (New York: Routledge).

United States Holocaust Memorial Museum (2001) *Teaching about the Holocaust: A Resource Book for Educators* (Washington, DC: United States Holocaust Memorial Museum), http://www.ushmm.org/education/foreducators/nesse/pdf/teaching_holcaust.pdf, date accessed 23 September 2010.

B. J. Wagner (1998) *Educational Drama and Language Arts: What Research Shows* (Portsmouth, NH: Heinemann).

B. J. Wagner (1976) *Dorothy Heathcote: Drama as a Learning Medium* (West Haven, CT: National Education Association).

W. Ward (1952/1981) *Stories to Dramatize* (Louisville, KY: Anchorage Press).

W. Ward (1947) *Playmaking with Children* (New York: D. Appleton-Century Company).

W. Ward (1939) *Theater for Children* (New York: D. Appleton-Century Company).

W. Ward (1930) *Creative Dramatics* (New York; London: D. Appleton and Company).

B. Warren (1995) *Creating a Theatre in your Classroom* (North York, Ont: Captus University Publications).

J. Watanabe and J. Neelands (2009) *Using Drama as a Medium of Instruction* (Tokyo: Bansei Shobo Publications).

B. Way (1998) *Development through Drama* (Amherst, NY: Humanity Books).

B. Woolland (1993) *The Teaching of Drama in the Primary School* (London; New York: Longman).

## Applied drama and theatre in communities

C. Baim, S. Brookes and A. Mountfound (2002) *The Geese Theatre Handbook* (Sherfield-on-London: Waterside Press).

J. Bergman and S. Hewish (2003) *Challenging Experience: An Experiential Approach to the Treatment of Serious Offenders* (Bethany, OK: Wood N Barnes).

A. Blatner and D. Wiener (eds) (2007) *Interactive and Improvisational Drama: Varieties of Applied Theatre and Performance* (Lincoln, NE: iUniverse).

A. Boal (2002) *Games for Actors and Non-Actors* (A. Jackson, trans.) (London; New York: Routledge).

A. Boal (1979) *Theatre of the Oppressed* (A. Jackson, trans.) (New York: Theatre Communications Group).

A. Bogart (2001) *A Director Prepares: Seven Essays on Art and Theatre* (London and New York: Routledge).

N. Bowles and M. E. Rosenthal (eds) (2000) *Cootie Shots: Theatrical Inoculations Against Bigotry for Kids, Parents and Teachers* (A Fringe Benefits Project) (New York: Theatre Communications Group, Inc.).

E. Boyer (1992) *Cornerstones for a New Century: Teacher Preparation, Early Childhood Education*, a National Education Index (New Haven, CT: NEA Professional Library).

D. Braverman and C. Supple (2002) *Playing a Part: Drama and Citizenship* (Stoke on Trent; Sterling, VA: Trentham).

S. Brecht (1988) *Peter Schumann's Bread and Puppet Theatre*, vol. 2 (London: Methuen).

T. Bridal (2004) *Exploring Museum Theatre* (Walnut Creek, CA: Altamira Press).

L. D. Byam (1999) *Community in Motion: Theatre for Development in Africa* (London: Bergin and Garvey).

D. Cocke, H. Newman and J. Salmons-Rue (eds) (1993) *From the Ground Up: Grassroots Theater in Historical and Contemporary Perspective* (Ithaca, NY: Cornell University).

C. Cohen, R. Gutiérrez Varea and P.O. Walker (eds) (2011) *Acting Together: Performance and Creative Transformation of Conflict, Volume I: Resistance and Reconciliation in Regions of Violence* (Oakland, CA: New Village Press).

J. Cohen-Cruz (2010) *Engaging Performance: Theatre as Call and Response* (New York: Routledge).

J. Cohen-Cruz (2005) *Local Acts: Community-based Performance in the United States* (New Brunswick, NJ: Rutgers University Press).

J. Cohen-Cruz (1994) *Playing Boal: Theatre, Therapy, Activism* (London; New York: Routledge).

C. Conroy (2009) *Theatre and the Body* (Basingstoke: Palgrave Macmillan).

R. Courtney (1968) *Play, Drama and Thought* (New York: Drama Book Specialists).

E. G. Craig (1912) *On the Art of the Theatre* (Chicago: Browne's Bookstore).

J. Dolan (2010) *Theatre and Sexuality* (Basingstoke: Palgrave Macmillan).

P. Duffy and E. Vettraino (2010) *Youth and Theatre of the Oppressed* (New York: Palgrave Macmillan).

P. Freire (1974/2007) *Education for Critical Consciousness* (New York: The Continuum International Publishing Group, Inc.).

P. Freire (1970/2000) *Pedagogy of the Oppressed* (New York: The Continuum International Publishing Group, Inc.).

H. Freshwater (2009) *Theatre and Audience* (Basingstoke: Palgrave Macmillan).

S. Ganguly (2010) *Jana Sanskriti: Forum Theatre and Democracy in India* (New York: Routledge).

A. Ghosh, D. D. Costa, G. Deshpande, H. Tanvir, M. Hashmi, S. Hashmi and S. Deshpande (S. Deshpande, ed.) (2007) *Theatre of the Streets: The Jana Natya Manch Experience* (New Dehli, India: Janam).

S. Grady (2000) *Drama and Diversity: A Pluralistic Perspective for Educational Drama* (Portsmouth, NH: Heinemann).

J. Grotowski (1968) *Towards a Poor Theatre* (New York: Simon and Schuster).

M. Haarbauer (2000) *Seasoned Theatre* (Portsmouth, NH: Heinemann).

J. Harvie (2009) *Theatre and the City* (Basingstoke: Palgrave Macmillan).

J. F. Hayes and D. N. Schindel (1994) *Pioneer Journeys: Drama in Museum Education* (Charlottesville, VA: New Plays Books).

N. Holdsworth (2010) *Theatre and Nation* (Basingstoke: Palgrave Macmillan).

C. Hughes (1998) *Museum Theatre: Communicating with Visitors through Drama* (Portsmouth, NH: Heinemann).

E. Hurley (2010) *Theatre and Feeling* (Basingstoke: Palgrave Macmillan).

A. Jackson and J. Kidd (2011) *Performing Heritage: Research, Practice and Innovation in Museum Theatre and Live Interpretation* (Manchester: Manchester University Press).

A. Jackson (2007) *Theatre, Education and the Making of Meanings.* (Manchester: Manchester University Press).

T. Jackson (1993) *Learning through Theatre: New Perspectives on Theatre in Education* (London; New York: Routledge).

J. Kelleher (2009) *Theatre and Politics* (Basingstoke: Palgrave Macmillan).

R. Knowles (2010) *Theatre and Interculturalism* (Basingstoke: Palgrave Macmillan).

S. Kuftinec (2003) *Staging America: Cornerstone and Community-based Theater* (Carbondale, IL: Southern Illinois University Press).

T. Kushner (1993) *Angels in America, Part One (Millennium Approaches) and Part Two (Perestroika)* (New York: Theatre Communications Group).

R. Landy (2004) 'Standing Tall: Study guide' (peggysternfilms.com).

R. J. Landy (1982) *Handbook of Educational Drama and Theatre* (Westport, CT.: Greenwood Press).

W. J. Lement (2005) *And Justice for Some: Exploring American Justice through Drama and Theatre* (Portsmouth, NH: Heinemann).

J. Malik'pūr (2004) *The Islamic Drama* (London: Frank Cass).

H. Nicholson (2009) *Theatre and Education* (Basingstoke: Palgrave Macmillan).

H. Nicholson (2005) *Applied Drama: The Gift of Theatre* (New York: Palgrave Macmillan).

C. J. Odhiambo (2008) *Theatre for Development in Kenya: In Search of an Effective Procedure and Methodology* (Eckersdorf: Pia Thielmann and Eckhard Breitinger).

I. Opie and P. Opie (1969) *Children's Games in the Street and Playground* (Oxford: Clarendon).

J. O'Toole, M. Stinson and T. Moore (2009) *Drama and Curriculum: A Giant at the Door* (New York: Springer).

J. O'Toole, B. Burton and A. Plunkett (2005) *Cooling Conflict: A New Approach to Managing Bullying and Conflict in Schools* (French Forest, NSW: Pearson/Longman).

L. Pilkington (2010) *Theatre and Ireland* (Basingstoke: Palgrave Macmillan).

P. Pitzele (1998) *Scripture Windows: Towards a Practice of Bibliodrama* (Los Angeles: Torah Aura).

P. Pitzele (1995) *Our Fathers' Wells: Personal Encounters with the Myths of Genesis* (San Francisco, CA: Harper Collins).

C. Poulter (1987) *Playing the Game* (Oxford: Macmillan Education).

M. Prendergast and J. Saxton (eds) (2009) *Applied Theatre: International Case Studies and Challenges for Practice* (Chicago, IL: Intellect/University of Chicago Press).

T. Prentki and S. Preston (2009) *The Applied Theatre Reader* (London; New York: Routledge).

P. Rae (2009) *Theatre and Human Rights* (Basingstoke: Palgrave Macmillan).

D. Rebellato (2009) *Theatre and Globalization* (Basingstoke: Palgrave Macmillan).

N. Ridout (2009) *Theatre and Ethics* (Basingstoke: Palgrave Macmillan).

M. Rohd (1998) *Theatre for Community, Conflict and Dialogue: The Hope is Vital Training Manual* (Portsmouth, NH: Heinemann).

S. Ruhl (2010) *Passion Play: A Cycle* (New York: Theatre Communications Group).

J. Saldaña (ed.) (2005) *Ethnodrama: An Anthology of Reality Theatre* (Walnut Creek, CA: AltaMira Press).

J. Saldaña (1995) *Drama of Color: Improvisation with Multiethnic Folklore* (Portsmouth, NH: Heinemann).

R. Schechner (2003) *Performance Theory*, vol. 10 (New York: Routledge)

R. Schechner (1985) *Between Theater and Anthropology* (Philadelphia, PA: University of Pennsylvania Press).

M. Schutzman and J. Cohen-Cruz (eds) (2006) *A Boal Companion: Dialogues on Theatre and Cultural Politics* (New York; London: Routledge).

P. Schweitzer (2006). *Reminiscence Theatre: Making Theatre from Memories* (London: Jessica Kingsley Publishers).

J. Shapiro (2000) *Oberammergau: The Troubling Story of the World's Most Famous Passion Play* (New York: Pantheon).

Y. Sleip, K. Weingarten and A. Gilbert (2004) *Narrative Theatre as an Interactive Community Approach to Mobilizing Collective Action in Northern Uganda* (Washington, DC: American Psychological Association).

P. Stern (producer) (2003) Standing Tall (film) (peggysternfilms.com).

A. Strimling (2004) *Roots and Branches: Creating Intergenerational Theatre* (Portsmouth, NH: Heinemann).

E. Swados (2006) *At Play: Teaching Teenagers Theater* (New York: Faber and Faber).

P. Taylor (2011) *Theatre Behind Bars – Can the Arts Rehabilitate?* (Stoke-on-Kent: Trentham).

P. Taylor (2003) *Applied Theatre: Creating Transformative Encounters in the Community* (Portsmouth, NH: Heinemann).

J. Thompson (2009) *Performance Affects: Applied Theatre and the End of Effect* (New York: Palgrave Macmillan).

J. Thompson (2003) *Applied Theatre: Bewilderment and Beyond* (New York: Peter Lang).

J. Thompson (1998) *Prison Theatre: Practices and Perspectives* (London: Jessica Kingsley).

L. Tocci (2007) *The Proscenium Cage: Critical Case Studies in U.S. Prison Theatre Programs* (Amherst, NY: Cambria).

V. Turner (1982) *From Ritual to Theatre: The Human Seriousness of Play* (New York: Performing Arts Journal Publications).

J. Willet (1964) *Brecht on Theatre* (New York: Hill and Wang).

R. Wooster (2007) *Contemporary Theatre Education* (Exeter, Bristol; Chicago, IL: Exeter Intellect).

## Drama therapy

A. Artaud (1958) *The Theatre and its Double* (New York: Grove Press).

A. Bannister (1997) *The Healing Drama: Psychodrama and Dramatherapy with Abused Children* (London: Free Association Books).

E. Berne (1964) *Games People Play: The Psychology of Human Relationships* (New York: Grove Press).

A. Blatner (2000) *Foundations of Psychodrama: History, Theory and Practice*, 4th edn (New York: Springer).

A. Blatner (1996) *Acting-in: Practical Applications of Psychodramatic Methods*, 3rd edn (New York: Springer).

A. Boal (1995) *The Rainbow of Desire: The Boal Method of Theatre and Therapy* (London; New York: Routledge).

J. Casson (2004) *Drama, Psychotherapy and Psychosis: Dramatherapy and Psychodrama with People Who Hear Voices* (New York: Brunner-Routledge).

J. Chodorow (1997) *Jung on Active Imagination* (Princeton, NJ: Princeton University Press).

M. Cox and A. Theilgaard (1994) *Shakespeare as Prompter: The Amending Imagination and the Therapeutic Process* (London: Jessica Kingsley).

M. Cox (ed.) (1992) *Shakespeare Comes to Broadmoor* (London: Jessica Kingsley).

M. Csikszentmihalyi (1990) *Flow: The Psychology of Optimal Experience* (New York: Harper and Row).

T. Dayton (2005) *The Living Stage: A Step-by-Step Guide to Psychodrama, Sociometry and Group Psychotherapy* (Deerfield Beach, FL: Health Communications).

T. Dayton (2000) *Trauma and Addiction: Ending the Cycle of Pain through Emotional Literacy* (Deerfield Beach, FL: Health Communications).

T. Dayton (1994) *The Drama Within: Psychodrama and Experiential Therapy* (Deerfield Beach, FL: Health Communications).

A. Demasio (1999) *The Feeling of What Happens: Body and Emotion in the Making of Consciousness* (New York: Harcourt Brace and Co).

A. Demasio (1994) *Descartes' Error: Emotion, Reason and the Human Brain* (New York: Putnam).

G. Diener and J. L. Moreno (1972) *Goethe and Psychodrama: Psychodrama and Group Psychotherapy, Monograph No. 48* (Beacon, NY: Beacon House).

D. Dokter (ed.) (1998) *Arts Therapists, Refugees and Migrants: Reaching Across Borders* (London: Jessica Kingsley).

D. Dokter (ed.) (1994) *Arts Therapies and Clients with Eating Disorders: Fragile Board* (London: Jessica Kingsley).

P. Dunne (1992) *The Narrative Therapist and the Arts* (Los Angeles: Possibilities Press).

M. Eliade (1972) *Shamanism: Archaic Techniques of Ecstasy* (Princeton, NJ: Princeton University Press).

M. Eliade (1961) *The Sacred and the Profane* (New York: Harper and Row).

R. Emunah (1994) *Acting for Real – Drama Therapy Process, Technique, and Performance* (New York: Brunner-Mazel).

N. Evreinoff (1927) *The Theatre in Life* (New York: Brentano's).

J. Fox and H. Dauber (1999) *Gathering Voices: Essays on Playback Theatre* (New Paltz, NY: Tusitala Publishing).

J. Fox (ed.) (1987) *The Essential Moreno: Writings on Psychodrama, Group Method, and Spontaneity* (New York: Springer).

S. Freud (1911) *The Interpretation of Dreams* (trans. and ed. J. Strachey) (New York: Basic Books).

J. Gershoni (ed.) (2003) *Psychodrama in the 21st Century* (New York: Springer).

A. Gersie (1997) *Reflections on Therapeutic Storymaking* (London: Jessica Kingsley).

A. Gersie (1992) *Earth Tales* (London: Green Press).

A. Gersie (1991) *Storymaking in Bereavement* (London: Jessica Kingsley).

A. Gersie and N. King (1990) *Storymaking in Education and Therapy* (London: Jessica Kingsley).

Gong Shu (2003) *Yi Shu, the Art of Living with Change: Integrating Traditional Chinese Medicine, Psychodrama and the Creative Arts* (Taiwan: F. E. Robbins and Sons).

R. Grainger (1995) *The Glass of Heaven – The Faith of the Dramatherapist* (London: Jessica Kingsley).

R. Grainger (1990) *Drama and Healing: The Roots of Dramatherapy* (London: Jessica Kingsley).

R. Grainger and M. Anderson-Warren (2000) *Dramatherapy: Expanding Horizons* (London: Jessica Kingsley).

A. P. Hare and J. Hare (1996) *J. L. Moreno* (Thousand Oaks, CA: Sage).

J. Hillman (1983) *Archetypal Psychology* (Dallas, TX: Spring Publications).

J. Hillman (1983) *Healing Fiction* (Barrytown, NY: Station Hill Press).

P. Holmes, M. Karp and M. Watson (eds) (1994) *Psychodrama since Moreno* (New York: Routledge).

L. Hornyak and E. Baker (1989) *Experiential Therapies for Eating Disorders* (New York: Guilford Press).

K. Hudgins (2002) *Experiential Treatment for PTSD: The Therapeutic Spiral Model* (New York: Springer).

S. Hurley and N. Chater (eds) (2005) *Perspectives on Imitation: From Cognitive Neuroscience to Social Science* (Boston, MA: MIT Press).

V. Iljine (1910) 'Patients Play Theatre: A Way of Healing Body and Mind' (originally published in Russian, cited in H. Petzold. 1973) *Gestalttherapie Und Psychodrama* (Kassel: Nicol).

Institute for Developmental Transformations (2006) *Developmental Transformations: Papers, 1982–2006* (New York: Institute for Developmental Transformations).

S. Jennings (2011) *Healthy Attachments and Neuro-Dramatic Play* (London: Jessica Kingsley).

S. Jennings (ed.) (2009) *Dramatherapy and Social Theatre* (New York: Routledge).

S. Jennings (1995) *Dramatherapy with Children and Adolescents* (London: Routledge).

S. Jennings (1995) *Theatre, Ritual and Transformation: The Temiar Experience* (London: Routledge).

S. Jennings (ed.) (1987) *Dramatherapy: Theory and Practice for Teachers and Clinicians*, vol. 1 (London: Routledge).

S. Jennings (1973) *Remedial Drama* (London: Pitman).

D. Johnson and R. Emunah (eds) (2009) *Current Approaches in Drama Therapy* (Springfield, IL: Charles C Thomas).

P. Jones (2007) *Drama as Therapy: Theory, Practice and Research* (London: Routledge).

P. Jones (ed.) (1989) *Dramatherapy: State of the Art* (St. Albans: Hertforshire College of Art and Design).

C. Jung (1969) *The Archetypes and the Collective Unconscious*, 2nd edn (R. F. C. Hull, trans.) (Bollingen Series XX) (Princeton, NJ: Princeton University Press).

C. Jung (1963) *Memories, Dreams and Reflections* (New York: Vintage Books).

C. Jung (1921/1971) *Psychological Types* (reproduced in collected works), vol. 6 (Princeton, NJ: Princeton University Press).

M. Karp, P. Holmes and K. Bradshaw-Tauvon (eds) (1998) *Handbook of Psychodrama* (New York: Routledge-Taylor and Francis).

P. Kellermann (2007) *Sociodrama and Collective Trauma* (London: Jessica Kingsley).

G. A. Kelly (1955) *The Psychology of Personal Constructs*, vols. 1 and 2 (New York: Norton).

R. Landy (2008) *The Couch and the Stage* (Lanham, MD: Rowman and Littlefield).

R. Landy (2005) 'Three Approaches to Drama Therapy' (Video and DVD) (New York: New York University).

R. Landy (2004) 'Standing Tall: Study guide' (Boston: Fanlight Productions).

R. Landy (2001) *New Essays in Drama Therapy – Unfinished Business* (Springfield, IL: Charles C Thomas).

R. Landy (1996) *Essays in Drama Therapy: The Double Life* (London: Jessica Kingsley).

R. Landy (1994) *Drama Therapy – Concepts, Theories and Practices*, 2nd edn (Springfield, IL: Charles C Thomas).

R. Landy (1993) *Persona and Performance – The Meaning of Role in Drama, Therapy and Everyday Life* (New York: Guilford).

M. Lindkvist (1998) *Bring White Beads When You Call on the Healer* (New Orleans, LA: Rivendell House).

M. Lowenfeld (1979) *The World Technique* (London: George Allen and Unwin).

C. Magai and J. Haviland-Jones (2002) *The Hidden Genius of Emotion* (Cambridge: Cambridge University Press).

R. Marineau (1989) *Jacob Levy Moreno 1889–1974* (New York: Tavistock/Routledge).

S. McNiff (1992) *Art as Medicine: Creating a Therapy of the Imagination* (Boston, MA: Shambhala).

J. L. Moreno (1985) *The Autobiography of JL Moreno M.D.* (abridged) (J. Moreno, ed.) (Moreno Archives) (Cambridge, MA: Harvard University Press).

J. L. Moreno (1953) *Who Shall Survive?: Foundations of Sociometry, Group Psychotherapy and Sociodrama* (Redlands, CA: Beacon House).

J. L. Moreno (1946/1994) *Psychodrama*, vol. 1 (New York: Beacon House).

J. L. Moreno (1941/1971) *The Words of the Father* (New York: Beacon House).

J. L. Moreno and J. Fox (1987) *The Essential Moreno: Writings on Psychodrama, Group Method, and Spontaneity* (New York: Springer Publishing Company).

J. L. Moreno and Z. T. Moreno (1969) *Psychodrama*, vol. 3 (New York: Beacon House).

Z. T. Moreno (2006) *The Quintessential Zerka: Writings by Zerka Toeman Moreno on Psychodrama, Sociometry, and Group Psychotherapy* (New York: Routledge).

F. Perls (1969) *Gestalt Therapy Verbatim* (Lafayette, CA: Real People Press).

H. Petzold (1973) *Gestalttherapie und Psychodrama* (Kassel: Nicol).

S. Pitruzzella (2004) *Introduction to Dramatherapy: Person and Threshold* (London: Routledge).

V. Propp (1968) *Morphology of the Folktale* (Austin, TX: University of Texas Press).

C. Rogers (1951) *Client-centered Therapy: Its Current Practice, Implications, and Theory* (Boston, MA: Houghton Mifflin).

B. Rothschild (2000) *The Body Remembers – The Psychophysiology of Trauma and Trauma Treatment* (New York: Norton).

J. Salas (1996) *Improvising Real Life: Personal Story in Playback Theatre* (New Paltz, NY: Tusitala Publishing).

G. Schatter and R. Courtney (eds) (1981) *Drama in Therapy*, vol. 1 (New York: Drama Books).

T. Scheff (1979) *Catharsis in Healing, Ritual and Drama* (Berkeley: University of California).

M. Schutzman and J. Cohen-Cruz (eds) (1994) *Playing Boal – Theatre, Therapy, Activism* (New York: Routledge).

P. Slade (1959) *Dramatherapy as an Aid to Becoming a Person* (London: Guild of Pastoral Psychology).

M. Stamenov and V. Gallese (eds) (2002) *Mirror Neurons and the Evolution of Brain and Language* (Amsterdam and Philadelphia, PA: John Benjamins Publisher).

A. Starr (1977) *Rehearsal for Living: Psychodrama* (Chicago, IL: Nelson-Hall).

P. Stern (producer) (2003) *Standing Tall* (film) (Boston: Fanlight Productions).

P. Sternberg and A. Garcia (2000) *Sociodrama: Who's in your Shoes?*, 2nd edn (Westport, CT: Praeger).

A. Timman Jacobse (1995) 'The Use of Dramatherapy in the Treatment of Eating Disorders' in D. Dokter (ed.) *Art Therapies and Clients with Eating Disorders* (Philadelphia, PA: Jessica Kingsley Publishers, Ltd.).

M. von Franz (1980) *The Psychological Meaning of Redemption Motifs in Fairy Tales* (Toronto: Inner City Books).

A. Weber and C. Haen (eds) (2005) *Clinical Applications of Drama Therapy in Child and Adolescent Treatment* (New York: Brunner-Routledge).

P. Weiss (1963/2001) *The Persecution and Assassination of Jean-Paul Marat as Performed by the Inmates of the Asylum of Charendon under the Direction of the Marquis de Sade* (Long Grove, IL: Waveland Press Inc).

A. Wethered (1973) *Drama and Movement in Therapy: The Therapeutic Use of Movement, Drama and Music* (Boston, MA: Plays Inc).

M. White (1998) *Papers by Michael White* (Adelaide: Dulwich Centre Publications).

M. White and D. Epson (1990) *Narrative Means to Therapeutic Ends* (New York: Norton).

D. W. Winnicott (1971) *Playing and Reality* (London: Routledge).

## Theatre by, for and with young people

S. Bennett (2005) *Theatre for Children and Young People: 50 Years of Professional Theatre in the UK* (London: Aurora Metro).

C. B. Chorpenning (1954) *Twenty-One Years with Children's Theatre* (Anchorage, KY: Children's Theatre Press.

N. Eek, A. M. Shaw and K. Krzys (2008) *Discovering a New Audience for Theatre: The History of ASSITEJ, the International Association of Theatre for Children and Youth* (Santa Fe, NM: Sunstone Press).

M. Etherton and J. Plastow (2006) *African Theatre: Youth* (Oxford: James Currey).

R. Fordyce (1975) *Children's Theatre and Creative Dramatics: An Annotated Bibliography of Critical Works* (Boston, MA: G.K. Hall).

M. Goldberg (2006) *TYA: Essays on the Theatre for Young Audiences* (Louisville, KY: Anchorage Press Plays).

M. Goldberg (1974) *Children's Theatre: A Philosophy and a Method* (Englewood Cliffs, NJ: Prentice-Hall).

C. Jennings (2005) *Theatre for Children: Fifteen Classic Plays* (New York: St. Martin's Press).

C. Jennings (1998) *Theatre for Young Audiences: 20 Great Plays for Children* (New York: St. Martin's Press).

C. Jennings and G. Berghammer (1986) *Theatre for Youth: Twelve Plays with Mature Themes* (Austin, TX: University of Texas Press).

J. Kase-Polisini (1986) *Children's Theatre: Creative Drama and Learning* (Lanham, MD: University Press of America.

N. McCaslin (1987) *Historical Guide to Children's Theatre in America* (New York: Greenwood Press).

N. McCaslin (1978) *Theatre for Young Audiences* (New York: Longman).

N. McCaslin (1971) *Theatre for Children in the United States: A History* (Norman, OK: University of Oklahoma Press).

M. Morton (1979) *Through the Magic Curtain: Theatre for Children, Adolescents, and Youth in the USSR: 27 Authoritative Essays* (New Orleans, LA: Anchorage Press).

L. Swortzell (1997) *Theatre for Young Audiences: Around the World in 21 Plays* (New York: Applause).

L. Swortzell (1990) *International Guide to Children's Theatre and Educational Theatre: A Historical and Geographical Source Book* (New York: Greenwood Press).

L. Swortzell (1986) *Six Plays for Young People from the Federal Theatre Project (1936–1939): An Introductory Analysis and Six Representative Plays* (Westport, CT: Greenwood Press).

C. Tolch and R. L. Bedard (1989) *Spotlight on the Child: Studies in the History of American Children's Theatre* (New York: Greenwood Press).

M. van de Water (2008) *Dutch Theatre for Children: Three Contemporary Plays* (Charlottesville, VA: New Plays Books).

M. van de Water (2006) *Moscow Theatres for Young People: A Cultural History of Ideological Coercion and Artistic Innovation, 1917–2000* (New York: Palgrave Macmillan).

D. Wood and J. Grant (1999) *Theatre for Children: Guide to Writing, Adapting, Directing, and Acting* (Chicago, IL: Ivan R. Dee).

# Index